WORK IN THE CANADIAN CONTEXT

Continuity Despite Change

Katherina Lundy

and

Barbara Warme

BUTTERWORTHS
Toronto

Work in the Canadian Context: Continuity Despite Change
© 1981 Butterworth & Co. (Canada) Ltd.

Printed and bound in Canada by Alger Press

The Butterworth Group of Companies

Canada:
Butterworths & Co. (Canada) Ltd., Toronto and Vancouver

United Kingdom: Butterworth & Co. (Publishers) Ltd., London

Australia:
Butterworths Pty. Ltd., Sydney

New Zealand:
Butterworths of New Zealand Ltd., Wellington

South Africa:
Butterworth & Co. (South Africa) Ltd., Durban

United States:
Butterworth (Publishers) Inc., Boston
Butterworth (Legal Publishers) Inc., Seattle
Mason Publishing Company, St. Paul

Canadian Cataloguing in Publication Data

Main entry under title:

Work in the Canadian context

Includes bibliographical references.

ISBN 0-409-84690-2

1. Labor and laboring classes — Canada —
Addresses, essays, lectures. 2. Industrial
sociology — Canada — Addresses, essays, lectures.
3. Division of labor — Addresses, essays, lectures.
I. Lundy, Katherina L. P. II. Warme, Barbara.

HD8106.5.W67   331'.0971   C81-095009-X

to Larry and Gordon

Contents

*Technological and Structural Change: Reorganizing Tasks and
Social Relations at the Work Place*

Occupational Fate in Changing Times

PART III

**Conflicts of Interest: Individual and Collective Strategies
for Coping with the Work Situation** 243

Worker Attitudes: Origins and Consequences

Worker Safety and Corporate Profits: A Question of Priorities

"Special People": Their Quest for a Better Life

Labour Unions: External and Internal Relations

List of Contributors

Grace M. Anderson, Wilfrid Laurier University.
Maureen Baker, University of Toronto.
Roy T. Bowles, Trent University.
Susan Clark, Mount Saint Vincent University.
Juanne N. Clarke, Wilfrid Laurier University.
Wallace Clement, Carleton University.
I. Coulter, University of Toronto.
Prudence Craib, Trent University.
Colin Flynn, University of Edinburgh.
Jack Haas, McMaster University.
O. Hall, University of Toronto.
Mary-Ann Haney, Trent University.
J.D. House, Memorial University.
Harish C. Jain, McMaster University.
M.J. Kelner, University of Toronto.
Graham Knight, McMaster University.
Graham Lowe, University of Alberta.
Malcolm H. MacKinnon, University of Toronto.
Patricia Marchak, University of British Columbia.
Victor Marshall, McMaster University.
R. Parsler, University of Stirling, Scotland.
M.-A. Robeson, University of Toronto.
William Shaffir, McMaster University.
Michael R. Smith, McGill University.
David Stager, University of Toronto.
Robert A. Stebbins, University of Calgary.
Marylee Stephenson, Nature Communications, Toronto.
G.L. Symons, University of Calgary.
Lloyd Tataryn, University of Western Ontario.
Jane Turrittin, York University.

Preface

We are grateful to our colleagues in many universities who encouraged us to undertake this project and who helped us to clarify the form it would assume.

The practical tasks involved in coordinating the work of a rather large number of authors was made easy and pleasurable by our contributors' cooperativeness, promptness and openness to editorial suggestion.

The following people generously gave us constructive criticism: Ellen Baar, Larry Lundy, Gordon Warme and, above all, Roy Bowles. His meticulously detailed and incisive commentary significantly influenced (and we believed improved), the final shape of the manuscript. Malcolm MacKinnon must also be thanked for his explanatory notes on some of the statistics used in the book.

Valuable services were provided by Iris Bent, Heather Spurll and Beverly Thomas.

Peter Horowitz and David Hogg, of Butterworths, supported us not only by showing enthusiasm for the project but also by placing company resources at our disposal. Our editor, Paula Pike, has been in all senses, third partner, performing tasks which made demands on her expertise, her time and her patience for minutiae.

It is an empirical question whether the aphorism "two heads are better than one" can be applied to academic undertakings. However, our collaboration has convinced us that two certainly do have more fun.

Kitty Lundy
The University of Toronto

Barbara Warme
York University

Introduction

The division of labour is a central feature of any society. Indeed, describing a society as "primitive" or as "advanced" essentially makes a statement about how its work is carried out. To an advanced society, one imputes a sophisticated technology, an industrial complex and a burgeoning service sector, as well as an educated and highly specialized labour force. Specialization brings with it centrifugal tendencies which require centralized control, typically provided through large formal organizations. The state of affairs described does not exist in a vacuum but, rather, is shaped by the interplay of history, geography and politics. In this book, we hope to demonstrate that work and occupations can only be studied gainfully by placing them in their social context, and that knowledge of how the division of labour is articulated is useful, even crucial, for interpreting society.

Examining work in a societal context must not blunt our awareness of the pervasive impact that work has on the individual. Despite contemporary rhetoric which heralds the transition from a society dominated by work to one dominated by leisure, the type of work an individual performs continues to have profound implications for his life chances. One must argue that it remains a critical factor in defining his social existence. As Bryant notes:

> *One's standard of living, style of life, political ideology, basic value orientation, choice of friends and spouse, health, daily routine, mode of child rearing, and general satisfaction with life, to name only a few considerations, may well be the indirect, if not direct, results of one's work speciality. We are shaped, molded, regulated, even assimilated by our work. Work is our behavioral product, but so, too, are we and our lives in many ways the products of our work (1972: XVII).*

The purpose of this anthology is to provide an opportunity for examining various dimensions of work, and for distinguishing characteristics and issues peculiar to Canada from those common to all industrialized societies. In pursuit of this goal, we sought articles which, together, would address a broad range of issues, and which would bring a variety of perspectives to bear on work in Canada — symbolic interactionist, quasi-functionalist, Marxist and other forms of conflict theory. An additional goal has been to expose students to diverse research techniques and to differing degrees of researcher "engagement."

An awareness of the need for a collection of studies on work in Canada emerged from our teaching, when we were obliged to spend *frustrating hours tracking down Canadian material which was scattered among books, journals, government documents and unpublished articles. Therefore, we decided to survey colleagues across the country to determine whether they shared the view that it would be useful, even though necessarily limiting, to attempt to reduce the scatter and make available to students a book which examines important dimensions of work in the Canadian context. The response, coming from virtually every university, was swift and affirmative; moreover, a number of those who responded offered to contribute an article. After surveying our collection of original articles and recent reprints, we pinpointed lacunae in important areas, and solicited contributions to cover them. Two of the latter are **Craib's*** article on the state of research and development, and **Jain's** on employment opportunities for Indians. The overall result is that fifteen of the twenty-two articles selected are original.*

Perhaps the most difficult, and certainly the most important, challenge an editor /alchemist faces is to pull out of the hat the hoped-for rabbit rather than, say, a wart hog or a butterfly. The editorial task is by no means entirely ex post facto, *in that there is a continuing interplay between what is available to put into the hat and what one hopes will come out of it. In our case, we sought to stress both the nature of work in an industrial society, and the specific realities of work in a nation characterized by high levels of foreign ownership, the overdevelopment of resource exports, and a state structure that plays a massive role in the economy (Drache, 1977). Secondly, we have been committed to a conception of the book which not only places occupations in their social context, but which also provides a dynamic rather than a static picture — hence, the historical dimension of many of the papers. This commitment has shifted the emphasis away from a more traditional in-depth analysis of specific work processes and specific occupations.*

The book is divided into three parts, covering work and the political economy, the division of labour, and processes of accommodation and conflict.** While such a division was part of the initial plan, it would have been more than magic if each article had fallen ever-so-neatly into only one of the intended categories. Indeed, some of our contributors may be surprised at the emphasis which this format lends to their paper. We trust, however, that they will not feel that their own intentions have

---

*To highlight connections among the articles in the book, contributors' names will appear in bold-faced type.

**By accommodation and conflict we refer to the processes that are set in motion by various interest groups to attain their respective work-related goals.

been distorted in an arbitrary way; certainly, there is considerable overlapping among the sections.

Although, like Ritzer (1977), we began our task with no ideological axe to grind, the final product does constitute a rather striking litany of problems, both at the level of social structure and at the level of everyday human experience. For example, the continuing quest to achieve greater control over the work process, and to maximize profit, has brought about rationalization of work in the office, as in the nickel mine. In turn, this has led to drastic changes in the tasks performed by workers, and in the way they feel about performing them. It is evident that, although Canada is an affluent country, for a significant segment of the labour force the quality of work life leaves much to be desired.

To the reader who is bothered by discovering contradictory findings, not to mention discrepant interpretations of what is found, we can only say that this dissonance reflects what is currently happening in sociology. Were there total consensus about the nature of the problems, then utopia would surely be just around the corner. We make no such starry-eyed claim. However, if the concern pervading many of the articles can be assumed to be widespread among social scientists, one is encouraged to hope that they will find ways of making their opinions known outside the ivory tower, and that these opinions will provide an impetus for action. One must not forget that students, too, are involved in the dialogue between the university and the larger society. For most of them, the tower is merely a way-station en route to the labour force; moreover, increasing numbers of students combine work and study. If education can fulfil, in even a modest way, its generic function of "leading out," then students will constitute one vital link in carrying these concerns forward.

REFERENCES

Bryant, C.D.
1972 *The Social Dimensions of Work*. Englewood Cliffs: Prentice Hall.
Drache, D.
1977 "Staple-ization: A Theory of Canadian Capitalism." In *Nationalism Imperialism and Canada*. J. Saul (ed.) Toronto: Between The Lines.
Ritzer, G.
1977 *Working: Conflict and Change*. Englewood Cliffs: Prentice Hall.

Part I

Work and the Political Economy

Paradox of Advancement and Underdevelopment

THE HARD FRONTIER: A "STAPLES" APPROACH TO THE CANADIAN ECONOMY

The influence of Harold Innis pervades much of the current analysis of Canadian problems, and this influence is apparent in the articles which have been selected for the first part of this book. A staples approach stresses the primacy of the flow of unprocessed raw materials (fur, fish, timber, wheat, oil) from hinterland regions to metropolitan centres, and the reliance of the hinterland on importation of capital and consumer goods from these metropolitan centres. It also stresses the many economic and social consequences of this type of asymmetrical exchange, involving the metropole in an upward spiral of development (more investment, more jobs, more skilled people, a stronger tax base, better services, etc.) and the hinterland in a downward spiral (capital leakage, fewer jobs, fewer skilled people, a weaker tax base, less political clout, more reliance on government funds, etc.). Thus, over the long run, differences between the metropole and hinterland tend to become exacerbated rather than eliminated, despite government strategies aimed at reducing regional disparities. Such an approach sheds light on the relationship between Canada and other industrialized nations, chiefly the United States. It can also be applied to internal relationships, such as that between the main staple-producing regions of Canada and the commercial centres of Toronto and Montreal. Furthermore, we have seen the emergence of regional centres of dominance (metropoles) within the hinterland itself, the most recent example being Calgary.

A historical perspective brought to bear on the Canadian situation reminds us that even as things have changed, they have stayed the same. While Canada's status has substantially remained that of a hinterland, the locus of dominance has shifted from France to Britain, to the United States. Not only has there been a shift in this locus, but there has also been a change in the nature of capital investment. British investment was mainly by way of loans, whereas American investment has been

1

marked by direct ownership of branch plants. Such ownership brings in its wake control over decisions concerning what Canadian workers will do, how they will do it and, indeed, whether they will work at all.

Innis viewed Canada as a "hard frontier," the penetration and development of which could not be accomplished by individual initiative alone; rather the exploitation of Canadian resources required "large accumulations of capital, corporate forms of business enterprise and state support" (Clark, 1968: 232). An unusual amalgam of government involvement and foreign ownership was necessary to meet Canada's capital needs. The attractiveness of the resource sector led to disproportionate investment in this area, promoting lopsided development. Moreover, economic development has also been truncated, inasmuch as most of the sophisticated technology now required by industry is imported. As Shepherd, in recommending an economic strategy for Canada, observes,

> It is disturbing to dwell on the notion that, having been structured primarily as a "hinterland" of initially the U.K. and the U.S. industrial base, policies for the development of the resource sector have resulted in a mining industry with no domestic mining machinery sector, a fisheries industry with limited processing capacity, and an agricultural industry with an inadequate agricultural machinery base. The failure to understand the necessity to conceptualize Canadian self-reliance has generated an unacceptable level of dependency, and a damaging truncation of the national potential represented by our resource wealth. (Shepherd 1979: 17)

The tendency to rely on imported technology is exaggerated by the fact that many of the large companies involved have their head offices outside of resource-producing areas, and are therefore not committed to strengthening the hinterland.

The three articles in this section all deal with aspects of dependency, how it affects the structure of various economic sectors, and the fate of workers in these sectors. **Craib**'s paper reflects a basic assumption of dependency theory, namely that "contemporary underdevelopment is in large part the historical product of past and continuing economic and other relations between the satellite underdeveloped and the now developed metropolitan countries" (Frank, 1969). **Marchak**'s paper applies this perspective in her examination of the B.C. forestry industry. Whereas the findings of **Craib** and **Marchak** provide supporting evidence for such a theoretical position, **House** shows that the development of the Alberta oil industry has not followed the negative course that dependency theory would lead one to expect.

THE ORPHAN STATUS OF CANADIAN RESEARCH: UNATTACHED AND
UNDERNOURISHED

*Craib's article draws attention to the fact that failure to produce
machinery is a long way down a road which begins with lack of
research. She notes that Canada lags behind other industrial nations in
expenditures on research, and that the money which has been spent has
not generated significant technological innovation. Most of our scientific
work has been pure research carried out under government auspices and
thus not directly oriented to practical applications. When the Canadian
government decided to become actively involved in sponsoring research,
a deliberate decision was made in favour of pure research, on the
assumption that this would enhance Canada's position in the international scientific community. However, in this state of affairs there exists
no ready channel between research and development. Corporations are
likely to conduct and develop their own research, most of which is done
outside Canada.*

*The profit motive is the driving force behind research and
development, since anticipation of a larger market is the rationale for
expanding industrial capacity. Because of the small size and the
dispersion of the Canadian market, foreign-owned corporations do not
deem it profitable to carry out their research and development here.
Likewise, Canadian firms, which tend to be smaller and less attractive
to investors than the large multinationals, and which are therefore
chronically faced with capital shortages, find it cheaper to import
developed technology (including machines) than to take the risk of
developing their own. Consequently, Canadian scientists and support
staff must either work in university or government laboratories, or
become part of the brain drain. Recent contractions in the international
economy have reduced this drain to a trickle, at the same time as
employment opportunities within Canada have decreased. The contraction has coincided with an expanded supply of highly educated people,
who must now compete for a small supply of appropriate jobs, with the
result that many are underemployed.*

REGIONAL UNDERDEVELOPMENT DESPITE RICH RESOURCES: THE
B.C. FORESTRY INDUSTRY

*Marchak's article illustrates the problems created by an economy
dependent on a staples industry that is controlled by monopolistic
multinational corporations. In her study of the B.C. forestry industry,
she notes that, despite long-term government subsidization aimed at
facilitating the creation of spin-off industries, the B.C. forestry industry
has failed to create them. A number of consequences flow from this.
Workers are in a weak bargaining position because employment is
unstable, and no alternative opportunities are available in a particular*

area. This instability generates "labour pools" which move around in quest of work. Like other migratory workers, these workers are thus denied the benefits and security enjoyed by much of the industrial work force.

Heavy reliance on the forestry sector leads to single-industry towns which are vulnerable because they prosper and decline with fluctuations in world prices of the staple. Moreover, such towns do not develop a full range of services, thus severely restricting job openings for women, who are largely excluded from employment in the forest industry itself.

THE ALBERTA SUCCESS STORY: A CHALLENGE TO DEPENDENCY THEORY?

Examining the human side of dependent development in the Alberta petroleum industry, **House** *provides an important caveat to the general argument that foreign ownership necessarily entails the adverse consequences referred to previously, such as underdevelopment and unstable employment. The Alberta oil industry, unlike the forestry industry in B.C., has succeeded in producing diversification of the economy, thus bringing prosperity to the whole region. The practice followed by multinational corporations of contracting out operations, for example, drilling, has led to active participation of small companies in the oil boom. This* modus operandi *has been favourable to the career mobility of well-trained individuals.* **House** *found that there are opportunities for moving horizontally, for example, from entrepreneur to executive to independent consultant, as well as for moving up within the multinational corporations. Not surprisingly, his respondents express high job satisfaction and tend to view their success "as a vindication of their free enterprise principles, rather than as a fortuitous result of a geological accident and the historical timing of the OPEC initiative in multiplying the price of oil." The question must nevertheless be raised: can this prosperity be maintained in the long run, when its impetus has come from a nonrenewable resource?*

For Alberta's oilmen the American dream has come true, at least for now. For the majority of Canadians, however, the ideology which encompasses belief in the inviolacy of the private sector, equal opportunity for those of equal ability and upward mobility through individual initiative alone, is like an ill-fitting suit of clothes. As countless studies have shown, this ideology does not correspond to the reality in North America as a whole; it is particularly inappropriate for Canada, because it fails to acknowledge the unique combination of factors which are characteristic of a hard frontier and which have shaped Canadian society right from the beginning. This uniqueness is investigated in a variety of ways throughout the book.

REFERENCES

Clark, S.D.
1968   *The Developing Canadian Community*. Toronto: Univ. of Toronto Press.
Frank, A.G.
1969   *Latin America: Development and Revolution*. New York: Monthly Review Press.
Shepherd, J.J.
1979   "An Economic Strategy for Canada: Our Political Economy Regained." In *Walter L. Gordon Lecture Series 1978–79*. Vol. III. Toronto: Omnigraphics.

Chapter 1

Canadian–Based Research and Development: Why So Little?

*Prudence W. Craib**

In the early 1980s, Canada is widely perceived to be a member of that enviable group of nations which leads the world in industrial output, national wealth and high personal living standards. Canada has also been a prominent participant in the fundamental transformation of the world's technology and economy which followed World War II. During this period, enormous investments have been made in the research, development, and marketing of new products and concepts, many of which have become an integral part of our economic and social systems. A very partial list of some of the most important of these revolutionary inventions must include: nuclear power generation and nuclear weapons; computer-controlled assembly lines; transistors with all their immensely important and indispensible applications; the microwave transmission towers and space satellites which have helped transform the world's communications systems; microwave ovens which have had an equally fundamental effect on the food industry; the jet engine, with its enormous impact on travel, transportation, communications, and warfare; aerospace research and development; xerox technologies, which together with systems of computerized knowledge storage, retrieval, and management, have revolutionized the flow of information and the nature of bureaucratic structures; the application of new chemical knowledge in the creation of new materials which are now used in fields as diverse as the fabrics we wear, the utensils we use daily, and the drugs which protect us from illness; and so on. It is self-evident that, in the modern era, new technologies have come to affect the development of whole nations and the well-being of the most remote populations. For example, in the industrialized nations the productiveness and hence the capacity to survive of whole segments of their economies have been challenged. Modern warfare has been revolutionized, and this has radically affected the international balance of power. Perhaps most profoundly, the balance of the world's total ecological system is seen by many to be under serious threat from the unknown and unpredictable effects of new and increasingly elaborate technical and social processes.

Canada as a society is generally perceived to have the characteristics basic to a member of the fortunate group of advanced industrial nations. She has superior levels of modern technological activity in many parts of the country and in some sectors of the economy. Standards of living are high, at least for a large and visible segment of the population in the major centres, and are

*I wish to acknowledge, with gratitude, my ongoing intellectual debt to my colleague, R.A. (Sandy) Lockhart, for his support in this and other related scholarly enterprises over the years.

comparable to those of similar groups in the United States, which by most criteria has the highest standard of living in the world. Political institutions have stability and continuity, and appear to be playing a guiding role in relation to issues which are subject to policy control. But the Canadian economy is a part of the capitalist world system, and as such manifests in an exaggerated form some of the more persistent problems which are increasingly seen to plague all advanced capitalist economies. Because Canada's economy is so profoundly integrated into the North American economic system, it is even more sensitive than the rest of the world to the fluctuations which occur in the giant United States economy. This is exacerbated by Canada's relative dependence on staple exports, which makes her much more vulnerable than most other advanced industrial nations to shifts in the structure and volume of demand for raw materials in the whole international capitalist system.

It is these latter tendencies which have, in recent years, led to a more critical evaluation of some important and persisting processes in Canadian society. Many analysts are increasingly concerned that an unprecedentedly large proportion of both Canada's primary raw materials sector, and her secondary manufacturing capacity are owned by foreigners. This raises some fundamental questions about the extent to which the state apparatus is in reality able to act as autonomously as is assumed to be the case in the usual Western economy. Also, a relatively small number of major multinational corporations exercise control over this large body of direct foreign investment in Canada. Such corporations have the usual democratic access to Canadian governments through their influence in local political processes, but they are frequently able to exercise further and important influences through their lobbies in Washington (Clement, 1977). In addition, the Canadian economy does not appear to be moving away from its historically heavy reliance on the export of largely unprocessed staple raw materials. This pattern began with the fur trade, and currently involves lumber, pulp and paper, minerals, and oil and gas. Finally, the secondary manufacturing sector itself is relatively poorly developed, and is undergoing a measurable decline. Not only is Canada importing an increasing proportion of the finished goods she uses, but Canadian manufactured goods are also tending to become less competitive in international markets and there is a growing imbalance between the export and the import of manufactured goods. This affects the balance of trade adversely, weakens the Canadian dollar, and ultimately reduces Canada's ability to continue to maintain high living standards.

It can also be pointed out that both the federal and provincial governments have been inconsistent and fitful in the ways in which they have addressed the issue of the possible need for the evolution of a coherent national economic policy. This may well be partially due to the widespread acceptance within many sectors of Canadian public opinion of the dominant private sector's perception that the Canadian economy is not really a separate entity, but is rather part of a North American economic unit, which is necessarily and appropriately dominated by the United States. Characteristics such as these are generally perceived to be more typical of the less developed countries than of the advanced industrialized nations.

Any analysis of how Canada has chosen to address the issues of scientific and industrial Research and Development must be viewed in the context of those complex and interlinked economic and political processes. There is widespread rhetorical support for the plea that government should facilitate the spending of a larger proportion of the Gross National Product (GNP) on Research and Development in order to improve her trading situation. But during the last two decades, she has spent less than 1 per cent of her GNP in this area. This compares poorly with West Germany (1.3 per cent), France (1.5 per cent), the U.K. (2.2 per cent), and the U.S.A. (3.1 per cent). The Japanese figure is currently almost double that of the U.S.A. Canada also differs from her competitors in that about 80 per cent of such research is performed by government supported agencies. In the United States, while it is true that much work done in the private sector is done under government contracts, about 70 per cent of total research and development is carried out by industry. The range of Canadian manufactured goods which are competitive in international markets is small, and getting smaller. This is occurring at the same time that it is becoming increasingly evident that it is in the areas of advancing technology that the greatest corporate and national gains in international markets can be made, and the relative wealth of individual nations thereby be retained, increased, or diminished.

In order to understand why, in the past, an expansion of the degree of financial support by government for research has not had the effect of expanding Canada's industrial sector as a whole, it is important, first, to examine the process of Research and Development more critically and, second, to relate this analysis to the specifics of the Canadian economic situation.

"R & D" is popularly used as almost a single word to describe the creation of new products. A surprisingly wide range of people in Canada see R & D as one smooth and flowing process in which basic research is followed inevitably by suitable commercial development and applications. It seems to be assumed that scientists are in communication with industrial corporations and are concerned about the ways in which their new theoretical insights can be used in practice. Corporations are often assumed to be willing, indeed eager, once the fundamental or pure research is done, to invest manpower and capital in the process of converting this new knowledge into some manufactured product which has practical use in the market place. The ultimate rewards of this R & D process are thought to be twofold. The direct profits made by the corporation which develops the product should thereby expand, and there should be an indirect profit to the Canadian economy at large if the product is marketed abroad, or if it displaces a product which would otherwise need to be imported.

The reality is somewhat different. There are at least three main models of the ways in which Research and Development tend to occur in advanced industrial societies. First, if a corporation is relatively large, it is likely to have its own research budget and establishment positioned near the head office. It is the managers of the corporation who make the final decisions as to whether it is worthwhile to undertake the often lengthy process of working out how to mass produce a new product, test its possibilities in the market place and then undertake the advertising which will make the public aware of the product, and choose it above the other competitive products in the field. A second type of R & D is one in which a large contractor such as the United States Pentagon, or the Canadian Ministry of Defence, will decide that a new product such as, for example, an aeroplane with specific capacities, or an advanced communications system is needed by the military establishment. The contract for such a product or product line is given to an appropriate "private" contractor, who then undertakes the preliminary research, receives financial and other assistance at all stages of development, and is assured of a market for the finished product. Many such "private" corporations commonly depend almost exclusively upon government contracts, although they may eventually also evolve commercial spin-offs. The third category is one in which basic research is carried out in a university or in a research institution and the practical and commercial development and applications of such research, which are usually of secondary importance to the scientists and researchers, are left to others to evolve. There are of course combinations and variations of these three models of different processes, but it is useful to distinguish broad differences of this kind.

The first two models are common in the United States, not only because it has a very large military establishment, but also because it has an economy dominated by very large corporations, many of which are multinational in range. The third model is more common in Canada, for reasons which will be explored later. These variations have frequently been overlooked by spokesmen from both the public and private sectors.

When the processes of R & D are set out in this way, it is possible to make some important distinctions about how they work in reality. One of the most basic consequences of this is that if new breakthroughs of knowledge have resulted from investments made by private corporations, they are seen as the private property of the corporation and are protected by exclusive patents. The intent is to acquire a competitive advantage and guard that exclusive advantage for as long as possible, by imposing stringent controls on the diffusion of the new knowledge. In very competitive and capital intensive "high technology" industries, this is often viewed as a profoundly patriotic pursuit of the national interest. The scientists who make new discoveries under these circumstances accept the limitations which commercial necessity imposes on the dispersal of what they have learned. They may perhaps make some aspects of such knowledge known to their peers, but only if no potential advantage to their commercial opponents can result. It is clearly understood that scientists in these situations will receive their career advancement and personal rewards within the framework of the corporation which employs them, and that these will tend to be correlated with the commercial advantage their discovery confers upon their employers.

By contrast, in the ideal university or Research Council situation, much greater emphasis is placed upon the independent pursuit by an individual or team of "fundamental" or "pure" scientific knowledge. It is frequently argued that in order to be truly original and creative such researchers should not be constrained by management concerns about possible commercial, or even national priorities. Therefore, the issue of whether or not research might have industrial possibilities is frequently viewed both as a matter of secondary importance, and also as somebody else's responsibility. Also, knowledge so acquired is viewed as private only while it is being developed. When in the opinion of the researchers there is enough information to provide a significant addition of new knowledge, this is disseminated as widely as possible by an announcement at an appropriate scientific conference, or publication in a suitable journal. At this point, the knowledge moves, in essence, into the public domain. The researchers who make such advances receive only part of their career rewards and prestige within the hierarchy where the work was done. They also greatly value the esteem of their peers within the international community of scholars who are engaged in related work and who have job mobility within this wider network. Such "pure" research tends to acquire very high status, in part because the process is one which emphasizes the autonomy of the individual or team who pursue knowledge for its own sake. It is contrasted to "applied" research which has to be repeatedly re-evaluated in terms of the overriding commercial needs of the sponsoring corporation.

The extent to which any body of research is transformed into developed and successful market products will depend to a significant extent upon the ways in which a particular country's attitudes toward, and methods of doing, R & D, are structured and supported, and how this is related to the economy as a whole.

When the Canadian Research and Development establishment is compared with that of the other Western industrial nations, and particularly with the United States, significant differences become apparent. As was stated earlier, in the United States all three models of R & D exist and the first two predominate. In Canada, the third model is more common. In this model the connection between achieving advances in "pure" research based in universities or institutes, and the further development of that research in industrial and commercial applications is much more tenuous. Why should this model be the dominant one in Canada? Because Canada, unlike all the other advanced industrial nations, has an economy in which the very core of both the primary extractive and the secondary manufacturing sectors is not made up of locally-owned and controlled firms, but rather of the branch plants of many foreign-owned and very large multinational corporations, and in branch plants extensive R & D is seldom encouraged.

The historical roots of this situation lie in the "protective" tariffs which were established as part of the National Policy more than a century ago and which have been followed in their essentials by Canadian governments ever since. At the time the policy was introduced, Canada had a very small population, a very large land area, and an economy which was almost wholly dependent on the export of staple resources. Large amounts of both Canadian and foreign capital were needed to develop the infrastructure of transportation and services which were necessary to bring these goods to international markets. At this time, the industrial economy of the United States was growing very rapidly, and the U.S. was exporting goods to Canada in competition with new Canadian industries that were short of capital in their struggle to develop and grow. The political processes of the period were much influenced by the views of prominent merchant capitalists who were primarily interested in trade and commerce, rather than in developing secondary industry. It was the conviction of government that more local manufacturing production was needed and a policy of protective tariffs was introduced. It is important to be aware that this policy essentially protected products themselves, rather than the producers of the products. One of its consequences was to create an environment in which it became profitable for foreign-owned firms to found wholly-owned branch businesses in Canada. While this provided welcome jobs for Canadians, it tended to affect many local manufacturers adversely, because they were often relatively inexperienced and under-capitalized and were struggling to survive. They now found themselves competing with goods manufactured in foreign-owned branch plants which had access to the research, development, managerial, and marketing skills which had been developed in the larger and older markets south of the border. Many branch plants were able to avoid some of the difficulties inherent in production by importing components which had been manufactured elsewhere, and their essential function was often the quite limited one of assembling efficiently a number of premade parts. In addition, while in other industrialized countries, such as the United States, England and Germany, the banking system as a whole was deeply committed to providing the capital necessary for the growth of industry, in Canada the few large and dominant banks had relatively little interest in lending capital to small and tentative Canadian firms, when large and secure American-owned firms were equally available and producing many of the same products on a larger and more efficient scale.

The result was that, while the policy had the effect of substituting some local production for goods imported from outside the country and it encouraged the expansion of industry in general, it also had the effect of discouraging Canadian entrepreneurship, and made it increasingly difficult for fledgling Canadian-owned industrial firms to survive and expand successfully. In 1879 alone, 13 branch plants were started. In 1900 there were 66, in 1913 there were 450 (Clement, 1975: 74). By the beginning of the Depression, British and American firms accounted for well over half of the local production of electrical apparatus, chemicals, and automobiles. In the post World War II period, the degree of control by foreign investors, now predominantly American, of very large segments of both the primary and secondary sectors of the economy, has grown significantly. The situation in 1974 is reflected in Table 1–1. This period has also seen the evolution and growth of the powerful modern form of the multinational corporation. This process of the creation of corporations of increasing size, complexity, and range has been assisted by the development of new technologies of management, which are based on the computerization and cybernation of an increasing range of managerial and production processes. This has the effect of making it much easier to control the operation of foreign subsidiaries from the increasingly centralized core of the corporation.

Foreign direct investment has clearly had a number of profound consequences for the Canadian economy and political structure, but for the issue of Research and Development, one aspect of the phenomenon is of particular importance. Basically, the managers of the branch plants of foreign-owned corporations operating in the Canadian secondary manufacturing sector are expected to penetrate this, or any other, local market in the interests of products which are the result of technological advances which have been made elsewhere. Their responsibility is to maximize the profits made in all subsidiaries in the expectation that these profits can be used in the

Table 1-1

Foreign and Domestic Control: Major Nonfinancial Industries, 1974

	Number Foreign-Controlled Corporations	Number Canadian-Controlled Corporations	% Foreign Controlled by Number	% Canadian Controlled by Number	Average Asset Size Foreign-Controlled Corporation	Average Asset Size Canadian-Controlled Corporation	% Foreign Control of Assets
Petroleum and coal products	26	14	65.0	35.0	398.1	3.1	99.6
Metal mining	55	n.a.	n.a.	n.a.	n.a.	n.a.	n.a.
Communication	20	345	5.5	94.5	6.7	24.3	13.8
Tobacco products	17	3	85.0	15.0	52.8	n.a.	n.a.
Public utilities	39	363	9.7	90.3	16.3	71.0	2.4
Paper and allied industries	113	258	30.5	69.5	38.2	21.3	44.0
Transport equipment	158	382	29.3	70.7	30.3	n.a.	n.a.
Rubber products	34	43	44.2	65.8	30.0	1.5	94.1
Mineral fuels	235	238	49.7	50.3	28.8	9.3	75.4
Beverages	39	248	13.6	86.4	14.9	5.5	29.8
Primary metals	55	205	21.1	78.9	17.5	n.a.	n.a.
Nonmetallic mineral products	113	497	18.5	81.5	16.2	n.a.	n.a.
Transportation	217	2190	9.0	91.0	13.9	7.8	15.1
Textile mills	97	307	24.0	76.0	13.4	n.a.	n.a.
Food	223	1344	14.2	85.8	13.1	2.2	49.4
Chemicals and chemical products	298	294	50.3	49.7	12.1	3.3	78.8
Electrical products	193	271	41.6	58.4	13.0	4.9	65.3
Wood industries	100	1038	8.8	91.2	8.4	2.1	28.4
Other mining	203	976	17.2	82.8	9.8	n.a.	n.a.
Construction	196	8101	2.4	97.6	8.8	1.1	15.1
Machinery	225	395	36.3	63.7	8.7	2.2	69.2
Retail trade	383	10995	3.4	96.6	6.7	0.9	21.1
Services	584	7754	7.0	93.0	5.6	1.0	30.0
Metal fabricating	321	1449	18.1	81.9	5.5	1.7	42.0
Wholesale trade	1598	11036	12.6	87.4	4.4	1.4	31.2
Knitting mills	17	200	7.8	92.2	5.1	n.a.	n.a.
Miscellaneous manufacturing	255	762	25.1	74.9	4.0	n.a.	n.a.
Furniture industries	40	492	7.5	92.5	3.7	1.2	19.7
Storage	16	158	9.2	90.8	3.3	8.3	3.9

Continued on page 14

Table 1-1 — Continued

Foreign and Domestic Control: Major Nonfinancial Industries, 1974

	Number Foreign-Controlled Corporations	Number Canadian-Controlled Corporations	% Foreign Controlled by Number	% Canadian Controlled by Number	Average Asset Size Foreign-Controlled Corporation	Average Asset Size Canadian-Controlled Corporation	% Foreign Control of Assets
Printing, publishing and allied industries	61	763	7.4	92.6	3.6	n.a.	n.a.
Clothing industries	42	939	4.3	95.7	3.8	0.9	16.5
Leather products	25	200	11.1	88.9	3.0	n.a.	n.a.
Agriculture, forestry and fishing	105	3077	3.3	96.7	2.5	0.6	12.5
Total nonfinancial industries	6103	55439	9.9	90.1	12.2	2.4	34.0

Note: In manufacturing, firms with assets of $1 000 000 000 were unclassified as to ownership. There are good grounds for assuming the vast majority are Canadian controlled. Therefore, the figures in the Canadian-controlled column are in some cases overinflated and in others, underinflated.

Source: Statistics Canada, *Corporations and Labour Unions Returns Act,* Report for 1974, Part I — Corporations, Cat. No. 61-210, Supply and Services Canada, Ottawa, January 1977.

Source: The Weakest Link, Science Council of Canada Report #43, P. 91.

interests of the larger corporation, wherever it chooses. Quite often, the parent corporation does not wish to have products made in a local market, such as that of Canada, competing with similar products which are produced by their subsidiaries elsewhere, and many branch plants are prohibited from developing foreign markets independently. Branch plants in many industrial sub-sectors take a dominant share of the Canadian market, and they thereby create a situation which imposes narrow limits upon the range of opportunities available to Canadian-owned firms. Also, since Canadian firms are usually smaller than their branch plant competitors, they are unable to achieve comparable economies of scale. In addition, in many cases the central managers of foreign-owned corporations or subsidiaries decide the purchasing or diversification policies of all their branches, and as a consequence may well bypass products made by Canadian firms which have developed the technological capacity to supply these locally-generated needs. This, in turn, will affect adversely the economic development of the smaller industries that supply parts and services to larger ones. All these processes have had the cumulative effect of stunting or "truncating" the development of much of Canadian secondary industry.

Concern about the situation has existed for many years. In 1916 the federal government acknowledged, through the foundation of the National Research Council (NRC), that the low level of local R & D in Canada was a matter of some importance. The prominent industrial and university leaders who were appointed to the NRC were charged with the task of surveying and organizing existing research agencies in Canada. In their first study, they reported that Canada "was falling behind its industrial competitors in the fields both of pure science and industrial research." It was calculated that at that time in all of Canada there were only about 50 persons engaged in pure research. One of the reports relating to the period stated that: "Scientific research in Canada was practically confined to the laboratories of two or three of our universities, and one or two departments of government" (Eggleston, 1978: 5–7). After extensive deliberations, the NRC decided to recommend the foundation of a permanent central research institute in Ottawa, and in 1928 the government did approve the beginning of the construction of national laboratories and the appointment of a full-time director. However, the Depression was looming, and in the period between the foundation of the NRC and the beginning of World War II, much of the planned research was cancelled or severely reduced.

In 1949 the Massey Commission, having examined the principal agencies of basic and applied research in Canada, confirmed earlier findings that industrial research was not keeping pace with the general development of industry. The most important reason given was that so many Canadian firms were branches of British or American companies in which the main research work was done at the centre, and the Canadian branch confined its activities to turning out exact counterparts of British or American originals. The report also noted that Canadian schools of applied science were adversely affected by the limited opportunities offered to their students in Canadian industry. A significant proportion of the most important work being done in Canada during this period was based on a foundation of the military research, that had been undertaken under the pressures of the war-time situation. Among the new research areas which had been opened up were work on radar, jet propulsion and nuclear fission. In the medical field the team led by Dr. Frederick Banting had earned a Nobel prize for work on the development of insulin.

In part because of these successes, it was thought that a wider industrial expansion would be stimulated by more scientific research. In 1952, Dr. Stacie became president of the NRC, and his attitudes toward both pure and industrial research were to have a considerable influence upon the future of Canadian Research and Development during the critical post-World War II period. He was convinced that more basic research was needed, and that the universities and the NRC laboratories must play a unique role in doing this work. He resisted any attempts to modify the definition of the NRC as an institution of high international standing, performing the pure research its members judged to be significant. In a speech to the Chemical Institute of Canada in Montreal on October 17, 1956, his priorities and values, which epitomize those described earlier in the third model for research, emerge quite ?learly.

There are many reasons which justify fundamental work in a laboratory like the NRC. In the first place, there is every reason to make a contribution to Canada's position in fundamental science. If the work is of high quality it reflects favourably on Canada's general scientific standing, and on the reputation of the NRC, especially internationally, and as far as academic institutions are concerned. This has a highly beneficial influence on our ability to attract first-rate men, and brings to the laboratory on fellowships people from all over the world. Finally, the existence of a fundamental group for consultation and discussion has an extremely helpful influence on the outlook of those doing applied work, and on the general atmosphere of the laboratory. . . .

He made his views on applied research more explicit when he wrote to the Secretary of the Treasury Board on September 26, 1958 that he took the view that: " 'the sole function of the NRC is the performance of research' and that any (industrial or applied) testing it did was entirely incidental to such a function." (Eggleston, 1978: 355, 356).

That these views were not universally accepted was made clear a decade later, when the Glassco Commission stated that Canada's failure to keep up to world standards in the area of industrial research before the war had been partially made up since then, but that serious problems still remained. The Commission wrote that one of the original purposes of government in devoting money to research had been to encourage and stimulate Canadian industry, but that over the years this goal had been relegated to being little more than a distraction from the pure research conducted in the NRC and major universities.

By the 1970s the general level of awareness of these issues had risen sharply, and the issue of R & D was being analysed in the wider context of the total structure of industry. In 1972, the Gray Report on *Foreign Direct Investment in Canada* (1972: 405–407) describes the effects on Canadian industry of what it calls *truncation*. The report points out that:

A truncated firm is one which does not carry out all functions — from the original research required through all aspects of marketing — necessary for developing, producing and marketing its goods. One or more of these functions are carried out by the foreign parent of Canadian firms. . . . truncation normally maximizes the achievement of the global objectives of the parent firm and is from its point of view, a rational business decision. It does not necessarily maximize the profits of the Canadian subsidiary, or its contribution to the Canadian economy. *Depending on which activities are involved, truncation may mean less production for the Canadian market, less opportunity for innovation and entrepreneurship, fewer export sales, fewer supporting services, less training of Canadian personnel in various skills, less specialized product development aimed at Canadian needs or tastes, and less spillover economic activity and so on.* (Emphasis added.)

In the 1980s, there is wide agreement that the development or maintenance of both foreign and internal markets will depend significantly upon the kinds of industrial innovation which produces improved or new processes and products. But in the Canadian "branch plant economy," technology tends to be imported rather than developed at home. Thus scientists and technologists in foreign countries do the work which might have been done in Canada, had there been more Canadian-owned companies in the medium and high technology area. The products which are developed in the headquarters laboratories of multinational corporations are usually aimed at the total international market. If local research facilities are permitted to exist in countries other than the parent country, these tend to be support units, whose main functions are to ease the process of transferring the techniques developed in the parent laboratories, and to service the local plants, rather than to undertake original R & D. Frequently, Canadian branch plants are not permitted by the parent corporation to compete in export markets at all, and if they are, they are seldom in a position to export products which are unique in that they are based on independent innovation undertaken in Canada, and hence have a competitive advantage. The relative size of the firm also affects the extent to which it is viable for it to undertake original R & D. Most Canadian-owned firms are smaller than their branch plant competitors, and only a small proportion of them do any internal research at all. In the total Canadian economy, probably only about fifteen hundred firms are large enough to support intramural research, and of these the large majority are foreign controlled, and as a matter of policy do not conduct innovative R & D in Canada. As a result of these factors, much of the industry based on Canadian soil has little capacity to generate either independent technological innovations for Canada, or creative research and development opportunities for Canadians.

The underdevelopment of Canada's Research and Development capacity is an issue which may seem somewhat abstract to most people. However, it affects the lives of both individuals and institutions in some important ways. In particular, the kinds of job opportunities which are available for individuals with relevant scientific and technological skills are affected adversely at all levels of the social structure. It is conventional to discuss this issue in terms of the "brain drain" of trained scientists to other more technologically advanced countries, and this is understandably a problem. The history of the "brain drain" is a long one. As early as in 1919, one of the founders of the NRC made an estimate of the distinguished Canadian graduates who had moved to academic and scientific jobs in other countries. "There were hundreds of the brightest intellects this country has ever produced who had to go to the United States to earn a livelihood, and they are still there helping to staff the universities and *assisting in building up the great industries of that country*" (emphasis added) (Eggleston, 1978: 14).

The progressive truncation of potentially innovative establishments and processes within Canada's industrial economy has also meant that there are fewer jobs for a wider range of skilled people, and the jobs that do exist tend to be less challenging. For highly-skilled manual workers, the situation is also complicated by the fact that, traditionally, the Canadian education system has not been designed to develop indigenous training processes at this level, and corporations have therefore usually recruited such workers from Europe. This shortsighted policy now has the effect of reducing the kinds of job opportunities which can become available to Canadian-born youth. Also, there is some evidence that, as the Canadian and European economies get closer to each other in terms of living standards, Canada becomes less attractive to such workers, who are in high demand everywhere, and there are intermittent shortages of people with the skills that become essential during periods of industrial growth.

During the 1950s and the 1960s, the advanced industrial nations undertook a huge expansion of their educational systems. This was based on the widely-held assumption that they would only be able to maintain their competitive position in the world economy if they developed their "human capital" by raising the skills level of the whole labour force, and particularly the highly trained scientific and technological components of it. This policy, which was to have enormous unforeseen consequences for millions of people, was based on an analysis of only one side of the equation of labour supply and demand. The theory was that if people were more highly educated they would necessarily become more productive, and would in consequence have an effect on the economy analogous to that of yeast in bread, in that they would cause the economy to rise and expand and require yet more skilled and creative people. The basic assumptions which lay behind this "human capital" body of theories and policies have turned out to be largely fallacious (Lockhart, 1971, 1975, 1977). The economic systems of most countries have grown much more slowly than was predicted, and sufficient jobs for all of the large numbers of highly trained people being produced by the expanded educational system have failed to materialize.

By the early 1970s, it was becoming increasingly clear from the available data that a serious situation of maladjustment between supply and demand of educated people was developing. In the United States in 1968–69, there was a 30 per cent drop in the research jobs available for Ph.D. level chemists and physicists (Ellis, 1969). In Canada, there had been a relatively small expansion in the numbers of Ph.Ds in science who were employed in the private sector during the period of the nineteen fifties. Yet, in the same decade, the number of candidates who were working for Ph.Ds in science had risen from 155 to 595. (Levine, 1970).

Dr. L. Gray, Director of Atomic Energy Canada Limited, in a brief presented in 1968 to the Senate Standing Committee on Science Policy, analysed the dimensions of this growing imbalance.

In 1965 Canada had some 100,000 scientists and engineers, of which 15,000 were engaged in R and D. In 1978 we will have some 300,000 scientists and engineers, nearly three times as many as we have today. ... With increasing numbers at our universities going on to do post-doctorate work, we can expect a larger percentage of scientists and engineers to be available for R and D; perhaps as high as 20 per cent of this professional group. ... This means 60,000 R and D professionals. Hence, unless we can employ 45,000 new R and D professionals in the next ten years we will have trained a select segment of our coming generation at a very substantial cost only to find that they are either underemployed, unemployed or that they emigrate. (Gray, 1968)

This overproduction of highly skilled people has one very important ripple effect, which can best be described by the word "bumping." The term was originally evolved in industrial trade unions, where it means that more highly-qualified employees whose jobs become redundant, have a contractual right to displace employees who have fewer qualifications or less seniority. This process has also happened, less formally, within the ranks of the scientists and technicians who do R & D. Because there is a surplus of highly trained people, the paper qualifications a person needs to have in order to get a particular job, or pass a promotion barrier, tend to increase. As a consequence, the levels of formally certified skill of many sectors of the employed North American labour force have been rising steadily for two decades, but there is a growing body of evidence that the skills required to perform the job in reality have not expanded equally (Jaffe & Froomkin, 1968; Bright, 1958(a), 1958(b); Lockhart, 1978). If this process of "upgrading" had not been happening, the number of officially unemployed people holding the advanced qualifications appropriate for R & D, would have risen even more rapidly in Canada during the last two decades than has been the case. What appears to have happened is that there has been a progressive process of "*under*employment" in which the level of skills and knowledge at all levels of the occupational structure is rising, and it is mostly the least skilled people at the very bottom of the system who finally become "*un*employed." It is ironic that these increased rates of unemployment of the least educated people in the system are frequently cited by both labour economists and sociologists as proof that there is a need for even more education. Lockhart (1978: 147) argues that the reality is not that there is "too little work for the less educated, but rather the opposite, i.e., that more and more of those with surplus education relative to real occupational demand were being forced into competing for lower-level jobs, and thus were becoming not unemployed but underemployed."

The Canadian economy as it is presently structured cannot absorb all the skilled people the educational system produces, at levels appropriate to their education.

When this situation is discussed by the media or by policy makers, it is clear that there is considerable confusion about the labour demand side of this complex set of processes. One major analysis of the United States was made by

Folger et al. in 1970 and was particularly informative, because it was based
not on theories, but on an analysis of the available data on the real
relationship between the supply of highly educated manpower, and the
demand within the economy for the skilled people that were being produced.
He does not focus specifically on scientists, who are particularly affected by the
expansion and contraction of opportunities in R & D, but he makes the
following generalization.

> America has developed an educational system that produces more college
> graduates than are required to replace graduates leaving the labour
> force and more than are required to provide for the growth of the
> occupational structure. The additional college graduates over and above
> those needed for replacement and occupational growth are [thus]
> available to raise the educational level of occupations. A large part of
> this educational upgrading, as has been indicated, is occurring in
> managerial, sales and professional occupations where college graduation
> has not been in the past a requirement for obtaining a job. (Folger et al.,
> 1970)

A somewhat comparable study of Canada was published in 1971 by
Kushner and others. They attempt to soften the evidence of a serious
demand/supply imbalance by writing "the excess supply does not necessarily
imply unemployment [but] may simply lead to other utilization patterns" such
as, for example, the employment of Ph.Ds as school teachers (Kushner et al.,
1971). In 1970, the Science Council of Canada stated that "the performance of
industry has been most discouraging . . . there had been net decreases in the
amount of Research and Development actually performed in industry"
(*Vancouver Province*, June 30, 1969: 17).

The slowing down of the growth of the university system is a result, in
part, of the decline in the birthrate and subsequent reduction in enrolments.
This had the effect of severely limiting job opportunities for new graduates in
the university research and teaching sector.

In 1974, Edward Harvey published a more detailed overview of the
Canadian situation after conducting a direct survey of several cohorts of
university graduates, in order to find out to what extent their educational
achievements matched their eventual occupational destinations. One of his
major conclusions was that the average employment of university graduates
had declined significantly, both in terms of social prestige and relative
economic advantages, since the beginning of the 1960s.

The ongoing and increasing truncation of the Canadian industrial sector
which has been described in this paper has been further complicated by a
process of "deindustrialization." A number of industries are increasingly
unable to meet competition from new factories in countries in which labour
costs are lower, or capital investment in technology higher. These two ongoing
processes tend to exacerbate each other so that the deindustrialization issue,
which is also a concern to most advanced industrial economies, is particularly
acute here. On the whole, Canadian industry is not well structured, either in
terms of organization or in terms of attitudes, to deal with a growing range of
international technological and commercial challenges. The industrial sector
is conspicuous among Western nations for its relatively high costs, low

productivity, and lack of significant technological innovation. All of these accumulative economic and social processes are having an important and negative impact on the overall quality and nature of the work opportunities which are available to individuals. In addition, if these trends persist, it seems unlikely that it will be possible in the longer run to maintain the high standards of living which are part of the current experience and expectations of most Canadians.

REFERENCES

Bright, James R.
1958a *Automation and Management.* Cambridge, Mass.: Division of Research, Graduate School of Business Administration, Harvard University.

Bright, James R.
1958b "Does Automation Raise Skill Requirements?" *Harvard Business Review* Vol. 36: 85–98.

Britton, John N.H. and James M. Gilmour
1978 *The Weakest Link: A Technological Perspective on Canadian Industrial Underdevelopment.* Ottawa: Science Council of Canada, Background Study 43, Supply & Services.

Clement, Wallace
1975 *The Canadian Corporate Elite: An Analysis of Economic Power.* Toronto: McClelland & Stewart.

Clement, Wallace
1977 *Continental Corporate Power — Economic Linkages Between Canada and the United States.* Toronto: McClelland & Stewart.

Eggleston, Wilfrid
1978 *National Research in Canada: The N.R.C. 1916–1966.* Toronto: Clarke, Irwin.

Ellis, R.H.
1969 "Who Finds Jobs?" *Physics Today* (June): 117.

Folger, J.K., H.S. Astin, and A.E. Boyer
1970 *Human Resources and Higher Education.* New York: Russell Sage Foundation.

Gray, Herbert E.
1972 *Foreign Direct Investment in Canada.* Ottawa: Information Canada.

Gray, J. Lorne
1968 *Atomic Energy of Canada Brief,* submitted to the Senate of Canada Standing Committee on Science Policy, First Session, Twenty-eighth Parliament. Ottawa: Queen's Printer.

Harvey, Edward
1974 *Educational Systems and the Labour Market.* Toronto: Longmans.

Jaffe, A.J. and J. Froomkin
1968 *Technology and Jobs.* New York: Praeger.

Kushner, J., I. Masse, R. Blauner, L. Seroka
1971 *The Market Situation for University Graduates — Canada.* Ottawa: Department of Manpower & Immigration.

Levine, Oscar
1970 Unpublished research. Ottawa: National Research Council.

Lockhart, R. Alexander
1971   "Graduate Unemployment and the Myth of Human Capital", in D.I. Davies and K. Herman (eds.) *Social Space: Canadian Perspectives.* Toronto: New Press.

Lockhart, R. Alexander
1975   "Future Failure: the Unanticipated Consequences of Educational Planning," in R. Pike and E. Zureik (eds.) *Socialization and Values in Canadian Society.* Toronto: McClelland & Stewart.

Lockhart, R. Alexander
1977   "Educational Policy Development in Canada: A Critique of the Past and a Case for the Future," in R. Carleton, D. Colley, and A. MacKinnon (eds.) *Education, Change & Society: A Sociology of Canadian Education.* Toronto: Gage.

Lockhart, R. Alexander
1978   *Future Failure: A Systematic Analysis of Changing Middle Class Opportunities in Canada.* Unpublished Ph.D. Thesis, July 1978, The University of Essex.

Chapter 2

Labour in a Staples Economy*

Patricia Marchak

Defences for overcutting the forest on which the British Columbia economy depends are most frequently phrased in terms of protecting employment. They sound a paradoxical overhead noise against technological change that is designed in no small part to reduce employers' dependence on labour, while not in any way reducing the economy's dependence on the export of lumber, pulp, and newsprint to the United States. The effects of a concentrated, integrated staples industry include highly unstable employment conditions, the development of regional pools of labour which are used in several industrial sectors but for which no employer has long-term responsibility, uneven development of regions, and community instability. This paper is concerned with the political economy of the B.C. forestry industry and some of its effects on labour as revealed in a study of three communities during 1977–1978.

The three communities are representative of various patterns of dependency on the forestry staple. Mackenzie, a municipality of just over 5,000, began as a company town in the mid-sixties and is still dominated by its main employer, B.C. Forest Products (Noranda–Mead). Terrace is a much older community of about 10,000 (14,000 including surrounding communities). It has seen its pioneer sawmills taken over by Columbia Cellulose (U.S.) and then Canadian Cellulose (majority ownership by the B.C. government) as part of the package which included the now-antiquated Prince Rupert mill. There are two other, smaller forestry companies in Terrace: Price–Skeena (Abitibi) and Mcgillies and Gibbs (U.S.). Campbell River, with a population of 12,000, is also an older town though its growth has occurred largely since the 1940s. Although the Crown Zellerbach saw and pulp mill employs about a tenth of its population of 12,000 it has been able to take advantage of its proximity to Vancouver and Victoria to develop tourism and sports-fishing. There is also "some mining."[1]

ORGANIZATION OF THE INDUSTRY

The forestry industry in B.C. developed at the coast from about the 1880s, following the demise of the fur trade. Newsprint production sharply increased during the first war and afterward, in large part as a consequence of exemption for newsprint by U.S. tariffs.[2] Small lumber mills proliferated in the interior, serving a prairie and local as well as U.S. market, but the pulpmills were concentrated at the coast until the 1950s. The coastal timber is of exceptionally high quality, in high demand on world markets, and has low transportation costs via waterways.

*Reprinted with permission from *Studies in Political Economy: A Socialist Review*, Vol. 2 (Autumn 1979).

Depletion of coastal timber, technological change, and expanded markets provided the incentive for a post-war growth of pulpmill operations in the interior. Differentials in transportation costs were somewhat offset by improved methods of road building and the development of diesel trucks with wide, movable flatbeds capable of carrying more whole logs over longer distances. The discovery of means by which sawdust could be pulped where only chips and logs had previously been the raw material for pulpmills encouraged the construction of integrated saw and pulp facilities by large companies. Finally, new harvesting machines allowed for the cutting of vast quantities of timber for these mills.

The resource itself is owned by the provincial Crown, with the exception of about 5 per cent sold or given for railway grants prior to the first Forestry Act of 1912. The 5 per cent has been the most valuable timber and this still accounts for about 15 per cent of the annual export product,[3] but the remainder, and almost all of the interior timber, is leased under various legislative arrangements for periods ranging up to "in perpetuity." Even the shorter leases, however, are easily renewed.

As large companies added facilities in the interior, small mills were pushed out of business. There were 967 mills in 1961, 308 in 1976, a drop of 68 per cent. This process was blessed by a provincial government through legislation ostensibly designed to reduce air pollution from slash-burning by mills, requiring technical equipment too expensive for small mills, and through timber-leasing practices clearly and intentionally favouring large, integrated mills. With the sawdust method of pulping, and the improvements in transportation, there was a cost-advantage in situating large saw and pulp mills in the same location.[4] Large mills bought out small operators in order to obtain their timber reserves, and by the mid-1960s a few large companies controlled almost all of the timber throughout the interior. There are a few medium-sized nonintegrated mills with timber supplies which have managed to withstand the competition for resources. The few smaller mills which remain depend largely on cutting rights granted by large companies for "scavenging" on their lands, and sale of wood-chips to their pulp mills. Very few have independent resources.

Following the two Sloan Commission Reports in the 1940s and 1950s (a B.C. commission on forest resources) a program of "sustained yield" cutting was implemented, whereby a provincial forestry service was developed to monitor forest growth and reforestation, and companies were given specific quantities of timber for annual harvesting (known as "allowable annual cuts" on "timber quotas").[5] While there is a great deal of evidence that this program was observed as much in the exceptions as by the rules, there was at least an ideological acceptance of the need to provide for a renewable resource. Unlike minerals, trees are renewable in theory, but they take a century or more to grow, are subject to a plethora of diseases and fire hazards, and as yet — despite extensive research and experimentation — success in reforestation programs has not been remarkable. Despite denials by officials, there is widespread belief among forestry workers, that several areas of the province have been massively overcut and are in danger of running out of supplies within the next two decades.[6]

The 1978 Forests Act nonetheless provides for a cutting program that ignores sustained yield principles, substituting in their place quotas dependent as much on "the nature, production capabilities, and timber requirements of established and proposed timber processing plants," as on biological growth, ecological safety, or even markets.[7]

At present, ten companies control between 80 and 93 per cent of the forestry resource in each of the seven forestry districts, (via different licensing systems known as public sustained yield units and tree farm licences) and own about 35 per cent of the lumber facilities, 90 per cent of the pulp facilities, 100 per cent of the paper facilities, and 74 per cent of the plywood and veneer facilities. Five of these companies are foreign owned, and seven altogether are owned outside B.C.[8] Thirteen of the top twenty are foreign owned.

Forestry is, without a doubt, a staples industry in that it involves the extraction of a raw material, is shipped out to export markets in a relatively unprocessed state, and it dominates the regional economies throughout most of the province. It has not spawned either forward or backward linkages, and there is not a significant manufacturing industry connected either with wood products or with machinery and chemicals for the production of wood and paper. There is not even a substantial quality-paper products industry, by far the larger part of the resource being utilized for dimensional lumber, pulp, and newsprint.

Although the industry produces neither technically sophisticated products nor a range of manufactured items, it does produce its simple materials through a highly sophisticated imported technology. Logging has become increasingly mechanized. Sawmills were mechanized throughout the 1950s and 1960s, and newer mills are now partially "17" automated. Pulpmills have been automated for most of the post-war period, each few years allowing for extension of that process.

Markets are somewhat different in the three main sectors of the industry, and these differences affect labour. Lumber is sold on a vigorous market, except for sales to the Eastern seaboard of the United States. Here, three consortia dominate the marketing arrangements through access to transportation, storage, and distribution facilities.[9] Elsewhere, producing companies compete for sales through wholesalers and brokers on a per shipment basis, although the major companies still dominate in these markets. Sixty-eight per cent of the lumber is shipped to the United States.[10] In the two northern regions of our study, and in the south-eastern Kootenays, manufacturers stated that up to 80 per cent of their product has a United States destination. While foreign firms have guaranteed markets in their parent manufacturing firms in the United States and Japan, this edge has not been a disincentive to Canadian firms because of the strength of the U.S. market.

Pulp and newsprint markets, unlike lumber, are clearly oligopolistic. Entry into the industry is restricted by the long-term contracts, close connections between suppliers and purchasers, the extremely high capital investments in plant and equipment, and control of resources.[11]

Logging, unlike lumber and pulp or newsprint, operates on an "internal" rather than export market. Prior to the second war this internal market was an active and important one along the coast, where timber would be boomed or barged to manufacturers after sale by independent logging companies. Brokers and buyers would bid competitively for the timber. The integration of logging and sawmilling and pulp companies over the post-war period has undermined the effectiveness of this internal market. The majority of transactions today are not sales between sellers and buyers, both of whom are independent, but consist of trades between the large companies. A Task Force report in 1974 noted that:

> Today, these reciprocal sale or "swap" arrangements so dominate the log market that it is generally acknowledged that significant volumes of timber cannot be acquired by buyers who have nothing to trade. Few milling firms without linked logging operations are able to survive, and the inaccessibility of the market to independent buyers is particularly acute in periods of strong demand.[12]

In addition to exclusion of small and nonintegrated firms, this has meant that the relationship between log values and market price is artificially determined by the few large integrated companies. Further, since large mills operate most efficiently by mass producing essentially the same product rather than by cutting specialized products according to timber differences, the best utilization of different qualities and types of logs is an unlikely outcome of this market structure. Thus a more diverse manufacturing woods-products industry is prevented by the monopoly of resources by large firms. In the interior, a log market such as the Vancouver log market never developed, due partly to the relatively late growth of the industry in more remote areas and partly to the distances and costs of transportation.[13]

OVERALL EMPLOYMENT

About 9 per cent of all workers in B.C. are directly employed in the forestry industries.[14] Estimates of the total direct and indirect employment related to the industry have been calculated at 30 per cent.[15] The latter figure however does not tell much about the overall dependence on forests, because it includes the two major metropolitan areas which contain 56 per cent of the provincial population. Outside the lower mainland, almost every town and valley is dependent on forestry. In the towns where we conducted interviews, between 30 and 70 per cent of all adult men earned their incomes in forestry industries varying with the presence of other resource industries and government employment in the region. The remainder of the population, adult women and other men, are, of necessity, indirectly dependent on the viability of the industry. Shares of forestry employment by sector for production workers are approximately 18 per cent in logging (22 per cent including salaried workers); 27 per cent in lumber manufacture (32 per cent total); and 13 per cent in pulp and paper manufacture (18 per cent total).[16]

While the industry has expanded regionally and production rates have greatly increased in the past two decades, there are relatively small increases in employment of production workers. Production worker increases between 1963 and 1967 relative to production increases are 11 per cent to 67 per cent in logging; and between 1961 and 1976, 22 to 90 per cent in sawmills; 24 to 80 per cent in plywood and veneer; and 85 to 167 and 105 per cent respectively in wood pulp and paper. The larger increase in pulp-mill employment is connected to the rise in the number of mills between 1964 and 1973. There have been larger additions in the number of salaried workers, especially in pulpmills, though even where these are included the production rates per worker have all increased substantially. The increases, then, reflect investments in capital rather than increases in labour for production. It may be noted that 1976 was a "good" year for forestry, and employment was at record levels.[17]

Employment figures over the entire two decades show considerable variation, especially for logging and sawmills. The years 1970 and 1975 were slump years; 1969, 1973, and 1976 were strong years on export markets. In the period 1973 to 1976, sawmill employment of production workers first declined by nearly 10,000 workers (30 per cent of the 1973 total) then increased by nearly 6,000. Logging in the same period dropped nearly 5,000 workers, (23 per cent of the 1973 total) then added nearly 3,000. It would be difficult to avoid the conclusion that employment in these sectors is unstable, and that labour takes the brunt of market variance. While employment for salaried workers is not as variable as for production workers, the slump of 1975 affected them as well. They have not regained the levels reached in 1973–1974.

Unemployment rates in B.C. have generally exceeded the national average. Seasonal unemployment is a normal phenomenon for wood-workers, but a persistent and growing segment of the labour force encounters long periods of unemployment not attributable to the seasonality of logging. One study has provided evidence to the effect that unemployment in the forestry industries is particularly unstable, fluctuating directly with prices for wood products, and that unemployment in towns is greater, the greater the degree of dependence on the single staples production.[18] This underlines the weak position of labour in a nondiversified economy, especially in single-industry towns and regions. Since the surplus from the industry is not being reinvested in manufacturing facilities within the province (other than in expansion of the industry), this situation cannot be regarded as temporary.

Unemployment in the Terrace region in February 1978 was variously estimated by local residents at 15 per cent to well over 30 per cent. The Manpower office, which covers the entire northwest region, estimated that 2,500 unemployed applicants had registered at their office since January 1978. The population base for this is approximately 35,000 so the number represents about 22 per cent of the labour force (assuming a one-third labour force: population ratio). Statistics Canada also reported this figure as numbers seeking work in the region. This high rate was in part due to the prolonged closure of the Prince Rupert Mill, to which logs from the region would normally have been delivered.

Figures for unemployment become ambiguous in a region dependent on a single resource, where seasonal and other layoffs are part of "the normal package."

As our study indicates, extended seasonal layoffs lead to job search within the larger area. Labour migration is also characterized by the flow from one-company towns like Mackenzie and Kitimat, where housing is only available to employees. As a consequence neighbouring towns like Prince George or Terrace experience inflated unemployment rates.

Unemployment in forestry is somewhat masked by the interchangeability of unskilled workers and machine operators between forestry, mining, construction, and transportation. All of these sectors provide a substantial number of temporary jobs, and all are subject to considerable fluctuation in employment rates. Workers in one sector will move to other sectors between "preferred" jobs, so that unemployment rates for a region may not reflect the complete impact of a layoff or strike in the dominant industry.

The division of the labour force by sex which occurs throughout the economy is sharpened in resource regions, especially in company or otherwise single-industry towns. Women are rarely employed in logging or mills. Since there are few clerical positions available at mill sites, and they are not considered for managerial positions controlled by head offices (and normally subject to geographical mobility requirements), they are restricted to service and clerical jobs in the nonforestry private sector and government offices or service sectors. Many of these jobs are temporary and/or part-time, and almost all provide incomes close to the minimum wage levels. Nonetheless these jobs are integral to service, retail, and industrial operations: labour is required in restaurants, hotels, banks, stores, schools and hospitals. The wives of millworkers provide this labour, interspersing their periods of employment with periods of "homemaking, full time." Although their official unemployment rates have steadily increased throughout the 1970s, even these greatly under-represent their situation. For example, in the company town Mackenzie, there were a reported 115 applicants for a single post-office clerical position, 88 applicants for four cashiering jobs at a supermarket, and 77 applicants for six clerical positions in a mill.[19] In that same town, 15 out of 872 employees in the central mill during 1976 were women.[20] The number of positions available to women increases when the town has government offices, tourist facilities, or a regional shopping centre, as is the case in Campbell River. Nonetheless, the range of occupations remains limited mainly to services and clerical work. There are especially few openings for single women, and the wages are insufficient for their survival; thus daughters and estranged wives move out of resource towns.

LOGGERS

The logging sector of the industry has undergone substantial mechanization throughout the past decade. In one large camp where we conducted studies in 1977, 150 men were producing 24,000 cunits per day where it took 280 men to produce the same amount in 1967.[21] The cutback is attributable to a number of harvesting machines, especially useful on the flat terrain of the interior and the relatively small diameter trees there which permit machine operators to perform a range of tasks formerly requiring fallers, buckers, loaders, and numerous other specialized woodsmen. One faller and a skidder, together with a shearer or snipper machine, can now cut, delimb, and land 500 trees in a single day.

The composition of the remaining labour force has undergone a parallel change. A hierarchy associated with knowledge of the woods, experience, agility, and talent, has been replaced with one dependent entirely on seniority. Recruits are required to have general machine operation skills, and these are, for the most part, interchangeable with the skills required in construction.

The organization of the labour force has also undergone changes. Loggers can no longer obtain their own supplies and small independent companies have virtually disappeared. However, about half of all logging is contracted out to small firms, known in the industry as "stump-to-dump" contractors. These, in turn, sub-contract about half of the work to "owner-operators." The stump-to-dump contractors are allotted a territory by the large corporation, and are responsible for logging it at a set piece or total rate. They employ maintenance workers on an hourly basis, and that part of the machinery which is too expensive for single owner-operators. The owner-operators do most of the actual logging and trucking, using their own skidders, trucks and other equipment, on a piece-rate basis. They have strong incentives to work at high speeds for long days and to complete the job as quickly as possible. The large company thereby obtains its labour and machinery and high productivity rates without incurring long-term liabilities. The risks are all shouldered by contractors and owner-operators under these arrangements.

These small firms are still counted as independent companies and therefore show up on statistics as separate firms. They are, nonetheless, entirely dependent on big companies for contracts, and can be broken and put out of business by their employers. Among the reported practices are the granting of timber cutting rights on the least accessible, most rugged or swampy terrain in the harvesting area, and no renewals of contracts for firms which complain or make demands beyond conditions acceptable to other firms. While it is impossible to document either of these practices on the information available at present, there is little doubt that small contractors and their workers take for granted their inferior bargaining position and its consequences. The most accessible and least problematic terrains are logged by direct hourly employees of the large companies. This recognition notwithstanding, there is general agreement that the "best life" is that of the owner-operator, and such owners frequently consider themselves to be independent entrepreneurs.

The quality of work done by highly competitive small firms is widely acknowledged to be superior to that of hourly-paid workers in corporate employment. A Royal Commission of 1976 notes that "economies of scale in logging do not extend much beyond a single operation, and the efficiency of small enterprises is reflected in the extensive use of independent logging contractors by large firms."[22]

There is a noticeable difference in the camp culture and attitude toward employers between large corporate camps and small contractor camps (still called "gypo" operators, although the term originally referred to independent logging operations). The large operations are reportedly characterized by a great deal of theft of company property, apparently by both hourly and staff workers; by strict observance of union skill jurisdictions and seniority rules; by general indifference to the company and not infrequently to the union as well. Small operations, including many owner-operators on piece-rates whose equipment is a precious life-line to a sense of independence, display fewer signs of alienation. If a machine breaks down in a small camp, the operator finds a way of repairing it and other workers come to his aid if at all possible. Past histories of makeshift repairs are the body of folklore in a camp, and mutual obligations are taken seriously. Since piece-rates affect so many workers, there is a recognized incentive to put in as many hours as the daylight will permit, and to do routine repairs in evening hours. There are reportedly fewer thefts. In the camps we visited, although the comforts and food were inferior to large camps, and owner-operators were required to pay a daily board and room fee, distaste for large corporations as employers was expressed. This takes the form of unfocused hostility to "bigness" and general skepticism. Big business is blamed for overcutting and bureaucratic, oversupervised working conditions; unions are equally blamed for their contribution to alienating conditions of work; and governments are blamed for policies that allow not only overcutting but such events as flooding of valleys filled with timber for purposes of erecting dams. The "little" logger is a free-enterpriser with skepticism built on experience with any large institution.

In addition to the displacement of risk and obligation for the labour force, the large companies are supplied with a surplus of labour which has no legal claim on employers and which is available according to market demand. Such a surplus normally forces down the cost of labour, and the hourly rates are, in fact, sufficiently lower than the piece rates for owner-operators that workers strive to put together savings for their own machines in the hope of thereby attaining prosperity. The relative returns, however, are often illusory. The payments on machinery are extremely high and can be met only if owners are steadily employed for long periods of time. Repairs are also costly. The accident rate in small contractor camps is reported to be high.[23] If the contractor is involved in an accident with loss of time, or the stump-to-dump operator loses his contract, the machinery payments can't be met. Among the loggers we interviewed, a history of machine purchases, "independent" employment, accidents or lengthy layoffs, loss of machines, and re-employment on hourly wages was typical. The occasional "good year" in which such loggers "make a killing" remains, nonetheless, a strong incentive. Even in those good years, a "killing" turns out to be about the average salary of a lower to middle-management administrator in the company's head offices, and somewhat less than a supervisor in a pulpmill. For loggers on an hourly basis, there was no apparent difference between employees of small and large firms.[24]

The labour surplus is increased by the seasonality of the industry. Layoffs have always been part of a cycle dependent on weather. As road and transportation methods have improved, the need for layoffs due to weather has decreased, but overproduction and variable markets have become substitute reasons for regular annual layoffs. In addition, with big unions and big companies strikes are frequent. The strikes sometimes take the place of layoffs, since companies are not eager to solve labour problems when they are afflicted with oversupplies for their markets. In the integrated industry, shut-downs in one sector of the industry have repercussions throughout the other sectors: the closure of a pulpmill for renovations or a strike in the lumber mills will bring about closure of the woods or severe cutbacks in employment.

In the pre-war era these layoffs were dealt with by loggers through a variety of other seasonal employments. Since agriculture and fishing are now big businesses as well, with complex seniority rules, parallel technical developments, and decreasing employment opportunities, and since rural occupations on a small scale are no longer available in any substantial degree, the loggers have moved into a different organization of industries and employments. They have the option of taking unemployment insurance throughout a layoff (dependent on length of previous days worked), but while UI is helpful to employers by its ability to keep a reserve labour force in the region, it is generally unsatisfactory to the workers.

Our research found that while loggers relied on UI for short layoffs, they spent longer layoffs and strikes seeking work throughout the region. The work they found was mainly with other large companies, some in forestry, others in mining and industrial construction (where contracting is again a characteristic) and with government departments or corporations such as Highways or B.C. Hydro. These jobs are typically of temporary duration. They involve the same range of skills as are used by labourers and machine operators in forestry. Another study of loggers in 1973 found the same pattern. Cottell argued that:

> Security for these men lay in their mobility itself — the ability to find work with whatever industry or company it was available, and so be employed for as much of the year as possible. They took pride in the portability and variety of their skills, an ability to "do anything" and be a "jack-of-all-trades."[25]

What this amounts to, then, is the development of a regional labour force with certain minimal machine skills, which is available for a round of employments according to large company needs for temporary workers. The jobs done by these workers are necessary and anticipated, therefore one must conclude the organization is neither capricious nor stop-gap in nature.

All of the large corporations benefit from this arrangement, since all obtain their labour without long-term obligations, on an hourly pay basis, with minimal accumulation of seniority rights, and basically outside union protection. Of course the elasticity of labour also works against large company interests in the years of strong markets where these occur simultaneously in several industries. In 1972–73, for example, the turnover rate in mining, logging, and sawmills was well over 100 per cent as workers experienced a sellers' market. During this period, companies commissioned numerous studies of turnover rates, citing the costs of constant replacements and inexperienced workers.[26] It was a time of tougher bargaining by unions, and increases in hourly wages. The benefits were uneven, however, greater in the industrial towns than in more rural areas, and the long-term inflation of prices increased the gap. Nor did the shortage induce employers to expand their "permanent" work force.

Loggers, together with some sawmill and pulpmill workers, are represented by the International Woodworkers of America. This union bargains on a regional basis with an employers' council, representing the large national and international firms. Regional union offices cover extensive areas, with few permanent personnel. The bargaining coverage is variable: in the Northwest, it includes contractors with as many as 50 employees, together with their own employees; in parts of the central interior and Northeast, it provides no coverage to small-firm employees. The groups not covered include those whom the union has not organized, and those who have actively rejected organization. Unionization is strongest on the coast, which has been organized into large corporate production units as well for a much longer time. These varying situations may explain why the I.W.A. appears to lack affectionate local support throughout much of the interior. There are, however, three other, perhaps more pressing, reasons.

One is suggested by Lucas in his study of single-enterprise towns.[27] It is that the turnover in some of these communities is so great, there is no way to build up a continuing membership and leadership core for union locals. In company towns, as well, company recruitment policies can effectively neutralize or oust a union. In Mackenzie, nearly 57 per cent of those interviewed said they anticipated a move in the foreseeable future, only 13 per cent expected to reside there permanently, and our sampling data indicated a 20 per cent turnover in a single-month period.[28] The rates are not all this high, and they are much lower in larger and less isolated towns, but in all, the turnover reduces union strength.

In addition, where workers are frequently engaged in temporary jobs both in one town and in several throughout a region, they may not seek union membership and may not have the opportunity to participate in unions. The structure of unions, with their emphasis on seniority rights and exclusive jurisdictions, prevents the development of a strong, regionally organized labour force which includes construction, transportation, mining and forestry workers together and throughout their many employments.

The third reason is symbolized in the support given to the 1978 Forests Act up to the final few days of legislative debate, and a turnabout only after the NDP and numerous grassroots regional groups had expressed opposition. On the whole the legislation did not threaten the interests of secure and established hourly workers. It provided for further consolidation of timber rights for large companies, and provided only minimal protection to contractors and small businesses. It required no public hearings and protected secrecy for large companies and the government in other ways, especially regarding timber allotments and cuts.[29] Though this international union has Canadians as half of its total membership, it does not appear to have the internal momentum or gut-level sense of local interests to mount an independent policy opposition to corporate owners in the industry.

MILLING

In sawmilling, most observers agree that some of the most advanced, innovative, and efficient mills have been built by small companies. Moreover, I have found no evidence to suggest that, even among the large integrated corporations themselves, either technical or economic efficiency is correlated with corporate size.

In short, the extent of industrial consolidation has proceeded well beyond what can be considered to have been necessary to keep pace with technological change and efficiencies of scale.[30]

These observations in the Pearse Royal Commission Report echo the Sloan Commission of twenty years earlier and several task-force reports between the two. Yet none of these led to a move toward decentralization of the industry. The 1978 Forests Act that followed the Pearse Report ignored the implications.[31]

Sawmills and pulpmills are in different phases of development. Sawmills are mechanized, becoming automated; pulpmills are well into an automated stage. In addition, there are still some nonintegrated and medium-sized sawmills in existence and a few speciality-cut mills. The selling market is fairly competitive — though increasingly oligopsonistic on supplies. Pulpmills operate in an oligopolistic international market.

Both mechanization and automation lead to decreases in the labour component of production, but the decrease creates a higher ratio of capital to labour in automation, whereas mechanized industries are still labour intensive. Mechanization leads to a demand for unskilled workers; automation leads to a demand for skilled workers, and the ratio of skilled to unskilled is the reverse of that found in mechanized industries. Because unskilled workers are in greater supply (and the definition of unskilled keeps being upgraded so that this proportion does not substantially change over time), mechanized industries can obtain a labour supply without providing long-term job security.

In addition, capital-intensive industries are extremely costly to operate at less than continuous and full production. The more capital invested in machinery, and the more reliant the industry on skilled workers, the more incentive there is to employers to create a permanent and secure labour force. Less expensive investments create fewer cost penalties for labour turnover.

These differences are evident in the working conditions, wage differentials, and employment practices of sawmills and pulpmills even where the two are owned by the same company and agglomerated at the same location. Sawmills, with a very high proportion of all workers doing unskilled and machine operation jobs under supervision, have high turnover rates. The employers' problems with transience, although much modified by the sharp increase in overall unemployment in B.C. since 1975, are the workers' responses to sawmill conditions. The work is repetitive, monotonous, individuated (assembly-style), and performed in extremely noisy and dusty conditions. Furthermore, the wage-scale is lower than in pulpmills, although wages for the same skill-levels — especially in integrated mills, where the comparison is accessible — would be the same. Jobs allow for little personal discretion, choice of pace or variability of quantity or content in the work, less than is the case for many workers in logging (not yet fully mechanized) or pulping (automated). Tradesmen are the only workers exempt from the general description. A small contingent of tradesmen is required for servicing machinery, and these operate on a sellers' market and so have both higher wages and more discretion.

Sawmills react to fluctuations in world (mainly United States) markets by cutting back on production, and thus on workers. Layoffs, while not as much a regular part of the work cycle as for loggers, are a normal event in slow market years, and workers can anticipate these when they obtain information on lumber sales. Layoffs are allocated by seniority ranks, the least senior being the first to go. These fluctuations in the size of the sawmill labour force add to the overall transience in this sector.

Very large mills, particularly those which have substantial investments in machinery or have moved toward automation, may actually be less stable than smaller and less capitalized mills. Although they can withstand slow markets for longer periods than small mills, they have less flexibility in their operating costs and their owners have alternative locations for capital. Small mills might operate on a casual basis, where they can rely on a rural labour force which also farms, fishes, or engages in casual work elsewhere. They do not lose large overhead costs when they temporarily close or when they cut back a daily shift. When a large mill takes over the industry in a region, the work force is transformed into an industrial one, dependent on daily mill employment. Prolonged layoffs create extreme tension in the community, since it no longer has fall-back options. When this labour "problem" is added to the very high overhead costs large mill owners may choose to shut down a mill altogether rather than wait out a market. The mills most likely to undergo permanent closure when markets decline are those owned by foreign corporations which have other, more profitable investments elsewhere and no long-term need for the host community. This is especially true where other investments include mills in home territories. The U.S. conglomerate, Evans Products, for example, closed two mills in B.C. in 1974. In both cases the closures meant community instability because the mills had become the central employers in the region.

In order to obtain a stable core of workers, large mills have employed immigrants whose background is nonindustrial and whose alternative employment opportunities are limited. At the present time many of these are from Portugal and India. These workers are extremely stable and unwilling to support strikes or other labour resistance actions. Their reasoning is that their first priority is to obtain steady incomes for their families, and their orientation is toward kin groups rather than work.[32] In this respect they resemble many earlier immigrant groups. The consequence is that these workers accumulate seniority though few become supervisors or tradesmen because of language barriers. This creates resentment among other workers, and these immigrants become the object of derision and hostility which is frequently expressed outside the mills in the streets, beer parlours, and town life. The racism cuts across the working class, divides it and weakens its bargaining capacity.

Pulpmills require fewer workers whose market value consists of physical strength, but also few craftsmen whose particular knowledge of the industry is necessary. Papermaking, for example, is now a computerized procedure ensuring high quality consistency. Thus engineering degrees take the place of apprenticeships in the art of papermaking. The skills demanded in automated mills are basic literacy, sometimes arithmetical literacy, ability to read computer printouts, and ability to learn how to operate automated control panels. A high proportion of workers in pulpmills is on salary, since the operation requires continuous production and the skills are consistent with traditional perceptions of technical and clerical rather than manual labour. This is symbolized by job titles, where machine-tenders rather than machine-operators predominate. Formal education levels are higher than for sawmills, and higher for the younger age groups than for the same groups in logging and sawmilling. It is only in the pulping sector of the industry that any perceptible difference in occupational levels and salary is connected with differences in education, though in all of the sectors the educational levels have steadily increased. An increasing number of younger workers have university degrees.

The age distribution of pulp workers is skewed in favour of workers over 40, whereas workers in their 20s and 30s predominate in logging, and the distribution is more widely dispersed in sawmilling. In none of these industries in 1977–78 were there large numbers of workers under 25 years. This reflects the decline in new employment opportunities which especially affect the young entrants to the labour force. It also reflects company policies which favour married workers who are less prone to quit when they disagree or are dissatisfied.[33]

As a consequence of the differences in working conditions, job security and wages, there is an increasing distance between the material standards, educational and skill-levels, marketability, and lifestyles of pulpmill workers and those of saw and logging workers. The latter form the regional labour pool, mobile between jobs and available for various industrial employments throughout a region. The former become the stable core of industrial towns. The differences appear to be transferred in terms of opportunities to the next generation, but this must be stated tentatively because our sample is not large enough to provide compelling evidence, there are no secondary sources to test this, and the pulpmill industry of the interior is still too new to provide much inter-generational evidence. In our sample, the young recruits in a coastal pulpmill included more children of fathers in that sector than of fathers in sawmilling and logging, and altogether included a high proportion of children whose fathers were owners, managers, or skilled tradesmen. In the youngest age group (18–24), several workers were regularly employed during summers by the pulpmill, and were undergoing university educations in engineering during the winters; their fathers were pulpmill workers. Altogether there were very few immigrants in this work force except among tradesmen, and these were from industrial countries (a practice which allows employers to subsidize very little on-the-job apprenticeship training).

Among young loggers and sawmill workers, fathers were engaged in logging, mining, farming, and construction — mostly as labourers.

It should be noted that these "reserve" and "central" labour pools are both associated with large companies or with a mixture of large companies and their dependent contractors. In the company towns there is scarcely any "peripheral" industry in the form of genuinely small and independent businesses. The service sector consists of the local branches of the banks, Hudson's Bay, Weston's drugs (Tamblyn), the gas and oil companies, one or other of the large grocery chains, and machinery rental, sale, or repair shops such as Pacific Terex, Finning Tractors, Kal-Tyre and Acklands. These companies, together with government services, are staffed by the remainder of the male labour force and by women. In the larger or older towns, and those which are regional centres or closer to metropolitan areas, there is a peripheral sector of local retail shops and restaurants, but even in these towns the majority of smaller businesses are franchises, agencies, branches, or sub-sidiaries of large companies.

There is also a division between salaried and hourly employees. To some extent this is marked by income differentials over a several-year period, but more importantly, it consists of differentials in job security, upward mobility, and access to skill upgrading. Over time, salaried workers are more likely to experience increases in their marketable skills and bargaining position; hourly workers, though initial wages may be equal, are more likely to experience either no change or downgrading of skills and bargaining position. These differences are transmitted to a second generation, via greater residential stability, upwardly mobile role models, accumulation of savings, and access to education.

Although the hourly labour force in industrial towns experiences instability of employment and some portion of it annually seeks other temporary work, the overall wage structure is higher than in rural regions where communities lack either access to the resources or local employers. This population of both men and women annually works at a series of temporary jobs attached to forestry, highways construction, tourism, mining, and farming. Often such villages grew around small family mills which have since disappeared or which now operate occasionally on corporate contracts. The average annual income (including UI) is very much lower than that of workers in industrial towns, and a significant portion of its subsistence consists of exchanges of goods and services outside the money economy.[34] Again, the gap between this population and that in industrial towns cannot be explained strictly in terms of corporate versus peripheral sectors, because though its employment is invariably temporary and marginal, its round of employers includes large as well as small businesses.

CONCLUSIONS

There exists a body of theory for the industrial and social development of Canadian resource regions on which government and industrial policies are ostensibly based.[35] With minor variations, the theory posits an incremental growth in population size, employment, affluence, diversity of economic base, and stability and self-sufficiency of communities, around an initial staples base. Growth takes a sequential form by which the staples generate sufficient surplus to reinvest in further production facilities for new products out of the same staple (the forward linkages), and the machinery itself to produce both the original and new products (the backward linkages). These increments to the economic base will then demand a larger population of workers, and these in turn require more service and goods producing industries; an original resource community becomes a larger, more self-sufficient, and more stable town.

On the basis of this conventional theory, governments — both federal and provincial — have encouraged resource companies to establish facilities in hinterland regions. Large companies have been favoured with land grants, special legislation, and privileged access to resources, because, it is argued, large companies are more reliable (less likely to close down in a recession), more responsible (they have a long-term interest in the resource and the labour force), and more profitable (economies of scale produce higher returns to this economy as well as to the producer).

The forestry industry has had a century to generate "spin-off" industrial growth in resource regions. Large companies have had highly favourable conditions for developing local economies, creating stability and self-sufficiency of communities in which they have plants, and providing increasing levels of steady employment. They have had incentives in the form of long-term leases on their resource supplies and cooperative governments ready to supply infra-structure and helpful legislation. They have also had a labour force which is disciplined, schooled, and trained for an industrial society, a culture conducive to industrial development, and a physical environment suitable for a wide range of industries.

The evidence presented in this paper suggests, however, that the conventional theory cannot be sustained.

The alternative theory for the fate of a staples economy within monopoly capitalism rests on the assumption that industrial development will take place at the pace, in the form, and with the labour supplies and conditions which are most profitable to capital, and that stability will be determined by such factors as the relative profit incentives in various regions and the amortization costs of capital investments. It proceeds with no necessary expectations about the development of secondary industry, local utilization of surplus, or community growth and self-sufficiency. These are all functions of cost-accounting decisions, and the accounting is done by large companies in their own interests and [in those of] the class and metropolitan regions which most benefit from the extraction of resources from chronically underdeveloped regions.[36]

Public policy has been directed toward providing the resource and infra-structure for, and supporting the labour policies of, capital. The state has retained its ownership rights over most of the resource, but this has strengthened, not weakened, the position of capital. The state has to maintain a large forestry service, and provide a large share of the funds for infra-structure and resource renewal. The companies pay a fraction of these costs and obtain a degree of control only marginally smaller than appears to be the case in other areas, such as Nova Scotia, where the land can be privately owned.

With respect to Crown ownership of facilities, Canadian Cellulose, purchased under the NDP government, consists of three major properties, two of which are antiquated mills deemed to be of no further value by their former American owners. These mills would have been renovated by Columbia Cellulose and Crown Zellerbach, the former owners, if the resource on which they depended had been sufficient for long-term future exploitation. There was thus no threat to the industry in the purchase, and the subsequent Social Credit government managed to re-sell "shares" in the properties to the public in order to "re-establish free enterprise."

A B.C. government, dependent on the forestry and mining industries, highly dependent on the decisions of Canadian Pacific in its many roles in transportation, realty (Marathon), forestry (MacMillan Bloedel and Pacific Logging) and mining (Cominco), and on the banking policies of the big five in central Canada, is not in a strong bargaining position even if (in the entirely hypothetical case) it were to concern itself with workers and communities.

The long-term developments of this staples economy include widespread unemployment; steady decreases in labour control over pace and other working conditions even where the owner-operator form persists; skill debasement or machine-attendance as a substitute for skill; and disparities in rewards for participation. I would argue that these are not exclusively problems of capitalist economies, since precisely the same complex of conditions with the single exception of unemployment (which becomes underemployment instead) occurs within state monopoly industrial economies. Public ownership does not automatically lead to workers' control, community control, or self-sufficient regions. Both forms of monopoly have an imperative to destroy nonindustrial cultures where these compete for the resource or the territory containing the resource. In Northern B.C. this especially affects native peoples who had managed to retain a hunting economy prior to the growth of forestry industries in the interior.[37]

Alternative strategies could be genuine alternatives only if power were dispersed, decentralized, and inaccessible to any single group of directors. With respect to the forestry industry, decentralization is entirely possible, without a loss in industrial capacity and with a potential net increase in productivity, a potential net decrease in destruction of the resource. Logging and sawmills are both recognized to be more efficient on smaller scales, and speciality products based on selective logging would increase the diversity of economic base. The cost advantages of integrated facilities are not social advantages; they are merely advantages to capital and means of maintaining power over the industry. There is no reason to discard technological advantages of harvesting machines and efficient saws if these are, as they can easily be, situated in more and smaller locations under local control. Pulpmills are less easily dismantled. There is a strong argument in favour of large units, but there is an even stronger argument in favour of less reliance on pulp and newsprint production in the overall economy. At the present time the technology rather than the needs of workers, communities, or markets, determines the production rates.

One community group has analysed the concentrated foreign-owned forestry industry in the central Kootenays, and detailed an alternative. This would involve a number of small mills each locally owned (type of ownership not specified), small logging companies engaged in selective logging, and both logging and manufacturing being directed toward specialized products rather than mass production. These activities would be co-ordinated, together with resource utilization policies and reinvestment decisions, by a locally-based management committee. If both the resource and markets were accessible, this alternative would be feasible and it would significantly reduce the ecological damage presently occurring in local forest areas. There would be both a greater number of jobs and a greater range of occupational possibilities.[38]

The flaw in this plan, of course, is that neither the resource nor the market is accessible. Even if a provincial government were to radically alter resource policies in favour of small entrepreneurs, community-owned companies, or worker-controlled companies, these producers would require market access until their surplus could be reinvested in local communities and a more diverse range of industries. Protection of access would require cooperation at least at a national level; development would require financial support; and transportation of supplies as well as products would require a national-level government which is unable to ignore local needs and interests. In short, a small community cannot become independent or self-sufficient on its own, even where it has the resources and skills to produce a range of products. Without a restructuring of the larger economy, as long as the staple has market value or is depleted, a staples region will continue to produce staples. All that changes over time is labour, variable in more senses than one.

NOTES

1. Exploratory research was conducted in the Southeast region between 1974 and 1976. The major part of the study was conducted in Mackenzie (Northeast), Terrace (Northwest) and Campbell River (South Coast) in 1977–1978. This consisted of interviews with all adult residents of 385 households, and questionnaire data for all residents over 12 years of age in 319 households. There were altogether 1418 respondents, 748 of whom were interviewed. In addition, employers were interviewed, and data were gathered on regional economies and the industry. The research is still in progress, and analysis of interview and questionnaire data is not yet complete.

2. The exemption was brought about when the Hearst newspapers applied pressure on U.S. legislators. The suppliers in that country were claimed to be monopolistic in their pricing practices. For general histories of the industry see O.W. Taylor, *Timber, History of the Forest Industry in B.C.*, Vancouver: J.J. Douglas, 1975; Ed Gould, *Logging*, Saanichton: Hancock, 1975; and The B.C. Forest Industries *1965–66 Yearbook*, Section A, Vancouver: Mitchell, 1965.

3. Peter H. Pearse, Commissioner, Report of the Royal Commission on Forest Resources, *Timber Rights and Forest Policy in British Columbia*, Victoria: Queen's Printer, 1976, Vol. I, 23.

4. Discussions of economies of scale are given in James Dobie, *Economies of Scale in Sawmilling in British Columbia*, unpublished Ph.D. thesis Oregon State University, June 1971; R. Hayter, *An Examination of Growth Patterns and Locational Behaviour of Multi-Plant Forest Product Corporations in British Columbia*, unpublished Ph.D. thesis, University of Washington, 1973; Doreen K. Mullins, *Changes in Location and Structure in the Forest Industry of North Central British Columbia: 1909–1966*, unpublished M.A. thesis, U.B.C., 1967; and Ronald N. Byron, *Community Stability and Regional Economic Development*, unpublished Ph.D. thesis, U.B.C., 1976.

5. Gordon McG. Sloan, Commissioner, *Royal Commission on the Forest Resources of British Columbia*, Victoria, C.F. BanField, Printer to the King, 1945; and *The Forest Resources of British Columbia, 1956*, Victoria: Queen's Printer, 1957 (2 vols.).

6. Beliefs, at least where they run counter to official statements, are difficult to document. This statement is based on persistent concerns voiced by respondents in our study and by many others throughout the province. Since they must remain anonymous, I can only assert that the belief is widely held. The problem in most regions is nonselective cutting combined with damage done to the forest ecology by some cutting methods.

7. Government of British Columbia. The Forests Act, 1978, section 7 (3)(c). The concept of "sustained yield" is not defined in the new Act. Section (c) has equal status with other instructions regarding determination of cutting allowances based on forest composition and growth rates; the "short and long-term implications to the Province of alternative rates of

timber harvesting from the area," and "the economic and social objectives of the Crown. . . ."

8. MacMillan Bloedel is counted as a B.C. firm in this summary statement because the majority of its stockholders are in B.C., the head offices and most of the production facilities are in the province. Nonetheless, the largest single stockholder is Canadian Pacific Investments, with 13.5 per cent.

9. Pearse, op. cit., Vol. I, ch. 21 describes markets. The three marketing groups for the Eastern seaboard are MacMillan Bloedel, Eacom Timber Sales, and Seaboard Lumber Sales.

10. Ibid., Vol. I, Table 21.1, 291.

11. Pearse argues that B.C. companies are not leaders in price-determination, though they are important elements in the market, 293–294. This view is challenged by Richard Schwindt, who accords them much greater prominence, in "the Pearce Commission and the Industrial Organization of the British Columbia Forest Industry," *B.C. Studies*, No. 41 (Spring 1979): 15–16.

12. Task Force on Crown Timber Disposal, 1974, *Second Report*, 167–168, cited in Pearse, op. cit., Vol. I, 297.

13. Pearse, op. cit.

14. Ibid., Vol. I, Table 4.1, 36.

15. F.L.C. Reed and Associates Ltd., *The British Columbia Forest Industry, Its Direct and Indirect Impact on the Economy*, Report prepared for the B.C. Government, Department of Lands, Forests, and Water Resources, 1973, Table 7, 63.

16. Pearse, Vol. 1, Table 4.1, 36.

17. All employment figures cited in this section are from special runs provided by Mr. Tony Laanemae, Forestry Advisor, Statistics Canada, Vancouver Office, and Statistics Canada Annual publications on logging, sawmills, and pulpmills. Figures for 1961 employment in logging are not available in comparable form to subsequent years.

   It is the practice in the industry to base projections and summaries on good years. In the Reed publication cited above, for example, data for 1970 were the most recent data available, but data for 1969 were given as well because, in the opinion of the consultants, "1969 is a more representative year," F.L.C. Reed, op. cit., 9.

18. Byron, op. cit., 90–137.

19. Joan Kotarski, "Mackenzie Report," in *Northern B.C. Women's Task Force on Single Industry Resource Communities*, 1977, 90. The mill figure was given us by that company.

20. B.C. Forest Product, *Annual Report*, 1976, cited in Kotarski, op. cit., 90–94.

21. B.C. Forest Products camp, data provided by the company.

22. Pearse, Vol. I, 61.

23. I have no independent data to test this statement. Loggers themselves are the source, and the accident rates in small camps visited were indeed high, but comparative data for a large enough number of large and small camps have not been gathered.

24. For 1977 this might have ranged between $24,000 and $35,000. The majority of loggers earned between $14,000 and $24,000, and the annual figures appeared to vary considerably even for the same skill groups, because of layoffs, regional differences in amount of time worked, and whether workers had seniority.

25. Phil Cottell, "Loggers View Instability as Key to Maximum Employment," *B.C. Logging News*, January 1975.
26. Examples for the forestry industries are, B.C. Research, *Labour Instability in the Skeena Manpower Area*, Vancouver, 1978; A. Alexander and D.T. Bryant, B.C. Research, "Labour Turnover at Mackenzie." Prepared for B.C. Forest Products Ltd., Vancouver, 1974, and subsequent studies by this group. A study commissioned by Alcan received a wide reading. This was R.D. Algar et al. *Report of the Task Force on Hourly Employee Turnover*, 1973. The Skeena Manpower report was not well received because it discussed a problem that had ceased to be critical in the Terrace region by the time it was published.
27. Rex A. Lucas, *Minetown, Milltown, Railtown*, Toronto: University of Toronto Press, 1971, esp. 140–41.
28. Questionnaire data, Mackenzie.
29. For example, public hearings are not required for extensions of licences within a 25-year period, conversions from present tenures to what the Act calls "evergreen" tenures as established in 1978, new timber sales, or situations in which local residents are opposed to present logging practices of existing tenure holders. They are stipulated only for new tree farm and pulpwood harvesting licences, but given the present tenure holdings in the province these are less critical to future harvesting than any of the other licensing conditions. In addition, there is an explicit clause prohibiting the public from obtaining information from members of the Forestry Service regarding the buying, selling, or harvesting of timber on publicly-owned lands. Public servants who give out this information are subject to dismissal from their jobs (section 149(2)).
30. Pearse, op. cit., Vol. I, 61.
31. For example, there are no provisions for competition between companies at public auctions for either new forest or timber sale licences (sections 11 and 16). Continuing practices which have grown outside the law over the post-war period, the new Act actually protects a noncompetitive system of sealed bids, bonuses for bids, and preferences for "designated applicants" who may submit second bonus bids equal to the highest bid submitted by others, should any others happen to bid against established operators. It is left to the chief forester's discretion to determine who will be the "approved applicant."
32. Interview data obtained with the aid of translators. The kin-group orientation has also been noted by Annama Joy in studies of immigrant workers in the Okanagan currently in progress, and I am grateful to her for sharing her information.
33. The turnover reports cited above point out the advantages, and in all of the companies in which we did interviews mention was made of this preference.
34. Findings in exploratory studies in the Kootenay valleys. Reported in "Corporate and Non-Corporate Labour in a Hinterland Economy: the case of Forestry Workers in British Columbia," paper presented to the Poland–Canada Exchange Seminar, Poland, May 1977, and "Women in Corporate and Marginal Employment Situations in Hinterland Forestry Towns in British Columbia," presented to Conference on Recent Research on Women, Mt. St. Vincent University, Halifax, November 1976.
35. The theory is implicit throughout both federal and provincial regional reports and "social impact" studies conducted for new development proposals. At the level of theory, expansion around a staples base was

discussed by W.A. Mackintosh, "Economic Factors in Canadian History," *The Canadian Historical Review*, Vol. IV, No. 1, March 1923, 12–25, and by the neo-classical economists who followed him; and in B.C. the theory is expressed most eloquently in P.A. Shearer, (ed.), *Exploiting our Economic Potential: Public Policy and the British Columbia Economy.*

36. I am indebted to discussion of this theory in the many papers of the "Marginal Work Worlds Project" at the Institute of Public Affairs, Dalhousie University, Halifax. The problem of "ability" versus "willingness" to pay is discussed, especially, in papers by Martha Macdonald.

37. The destruction of Indian communities by large-scale logging over hunting and trapping grounds is dealt with in other papers, and has recently been discussed by Douglas Hudson in "Bush and Bulldozer: A Clash of Staples in Northern British Columbia," *mimeo* paper presented to Science and Technology Studies Colloquium, U.B.C., October 19–20, 1978.

38. Solcan Valley Community Forest Management Project, *Final Report*, 1974.

Chapter 3

From Farm Boy to Oil Man: The Human Side of Dependent Development in Alberta*

J.D. House

The Canadian province of Alberta provides a challenging case for proponents of dependency theory (Frank, 1967; Oxaal, Barnett and Booth, 1975). Any simple notions that foreign ownership and control, and the domination of a nation's (or, in this case, a province's) economy by the subsidiaries of multinational corporations with their head offices elsewhere, must *necessarily* entail underdevelopment, high unemployment and underemployment, and low incomes for the bulk of the local population, are clearly refuted in the case of Alberta. On the contrary, Alberta is one of the most prosperous areas in the world: unemployment is low, personal incomes are high, there is no sales tax, and the government coffers are overflowing with oil revenues. While much of Alberta's new wealth can be attributed to the fortuitous effects of the OPEC-induced oil crisis of the early seventies, the province was more developed than underdeveloped even before that. Indeed, most of the data upon which the following analysis is based were gathered from 1973 to 1975 *before* the current boom got underway (for an account of the latter, see Foster, 1979).

Earlier, I have attempted to explain aspects of this combination of foreign ownership and modern development, albeit dependent and uneven development (1977; 1978; 1980). In Canada, at least three factors are important: (1) the major oil companies prefer to man their Canadian operations with well-trained locals, even in senior positions; (2) the dominant position of the majors in this open resource industry still leaves many opportunities for small local companies in petroleum exploration and production; and (3) since the majors do most of their business on a contract basis, there is a great opportunity for the growth of the local drilling, service, and supply business. More recent events in the North Sea show that, in countries that are already fairly developed in terms of educational level, local infra-structure, and potential petroleum service and supply firms, the oil companies pursue a strategy of *incorporation* rather than *exploitation* as they adapt to a new region. In many ways, the companies' interests coincide with those of the local people (in the short run), who can reap personal benefits by gearing up to

---

*This article draws on material from Chapters 5, 6, and 7 of *The Last of the Free Enterprisers: The Oilmen of Calgary* (Toronto: Macmillan of Canada, 1980). The early chapters of the book analyse the social organization of the Albertan oil industry and the Canadian subsidiaries of the major oil companies, while the concluding chapter makes some general observations about the recent political economy of Canadian oil and its implications for various regions of the country.

43

satisfy the industry's needs. The local people are *seduced* rather than *raped* by the oil companies.[1]

My purpose here is to examine part of the *human* side of this dependent development as it is experienced in Alberta. I will not consider here the wider social implications of oil-related development, but will focus only upon the work experiences of people directly employed in the oil industry in Calgary. And, among these, my concern is only with professional, managerial, and entrepreneurial oilmen, not with either nonprofessional workers in the field or with the phalanx of female secretaries who serve the almost exclusively male oilmen within the many high rise office buildings that dominate the skyline of downtown Calgary. The research reported upon was carried out between 1973 and 1975. The main technique used was semi-structured interviewing with 121 people working in various jobs within the industry, supplemented by some direct observation at Imperial Oil's Calgary operations, and a mailed survey of a random sample of 350 Calgary oilmen.[2]

The social organization of the Canadian oil industry provides for a great variety of alternative career opportunities for professionally trained engineers, geologists, and geophysicists; and, secondarily, business graduates, chartered accountants, and lawyers. I will begin the analysis by examining the typical career patterns of Calgary oilmen; relate these to the nature and causes of job satisfaction within the industry; and conclude with a critical account of the main beliefs and dominant modes of thought of Calgary's oilmen.

OILMEN'S CAREERS: THE LUXURY OF CHOICE

As Tables 3–1 and 3–2 show, the oilmen of Calgary come mainly from western Canada, and from farming and working class backgrounds. Hence, the growth of the Albertan petroleum industry since the first major discoveries in the late 1940s has brought about a real transformation of one important sector of the local population. The current conservatism of Albertans, their close identification with the predominantly foreign-owned oil industry, and their tough determination to maintain control of their resources against the perceived incursion of the federal government, have to be understood against the historical background of the circumstances in which the oil industry grew to prominence. After the Second World War, what the Albertans feared more than anything else was a return to the dark depression days of the thirties. At best, the province seemed destined to continue as an underprivileged agricultural hinterland to the more prosperous industrial centre. Oil, at first viewed with suspicion by some, in the event has proven to be the godsent solution to Alberta's economic problems. In transforming the province's history, it has also transformed the personal careers of thousands of western Canadians. Notwithstanding that western Canadian agriculture is now a healthy industry in its own right, the title phrase, "from farm boy to oil man," captures the *symbolic* meaning of oil to many Albertans. Career accounts such as the following are common:

> I was born in Lethbridge, raised in Medicine Hat and Calgary. My dad was in the life insurance business. I guess I had my mind made up that I

was going to be a petroleum engineer when I was fifteen years old. This was the year when the Leduc discovery was being made. This was soon followed by Redwater. There was an awful lot of excitement and talk about the money to be made. It all sounded very logical to me, an industry that would be a good idea to get in on the ground floor. I worked with Imperial for one summer before I graduated, and got to know a little about the organization and its people, and I looked at some of the alternate offers from other major companies and I guess by the process of elimination I ended up with Imperial. I've stayed with them for 20 years. I've spent a year in Tulsa with the old Carter Research Laboratory there, and I've been on various assignments here and there.

This man's career was strictly with one major oil company. But one of the great advantages of the western Canadian oil industry, from the point of view of those who work in it, is that it provides great opportunities for free choices in terms of alternative career options for its professionally trained members. This luxury of career choice is basic to the generally high level of job satisfaction within the industry, and helps account for oilmen's strong commitment to their industry and resistance to changes in its organization. I will now describe, in ideal typical fashion, the various career options and patterns that professionally trained oilmen enjoy.

Table 3–1

Distribution by Place Raised, Random Sample of 349 Calgary Entrepreneurial, Managerial, and Professional Oilmen, 1974

Place	Number			%	
Canada		276			79.08
Western Canada		243		69.63	
British Columbia	17		4.87		
Alberta	135		38.68		
Saskatchewan	66		18.91		
Manitoba	25		7.16		
Ontario		21		6.02	
Quebec		4		1.15	
Atlantic Provinces		8		2.29	
United States		27			7.74
Great Britain		15			4.30
Other European		20			5.70
Other		11			3.15
TOTAL		349			100.07

Table 3–2

Fathers' Occupations of Random Sample of Calgary Oilmen, 1974 (Per Cent)

Professional	18.0
Management-Administration	8.3
Small Business	8.6
Clerical	9.1
Skilled Trades	14.3
Unskilled	12.0
Farmer	24.0
Salesman	5.1
Other	0.6
N = 348	100.0

THE INITIAL YEARS

The typical Calgary oilman studies engineering or geology at a western Canadian university. He gets his first exposure to the oil industry by taking a summer job with the Canadian subsidiary of a major oil company, which usually involves some practical field experience, such as working on a drilling rig. Upon graduation, the young professional goes to work for one of the majors or a large independent such as Dome Petroleum of Petro-Canada. His first year is mainly a training year, and may involve a trip to Houston or another international oil centre for a course in some aspect of petroleum technology. Then, he is assigned to a technical task group. Initially, his task assignment involves some fairly mechanical operation such as geophysical processing, well-logging, or computer simulation of particular oil and gas reservoirs. Later, if he shows promise, he is assigned to more challenging technical work like geophysical interpretation or the design of secondary recovery methods for producing wells. If he shows leadership potential, he may become a group leader after a few years.

After working for four or five years in such a technical capacity, the young oilman reaches a crucial career phase. In light of others' and his own assessment of his abilities, and of the career opportunities open to him, he must make a decision about what kind of long-term career he wants to pursue. There are numerous possibilities. If he decides to remain with his present company (a strikingly large number of Canadian oilmen have spent their whole careers with a single major company), his basic choice is whether to opt for a technical or managerial career.

TECHNICAL CAREERS

Technical careers appeal to people who like solving challenging technical problems, and who feel uncomfortable with having to co-ordinate and make decisions about personnel — to cope with "people problems," as oilmen put it. Successful professional technologists can enjoy interesting work, good salaries, job security, and a fair measure of prestige from those who depend upon their technical expertise. The following comments, by a researcher, illustrate the context of choice for one technical oilman:

I did my masters degree at the University of Alberta, and doctorate at the University of Calgary. I applied to Imperial because I wanted to stay in Calgary where I could work while I finished off the degree. I prefer the west, I have no desire whatsoever to go to Toronto. That means I probably can't go too far in the management line. Our major project is trying to investigate the thermal damage that can be done drilling through permafrost, mainly in the Delta area; and we have done some design for possible gas plant development in the Delta area. We don't have one project as such, but are involved in a number of projects.

If I did move, it would probably be as a consultant, but I don't think so, particularly with my lack of experience in the oil patch. In a big organization like Imperial, you get exposed to many people, conferences, meetings, trips; and there's an awful lot of support facilities to make the job much easier. And you have the freedom to work with the larger research group in Houston. These are conveniences you don't get in a small company. Of course, you can get lost in a big company, shuffled off into some job. . . . This doesn't happen too much, they keep moving people around.

Not all technical careers, however, are a matter of choice. Those whom management consider to be lacking in promise either as administrators or as high-level technical experts may be kept on for years doing the more routine kinds of geological, geophysical, and engineering work. These constitute the most dissatisfied subgroup of professional oilmen.

MANAGERIAL CAREERS

In order to make it to the top in the corporate sector of the oil industry, young oilmen must opt for managerial careers by making the crucial shift from the technical to the administrative organizational ladder. The option to attempt this move is not, of course, entirely up to them; but those with managerial aspirations can let these be known and, if they are considered to have promise, will usually be given a chance to prove themselves. The first level administrative appointment, as a leader of a project group, still involves a lot of technical work. This link helps ease the transition to the administrative ladder, where purely administrative and business concerns become proportionately more important as one moves up. Except for a few inhouse training courses, Canadian oilmen learn their managerial and business skills on the job.

The following is one man's account of his successful managerial career.

I took a general science degree in Manitoba. I was a kid from the farm. About the time I was ready to graduate I didn't have any firm ideas. An uncle of mine suggested that geophysics might be a good field, so I went to Toronto for a year of graduate school. Then I spent one summer in the seismic business in Alberta. Actually, how I was drafted into Imperial, my uncle was working for Imperial at the time. That was back in the early '50s. Our training program at that time involved a moderate amount of time on a seismic crew, six weeks in my case; and then I had a six weeks formal lecture-workshop type of course. Then I went to the Regina district as a trainee for a year or two, and I was on a crew for about a year and a half, and wandered around: Saskatchewan, Fort

Macleod, Red Deer to Calgary to Fort St. John. That was probably a low point in my career.

Then I went to the Edmonton office as a junior interpreter. I was fairly competitive. Then we had a bit of an internal reorganization within the Edmonton division and went to an area system — four areas with a junior technical man assigned to each. I didn't immediately get an assignment like that and it bothered me: I began to worry that obviously I'd been slotted and other people were going to get more responsibility. But then I got the responsibility for a specialized geophysical program. Then I got an assignment as an area geophysicist. I later had a transfer from that job as an area geophysicist to our research department, and after that I got into a straight staff job for about five years.

I moved to Toronto on the staff there, and then came back here as an area exploration manager, and now I'm manager of all our exploration operations. When the job was offered to me, it never occurred to me to consider turning it down. Not that I expected it at that time or at any particular time, but it was the next logical step in the system. In a big corporation, there's no such thing as standing still on the main line. In the future, as far as the main line path is concerned, that leads to Toronto. . . .

This man was a confident manager, and others in the department believed that his next move would indeed be to an executive position at the corporate head office in Toronto. The logic of a successful managerial career leads, as he points out, to a senior executive and eventually a board position.

Not all competent managers can, however, reach the top. Positions become scarcer and competition keener the further up the hierarchy one moves. Within the Canadian oil industry, however, these barriers to intracompany mobility are greatly mitigated by the presence of other career opportunities. Once they have gained their basic training in the majors, those oilmen who wish to can and do leave to take up new careers as consultants, as senior members of small oil companies, or even to set up their own oil company or consulting firm.

CAREERS IN SMALL COMPANIES

The structure of the Canadian oil industry, with its combination of majors, large independents, small oil companies, and consulting firms, opens up a great variety of job opportunities to trained professional oilmen. One of their most important career decisions concerns whether they should stay with a large company, or leave for a new challenge with a smaller company or as a consultant. Opinions vary as to the relative merits of large versus small companies. Technical professionals in the former argue that only the majors and largest independents have the capital and resources to be involved in the most interesting and challenging exploration and engineering problems. And they enjoy the opportunity to work with other experts in their fields. In one man's words: "I see this position as being where the action is." Corporate managers enjoy their economic power, and the experience of being intimately involved in the big decisions that affect the country's future.

The majors, however, cannot provide challenging managerial jobs to all who seek them. Many leave because they feel frustrated and lost within the big organizations, and because their career opportunities there seem restricted and dull. Small companies complement and reinforce this pressure to leave. They are always on the look-out for well-trained geologists, geophysicists, and engineers. To compete with the greater job security and prestige of the majors, they offer higher salaries and fringe benefits, such as memberships in the Petroleum Club and various recreational clubs in the city. The scope of activities associated with any formal position is greater within the small companies, there are far fewer steps to senior managerial slots, and less competition among would-be executives.

The following account of a successful career with a small company is by a man who had worked for a large, international British firm which was bought out by a major. He was then approached by its directors to manage a small Albertan company.

> That was in 1952. There was this little entity which had just been financed by a group of Bay Street financiers. We bought out some properties, and I was able to go back to my friends in ———— whom I had left three or four years before, and I had by that time developed sufficient assets to ask them to invest in our company. They agreed, so I raised quite a bit of money on the basis of the reserves that we had managed to put into the group of companies, and from that point we were able to use that money to buy further assets and so on and we built up the company from that point.

This man is currently the chairman of the company, which is becoming a large Canadian independent. Career success in small companies becomes more a function of building up the enterprise as a whole than of moving up an organizational hierarchy. This applies as well to consultants' careers.

CAREERS AS CONSULTANTS

An increasing proportion of the work done in the petroleum industry is contracted out to consultants of various kinds. Oilmen may leave the large companies, where they get their basic training, at any point in their careers to enter consulting, but three main patterns can be distinguished. The first is to leave early in one's career, when one has become well-trained as a petroleum engineer or geologist. People choosing this option continue to do the same type of work, but on a contract basis with numerous different companies. This gives them greater freedom and autonomy in their work, in that they can work in their own time, and can take longer holidays. In expansionary phases of the industry they do well financially, but they are vulnerable to economic recessions. To gain a measure of security, they often associate themselves with larger consulting firms on a sub-contract or fee basis. In general, they do not expect to get wealthy as consultants, but prefer the greater autonomy to the greater security of working full-time for an oil company.

The second career phase, when moving into consulting is a likely option, occurs when one reaches a career peak within a large oil company, either as a high-level technical expert or as a middle-level manager. People in the former category can become technical consultants; they are in high demand from smaller oil companies, and even from the large independents and majors for certain specialized problems. These experts enjoy high incomes and prestige within the industry.

So do those senior oilmen who exhibit a third pattern. Late in their careers, sometimes even after formal retirement, they decide to become consultants, offering business expertise and deal-making ability to interested clients. The following account is by a man who grew up with the industry in Alberta while working his way up to a high-level position in a major, left to work overseas, and then returned to Alberta as a consultant.

I have an academic background in geology, and my connection in exploration dates as far back as 1934 here in Alberta. In that period of time I sort of lived and worked along the foothills and in the Arctic. After that period and for the next ten years I worked in the head office of the company in Toronto. I did some short-term assignments for the parent company, in Cuba before Castro, in Venezuela. And I worked in resource research in short-term assignments in Tulsa and Houston and New York. So I drifted around a little bit in this hemisphere. Then, after Leduc, I came back to Calgary as general manager for the company for all of western Canada, and I was on the board. This was in the '50s and early '60s. Then in the middle '60s I left the company and I went overseas and I worked the Eastern Hemisphere, Sydney, Australia for a little while and from there I went to London, England and was involved in the North Sea and the Mediterranean and Europe.

When I came back here, I went into consulting. Now I'm walking the other side of the street, I'm an independent consultant. Essentially, I'm giving advice to independent companies. And I'm a director in ———————— (a medium-sized Canadian independent with interests in the North Sea).

This man's career sums up very neatly what I mean by the "luxury of choice" enjoyed by professionals in the Canadian oil industry. Through the combination of structurally available opportunities and his own free choices at various points, his career, as he reconstructs it, has come to include phases as a technical professional in Canada, the United States, and South America; a senior manager and director in a Canadian major; a manager with various affiliates of multinationals and smaller companies in Australia and Europe; an independent consultant making a living by selling his knowledge and expertise gained through his multifaceted experience; and a director of a rapidly growing Canadian independent intimately involved in the international oil business. His career epitomizes what it means to be a Canadian oilman. The luxury of choice entails high levels of job satisfaction for most oilmen.

JOB SATISFACTION

Our survey data give striking evidence that Calgary oilmen are highly satisfied with their jobs, and feel little alienation from their work. This is clearly indicated in Figures 3–1 and 3–2 which show high scores for overall job satisfaction and low scores for alienation.[3] Eighty-eight per cent of the oilmen sampled scored above the median value on the scale for satisfaction, and 98 per

Figure 3-1

Job Satisfaction of Sample of Calgary Oilmen

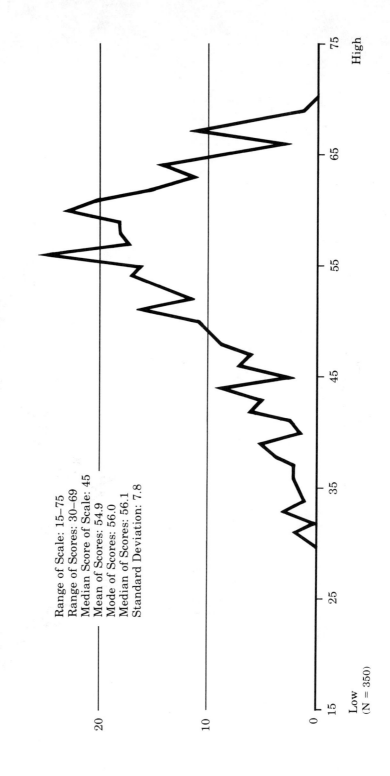

Range of Scale: 15–75
Range of Scores: 30–69
Median Score of Scale: 45
Mean of Scores: 54.9
Mode of Scores: 56.0
Median of Scores: 56.1
Standard Deviation: 7.8

Low
(N = 350)

High

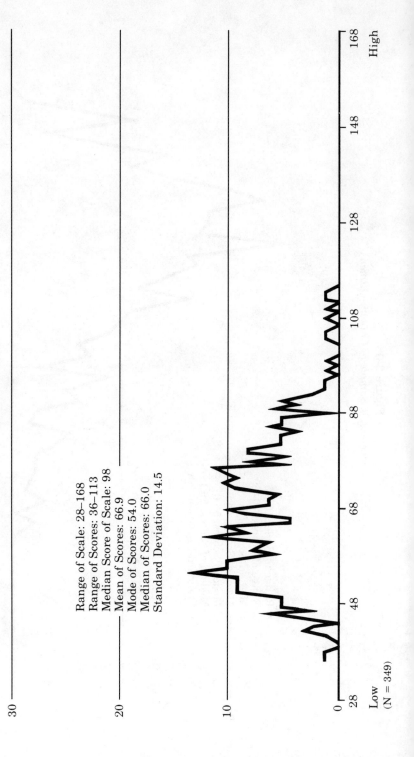

Figure 3–2

Subjective Alienation of Sample of Calgary Oilmen

Range of Scale: 28–168
Range of Scores: 36–113
Median Score of Scale: 98
Mean of Scores: 66.9
Mode of Scores: 54.0
Median of Scores: 66.0
Standard Deviation: 14.5

30

20

10

0

28   48   68   88   108   128   148   168

Low   High
(N = 349)

cent below the median scale value for alienation. Whereas only 2 per cent of oilmen scored above the scale median on alienation, an earlier study found scores ranging from 19 to 93 per cent on the various alienation subscales for three groups of blue collar workers (Shepard, 1973: 75). The data from personal interviews are consistent with and thereby lend validity to this claim. The findings also appear to be reliable, as they are consistent for the various subscales. Job satisfaction frequency distributions are skewed toward the high ends of the scales for pay, recognition and accomplishment, advancement, commitment, co-workers, and supervisors; while alienation scores are skewed toward the low ends of the scales for powerlessness, meaninglessness, instrumental work orientation, self-evaluative work involvement, and isolation from the goals of the industry. The powerlessness and meaninglessness scales are particularly striking for their low scores.

Although the survey data preclude our getting at the underlying causal processes for the above findings, we were able to discover important leads by establishing the organizational and work correlates of job satisfaction and alienation. In investigating these, we used a variety of statistical procedures for exploring the data along the lines suggested by Glaser and Strauss (1967) rather than the more usual hypothesis-testing format familiar to sociologists. Although a few variables, such as organizational level, appeared to be related to satisfaction and alienation in simple cross-tabulations, these relationships proved to be weak when controlled for other variables. Indeed, the data are striking for the variables that are *not* significantly correlated with job satisfaction and alienation. These include: occupation, intracompany mobility, age, years working in the industry, years with present company, and education.

In manipulating the data further through a variety of statistical procedures, it was clearly shown that the most important variable in explaining both job satisfaction and alienation is *achievement opportunity*. This variable refers to one's perceived opportunity to involve oneself in and to complete challenging and interesting pieces of work. It is not achievement in the sense of upward mobility. The questions which comprised this scale (modified from Patchen, 1970: 98, 75, 77) were as follows:

In connection with your job, how much chance do you get:

a. to do the kind of things you're best at?
b. to show your full potential?
c. to learn new things?
d. to see your projects or assignments fully completed?

The nature of the work itself, then, appears to be the key variable in explaining high job satisfaction and low subjective alienation. Oilmen who answered "a good chance" or "an excellent chance" to the above questions enjoyed their work and felt fulfilled in it; and the oil industry in Calgary provides this kind of opportunity to most of its entrepreneurs, managers, and professional workers.[4]

The overwhelming importance of the nature of the work itself is further shown by the other main variables that correlate with job satisfaction. These are *job involvement* and *job participation*. People who feel deeply involved in their jobs, and feel that they themselves participate in scheduling their own work and deciding how their tasks are to be done, tend to be highly satisfied. Turning to alienation, achievement opportunity and job involvement again show up as important, as well as two other variables. The more important of these variables is *participation in decision making*. Those who score high on decision making score low on alienation. This suggests that, in addition to the nature of the work itself, one's actual participation in decisions about the organization and about other employees affects one's subjective alienation, but not one's job satisfaction. Alienation is also related to *job codification*. The more formalized one's working conditions, the more alienated one feels.

These quantitative data are highly suggestive for understanding the proximate causes of the high level of job satisfaction reported by most Calgary oilmen. They are supported in greater depth, and rounded out in terms of the larger structural context in which the oilmen work, by the qualitative data collected from personal interviews. Most interviewees cited the interesting nature of the work itself, and their autonomy to run their own tasks, as the main reasons. The interview data also give another insight, not discovered by the survey, into the context of job satisfaction within the industry. This is the great variety of *sources* of satisfaction that different individuals find in different jobs. They run the whole gamut of positions within the industry.

> *Research Engineer.* It's interesting work, challenging. I think what makes it even more exciting is that you're on the very forefront of technology.

> *Geologist.* There's never a dull moment. One of the nice things is that it's not as much routine as you'd think, 'cause every morning something else will happen. And one of the interesting things is you're on top of our current activity, knowing exactly what's happening in your part of the world.

> *Senior Manager.* I don't have any frustration whatsoever; I feel that I haven't been inhibited from making decisions that I thought were important simply because I had to go through some prearranged formal ritual. I think it's one of the best jobs in the country; it's involved in a business that's critical. I feel myself part of the team responsible for one of the most important industries in Canada.

> *Small Company Manager.* The thing I like about working for an independent or small company is that you're part of the decision making and anything that happens you know about. It's part of your life, and everything that happens directly affects you. I find that really is the best part of working in the business.

> *Consultant.* Well, personally, I really can't say anything nasty about the oil industry. It has been exceptionally good to me; I've enjoyed every minute of it; I enjoy the people who are in it; I would never leave it.

Underlying this high level of job satisfaction is the luxury of career choice that oilmen enjoy. They assess alternative career routes in light of their own interests, and, to a large extent, can choose the path that gives greatest satisfaction. For the most part, only those who get stuck at low level technical jobs and others who "peak out" as middle level managers become disinterested

Figure 3–3

Economic Conservatism of Sample of Calgary Oilmen

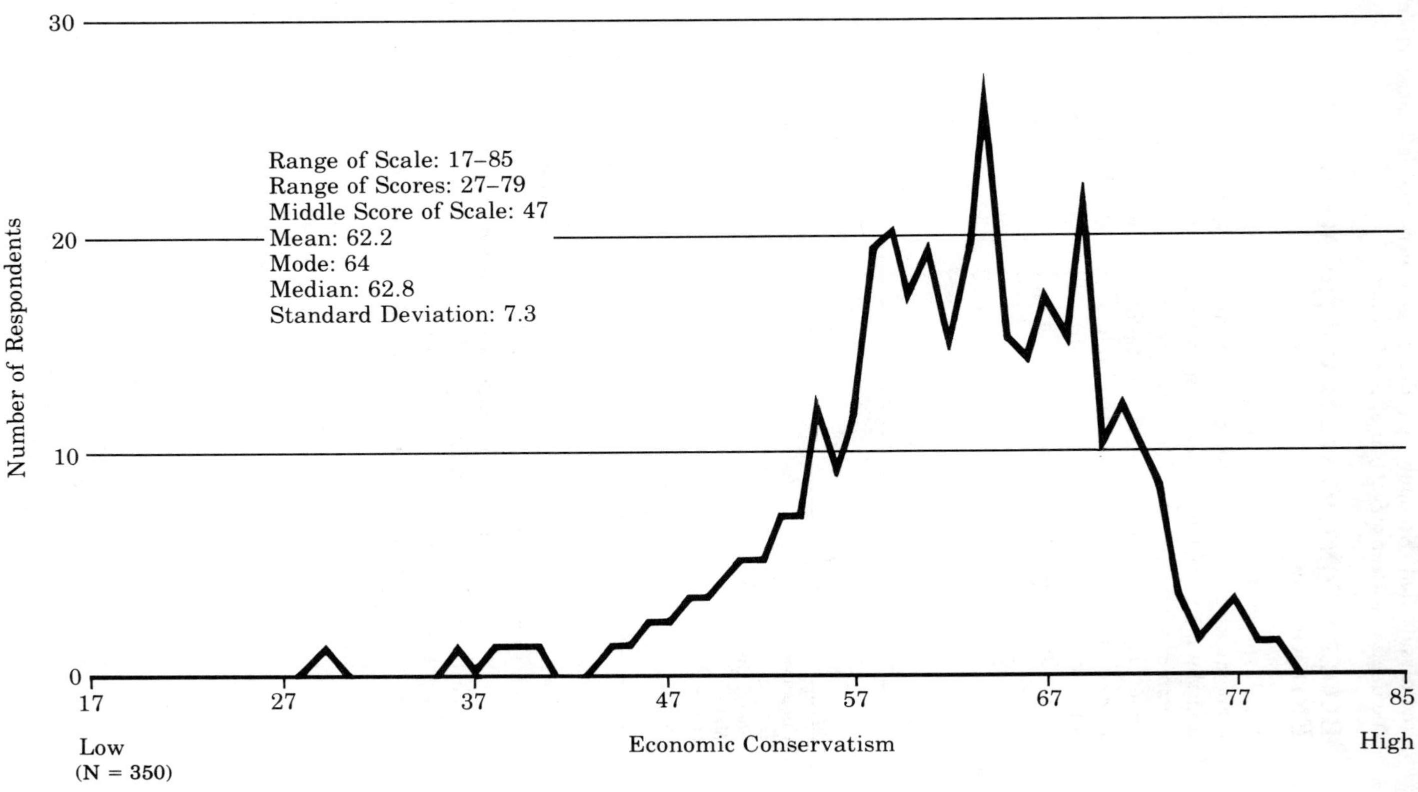
30
20
10
0
Number of Respondents
Range of Scale: 17–85
Range of Scores: 27–79
Middle Score of Scale: 47
Mean: 62.2
Mode: 64
Median: 62.8
Standard Deviation: 7.3
17
27
37
47
57
67
77
85
Low
(N = 350)
Economic Conservatism
High

and dissatisfied. No doubt, challenging careers and job satisfaction underlie the deeply felt conservatism of most oilmen.

BELIEFS: CONSERVATISM AND THE MYTH OF FREE ENTERPRISE

It will surprise no one to learn that Canadian oilmen are conservative in their economic thinking and political allegiances. Yet, the unanimity of their views, and the depth of feeling with which they are held, are striking. Figure 3–3 summarizes the results of our survey on the Minnesota economic conservatism scale. At the political level, these beliefs lead to a preference for the Progressive Conservative party (Table 3–3). It should be noted, however, that many oilmen feel that no current political party fairly represents their views and interests — they are all too "socialistic."

Table 3–3

Political Party Preference for Sample of Calgary Oilmen

| | Federal | | Provincial | |
	Number	Per Cent	Number	Per Cent
Conservative	246	75.7	249	78.8
Liberal	69	21.2	5	1.6
Social Credit	7	2.2	56	17.7
NDP	2	0.6	5	1.6
Other	1	0.3	1	0.3
Totals	325		316	

The survey data clearly confirm that oilmen are economically and politically conservative, but they fail to say much about the qualitative aspects of their thinking or about the depth of feeling with which their beliefs are held. One of the most striking findings of the survey, however, was the extent to which respondents felt called upon to add additional comments about their political and economic views, either on the economic conservatism scale questions, on the question about political allegiance, or in the space at the end where respondents were invited to add further comments. The oilmen clearly felt frustrated by the forced choice questions of the survey, and were concerned that their views were being distorted. For example, when asked whether they agreed with the statement "without sweeping changes in our economic system, little progress can be made in the solution of social problems," many oilmen would agree with the statement, but not in the way that the (presumably liberal) phraser of the question meant. Oilmen feel that there should be sweeping changes toward a more *laissez-faire* system, not toward the more socialistic system that they assumed the statement implied. Similarly, in the question on political affiliation, some respondents pointed out that, although they supported the Progressive Conservative party, they did so merely because they considered it to be the least of three evils. From their perspective, Pierre Trudeau was only slightly less socialistic than David Lewis, and Peter

Lougheed was not far behind. As one respondent wrote: "I am violently antisocialism, and, therefore, very anti-Trudeau, but not necessarily conservative."

These unsolicited comments capture the depth of emotional reaction stirred up within the Calgary oil community in 1973 and 1974, as federal and provincial governments and the informed public attempted to adapt to a radically changed world energy situation initiated by the members of the Organization of Petroleum Exporting Countries. Included in this reaction was an apparent attack upon the hitherto undisturbed Canadian oil industry. More recently, of course, the oil industry in western Canada has adapted very successfully to the new circumstances, and Albertan oilmen are reaping profits beyond their wildest dreams when the research reported on here was conducted. Oilmen interpret their own new wealth as a vindication of their free enterprise principles, rather than as a fortuitous result of a geological accident and the historical timing of the OPEC initiative in multiplying the price of oil.

CONCLUSION

The oilmen of Calgary form a tightly knit occupational community. The flexible social organization of their open resource industry creates a luxury of career choices for professionally trained people. This allows individual talents and aspirations to settle into suitable niches within the oil patch; the oilmen can make it as technical experts, corporate managers, as entrepreneurs in small companies or as consultants. In whatever capacity, most oilmen find their work challenging and stimulating, and this is reflected in their high level of job satisfaction and low degree of subjective alienation.

Contrary to the expectations of a simplified dependency model of development, these western Canadians constitute a privileged stratum within contemporary capitalism, despite their hinterland origins and despite the high degree of foreign ownership in the Canadian petroleum industry. Theirs is a classic case of *dependent development*, rather than underdevelopment. This paper has focussed upon the human side of this dependent development, and has shown that Canadian oilmen enjoy their status and that they explain their privileged position to themselves in terms of a straight-forward brand of free enterprise conservatism. Except for a few expressions of discomfort at the high degree of foreign ownership in the industry, Canadian oilmen are content with their lot. They attribute their good fortune to their own efforts rather than to their being "in the right place at the right time"; and, given the oilmen's renewed power within the Canadian social mosaic, their heavy-handed conservatism augurs poorly for the prospects of a more liberal and humanitarian approach to regional and class differences within this country.

NOTES

1. I am grateful to Sheena Findlay for suggesting this metaphor. We might add that the seduction may prove to be enjoyable only while the affair lasts. When the petroleum reserves run out, so will the oil seducers.
2. For a detailed discussion of the research methods, see the methodological appendix of *The Last of the Free Enterprisers*.

3. By "alienation" here, I mean subjective alienation, the extent to which oilmen *feel* themselves to be psychologically disassociated from the work they do. I am not referring to alienation in an objective Marxist philosophical sense.
4. Again, the reader should be reminded of the limits to the scope of this analysis. I am not suggesting that all groups working in the oil industry are satisfied.

REFERENCES

Foster, Peter
1979 *The Blue Eyed Sheiks: The Canadian Oil Establishment.* Toronto: Collins.

Frank, Andre Gunder
1967 *Capitalism and Underdevelopment in Latin America.* New York: Monthly Review Press.

Glaser, Barney G. and Anselm Strauss
1967 *The Discovery of Grounded Theory.* Chicago: Aldine-Atherton.

House, J.D.
1977 "The Social Organization of Multinational Corporations: Canadian Subsidiaries in the Oil Industry." *Canadian Review of Sociology and Anthropology* 14: 1–14.

1978 "Oil Companies in Aberdeen: The Strategy of Incorporation." *The Scottish Journal of Sociology* 3: 85–102.

1980 *The Last of the Free Enterprisers: The Oilmen of Calgary.* Toronto: Macmillan of Canada.

Oxaal, Ivar, Tony Barnett and David Booth (eds.)
1975 *Beyond the Sociology of Development.* London: Routledge & Kegan Paul.

Patchen, Martin
1970 *Participation, Achievement, and Involvement on the Job.* Englewood Cliffs, New Jersey: Prentice-Hall.

Shepard, Jon M.
1973 "Technology, Division of Labor, and Alienation." *Pacific Sociological Review* 16: 61–88.

Part II

The Division of Labour
Who Does What, Where and How

It is characteristic of modern society that work has become a sphere of human activity distinct from nonwork or leisure activities. Work activities themselves have become highly specialized but, as Durkheim noted, increasing differentiation of functions brings with it increasing interdependence of the groups and individuals performing them (the disruption caused by strikes is a rather dramatic reminder of just how interdependent we are). Given this interdependence, we cannot merely analyse the internal structure of an occupation, but must also examine its position relative to other occupations in a particular society at a particular point in time.

Another aspect of the division of labour to be noted is the shift in the numerical distribution of workers among occupational sectors. In the early days of industrialization, the most pronounced change was from the primary sector (mining, fishing, agriculture) to the secondary one of manufacturing. More recently, the most rapid growth has taken place in the tertiary or service sector. This growth has been spurred by a number of developments. Better-educated individuals create both the demand for more sophisticated services (for example, in the health and welfare fields), and the manpower to satisfy this demand. Moreover, as access to higher education is broadened, a push factor is created for jobs which utilize this education. A striking example is provided by the Quiet Revolution in Quebec. Secularization and rapid expansion of the educational system brought in their wake a demand for appropriate jobs. This demand, in turn, stimulated further government expansion.

WHO DOES WHAT?

While Durkheim was concerned with the division of labour as a vital aspect of society as a whole (a macro-sociological approach), occupational sociologists have tended to focus on mechanisms by which tasks are allocated to appropriate individuals, the criteria by which appropriateness is defined, and the rationales used for grouping occupations into categories.

According to the ideology of Canadian society, tasks are allocated to individuals on the basis of their achievements and competence. In practice, ascription continues to play an important role in the allocation of tasks, and in the definition of what kinds of persons are suitable for performing certain work. Ascription refers to the assignment of individuals to categories, based on such characteristics as age, gender and ethnicity. Categorization has far-reaching consequences for steering individuals into certain types of work, while excluding them from others. Once in existence, this sorting process operates at many levels. It is perpetuated through socialization which transmits a certain level of expectations, and by vocational training which prepares people for positions consistent with their anticipated status. Individuals thus raised are unlikely to challenge the legitimacy of the sorting process, and to test the strength of barriers. Ironically, then, discrimination continues with the compliance of its victims. However, in Canada discriminatory practices are not allowed to proceed unchecked, since they violate the societal ideal that those of equal ability must have equal opportunity to enter the occupation of their choice, and to progress within it on the basis of performance.

The disjunction between ideal and practice as manifested in job allocation has been extensively discussed in the sociological literature (Krause, 1971; Merton, 1968; Porter, 1965). Students of the division of labour have found it useful to group work into categories based on certain characteristics. Occupations can be distinguished and grouped according to a variety of criteria. Krause (1971), for example, subsumes occupations under institutional sectors — health, education, the military, and so on. Hall (1975) and others concerned with the ranking of occupations have used the broad groupings of Professional and Managerial, White Collar and Service, and Blue Collar and Primary workers.

*Traditionally, these groups have indicated differing rewards in terms of pay, power and prestige, with professions being at the high end of the scale and the blue-collar sector at the low end. Professions have for the most part maintained their pre-eminent position, with some internal realignments such as that suggested by **Clarke**'s article on the clergy, and demonstrated by **Stager** and **Meltz**'s analysis of relative earnings. It is doubtful, however, whether white-collar workers have maintained an advantaged position vis-à-vis blue-collar workers, for large-scale unionization has enhanced the power and pay of the latter. Because of the historically close relationship among pay, power and prestige, it will be interesting to discover whether an unambiguous redistribution of prestige between white- and blue-collar occupations will occur in the future.*

WHO DOES *WHAT*?

When we referred to ascription, we noted that the allocation of individuals to occupations is a mechanism that utilizes the aspirations and expectations engendered in people as they are prepared for functioning in society. Formal education plays a vital part in this socialization process. The role of education is, of course, complex.

The quality and amount of education an individual receives is heavily dependent on socio-economic origin; at the same time, the educational level one achieves affects occupational opportunity. Moreover, education has critically affected the relative position of occupational groups. On the one hand, the educational attainment of professionals has remained far above that of the general population, entrenching their position at the top of the hierarchy. On the other hand, the society-wide upgrading of education has served to level differences between white- and blue-collar workers — a phenomenon noted by Mills some time ago (1951).

A DYNAMIC APPROACH

In organizing this second part of the anthology, we sought to give weight to the structure *of work (see especially* **Stephenson** *and* **Clark***) in the fundamental sense of examining under what conditions a certain combination of tasks is defined as work. A second objective was to delineate how this task combination and the social relationships associated with it are rearranged with the introduction of new technology. As the articles by* **Lowe, Bowles** *and* **Haney,** *and* **Clement** *demonstrate, these changes are one facet of more general societal change.*

Attention to work processes *is provided by the articles which address various aspects of negotiating role relationships. Negotiation, here, refers to the constant jockeying that occurs as groups and individuals seek to redefine their relationships in ways most advantageous to themselves, but which also facilitate the effective performance of their work. Thus, respect for his authority gratifies the policeman as an individual, reaffirms the occupational status of policemen as a group, and makes easier the upholding of law and order.*

A further dimension of the dynamic nature of work is explored by the articles that address historic changes which have taken place in the relative rewards obtained by different occupations. **Clarke** *enables us to see how change in society is translated at the level of a particular occupation. She argues that, as religion has come to lose its central role, the power and prestige of the clergy have diminished.*

THEORETICAL PERSPECTIVES

Earlier, we mentioned that the papers in this anthology reflected a diversity of analytic perspectives. We have deemed it useful to group the articles in this part of the book on the basis of shared perspectives.

Haas et al., *Kelner* et al. and *Stebbins* and *Flynn* approach their respective topics in a manner compatible with the Symbolic Interactionist orientation. Symbolic Interactionism focuses on the ways in which human beings interpret the meaning of situations, and the ways in which such interpretations influence subsequent behaviour. The emphasis, then, is on the active part individuals take in fashioning their environment, and on the negotiating processes involved in interaction. Students would do well to study these papers in terms of the various negotiating processes which are examined. *Turrittin's* article, albeit more implicitly, also refers to negotiating processes — in this instance, between employer and employee in the context of the household.

The articles just mentioned underline the emergent quality of interaction. By contrast, **Lowe, Bowles** and **Haney**, and **Clement** pay great attention to the ways in which behaviour is constrained by the environment and by the relative position of the actors. This is not to imply that people act like robots in simply responding to external stimuli; they do not. As Marx noted, individuals make their own history, but not under conditions of their own choosing.

Lowe, Bowles and **Haney**, and **Clement** present a historical and structural analysis of occupational change. In other words, they trace the evolution of relationships between general variables such as, for example, technology and organizational size (new technology becomes more profitable as if it is instituted on a large scale). While **Lowe**, and **Bowles** and **Haney** draw somewhat on the Marxist tradition, **Clement's** analysis falls squarely within this perspective. Marx focused on the inequality of power between owners and workers, an inequality which arises from their different relations to the means of production. The Marxist perspective points to the pervasive influence of the economy on other societal institutions, such as education, religion and law.

What follows is a brief discussion of the papers in this part of the book. With each paper, our purpose has been to identify the main issues, to provide links with other papers in the book and, where appropriate, to raise questions of wider concern to social scientists. Our headings are intended to capture the articles' essential contribution to the general themes that run through the anthology. These headings are not to be confused with the authors' own titles.

WHAT IS WORK?

Stephenson and **Clark** address the basic conceptual issues of what constitutes work in our society. It is perhaps ironic that they furnish such a useful definition and analysis of work while discussing domestic labour, which has traditionally not been viewed as "real" work. Traditional analyses of housework have employed a circular argument. It is not regarded as real work because it is not remunerated by a salary *or wage; on the other hand, it is not remunerated because, being privatized and performed by family members, it is not designated as work. Moreover, for the most part, housework is done by women, so we get an interplay between the low prestige assigned to the work and that brought to it by the recruit.*

ARM'S LENGTH RELATIONSHIPS IN AN INTIMATE SETTING

Turrittin's paper can be usefully linked to a number of other articles in this book. As do Stephenson and Clark, she investigates domestic work, but she also explores the asymmetrical power relationships between domestic workers and their employers, and the strategies the workers use to reduce this asymmetry.

Turrittin's examination of West Indian domestics highlights the vicious circle involved in ranking occupations. Being black, poor and female tends to confine opportunities for these people to culturally devalued work. The same phenomenon is apparent at the opposite end of the spectrum. Valued occupations attract prestigeful recruits who, by virtue of their characteristics, reinforce the prestige of the occupation (hence attempts on the part of aspiring professions, such as social work and teaching, to enhance their status by recruiting males); in turn, membership in a prestigeful occupation in and of itself confers prestige on even the most lacklustre individual.

As so many articles in this book demonstrate, technology has revolutionized work in many ways. Housework, too, is constantly being reshaped by new labour-saving devices. But their availability has raised standards of cleanliness, with the result that some of the time saved from drudgery is expended in meeting these new standards. Furthermore, much time is spent in making selections from among a wide range of consumer goods. Both Turrittin, and Stephenson and Clark stress that, despite the advent of labour-saving technology, an irreducible residue of housework must be done in the good old-fashioned way. This is partly due to the largely inflexible, continuous, often unpredictable demands of childcare. Because of the nature of housework, then, it is difficult to apply standards of efficiency even when the tasks are performed by employees. The low rewards of these paid workers reflect the impossibility of rationalizing all aspects of the job.

PROFESSIONALIZATION: THE TRANSITION FROM APPRENTICE TO MASTER

Adult socialization refers to the process by which individuals are prepared, by what is taught formally and "caught" informally, to fill designated positions in work or social settings. The "catching on" process includes learning the ropes, the rules that must be followed conscientiously and those that can be safely ignored some of the time, and adopting appropriate values and behaviours. Professionalization is a particular case of such adult socialization, one that is concerned with the transformation of students into full-fledged physicians, lawyers or clerics.

Earlier, we noted that educational attainment has been one important factor responsible for professions being able to maintain their dominant position. Students of professions have long recognized, however, that the making of a professional involves far more than lengthy formal training; the whole process of adult socialization serves to establish professional identity, which is so crucial in carrying out a powerful social role. Given the power and prestige accorded to physicians in our society, it is understandable that the experience of becoming a physician (medical socialization) has received a great deal of attention from social scientists. Haas, Marshall and Shaffir focus specifically on the ways in which first-year students at an innovative medical school are initiated into the professional culture. They look at the nature of the "ritual ordeal" students undergo, how students respond to it, and how, in contrast to that of the traditional medical school, these responses are shaped by a training program which incorporates clinical exposure from the very beginning, and which eschews formal tests in favour of continuing self- and peer-evaluation.

The authors, then, stress the importance of the context in which professionalization takes place. They echo the view of Christie and Merton (1928) that "the learning and performance of students vary not only as their individual qualities vary, but also as the social environment provided by the school varies." Through being forced to cope with uncertainty and anxiety, and through being aware that this trauma is shared, the student is gradually transformed into the full-fledged physician, able to define his role not only to himself, but also vis-à-vis peers, patients and the society at large.

PROFESSIONALIZATION: A PROCESS FOR ACHIEVING COLLECTIVE UPWARD MOBILITY

Wilensky (1964) and others have argued that occupations seek to transform themselves into full-fledged professions by a series of steps which include transfer of their training program to the university setting, commitment to the occupation as a life-long career, and adherence to a code of ethics. Professionalization has been deemed desirable because of the high material and symbolic rewards professions enjoy. One key ingredient of the symbolic rewards is the broad societal mandate of professions to recruit, train, certify and discipline their members. Linked to this is society's legitimation of the occupation's claim to exercise exclusive control over a body of skills.

Kelner, Hall and Coulter focus on chiropractic, an occupation aspiring to become a profession, and one which has consolidated and expanded its position in the health field. This position has been a controversial one from the beginning, for public acceptance of chiropractors has stood in marked contrast to their rejection by the medical profession, at least in its official pronouncements. Here, we see an example of negotiating processes which involve what the authors call "a good deal of pushing and shoving," as physicians seek to protect their hegemony in the health care field against intruders. The authors also show, however, that despite this professed rejection, in practice physicians and chiropractors are embedded in a web of relationships, with the patient at the centre. Once the patient decides to consult a chiropractor who may then order procedures which must be carried out under medical auspices, the links between chiropractor and physician are reinforced. Over time, these links are taken for granted by both groups.

PROFESSIONALIZATION: UPGRADING AN OCCUPATIONAL IMAGE

*The paper by **Stebbins** and **Flynn** includes elements of the two aspects of professionalization first discussed in the previous two papers. On the one hand, police officers seek to upgrade their occupational image and broaden their mandate by undergoing further training. On the other hand, this training is intended to foster relationships with clients that are marked by the detached concern (Lief and Fox, 1963) which is considered characteristic of professionals. In other words, concern with the welfare of the client must be combined with sufficient detachment to allow the professional to deal effectively with a given situation. This article, however, focuses primarily on a third facet of professionalization, namely the strategies used by an occupational group to renegotiate its position in society, that is, to come closer to being accorded the status of a profession.*

*   **Stebbins** and **Flynn** evaluate a training program aimed at influencing the ways in which policemen in St. John's, Newfoundland, define situations encountered in their work. This definition includes self-perception, how policemen think others perceive them, and interpretation of others' motives and actions, for example, deciding whether a citizen is deliberately committing an offence.*

*   The authors found that trainees learned to define their role in a broader and more positive way, in other words, not only as policemen, but as mediators of conflict and as "competent protectors of the public welfare." Concomitantly, trainees also exhibited a clearer understanding of broad community goals; thus, their concern was not confined to making an arrest, but rather extended to the rehabilitation of the offender and the prevention of crime.*

*   A number of articles in this book suggest ways in which sociological knowledge could be used for improving the lot of the workers concerned. **Stebbins** and **Flynn** demonstrate that a practical program, designed on*

the basis of a symbolic interactionist perspective, can help policemen–students to perform their role more effectively and to feel more positive about it. If credence can be given to the arguments in favour of job enlargement (Herzberg 1959, 1966; Likert, 1962), then we can assume that programs such as this can make work more satisfying for policemen.

CLERICAL WORKERS: DOWNWARD MOBILITY IN THE
WHITE-COLLAR FACTORY

The groups discussed thus far possess a high degree of occupational consciousness. Among professionals, this consciousness is deliberately inculcated through intense and lengthy socialization, and reinforced by the peer pressure of a tightly-knit community (Goode, 1957). For policemen, there are a number of factors (working shifts, the visible symbol of the uniform and the possibility of an adversary relationship with various segments in the community) which isolate them and heighten the sense of shared fate with their co-workers.

By contrast, office workers have traditionally had a low degree of occupational consciousness, in part because many of them identified with their employers whose ranks they eventually hoped to join (Mills, 1951; Krause, 1971). Such aspirations were not totally unrealistic when white-collar workers were few in number, predominantly male and better-educated than the majority of the population. Lowe traces the evolution of corporate capitalism in Canada, the accompanying transformation of the office and the devastating consequences of these developments for office workers. For the clerical labour force as a whole, these developments included an explosion in numbers, feminization, the emergence of a superordinate stratum of expert salaried managers, and a revolution in office technology which eliminated some jobs and routinized others. The individual workers faced a severe reduction in the scope of their tasks, and decreased autonomy over the manner and order of performing them. Whereas in earlier times the clerk had been in personal contact with his employer, the modern clerical worker is an anonymous cipher in a white-collar factory, integrated into the bottom ranks of a hierarchy which she has virtually no hope of ascending.

This combination of factors has resulted in downward mobility for clerical workers. As we noted earlier, they no longer enjoy material rewards higher than those of blue-collar workers. Indeed, average clerical earnings have dropped far below those of the unionized segment of the manual labour force. The influx of women has depressed the status of office workers, and technological innovation has made them more easily substitutable. A copy typist had to be able to copy accurately; virtually anyone, however, can operate modern reproduction equipment, and accuracy is built into the machine.

Lowe's article draws attention to the ways in which transformation of the Canadian office has provided a changing context for the occupational groups that must interact within it. **Bowles** *and* **Haney's** *study of the timber industry likewise demonstrates how the various phases of forest exploitation (the square timber trade, local sawmilling, industrial sawmilling and the pulp and paper industry) have provided differing contexts in which work is carried out, and differing occupations to do this work. Like* **Lowe**, *and like* **Clement** *whose article follows in this subsection,* **Bowles** *and* **Haney** *present a historical analysis of the impact on an occupation of technological and structural change. Students should note that, in discussing a staples trade, the* **Bowles** *and* **Haney** *article is also related to the section on the political economy, and specifically to* **Marchak's** *study of the B.C. forest industry.*

Bowles *and* **Haney's** *historical survey of the timber trade in Ontario and Quebec analyses the internal diversity of this industry. Whereas square timber has been a major staple export since the Napoleonic Wars, development of a pulp and paper industry had to wait until the technology for manufacturing paper from wood became available at the end of the nineteenth century. Because the manufacture of pulp and paper required heavy capital investment, ownership was concentrated in the hands of large corporations. Corporate ownership and permanent work establishments meant that workers were part of a hierarchy and lived in settled communities. In contrast to this state of affairs, those employed in the square timber industry were less regimented, but had to make do with living in a succession of camps, populated entirely by males. However, the diversity in occupational structure that has characterized the timber industry should not obscure the fact that although there are variations in the work and life experiences of individuals all depend on an industry which shares with other staple producers contingencies such as vulnerability to fluctuations in international demand and prices. From this point of view, they share a common fate, and one that is, as we have seen, markedly Canadian.*

TWO FACES OF TECHNOLOGY: SKILLED MACHINES AND DESKILLED WORKERS

Earlier, we pointed out that **Clement's** *perspective was Marxist. Accordingly, he views technology as an instrument of capitalist ownership which is used to institute social arrangements at the workplace that benefit owners at the expense of workers. In other words, the subordination of workers does not simply or necessarily follow from a particular technology, but rather from the way this technology is used by those who control it.*

Like the other two articles in this sub-section, **Clement's** *is a historical analysis, in this case delineating the ways in which the division of labour has changed in mining. As ownership of mines has passed from owner-operators to petty capitalists to large corporations,* *the autonomy of the miner has been progressively undercut.*

Reductions in autonomy have gone hand in hand with reductions in skills required of workers. As tasks are fragmented, those who perform them become more easily substitutable. Through the introduction of modular training (MTS)* the expertise of even the most skilled craftsmen has become attached to specific equipment. Thus, these craftsmen lose the more general skills which are easily marketable, and become increasingly dependent on their present employer.

One reason why multinational mining corporations have made huge investments in the latest technology available is that this technology has helped to subordinate a work force with a long tradition of militancy. For the mine worker, the subordination has been two-pronged: he is more easily substitutable by the employer and, at the same time, his own ability to switch employers has been diminished with the narrowing of his skills.

Students should note that umbrella terms such as "clerk" or "miners" draw attention to the work performed by members of these groups; at the same time, unqualified use of these terms may conceal important differences. For example, **Clement** *observes that surface miners have always been subject to closer supervision than those working below ground. Gouldner noted a similar distinction in his study of a gyprock enterprise (1954).* **Bowles** *and* **Haney**'s *examination of the timber trade demonstrates that much can be learned from focusing on the internal diversity of an industry.*

CONTINUITY AND CHANGE IN RELATIVE OCCUPATIONAL
EARNINGS: AN OVERVIEW

It should be noted at the outset that, as economists, **Stager** *and* **Meltz** *use a vocabulary which is somewhat different from that found in most of the articles in this book. The authors provide a macro analysis of relative occupational earnings which they define as "the average annual earnings of the total wage and salary earners in the labour force." In other words, they examine whether, and in what direction, occupational earnings have changed over time in relation to the total labour force. For example, the relative earnings of physicians declined between 1931–1941, again slightly from 1951–1961, but increased sharply between 1961–1971.* **Stager** *and* **Meltz** *do not examine variations of earnings within an occupation, such as in the case of physicians, income differences between specialists and general practitioners.*

This approach permits observations about the relative position of specific occupations, and also about changes in the overall shape of the

---

**"Modular training means that each operation is broken down into its parts and these parts become interchangable and can be arranged in a variety of ways."*

labour force wage structure, that is, how the gap between occupations and occupational groups (e.g., as between white- and blue-collar workers) has widened, narrowed or remained stable. Such an analysis belies the notion that occupations stand in a constant "historical" relationship to each other; rather, it shows that their relative positions can change over time.

An important point stressed in the article is that an increase in absolute earnings can go hand in hand with a decline in relative earnings. Indeed, this is what happened to the clerical workers discussed earlier by **Lowe**, *who have steadily lost ground since 1931 (with a slight upswing between 1941–1951).* **Lowe** *argued that by 1931 the transformation of the office had been completed.*

What are the main determinants of patterns of change in relative earnings? Stager and Meltz explore the influence of age (as a proxy for years of experience in the work force), education, industry, and region on average (mean) earnings of an occupation. Age and education were found to have the greatest impact, an impact which has been consistently strengthened in each of the four decades examined. Although the authors do not draw this inference, it would seem that occupations which seek collective upward mobility (e.g., chiropractors) can justify demands for stiffer educational requirements by pointing to the positive association that has historically existed between education and income.

THE FATE OF THE CLERGY IN A SECULAR ERA

Max Weber described the transition from a world dominated by religion to one in which people increasingly interpreted reality according to what they perceived through their senses. **Clarke** *argues that the fortunes of an occupation concerned with conveying supernatural explanations to the public will vary with the degree to which such explanations are accepted in a society at a given point in time. She examines the ways in which the secularization of society generally has been reflected in the decline of the clergy in terms of social power, earnings and prestige relative to other professionals, specifically physicians.*

Whereas several articles in the book focus on how the state of technology has influenced occupational fate, secularization in the sense of Zeitgeist, *the spirit of the times, provides the context for* **Clarke**'s *examination. Her focus, then, is not on the work the clergy performs but, rather, on the importance members of society attach to this work.*

At a more general level, she looks at the transformation of the relationship between church and state, with the latter assuming increasing control, particularly in education. Here, it is interesting to note that the "deconfessionalization" of the educational system took place much earlier in Ontario than in Quebec, where no provincial ministry of education existed until 1964.

THE MORE THINGS CHANGE, THE MORE THEY STAY THE SAME

What has been referred to in the literature as a "segmentation perspective" (reviewed in Clairmont et al., 1980), views the economy in terms of two or more separate and self-perpetuating sectors which are characterized by unequal rewards. Clairmont uses such a perspective to examine low-wage work in the Atlantic provinces. In his analysis of the Newfoundland fishing industry (1972), Brox draws attention to the sharp cleavage in the province's economy:

> *The most striking features of Newfoundland's economy is the dualistic nature of its development. On the one hand, there are modern, sophisticated, up-to-date industries. On the other, economic practices and techniques exist that appear to be almost medieval, such as inshore fishing and especially the processing of salt fish, where no innovation whatsoever seems to have taken place, either in tools or work methods. . . . Most noteworthy is the fact that the traditional fishing population is not mobilized for the trawler fleets — the latest innovation in Newfoundland fishing technology. Traditional inshore fishing continues alongside commercial, large-scale trawler fishing in striking contrast to Scandinavia and especially Iceland, where modernization seems to take place simultaneously in all sectors and regions.*

*In tracing developments of the Newfoundland fishing industry from the first settlements until today, **Parsler** argues that, until the middle of the century, and despite the vicissitudes of military and political events, the lives of the fishermen and their families remained fundamentally unchanged. Each community was characterized by extreme isolation and an economy based on a barter system in which fish was exchanged for goods brought from abroad by merchants. This exchange was mediated by a local merchant class which exploited the fishermen, using a number of mechanisms to keep them in perpetual debt. Patently, rich fishing grounds did not produce rich local fishermen.*

Eventually, however, fishing and processing became enmeshed in the familiar pattern of "low-cost large-scale production, increasing division of labour and an increasing administrative bureaucracy." In the wake of these innovations came a resettlement program which was intended to improve the lot of subsistence fishermen. This goal was not attained, but a host of kinship-based cultures were destroyed in the attempt. Change has come to Newfoundland with modernization and political integration with Canada, but poverty has remained a constant.

THE WORKER AND HIS JOB IN CANADA TODAY

Some of the articles do focus on the perception of work experience, or the *socialization process, but the structural emphasis which emerges cannot begin to convey the rich and variable texture of day-to-day work experience for real people. This experience, so crucial in bestowing a sense of identity, may be woven from a variety of skeins: realistic aspirations or dissapointment and compensatory dreams (Chinoy, 1955; also see **Knight's** article here); challenge or boredom; the stress of too many decisions to make or the strain of too few; the exhilaration of achievement and fulfilment, or soul-destroying alienation, stemming perhaps from separation between conceptualization and execution of tasks (Braverman, 1974; Rinehart, 1975). In short, work may constitute anything from a source of intense personal satisfaction to a "Monday through Friday sort of dying" (Terkel, 1972).*

*The essence of a sociological approach, however, is to locate work in a social and institutional matrix, and to demonstrate its links to technological, political and economic developments. These developments keep the matrices in a constant state of flux, with the result that tasks performed by individuals with the same occupational title vary significantly over time, as demonstrated by **Parsler's** paper on fishermen in Newfoundland, and **Bowles** and **Haney's** discussion of workers in the timber industry of Ontario and Quebec. Any perspective is necessarily partial, but a structural perspective allows one to trace how the contexts evolve in which individuals experience their work.*

REFERENCES

Braverman, H.
1974   *Labor and Monopoly Capital: The Degradation of Labor in the Twentieth Century.* New York: Monthly Review Press.

Chinoy, E.
1955   *Automobile Workers and the American Dream.* New York: Doubleday.

Christie R. and R.K. Merton
1958   "Procedures for the Sociological Study of the Values Climate of Medical Schools." In *The Ecology of Medical Colleges.* H.H. Gee and R.J. Glaser (eds.) Evanston: Association of American Medical Colleges.

Clairmont, D.A., M. Macdonald and F.C. Wien
1980   "A Segmentation Approach to Poverty and Low-Wage Work in the Maritimes." In *Structured Inequality in Canada.* J. Harp and J.R. Hofley (eds.) Scarborough: Prentice Hall.

Goode, W.
1957   Community Within A Community: The Professions. *American Sociological Review.* 22(2): 194–200.

Gouldner, A.W.
1954   *Patterns of Industrial Bureaucracy.* New York: Free Press.

Hall, R.H.
1975   *Occupations and the Social Structure.* Englewood Cliffs: Prentice Hall.

Herzberg, F., B. Mausner and B. Snyderman
1959   *The Motivation to Work.* Second Edition. New York: Wiley.

1966   *Work and the Nature of Man.* New York: Mentor Books.

Krause, E.A.
1971   *The Sociology of Occupations.* Boston: Little Brown.

Lief, H.I. and R.C. Fox
1963   "Training for 'Detached Concern' in Medical Students." In *The Psychological Basis of Medical Practice.* H.I. Lief et al. (eds.) New York: Harper and Row.

Likert, R.
1962   *New Patterns of Management.* New York: McGraw-Hill.

Merton, R.K.
1968   *Social Theory and Social Structure.* New York: The Free Press of Glencoe.

Mills, C.W.
1951   *White Collar.* New York: Oxford University Press.

Porter J.
1965   *The Vertical Mosiac.* Toronto: University of Toronto Press.

Rinehart, J.W.
1975   *The Tyranny of Work.* Don Mills: Longman Canada.

Terkel, S.
1972   *Working.* New York: Avon Books.

Wilensky, H.I.
1964   "The Professionalization of Everyone?" *American Journal of Sociology.* 70(2): 137–158.

Chapter 4

Housework as Real Work

Susan Clark
Marylee Stephenson

INTRODUCTION

Feminist researchers in a variety of fields of study have recently been looking at many issues from a new perspective.[1] Frequently, topics and issues have been studied in sociology and other disciplines from an implicitly biased perspective, although claims have been made about the objectivity and universality of the methodologies and theories used. For feminist scholars, the most significant biases they have attempted to redress are sexist biases — in particular, unsubstantiated assumptions about the life experiences of women which are based on partial or incomplete information or on conclusions drawn from men's experiences. Because of this concern about the research methods and the topics studied, feminist researchers are questioning and revising knowledge about issues which were previously seen as unproblematic. One issue in which this process is very evident is work, clearly a central aspect of human life. Critical attention to the concept of work is indeed a prime example of the revisions which feminist researchers see as essential to current research activities.

Work, as a major activity in people's daily lives, regulates in some way virtually everything else we do. We frequently may not analyse this in our day-to-day lives, but simply take it for granted as the way in which things normally occur. If we do consider the impact of work on our lives, however, it becomes evident that we are highly constrained by work activities. This is apparent in the short run in our daily routines, pertaining as it does to when we get up or go to bed, when and where we eat certain meals, and the time available for leisure pursuits in nonworking hours. Over a longer time span, work affects when (or if) we take holidays, where we live and the organizations to which we may belong. For many of us, work is the activity around which we also make long-term decisions in relation to plans for the sort of lives we would like to lead or our educational goals. There are other long-term decisions it affects, such as whether we will move considerable distances to secure employment, or accompany a spouse or partner who must move for work.

In fact, work activities probably provide a much more rigid framework — both temporal and spatial — within which people operate than is usually acknowledged. Since wages and salaries are frequently attached to many kinds of work, it has a further constraining effect on other, or nonwork, activities. This is evident insofar as the amount of money a person or family has available will influence the goods and services bought, whether one considers housing and food, or leisure time pursuits such as sailing or softball.

TRADITIONAL DEFINITIONS OF WORK

The definition of what constitutes work has been the subject of a long and continuing debate. A minimum definition revolves around the idea that the human species has to expend energy and undertake activities in manipulating its environment to meet basic needs for shelter and food, in order to allow people to survive and reproduce.

The human species, however, has the ability consciously to modify and elaborate its needs for survival and the means of fulfilling these needs. Because of our capacity for self-awareness (in both historical and present-day contexts), we reflect on our condition and constantly re-define and re-evaluate the activities which constitute the human experience. The implication of this is that we are not satisfied with only minimal or simple levels of survival. We also have a whole series of needs relating to social and psychological well-being. For example, over and above the "basic" needs for food, clothing and shelter, there are needs for contact and interaction with other people, for recreational and physical activities, and for aesthetic and spiritual experiences.

In comparison with traditional hunting and gathering or other nonindustrial societies, the way in which we satisfy our needs for food, shelter and clothing, and for nonmaterial needs, is complex and dependent on sophisticated technology. Whereas people in the former types of societies satisfy their needs primarily through their own production of the goods and services they require, in industrial societies we typically provide for most of our needs for goods, and many of our needs for services, by buying them. And, of course, we are able to buy these commodities and services because we (or someone to whom we are closely attached, i.e., spouse, parent, offspring) sell our labour and are paid a wage or salary for doing so.

Because different types of work are differentially evaluated and thereby have varying levels of pay attached to them, the type and allocation of work among people is a major concern within industrial societies. Thus we are faced with the familiar situation in which certain types of work are characterized by elaborate procedures for the selection and training of workers, by a demand for specific and sophisticated knowledge, and are then frequently accompanied by high pay and prestige. The obverse of this, of course, is that low pay and prestige are given to those work activities which are seen to be easily learned by nearly anyone, and where the training period is believed to be short.

But in both extremes, whether we consider physicians and scientists or litter-gatherers and newspaper sellers, and all the occupations between, there are certain common criteria in the *traditional* scholarly or popular definitions of work. In essence, people are engaging in activities that some segment of the society values sufficiently to pay for the labour being expended — whether manual or intellectual, or some combination of the two. This familiar picture of work reflects a common tautological definition of work — a person gets paid for doing work and we know it is work because it is being paid for.

WOMEN, WORK, AND HOUSEWORK

How then does this relate to our central concern of analysing work with the aid of a feminist perspective? In general terms, we could say that most adult men (between their early 20s and mid-60s) in Canada work for pay, usually away from their homes, and engage in social life with family and friends, as well as undertaking the necessary activities of eating and sleeping or personal maintenance. Men's activities, therefore, fit reasonably with the common definition of work. The picture for most adult women, however, is quite different.

Close to half the adult female population does engage in work for pay at any given time. However, *whether or not* they are in the paid labour force, virtually all women are engaged in unpaid labour in the home for a husband, children or other family members. Women are typically responsible for maintaining some of the physical aspects of a home, for caring for children, and for providing services such as meals and laundry. (They also spend some time in socializing and on their own personal care. They must, too, be a central source of emotional support for the other household members, and a source of sexual access for their partner). It is this enormous amount of unpaid labour by women which causes the significant variation between their life experiences and those of men. Yet, we find a commonly held assumption that housework, that is, all the activities undertaken to maintain the members of the household, both physically and socially, and the maintenance of the physical structure of the home, is not "real" work.

There are several indications of the fact that housework is not defined as work or "real" work. One indicator can be found in certain government policies and programs which are based on the assumption that housework is not a productive economic activity. Secondly, the attitudes and behaviour of people toward the work performed by housewives indicates that housework is not regarded as work in the same way as other occupations are seen to be work. A further indication of the belief that housework is not work is found in the scholarly descriptions of work performed in industrial societies. Researchers have typically not studied and analysed housework and housewives in the same way in which they have studied other occupations or work situations. Let us look at each of these indications in somewhat more detail.

GOVERNMENT ATTITUDES AND POLICY TOWARD HOUSEWORK

The poverty in which many women, and especially elderly and widowed women, find themselves is a result of government and social economic policies. Women in Canada do not have the same social security coverage as do men. In general, this inequality in coverage arises because governments do not view housework as an economic activity which should entitle people to the same benefits as those who undertake work in the paid labour force. For housewives, there is no accident, disability or sickness assistance. Thus, if a housewife becomes disabled, there is no recognition that the tasks she formerly performed will still need to be done and that it may be necessary to hire someone to do the work for which she was previously responsible.[2] The inadequate social security coverage for women outside the paid labour force is probably the single most important gap in our social security system at this time. Nowhere is this more evident than on the question of pensions. So, many elderly women in Canada spend the last years of their lives in poverty because of government policies on pensions. Both the Canada Pension Plan and the Quebec Pension Plan are established such that housewives cannot make contributions to them and therefore cannot derive any benefits. At the time of writing (September 1980) the federal government has announced its intention to allow housewives to make voluntary contributions to the CPP. This is planned for two years hence. It will be interesting to follow the course of this plan. It is by no means a simple issue.

The only recognition of the housewife's contribution to the economic well-being of the whole family comes at the time of divorce when the accumulated pension credits may be split between the husband and wife. Surviving spouses' benefits under the Canada Pension Plan averaged less than $100 a month in 1978.[3] Policies governing private pension plans are equally problematic for housewives. Less than 50 per cent of the male labour force participates in a private pension plan and, despite the money paid into the plan, women may find themselves very disadvantaged should they outlive their husbands, as the majority of them do.[4] At the present time, private pension plans are not required to include survivor's benefits. At their husband's deaths, therefore, many women find that the pension is no longer paid or, if it does continue, it is a substantially reduced percentage of the amount received when the husband was alive.[5]

The government, in fact, seems to accept virtually no responsibility for housewives and their economic well-being, and certainly makes little provision for them when they are elderly. Prevented from participating in the CPP/QPP, they are given no protection with regard to the private plans of their husbands. Current policies of governments thus reinforce the idea that housework is not work, and further seem to imply that housewives are so unimportant that they do not merit recompense for decades of essential labour in the home, or protection of economic needs throughout their lives.

A major and unequivocal indication that the government does not consider housework to be an economic activity is the fact that housework is not a part of the calculations of the economic activity of the country, that is, it is not included in the Gross National Product (GNP). Whether one considers the GNP to be simply a measure of economic activity or a measure of economic well-being, it is difficult to justify the omission of housework. It does result in the production of goods and services, which the GNP purports to measure, and the provision of those goods and services is important to the economic well-being of individuals. The possibility of including housework in the GNP goes back to at least the 1920s, and during the subsequent discussion and debate — primarily among economists — no one has developed a significant or convincing argument for the exclusion of housework. In fact, virtually all the debate centres around *how* to measure the economic value of housework, and not around whether it should be measured.[6] Considerable attention has been given to the different ways in which the value of housework could be measured, but it is clear from the discussions that there is no insuperable problem in including the value of housework in the GNP. Rather, it has been decided not to include it because governments have not been willing to recognize the economic value of housework. In fact, the most common estimate is that housework would increase the GNP of Canada by approximately 33 per cent.

If the federal government through its economic policies indicates that housewives do not make an important economic contribution to the family and society, a similar attitude was also reflected until very recently in the divorce legislation of most provinces. At the time of divorce, courts typically took a very narrow definition of who owned the assets acquired during marriage. If the wife, for example, could not prove that she had made a substantial and direct monetary contribution to the acquisition of a house, car or other items, then it could well be ruled that she had no claim on the possessions and would receive no share in them. In the case of property, for instance, it was virtually essential that the wife's name be entered in the title to the property.[7] Thus, the value of the goods produced by the housewife and the services performed was denied.

That some change may be on the horizon is shown in the assumption behind new legislation in Ontario and Nova Scotia that marriage is a joint endeavour. Spouses contribute to the marriage, either through bringing income into the household, or through the provision of services. Both types of labour are necessary and should, therefore, entitle both spouses to a share in the assets of the marriage if a divorce takes place. It is still the case, however, that not all assets will necessarily be shared. Business assets have proved to be a major point of contention and are typically divided at the discretion of the judge. The idea that households require both salaries and services, and that wives and husbands may contribute different shares of these essential requirements, is only recently being reflected in certain of our laws, and has by no means been fully accepted as the principle on which households are normally organized.

POPULAR ATTITUDES TOWARD HOUSEWORK

The lack of acknowledgment that housework is work of economic value or "real" work is not, of course, just confined to governments. It is probable that most Canadians do not view housework as real work and certainly many of us have heard women answer the question: "What do you do?" by saying "Oh, I'm just a housewife." Too many housewives have themselves accepted the common evaluation of their role as unimportant and insignificant within the economic system. Galbraith[8] has explored the advantages to the economic system of maintaining women in traditional housewife roles. Although his analysis relates more to middle- and higher-income families, it is of importance because more women in these income brackets are housewives and these families have lifestyles to which less well-off people may aspire; in this sense, the families about which Galbraith writes can be seen as important trend-setters. Housewives are induced to remain in an often undesirable role by what Galbraith terms "convenient social virtue."

> The convenient social virtue ascribes merit to any pattern of behavior, however uncomfortable or unnatural for the individual involved, that serves the comfort or well-being of, or is otherwise advantageous for, the more powerful members of the community. The moral commendation of the community for convenient and therefore virtuous behavior then serves as a substitute for pecuniary compensation. Inconvenient behavior becomes deviant behavior and is subject to the righteous disapproval or sanction of the community. The convenient social virtue is widely important for inducing people to perform unpleasant services. . . . The ultimate success of the convenient social virtue has been in converting women to menial personal service.[9]

Galbraith's thesis is that housewives are an essential part of the economy to the extent that they administer a household, and thereby create the possibility for affluent households to possess, maintain and use the many consumer goods available. Without this household manager, the consumption of consumer items would not be so great, resulting in significant consequences for the economic system. In the interests of maintaining the status quo, therefore, it is advantageous to convince all members of the society that women's place is in the home — that being a housewife is not a mere job but entails qualities of an incalculable nature that only women possess. In this way, the economy is maintained at minimal economic cost. Consequently, it is not surprising that people, including housewives themselves, look upon housework, not as a job to which certain rights and benefits should accrue, but as a calling to which women are ideally suited.

SCHOLARLY ATTITUDES TOWARD HOUSEWORK AND THE STUDY OF IT

As Galbraith implies, if we had a more informed understanding of the position of housewives in society, many of our common assumptions about the importance and usefulness of housework would be challenged. When we look to scholarly research for such assistance, however, we find that very little research has been conducted in this area. It is not until the mid-1960s that one begins to find sociological studies of housewives and their work. Prior to this time, studies of housework are few and far between, so that our understanding of housework and what it means to be a housewife has been based on impressions and less-than-adequate information.[10]

The paucity of description studies about housework is also related to the fact that housework is not treated within the common theoretical frameworks found within sociology. It is difficult to know whether the lack of attention given to housework in empirical studies is a reflection of housework not being dealt with in our theories about society or vice versa, that is, because housework is not analysed within our theoretical approaches, researchers have not thought it to be a topic worthy of study. Empirical research and theory should go hand in hand, but whatever the links between the two, it is evident that a major part of women's lives has not been subjected to the same intensity of research and analysis as that which has been given to men's lives and to work performed for pay. The relatively recent debate among researchers within the Marxist tradition indicates the basic level at which our analysis of housework stands, since there is a lack of agreement as to how one views the economic worth and value of housework.[11] Lack of agreement on such basic issues reflects, in part, the preliminary nature of the analysis and concern with housework, although there is no disagreement that housework does contribute to the overall maintenance of the economic system.

If we look at the classic articles and debates dealing with inequality and its relation to the occupational system,[12] the activities performed by women in the home are not part of the situation to be analysed. Typical of this approach is the work of Davis and Moore; while they claim to be explaining all inequality, they deal, in fact, only with inequality in industrial societies where money is the medium of exchange. The lack of monetary rewards attached to housework, therefore, precludes the consideration of housewives as an occupational category.

It is this aspect of housework — the lack of monetary rewards for the goods and services provided — which seems to create most difficulty in considering housework as work. Definitions of work or occupations in sociology are nearly unanimous in using wages or salaries as one of the fundamental defining characteristics. It is evident, however, that researchers are aware that this has not always been the case, and that even in industrial societies not all work is rewarded by wages. Despite acknowledging this fact, researchers usually go on to ignore that part of society where work is done without pay, and concentrate their comments and studies on workers who are paid.[13] The International Encyclopedia of Social Sciences provides an example of this. Under the definition of workers, Sills writes:

> Workers are those who produce or transform goods or provide services for their own consumption and for that of others. Money payment for work does not always accompany its performance although this is general in advanced economies.[14]

Despite this caveat, however, Sills' subsequent discussion relates to workers receiving wages for their efforts.

THE FUNCTION OF HOUSEWORK

Moving from these common definitions of occupations and work, it is not surprising that, until very recently, scholars have largely ignored housework as an activity worthy of study. Within empirical studies of work and occupations, little attention is given to housework and the occupational role of housewife or homemaker. Sociologists, writing about the place and functions of work in modern societies, exclude housework although their analyses could fairly easily accommodate this activity. Slocum,[15] for instance, gives a comprehensive overview of the functions of work in modern industrial societies. He suggests that work is a source of subsistence, regulates activities, provides patterns of association, contributes to a public identity and meaningful life experience, and determines social status. To what extent does housework fulfill these functions for many women? Can it therefore be considered work in the same way as being a farmer, a professional or working in another occupation?

If we consider just those women who are married and who do not work for pay in the labour force (3,080,204 or 55.9 per cent of married women in Canada in 1977), being a housewife is for most of them their sole source of subsistence. Although housewives are not paid for their work, there is a clearly defined exchange of goods and services between wives and their husbands. In return for taking care of the home, the children and the husband, a housewife is entitled to be supported by the husband. That this is one of the intentions behind the relationship between husbands and wives is evident in the legal system, where nonperformance of the obligations of the husband to support his wife or of the wife to perform her role in providing services (including sexual services) is grounds for the termination of a marriage. For housewives, therefore, it is clear that housework is their normal means of subsistence.

If one considers the other functions of work, housewives are not a unique category of workers. We suggested earlier that work is the major activity in people's lives, around which they regulate other decisions and events. Since work is the activity with the most external constraints attached to it, we make this the base around which we organize everything else. The work undertaken by housewives is no exception. Many of the activities housewives perform have to be done at particular times because of the constraints imposed by the schedules of other members of the household. This is evident in the timing of meals, which have to be prepared so that husbands can arrive at their work place at the correct time, and so that children can arrive on time for school. Even evening meals may have to be served at specific times so that household members can participate in organizational activities, whether of a leisure or work nature. Within the framework of providing meals at particular times, housewives have to perform the other aspects of their work. Although they are sometimes viewed as being lucky because they have more flexible time schedules than many other workers, in reality this flexibility may not be as great as is first supposed. Shopping, for instance, is dependent on the hours during which stores are open, and even scheduling the laundry has limits related to the amount of clothing the family has and therefore to how frequently clothes are washed, as well as to standards of cleanliness and, perhaps, the weather. For housewives with small children, their use of time is constrained by the waking and sleeping hours of children, by their feeding times and by the availability of babysitters. The time a housewife goes to bed in the evening is probably related to the time at which breakfast has to be ready, and that, in turn, is probably dictated by her husband's work schedule.

Clearly, like other forms of work, housework requires a major and organized time commitment. Housewives, in common with other workers, also have leisure time. The use of this time is determined by such factors as how much time is available in the evening and the resources accessible to the housewife within both the family and the community. Being a housewife imposes constraints within the work situation similar to the constraints which characterize other occupations. As do most work roles, this occupation creates patterns of association with other people. In this respect, a complaint sometimes voiced by housewives is that their work role severely limits the people outside the family with whom they can meet. Loneliness and isolation can be seen as functions of being a housewife, although the extent to which these are experienced by all housewives appears to vary according to such factors as educational level and family income.[16] Nevertheless, housewives are generally confined for a large part of the day to interaction with children, other housewives and the occasional service person. They have a pattern of association different from that of other workers but, as with other workers, this pattern is heavily determined by their work role. Other patterns of association are also evident in relation to the mass media. Television programming, for instance, is oriented toward housewives (or what T.V. networks assume housewives wish to see) during the day, and a different set of programming comes into play in the late afternoon and evening. In this regard, too, housewives operate within informational and entertainment systems different from other workers.

What of the other functions of work? It provides an identity for the individual. In describing themselves, people usually make some reference to their occupation, stating that they are teachers, secretaries or whatever. Housewives are certainly no exception to this rule, but see that position as being a major descriptive characteristic of who they are. Women define themselves, at least in part, as housewives. Although they may see it as a major source of identity, women do not necessarily view the role as one which is of particular importance. In their denigration of this role, they are in part reflecting what may be the commonly-held views about being a housewife — that it is a job which does not need any particular skills or abilities, one which can be done by virtually anyone and which is probably not all that necessary anyway.

The argument that work can provide an identity and meaningful life experience, can be applied quite readily to the role of housewife and to the work a housewife performs. We have already noted that "housewife" is a completely recognizable *social* category. It may be seen positively (a good homemaker, beloved mother and wife), or negatively ("just a housewife") but it is *there* as a well-known, if often little understood, membership category in our society. Being a housewife can organize a woman's life, can give it order and meaning by virtue of her knowing she is the one expected to be centrally responsible for the care and maintenance of a whole household. She will have learned as a young person much of what is expected of her, and she will continue that learning through most of her life. To a certain degree, she can shape how she carries out this responsibility, and may evaluate her success according to the standards she evolves for herself.

A final function of work is that it is a primary determinant of social status. To what extent does being a housewife determine a woman's social status? Again, the lack of income for the work she performs creates difficulties in using the common measures of social status — educational attainment and income level. Prestige rankings of occupations usually omit the role of housewife; this omission both reflects and reinforces the idea that being a housewife is not an occupational category. As sociologists generally assess the status of a family by the occupational status of the head of the household — nearly always the husband for married couples,[17] — women, whether housewives or in the paid labour force, are not seen to contribute to the social status of the family.

Stratification studies are deficient in their analysis of social status insofar as very little research has been directed toward a more comprehensive analysis of family status. There is also the question of whether housewives have a social status independent of that of their husbands. The little evidence we have to date on this issue raises interesting questions. Eichler reports that respondents in her study had little difficulty in ranking the occupation housewife, which was seen as an occupation of medium prestige. It also appears to be the case

> ... that when the husband's occupational standing is higher than that of a housewife he lends some of his prestige to his housewife-wife, but when his occupational prestige is lower than that of a housewife he depresses her social standing. If this generalization can be confirmed in other research, it suggests that studies which use the occupational prestige of husband in one-job families as an indicator for both spouses have slightly overestimated the family's social standing in the case of husbands with

Table 4–1

Time Spent on Various Activities by Married Women and Men with One or More Children (Time in Minutes)**

	Paid Work	Cooking	Home Chores	Laundry	Marketing	Total Housework	Gardening/Animal Care	Errands/Shopping	Other House	Total Other House
Housewives — Weekday	—	97.0	149.5	81.1	65.0	326.8	31.3	38.4	46.4	54.9
Housewives — Sunday	—	86.8	126.5	67.1	43.0	244.8	47.1*	108.3*	24.2	51.0
Employed Women — Workday	466.1	58.0	68.5	58.4	48.4	155.7	30.3	21.1	27.6	34.4
Employed Women — Day Off	357.5	69.7	115.9	91.0	77.0	233.0	38.4*	24.4*	43.5	55.2
Employed Men — Workday	520.3	27.4	35.3	95.0*	41.3	52.7	51.5	24.6	54.5	57.3
Employed Men — Day Off	483.6	28.96	52.6	15.0*	48.6	67.6	43.0	51.5	118.1	118.0

**For a description of the activities, see Appendix "A."
*Average based on fewer than 10 people.

high prestige occupations and have slightly underestimated the family's social standing in the case of husbands with low prestige occupations.[18]

Eichler's study suggests that people are capable of viewing the prestige of housewife in the same way as other occupations, and that housewives do indeed derive at least some of their social status from the work they perform for their families. The issues certainly warrant further investigation; since housewives also derive status from their husbands it makes for quite a complex situation which is not yet fully understood.[19]

HOUSEWORK AS A DAILY EXPERIENCE

To understand further how housework may accurately be considered as an occupation, it is useful to describe in some detail the daily round of housework activities for the woman in the home. Studies of the way in which housewives use their time and of the activities they perform are available for several countries and over fairly long time-spans. Evident from these studies are the continuing demands on housewives, despite changes in technology and differences between countries. Vanek[20] demonstrates that over the fifty-year period from 1920 to 1970, housewives have not decreased the number of hours they spend in housework, although the time spent on particular tasks has changed. The increasing availability of labour-saving appliances has not reduced the time devoted to activities such as laundry, since we now have many more clothes to wash and our standards of cleanliness are such that we wash clothes, bed linen and the like more frequently. The whole process of

Table 4–1

*Time Spent on Various Activities by Married Women and Men with One or More Children (Time in Minutes)***

Total Child Care	Sleep	Total Personal Needs	Radio	TV	Read Newspaper	Read Magazines	Total Mass Media	Total Leisure	Total Free Time	Total Study and Participation	Total Non-Work Travel
119.8	475.6	638.8	33.0	126.3	32.1	59.3	140.9	169.7	319.8	116.5	59.6
153.7	509.9	669.8	30.0*	157.4	26.0	100.2*	154.2	185.0	344.8	153.0*	51.6
54.9	436.2	593.3	24.7*	94.6	37.3	59.2	97.2	109.7	185.7	111.0	49.3
89.1	512.4	687.4	27.5*	124.8	29.1	77.2	147.5	175.2	340.8	163.7	74.3
43.7	439.4	593.7	39.0	130.0	39.5	54.7	144.5	108.3	243.0	159.2	48.8
63.2	486.1	667.3	63.2	174.5	37.3	89.8	199.2	207.9	425.4	141.8	68.2

**For a description of the activities, see Appendix "A."
*Average based on fewer than 10 people.

consumption now takes far more time than it did 20 or 30 years ago — there is more to shop for, for instance, and we spend more time deliberating about our choices. In reviewing time-use studies in various countries, Robinson[21] concludes that the increase in shopping time is the single most important change in time used to maintain the household.

It would appear, therefore, that our expectation that housewives do a full day's work as their share in maintaining the family and home is fully realized. If we look in more detail at the use of time by people in Halifax,[22] we can obtain a fuller appreciation of how a housewife's day and week are put together.

Table 4–1 presents, in some detail, the activities different groups of people undertake and the average length of time they spend on them. All the people represented in the table are married and have at least one child under 18 years. This table shows people's activities on a normal day — a weekday for housewives and a work day for women and men in the labour force — and on a day off. This day off is Sunday for housewives, and typically, a weekend day for the other people; although in some instances the day off is during the week.

If we compare housewives with men and women in the labour force, interesting differences are apparent. Housewives have much less variation in time use across the week, indicating that one day is very much like another, whether it is a weekday or a Sunday. On weekdays, housewives work an eight-hour day at housework, other household obligations and child care, and on Sundays they are still working something slightly over seven hours. The 50–60 minutes saved from their usual responsibilities results in an extra half hour in bed and a further twenty-five minutes of free time.

Employed men are the group with the most variation between days at work and days off. In comparison with employed women, on work days employed men spend about fifty minutes a day more at their main occupation and travel somewhat further to get to and from work. This travelling involves an additional ten minutes a day. Since we know that women are more likely than men to be employed on a less than full-time basis, these results are not surprising. If we look just at the time spent in the main occupation and travelling to work on work days, this accounts for 432 minutes for women and 491 minutes for men. The time housewives spend on their work is 501 minutes although this, of course, involves no time for travel to work, since housewives are at their place of work as soon as they get up. If, however, we include the household and child care responsibilities men and women take on in addition to their work in the labour force, we find that on work days women average a further 245 minutes, and men 154 minutes. When these figures are added to their total paid work hours, men work approximately 10¼ hours a day, and women 11½ hours.

On days off, employed women and men reduce the total number of hours in all types of work to 6 hours and 4 hours respectively; except for the 7 per cent of men who spend 7 hours doing activities associated with work, despite officially having a day off from employment. For these men, total work time is essentially the same for work days and days off.

It is apparent from these data that women who are in the labour force have very heavy responsibilities. An average work day involving 11½ hours of work includes four hours of household and child care activities, 1½ hours more than men in situations similar to themselves. And while men do increase their contributions to household work on days off — from 2½ hours to slightly over 4 hours, this is not as great an increase as for the women (4 hours to 6¼ hours) who are presumably attempting to catch up with the household chores which they were unable to perform during the week. While many men relax on days off and have the highest amount of free time of the groups being discussed, most employed women are still putting in over 6 hours of work.

Thus we have three distinct patterns of time use for these groups: (1) Housewives spend 7½ – 8 hours on household and child care work a day, every day, and have considerable free time with only slight variations between Sundays and other days. (2) Employed women spend less time in employment than men, but spend considerable time on household tasks once they arrive home, and have a relatively short time for free-time activities. On days off, they increase considerably time spent on the household and its members. They increase their sleep time by over an hour and their free time by a paltry 25 minutes. (3) Employed men work about an 11-hour day including 2½ hours on the household, most of which time is given to household chores such as repairs and maintenance of the physical structure. The time given over to these tasks increases considerably on days off, although the largest change in time use comes with the additional 3 *hours* these men gain for free-time activities and about 45 minutes given over to extra sleep. Most men really do have a day off from work.

The figures for the time spent in certain activities, however, do not reveal the total picture. Another factor which has to be considered is the extent to which all members of a particular group are involved in particular activities. Table 4–2 presents the participation rates, that is, the percentage of a group which performs the specified activity during the course of a week, for various countries. What is evident is the universality of women's participation in the day to day running of the household versus the much more selective nature of men's participation. This is the case whether one considers cooking and laundry, for example, or child care.

It seems evident that expectations about the maintenance of a household — both of the people and the physical structure — are such that housewives in different decades and in different countries are required to perform a full day's work to meet these obligations. Housewives in Canada appear to come closest to the old union ideal of 8 hours work, 8 hours play and 8 hours sleep. Where they differ is in the fact that they rarely have a day off. Nevertheless, the consistency of the demands on their time should lay to rest the notion that what housewives do is not necessary real, or productive work and is merely something which is conjured up by them to get them through the day. That women also find it necessary to spend 4 hours a day on household obligations in addition to their paid work, and men 2½ hours, is a further indication of its essential nature.

A rethinking of the housewife's work role in our society is long overdue. Policy makers are reluctant to undertake the radical rethinking necessary to admit housewives into the mainstream of Canadian society, and Canadians in general have not been challenged to analyse their assumptions about the importance of housewives to the well-being of individuals and the society. The responsibility for this lack of understanding at all societal levels must in part rest with social scientists who, too, accept the status quo and do not deem it necessary to explore such a significant part of women's lives and the human condition.

What are the possibilities for change? The most apparent signs of change have occurred in the area of matrimonial property laws, where the idea that a household is maintained by wages and services has begun to be appreciated. While such changes are significant, they only affect a minority of women and only become relevant at the end of a marriage; no equality in access to assets is assured during a marriage. If, as we have argued, one should regard housework as an occupation similar to many others, should the idea of wages for housework receive more support?

Wages for housework is an appealing concept, because it would mean that housewives could fit quite easily into the ongoing social security system. But who would set and pay these wages, and is the payment of a salary the only effective way to ensure that housewives do receive benefits equal to other occupational groups in society? Eichler[23] has reviewed the possibilities of wages for housewives and makes a good case that women who are looking after children at home should receive a wage from the government, since the rearing of the next generation concerns society in general. With regard to housework, however, it can be argued that all adults are equally capable of performing these duties, and that we should not continue to encourage a special class of people to be more or less solely responsible for these activities. This maintains those people, women, in a highly stereotyped, undervalued, and virtually

Table 4–2

The Percentage of Married Employed Men and Women and Married Housewives Who Engage in Specified Activities During a Week, for Selected Countries and Activities

		Bulgaria	France	W. Germany	E. Germany	Hungary	Poland	U.S.A.	Yugoslavia	Canada
Main Jobs										
(Paid)	M	84.0	79.5	71.0	73.6	86.3	83.3	76.3	83.4	77.2
	F	77.6	76.7	66.4	62.9	78.6	77.2	68.6	82.7	66.3
	H	—	—	—	—	—	—	—	—	—
Cooking										
	M	20.2	34.9	7.0	52.5	26.1	38.8	23.3	27.8	25.5
	F	77.1	93.3	89.1	96.9	96.7	96.9	95.1	95.6	80.6
	H	94.8	99.9	95.3	100.0	99.5	99.8	99.5	97.9	97.3
Home Chores										
	M	23.0	33.2	14.8	44.9	29.7	33.7	26.5	17.5	26.1
	F	71.5	96.8	91.2	94.5	96.2	90.8	85.0	90.2	82.2
	H	96.5	99.7	96.0	98.8	98.9	98.3	99.0	95.9	97.6
Laundry										
	M	2.9	6.8	2.4	13.2	3.6	13.0	1.5	8.2	2.1
	F	32.4	62.2	47.4	60.8	62.0	58.0	46.5	62.1	33.7
	H	51.3	75.8	45.9	76.6	68.7	69.7	63.6	64.1	62.0
Marketing										
	M	30.1	29.0	17.0	26.8	25.5	23.4	25.8	18.4	31.7
	F	34.2	56.6	53.1	62.3	67.4	56.4	42.0	50.1	40.6
	H	50.6	73.7	69.2	79.3	73.7	82.1	46.0	62.4	44.9
Garden Animal										
Care	M	10.3	11.8	7.7	11.7	5.5	12.9	31.8	8.9	7.9
	F	7.0	14.2	6.2	14.0	10.9	24.4	36.0	7.5	13.9
	H	21.4	17.5	8.3	12.5	17.4	41.5	31.3	10.8	16.3
*Basic Child										
Care	M	12.8	27.5	4.5	20.8	19.6	17.5	17.3	15.5	22.4
	F	27.9	72.0	59.5	62.9	62.3	56.1	62.0	59.7	57.4
	H	56.4	89.2	64.7	85.2	70.7	70.4	82.4	72.1	80.0

Notes: M = married employed men
F = married employed women
H = housewives — married women not in the labour force.
*For Canada and for all countries with respect to Basic Child Care, only married people with at least one child under 18 years living at home are considered.
Source: Data for Bulgaria, France, W. Germany, E. Germany, Hungary, Poland, U.S.A. and Yugoslavia are taken from Szalai, 1972, pp. 601–613; data for Canada from the Dimensions of Metropolitan Activities Survey, see Elliott, Harvey and Procos, 1973.

unchanging work and social setting. Even adequate pay would not significantly alter the housework/female equation of our social expectations of proper adult behaviour.

The issue of income security and pensions, however, is well within our capability to solve. Pensions do not have to be tied to participation in the paid labour force, companies could be required to provide survivor benefits, and governments could ensure minimum annual incomes for individuals and families. Economic security is, therefore, a major concern which could be resolved.

But what of the psychological costs of being a housewife — the loneliness, the monotony and the never-ending nature of the job, health problems, and the lack of self-esteem which can be associated with the position? We do not know as yet the extent to which these problems are experienced by Canadian housewives, and whether they are experienced equally at all income levels. Partial evidence suggests that housewives in higher income groups and with higher levels of education lead more varied lives than lower-income women. This indicates that the problems associated with being a housewife will be different in some ways for different groups. And, certainly, the move into the labour force brings with it attendant problems, not the least of which is a greatly extended work week, a hectic schedule and the reality of paid work which often is not particularly interesting, challenging, or well paid. To create major changes within the family situation, therefore, without concomitant changes in the work situation of women is to bring about quite limited change which can, in fact, increase the female dilemma.

Although economic realities force many women into the labour market, and current expectations are such that women are still required to do most of the housework, some of the economic and psychological pressures on housewives and their families could be alleviated by changes in government policies and the encouragement of different attitudes among Canadians. The recognition of the economic value of housework would constitute appreciation of the work undertaken by housewives, and an entitlement to some of the benefits which other workers have would be a step in the right direction. What is also essential is a major commitment on the part of researchers to understanding the lives of women. That housework is real work, that it produces goods and services, and that it definitely orders a woman's everyday life in a physical, psychological, and social sense, cannot be denied. Without this fuller understanding, our knowledge of human societies is incomplete and our policies and programs will necessarily be implemented in a less than satisfactory way.

NOTES

1. This new scholarship is evident in journals such as *Signs: A Journal of Women in Culture & Society, Atlantis: A Women's Studies Journal* and *Resources for Feminist Research.*
2. Social service agencies typically intervene only when the family is in crisis and there is the possibility, for instance, of children being abused. At that stage, services such as a homemaker service may be made available.
3. *Women and Poverty, 31.*

4. The National Council of Welfare estimates that the wife will outlive the husband in 67 per cent of marriages. See the report, *Women and Poverty.*
5. Although housewives are at the greatest disadvantage with regard to pensions, it should be noted that women in the paid labour force are also in a disadvantaged position with regard to pensions because family obligations influence their work patterns. Part-time workers (70.9 per cent of whom are women in 1977) are usually not entitled to be in company pension plans; intermittent work histories (because of withdrawal from the labour force to look after children) reduce the total contributions made to pension plans; and since pension plans are generally income related (the higher one's income, the higher one's pension) and women earn substantially less than men (57.8 per cent of men's earnings in 1977) women will on average have smaller pension benefits than men.
6. See, for example, Hawrylyshyn 1974a, 1974b, 1975; Ann Crittenden-Scott, 1972; Chong Soo Pynn, 1969; Walker and Granger, 1973.
7. See Linda Silver Dranoff, 1977 for a review of some of the landmark cases.
8. Galbraith, 1973.
9. Galbraith, 1973, 30–31.
10. Walker and Woods, 1979, 314–320 list publications on household use of time 1915–1975; recent studies of housework include Gavron, 1966; Lopata, 1971; Oakley 1974a and 1974b, Glazer-Malbin, 1976.
11. Seccombe, 1973 and 1975, Coulson et al., 1975, Gardiner, 1975.
12. K. Davis and W. Moore, 1945 and critique by M. Tumin, 1953.
13. Caplow, 1954, is unusual in directing attention to the work of housewives. That Hall, 1975, relies heavily on this work indicates that there had been little research on housework in the intervening 20 years.
14. *International Encyclopedia of Social Sciences*, 1968.
15. Slocum, 1974.
16. Clark and Harvey, 1975.
17. It was only in 1976, for instance, that Statistics Canada ceased to automatically consider the husband as head of the household for a married couple. Aker, 1973, indicates similar problems with research in stratification.
18. Eichler, 1976.
19. Eichler, 1976 and 1977.
20. Vanek, 1974.
21. Robinson, 1971.
22. Elliott, Harvey and Procos, 1973; Harvey and Clark, 1973.
23. Eichler, 1980.

REFERENCES

Acker, Joan
1973   "Women and Social Stratification: A Case of Intellectual Sexism," in *Changing Women in a Changing Society*, Joan Huber (ed.) Chicago: University of Chicago Press, 174–183.
Bart, P.
1972   "Depression in Middle-Aged Women," in *Woman in Sexist Society* Vivian Gornick and Barbara Moran (eds.) New York: Basic Books, 163–186.
Bernard, J.
1972   "The Paradox of the Happy Marriage," in *Woman in Sexist Society* Vivian Gornick and Barbara Moran (eds.) New York: Basic Books, 145–162.

Caplan, Theodore
1954   *The Sociology of Work*, Minneapolis: University of Minnesota Press.

Clark, Susan and Andrew S. Harvey
1975   "Women are Not all the Same," *Housing & People* Vol. 6, No. 1 (Spring).

Clark, Susan and Andrew S. Harvey
1976   "The Sexual Division of Labour: The Use of Time," in *Atlantis* Vol. 2, No. 1: 46–65.

Cook, Gail A. and Mary Eberts
1976   "Policies Affecting Work," in *Opportunities for Choice* Gail A. Cook (ed.) Ottawa: Information Canada 1976.

Coulson, M., Branka Magas and Hilary Wainwright
1975   "The Housewife and Her Labour Under Capitalism — A Critique," in *New Left Review* Vol. 89 (Jan.–Feb.): 59–71.

Crittenden-Scott, Ann
1972   "The Value of Housework," in *Ms* (July): 56–59.

Croll, David A.
1980   "Retirement Without Tears: The Report of the Special Senate Committee on Retirement Age Policies. Hull, P.Q.: Minister of Supply and Services, review by Jean Elliott in *Atlantis* Vol. 5, No. 2 (Spring): 216–218.

Davis, K. and W.E. Moore
1945   "Some Principles of Stratification," in *American Sociological Review* Vol. 10, No. 2: 242–249.

Dranoff, Linda Silver
1977   *Women in Canadian Law*. Toronto: Fitzhenry & Whiteside.

Eichler, M.
1980   *The Double Standard* London: Croom Helm.
1977   "Women as Personal Dependents," in *Women in Canada*, Marylee Stephenson (ed.) Toronto: General Publishing, 51–69.

Eichler, M., Neil Guppy and Janet Siltanen
1976   "The Prestige of the Occupation Housewife," in *The Working Sexes* P. Marchak (ed.) Vancouver: Institute of Industrial Relations.

Elliott, David, A.S. Harvey and D. Procos
1973   "An Overview of the Halifax Time-Budget," Halifax: Institute of Public Affairs, Dalhousie University.

Galbraith, J.K.
1973   *Economics and the Public Purpose*. Boston: Houghton-Mifflin.

Gardiner, J.
1975   "Women's Domestic Labour," in *New Left Review* Vol. 89 (Jan.–Feb.): 47–59.

Gavron, Hannah
1966   *The Captive Wife*. London: Routledge & Kegan Paul.

Malbin, Mona Glazer
1976   "Housework," in *Signs* Vol. 1, No. 4, (Summer) 6: 905–922.

Gronau, Reuben
1973   "The Intrafamily Allocation of Time: The Value of the Housewives' Time," in *American Economic Review* (Sept.).

Hall, Richard H.
1975   *Occupations and the Social Structure*, New Jersey: Prentice-Hall.

Harvey, Andrew S. and Susan Clark
1973 *Descriptive Analysis of the Halifax Time-Budget.* Halifax: Institute of Public Affairs, Dalhousie University.

Hawrylyshyn, Oli
1974a *A Review of Recent Proposals for Modifying and Extending the Measure of the GNP.* Ottawa: Statistics Canada (Dec.).

1974b *The Value of Household Services: A Survey of Empirical Estimates.* Ottawa: Statistics Canada, Non-Market Activity Project, Working Paper No. 1 (Dec.).

1975 *Evaluating Household Work: Theoretical and Methodological Approaches.* Ottawa: Statistics Canada, Non-Market Activity Project, Working Paper No. 2 (May).

1968 *International Encyclopedia of the Social Sciences* New York: MacMillan & Co. and The Free Press.

Kitchen, Brigitte
1980 "Women and the Social Security System," in *Atlantis* Vol. 5, No. 2 (Spring).

Lopata, Helena Z.
1971 *Occupation Housewife.* New York: Oxford University Press.

Meissner, M. et al.
1975 "No Exit for Wives: Sexual Division of Labour and the Culmination of Household Demands," in *Canadian Review of Sociology and Anthropology* Vol. 12, No. 4 (Part I): 424–439.

National Council of Welfare
1979 *Women and Poverty.* Ottawa: Supply and Services.

Oakley, Ann
1974a *The Sociology of Housework.* New York: Random House.

1974b *Women's Work: The Housewife Past and Present.* New York: Random House.

Pynn, Chong Soo
1969 "The Monetary Value of a Housewife," in *The American Journal of Economics & Sociology* Vol. 28, No. 2 (April): 271–284.

Robinson, John B.
1971 "Historical Changes in How People Spend Their Time," in *Family Issues of Employed Women in Europe and America*, Andrée Michel (ed.) The Netherlands: E.J. Brill, 143–153.

Seccombe, Wally
1973 "The Housewife and Her Labour Under Capitalism," in *New Left Review* Vol. 83, (Jan.–Feb.): 3–24.

1975 "Domestic Labour — A Reply to Critics," *New Left Review*, Vol. 94 (Nov.–Dec.): 85–96.

Slocum, Walter
1974 *Occupational Careers.* Chicago: Aldine Publishing.

Smith, Dorothy E. and Sara J. David
1975 *Women Look at Psychiatry.* Vancouver: Press Gang Publishers.

Smith, Dorothy E.
1977 "Women, The Family and Corporate Capitalism," in *Women in Canada*, Marylee Stephenson (ed.) Toronto: General Publishing, 17–48.

Szalai, A. (ed.)
1972 *The Use of Time.* The Hague: Mouton.

Tumin, M.
1953   "Some Principles of Stratification: A Critical Analysis," in *American Sociological Review* Vol. 18, No. 4: 387–394.
Vanek, Joann
1974   "Time Spent in Housework," in *Scientific American*, (Nov.): 116–121.
Walker, K.
1969   "Homemaking Still Takes Time," in *Journal of Home Economics* Vol. 61 (Oct.): 621–624.
Walker, K. and M.E. Woods
1976   *Time Use: A Measure of Household Production of Family Goods and Services*. Washington, D.C.: The American Home Economics Association.
Walker, Kathryn E. and William H. Ganger
1973   *The Dollar Value of Household Work*, Cornell: New York State College of Human Ecology, Cornell University, Consumer Economics and Public Policy No. 5 Information Bulletin 60.

Appendix A: Description of Activities

1. Total paid work: regular work at the job, overtime and second jobs, work brought home, waiting or interruptions during work, time spent at the workplace before and after work, regular breaks, e.g., coffeebreaks, travel to and from work

2. Cooking: preparation of food

3. Home chores: washing and cleaning up after meals, cleaning the house indoors, e.g., vacuuming, making beds, washing floors, outdoor cleaning, e.g., disposal of garbage, sweeping the steps.

4. Laundry: washing clothes, ironing, mending clothes

5. Marketing: purchasing of everyday goods, e.g., food and groceries

6. Total housework: summation of items 2, 3, 4, 5

7. Garden and animal care: mowing the lawn, planting, raking leaves, feeding pets

8. Errands, shopping: purchasing durable consumer goods, administrative services, e.g., banking, government and repair services

9. Other household obligations: repairs and maintenance of the house, e.g. painting, decorating, maintenance of furnace and other heating systems, paying bills, at home

10. Total other household obligations: summation of items 7, 8 and 9

11. Child care: feeding, washing, dressing babies and young children, help with homework, playing with children indoors and out of doors, reading and talking with children, babysitting, visiting doctor or dentist for a child

12. Sleep: regular night-time sleep, or day-time sleep if working night shifts

13. Total personal needs: sleep, eating at home, work or restaurant, personal care, e.g., taking a bath, washing of hair.

14. Total non-work travel: travel associated with children, shopping, leisure activities, attendance at educational classes, organizations

15. Total study and participation: attendance at educational classes, religious, political, civic and professional organizations

16. Radio: listening to the radio as a major activity, i.e., if preparing breakfast and the radio is on, the major activity would be meal preparation, not listening to the radio

17. Television: watching television as a major activity

18. Reading newspapers

19. Reading magazines

20. Total mass media: summation of 16, 17, 18, and 19; attendance at movies and reading books

21. Total leisure: visiting with friends at home or elsewhere, parties, in taverns and lounges, conversation, active sports, taking a walk, attendance at sports events and cultural institutions, e.g., museums, art galleries, hobbies, private correspondence, resting, relaxing

22. Total free time: summation of travel associated with leisure activities, attending educational classes, organizations, total mass media and total leisure.

Chapter 5

"Doing Domestic" — Work Relationships in a Particularistic Setting

Jane Turrittin

INTRODUCTION

The work relationships between domestic workers and their employers described in this paper are of interest because they are not typical of employer–employee relationships in our economy. The work done within private households is "interstitial" to the main thrust of our economy; the particularism characteristic of social interaction between domestics and their employers within the private settings of the employer's household contrasts sharply with the universalism characteristic of social interaction in more public industrial and bureaucratic work settings. The structure of social inequality brings together a domestic and her (or his) employer and creates a situation of dependency which is the context in which the particularistic interaction between them emerges. Two aspects of this interaction — the conditions of servitude and the patron–client relationship — will be examined. In addition, the working conditions of domestics, the relationship between the availability of domestic work in Canada and our immigration patterns and policies, and attempts to reform these, will be discussed.

DOMESTIC WORK IN AN INDUSTRIAL SOCIETY

Within our present economic system, not all forms of work are amenable to the rationalization and standardization which can render labour not only useful but profitable. Certain aspects of the work necessary to maintain a home and raise children, for example, defy further efforts at standardization. It is possible that the work involved in child care, preparing meals, and maintaining personal property is one of the last pockets of work which cannot be successfully commercialized.

There have been efforts to rationalize and commercialize work done within the home. Many tasks formerly done by independent household producers, such as baking bread and making clothing, have now been successfully taken over by the industrial sector and their production rationalized and made profitable by entrepreneurs. Indeed, entrepreneurs have been successful in making available to consumers not only a wide variety of products, but an increasing number of services. Today we can take our shirts to the laundry and eat our meals at fast food or gourmet restaurants. But because it is too costly for most of us to make use of these services continually, domestic labour within the household still is characteristic of family life and is still largely part of the role-expectation of women in our society.

93

One explanation of why domestic work has been so resistant to capitalist penetration is made by E.R. Blumenfeld and S.A. Mann, who suggest that the services necessary to maintain a household are characterized by a "gap between production time and labour time", and that "within this production time labour is used sporadically" (1979: 33). This "nonidentity of production time and labour time" may lead to the underutilization of labour. For example, while the preparation of a meal may take a relatively long time, the actual labour expended in preparing the meal is sporadic; after the potatoes have been peeled and put to boil, one must simply watch the pot. Because labour is not productive all the time, it has been difficult to make housework profitable.

Whether the gap between labour time and production time necessarily leads to the underutilization of labour, as Blumenfeld and Mann suggest, can, however, be questioned. Housework involves the co-ordination of a multiplicity of tasks, which can be carried out intermittently. While one is waiting for the pot to boil, one can put in a laundry, answer the door, or diaper the baby. In addition, the degree of productivity of household labour would differ depending upon the size of the family, stages in the life cycle of family members, presence of supplementary helpers, and so on. Because of the difficulty of shortening the time expended to complete many household tasks, however, it has not been possible to rationalize some services which household members inevitably require.

The socially necessary labour time required in the home to maintain the household, then, differs qualitatively from the socially necessary labour time required in the market (e.g., by commoditized goods and services such as processed food and goods), and thus domestic work falls outside the sector of the economy premised on the "profit ethic." Employer–employee interaction within the setting of the private household is of interest, then, precisely because the household has not been capitalized.

Before examining the particularism characteristic of the work relationships of domestics and their employers, some basic information about domestic workers and their working conditions in Canada will be presented.

Because of lack of continuity in the manner in which service workers are reported in the Census, it is not possible to present a reliable estimate of the number of domestic workers in Canada today. Not only has the way in which service occupations are classified been changed by Statistics Canada between 1961 and 1971, but the occupational breakdown under the broader heading of "Personal Service Occupations" does not include domestics as a separate category.[1] In this paper a domestic worker is defined as anyone "employed directly by the householder" (Women's Bureau, Ontario Ministry of Labour, 1976: 2). It should be noted that workers who perform domestic work but are employed by an agency or organization are excluded from this definition, because the legal status of such workers differs substantially from domestic workers who work out an individualized contract with their employers. Domestic workers may be further sub-divided into a number of categories, such as babysitters, cleaning women, housekeepers, senior citizen caretakers, and maids/valets (Saskatchewan Department of Labour, 1977: 2).

The work done by a domestic worker varies with the special needs of her employer's family and may span a variety of responsibilities, including child-care, partial child-care combined with total responsibility for the household, "light housekeeping," laundry, some food preparation and shopping. The 1961 Census reported 129,244 female workers counted as babysitters or employed as maids or related service workers — a ratio of one domestic to every thirty-five households (Leslie, 1974: 76), while the 1971 Census reported 76,650 women working as babysitters or in personal service occupations "not elsewhere stated." Perhaps the most reliable estimate comes from a special survey of the 1973 Labour Force, which estimated that 8 per cent of 534,000 Canadian households paid for domestic services in that year. However, statistics available in government publications underestimate the actual numbers of women who do domestic work because many domestic workers, wishing to avoid taxation, do not declare themselves as employed.

Statistics do indicate a disproportionately large number of immigrant women as compared to native-born Canadian women employed as domestic workers. In 1971, 25.2 per cent of a total of 34,425 individuals classified in the "personal service" occupational category were immigrant women who had come to Canada in the previous ten years (Boyd, 1977: 239). In addition, a slightly larger percentage (19.6 per cent vs. 16.3 per cent) of foreign-born than native-born women were reported as being in "service occupations" in 1971 (Boyd, 1977: 241).

At least two aspects of these statistics on domestic workers need clarification. First, we need to know whether, in fact, the number and proportion of domestic workers is on the decline or on the increase. We know that, historically, the proportion of women doing domestic work declined dramatically about 1920 when wage-labour became an attractive alternative to domestic work for young working girls, many of whom came from rural areas. In the twenties, the availability of wage-labour in the industrial sector not only coincided with "modernization" of household technology, but also with urbanization. While American data suggest a recent decline in the demand for domestic workers, it is possible that, because of the increasing numbers of married women entering the labour force in Canada, the proportion of and demand for domestic workers may actually be on the increase. Second, we need to know the proportion of domestic workers who are immigrant women. We know this proportion is substantial but, without better data, it is difficult to describe long-range trends.[2]

It is well-known that domestic workers are among the most poorly paid workers in the country (Women's Bureau, Ontario Ministry of Labour, 1976: 12–13; Turrittin, 1975: 68). Sheila Arnopoulos reports, for example, that live-in domestics "usually earn less than half the minimum wage . . . and are clearly the most disadvantaged group among immigrant women in the Canadian labour market" (1979: 23). Pay and working conditions of domestic workers who are sponsored to Canada by employers on temporary work permits reflect current government and employer expectations about acceptable working conditions and salaries. In 1979, such women were to be paid $75 per week in addition to room and board for a 45-hour work-week. They were also to be given two consecutive days off each week and two weeks annual paid holiday. At present the Department of Manpower and Immigration has no authority to enforce these standards and there is little way of knowing to what degree they are maintained. It is certain that many domestic workers do not enjoy such favourable working conditions (Farkas, 1978; Arnopoulos, 1979).

Our information about domestic employers is impressionistic and much more information about them is needed as a basis for the formulation of policy. It is probable that the majority of employers are households in which either both parents must work in order for the family to attain the lifestyle to which they aspire, or households which are supported by a single parent. A survey made by the Saskatchewan Department of Labour in 1975, which included domestic employers (as well as employees) as respondents, found that most requests for domestic help in Saskatchewan came from "single-parent families, particularly by working mothers" (1977: 5), who had incomes substantial enough — an average of about $15,000 annually — to afford the costs of "domestic services particularly for child care" (1977: 5). The results of the Saskatchewan survey cannot be used as a basis on which to make generalizations about domestic employers across the country, however, and national and provincial surveys of such employers would be most useful.

Likely, a small proportion of domestics are employed in households of middle-class professionals such as doctors and lawyers, in which the mother, perhaps motivated by the women's liberation movement, has returned to university or re-entered the labour force, not because of economic need but because of personal interest. A spokeswoman for a union of domestic workers in Quebec, Les Aides Familials, has interpreted this situation as "out and out exploitation and it's women exploiting women" (Toronto *Globe and Mail*, Dec. 27, 1974: 13). Given the premise of solidarity between women characteristic of the women's movement, it is a sad commentary on our social system that the liberation of middle-class women is often possible only because they, as privileged women, can hire other women at low wages to do their domestic work.

RECRUITMENT OF DOMESTIC WORKERS FROM PARIAH GROUPS

As an occupational option, domestic work has emerged because of the existence of social inequalities, and domestic workers have most often been recruited by the advantaged class from the disadvantaged sectors of the population. Historically, the demand for domestic workers in Canada has not been filled by lower-class women, who share with their employers a low evaluation of domestic work; domestic workers have, therefore, had to be recruited from among members of pariah groups. Nevertheless, both domestics and their employers have viewed the availability of domestic work as a means of promoting the upward mobility of the domestic worker.

A pariah group is a

> group of outsiders called upon to perform some task which is either
> contradictory to the values of or beneath the dignity of the host society,
> even though it is essential to the functioning of that society. . . . (Rex,
> 1973: 215).

When not only class but cultural differences between domestics and employers are great, the availability of domestic work is seen as a means of acculturating women from the culturally subordinate group to the life-ways of the culturally dominant group. Domestic workers can learn the life-ways and language of their employers while performing work for them. Thus, women from subordinate cultural groups who work as domestics have been significant agents of change in situations of social contact.

During the colonial era in Canada, a small number of black slaves were brought into both Upper and Lower Canada from the Caribbean to do domestic work, but colonists also recruited domestic workers from among Native Peoples. The French called these Native domestic servants "panis." In the Arctic today, Native women do domestic work for southern Canadians who have come up to bring social services to the North, and such Native women, to some degree acculturated to southern ways, are significant agents of change in northern communities.

During the period of the expansion of the prairies in Canada, domestic servants, not distinguishable from their employers in terms of race or culture, but rather in terms of class, were recruited from rural areas of the British Isles. Domestic work was seen as a means of promoting mobility by both employers and employees, however, and Canadian immigration officials recruiting Scottish lasses to come to Canada as "female servants, held out to them the possibility of marrying bachelor farmers," whereafter they could "assume the dignity and responsibility of an employer rather than of an employee" (Leslie, 1974: 108).

The Canadian government has continually attempted to meet the demand for domestic workers in this country by arranging for the immigration of women from minority or pariah groups, and exceptions to exclusionist immigration policy have been made to allow entry into Canada of this special category of woman worker. Although the Immigration Act of 1927, in force until 1967 when the present liberal immigration legislation was enacted, prohibited entry into Canada of individuals who were unsuitable with "regard to climatic . . . conditions," it is estimated that almost all of the three to four thousand West Indians who entered Canada between 1925 and 1964 were women seeking domestic employment. The number of West Indians entering Canada in the late 1920s is reported by Ida Greaves as follows (1930: 56):

Year	Men	Women
1926	4	49
1928	4	84
1929	11	85

The demand for domestic workers, together with the social and cultural disparities between Canada and the Caribbean, and the prevalence in Canada of the stereotype of the West Indian domestic, a stereotype rooted in the colonial past, underlay the development of the Canadian–West Indian Female Domestic Scheme. In effect between 1955 and 1967, this scheme legitimated recruitment of domestic workers from a pariah group. In order to be eligible for the scheme, the women had to meet several criteria — they had to have the equivalent of Grade 8 education, be single and in good health, be between the ages of 18 and 35, and they had to agree to work in Canada as domestics for one year, after which time they could move out of domestic work into other types of jobs. The availability of this scheme enabled over 3000 West Indian women to migrate to Canada, where they learned Canadian ways while working as domestics. Many later moved out of domestic work into more satisfying and better-paying jobs. (Bled, 1965; Henry, 1968; Turrittin, 1975). The scheme became anachronistic after the enactment of the Immigration Act of 1967, but the demand for domestic labour continued to motivate substantial numbers of West Indian women to come to Canada and do domestic work. However, in 1973, a change in the Immigration Act made illegal the former practice of coming into Canada as a visitor, securing domestic or other kinds of employment and then applying for landed immigrant status from within the country.

It is instructive that, despite this change in the Immigration Act, which effectively stopped migration to Canada of lower-status West Indians over the age of 15, the government made provision to continue to meet the demand for domestic workers by initiating a system of work permits. Under this system, workers are allowed to come into Canada on work visas, but are not able to apply for landed immigrant status from within the country. The work visa can be renewed a number of times but, after the expiry of their visa, workers must return to their own country. Thus, by creating an alternative route to Canada, the government has again circumvented the Immigration Act to meet the demand for domestic employees.

The relationship of Canadian immigration policy to the recruitment of domestic workers conforms to a more general pattern in which distinctive groups of workers have been recruited in response to demand for particular kinds of work. Updated statistics on the number of women who have made use of this scheme to come to Canada as domestics are not available, but the numbers are thought to be substantial. Arnopoulos reports that between 1973 and 1976, 4,269 or 40.7 per cent of the 10,482 workers who came to Canada on "In Homes Domestic Service Occupations" were from the West Indies (1979: 61). Because the work visa system does not permit domestic and other workers the opportunity to move out of their initial work situations in Canada into the wider labour market (an opportunity they have had in the past) it denies to them the opportunity of making their dream of upward mobility a reality. It is therefore a discriminatory policy and represents a regressive step in Canadian immigration policy.

INEQUALITY AND DEPENDENCY

Inequities underlie the way in which work relationships are structured in many work settings, but a number of factors result in the structuring of the work relationship between domestics and their employers in ways which differ qualitatively from most work relationships. In effect, the structural and economic inequality which bring together a domestic and her employer put the domestic in a situation of inadequacy (Memmi, 1965); her well-being is unusually dependent upon how her employer treats her.

The nature of the domestic's work setting and of her contract with her employer contribute to her dependency. The employer's home is not the "neutral" factory or office setting of most other workers. In addition, and related to this, since their relationship is dyadic, a domestic works out an individualized personal contract with her employer. This is in contrast to the collective agreement between most workers and employers. Thus, the domestic employee–employer relationship is shielded from public scrutiny to an unusual degree. Further, most domestic workers lack occupational alternatives, either because they lack certain skills or because they are discriminated against. Because it is difficult for them to leave domestic work, they have little personal sanction against their employers. As John Rex writes:

> Domestic service is one of the least free forms of labour, in that the servant is thought of as participating only indirectly in the market, relying for his income and welfare, to some extent at least, on the benevolence with which the master administers his private household. (1973: 278)

Because of the excessive dependency of a domestic on her employer, which results from the inequities between them, the employer has a great deal of discretionary power with respect to the way in which they interact. If employers choose to play down the inequities, as they would in a situation in which they are in great need of domestic help, there is a tendency for the patron–client relationship to develop, and there is a long tradition of paternalism and benevolence toward servants which favours the emergence of this type of relationship. On the other hand, given the privacy of the household, if for whatever reasons the employers choose to emphasize the inequities which exist between themselves and their domestic, the conditions of servitude may emerge. Over a period of time a domestic employee–employer interaction may include both tendencies — the lop-sided friendship characteristic of the patron–client relationship on the one hand, and out-and-out exploitation on the other. The alleged egalitarian child-centered middle-class family, promoting equality between husband, wife and children, should not be thought of as guaranteeing similar egalitarian relationships when it comes to hiring help.

THE CONDITIONS OF SERVITUDE

Conditions of servitude can develop when individuals deny their sentiments and do not allow them to intrude on their interaction, so that communication is limited to the task at hand. It is characteristic of slavery that slaves are treated by their masters as objects, not sentient human beings, but in so treating their slaves, masters also deny or repress their own feelings toward their slaves. Slavery entails the denial of affect, and servitude occurs when one individual can treat another not as a subject but as an object.

A slave has been defined as an individual who is the "property of another, politically and socially at a lower level than the mass of the people, and performing compulsory labour" (H.J. Nieboer in Park and Burgess, 1921: 676). While no one today can legally be the property of another, if a domestic is isolated in the private home of her employer, if she has little access to alternate work, if her financial and social dependence upon her employer is "total," and her employer takes advantage of this, a kind of servitude can emerge.

Even though slavery is reprehensible to us, some domestic workers are treated "as if" they were the property of their employer.

The first three months I worked for the Xs were pretty good. I had Thursday afternoons and Sunday off and they used to pay me promptly. I have a daughter (back home on the islands) — my mother is raising her. But after three months they began to forget to pay me. The 15th would go by and then two or three more days and no money. So I spoke to the lady, and she called her husband, and they made a special trip to pay me. It was a Thursday and I wanted to do some shopping. You know, you only get half a day and that doesn't give you much time. But it continued, their being late paying me. So after the third or fourth time I just quit. I said, "I just won't make a bed." They said to me, "Rose, you didn't do this or that." And I said, "You didn't pay me. I am working here for money and no other reason. That is the agreement we made. You are to pay me for my work." Then she hugged me up, and got the money, and said they appreciated all that I did. (Extract from an interview with a former West Indian domestic — Turrittin, 1975: 72)

The prevalent attitude of most Canadians toward domestic work — that as traditional women's work it is demeaning, requires little skill, etc., is shared by many domestic workers, and there is little doubt that domestic workers are viewed as socially inferior to "the mass of the people" because of the kind of work they do. One former domestic worker referred to domestic work as "a bottom of the barrel job." The social stigma attached to the occupation of domestic, however, is not enough to explain the degree to which domestic workers are excluded from legislation protecting workers' rights. A recent report by the Women's Bureau of the Ontario Ministry of Labour, after examining legislation covering domestic workers in Ontario, concluded that, unlike any other category of workers in that province,

domestic workers ... are ... excluded from most of the legislation designed to regulate standards for workers. They are specifically excluded from much of the Employment Standards Act, and all of the Human Rights Code, the Labour Relations Act and the Workmen's Compensation Act. Although there are other groups of workers excluded from these Acts, *no other group* [author's emphasis] is excluded from all four major pieces of Ontario labour legislation. (1976: 17)

The degree to which domestic workers are excluded from protective labour legislation differs by province, and coverage in Prince Edward Island is better than in Ontario. Most domestics are employed in Ontario, however, and it is relevant to use the legislation of that province to illustrate the degree to which domestic workers are "politically at a lower level than the mass of the people."

Because domestic workers in Ontario are not covered by the Employment Standards Act,[3] domestic employers do not have to conform to certain standards in working out an agreement with their employees over such conditions as wages, hours of work, overtime pay, and vacation pay. Whatever is agreed upon by a domestic and her employer is legal. Lack of protection under existing labour legislation means that unionization efforts by domestics are futile, since "any union of household workers could not use the Act's certification procedures to obtain recognition and would, therefore, need to rely on voluntary recognition by the employer(s)" (1976: 23). Although most household workers receive medical coverage, their exclusion from the

Workmen's Compensation Act in Ontario means that if they suffer a serious injury on the job, such as a back injury or a bad burn, they have no legal right to compensation.

Further illustration that domestic workers are denied rights extended to other categories of workers is that they are "the sole group of workers" (1976: 23) excluded from the Human Rights Code. Section 4(8) "does not apply to a domestic employed or to be employed in a single family residence" (1975: 8). It is therefore legal in Ontario to discriminate in the hiring and firing of domestic workers.

It is relatively easy to adduce evidence in support of the final criterion for determining if the conditions of servitude exist — performance of compulsory labour (Turrittin, 1975; Women's Bureau, 1976; Arnopoulos, 1979). A journalist's account of one domestic worker's tasks is summarized below:

> "Y's" boss had two grown sons, a daily visiting daughter and her baby, and two dogs. She worked from 8 a.m. to 10 p.m. by which time she had washed the supper dishes, cleaned the kitchen and served the evening snack. She was allowed out of the house only twice from Monday to Friday for her French conversation course (Farkas, 1978: 17).

Sheila Arnopoulos reports:

> Josie L., 24, works for a Montreal family with three pre-school children. In the winter her duties start at five in the morning when she gets up to turn up the furnace, and frequently end at midnight when she washes up dishes after evening guests have left. In addition to childcare, housecleaning and cooking during the day, Josie must be available to babysit in the evening. This means she is on duty virtually 18 hours a day or 90 hours a week. Although Josie is supposed to be free every weekend, usually she is off only every second weekend. Even then, she is asked to work or babysit if she stays at home (1979: 29).

Little wonder, then, that many domestic workers feel they are performing compulsory labour.

> I did not like the family I worked for, although the salary was okay. I had to do everything — get up at 7, and still at 8 in the evening I would be in the kitchen — clean, cook, babysit, wash, everything. This family had three children. They even asked me to make the beds on Sunday, my day off. After three months I decided I wouldn't take any more of this nonsense and I quit. I went to Manpower to enquire whether I was free to leave, since I had paid my own fare (to Canada from the West Indies). Manpower was willing to find a room and help me get another job, but I would have to pay them back. Instead I went to a personnel agency where I got a job as a live-in babysitter. This was with a family in (another) area. The pay was better and the family nice. (Extract from an interview with a former West Indian domestic — Turrittin, 1975: 73)

The foregoing provides support for the assertion that when employers exacerbate the inequities which exist between themselves and their domestic employees, the conditions of servitude can characterize the work situation.

PATRON–CLIENT RELATIONSHIPS

In contrast to treating a domestic as an object, which occurs in the conditions of servitude, the patron–client relationship involves treating a domestic as a person in her own right. When employers and domestics attempt to play down the inequalities which exist between them, the lop-sided friendship characteristic of patron–client relationships may emerge (Wolf, 1966: 16). An informant's statement that "you expect to have a personal relationship with your employer, woman-to-woman," illustrates Wolf's point that the patron–client relationship is premised on the engagement of at least a "minimal degree of affect." One motivation for the friendly interaction which characterizes the relationship may be the desire by both employer and domestic to seek out meaningful personal relationships to counter not only the general anonymity of urban life but the isolation of the household in which they find themselves (Wolf, 1966: 16). Another motivation may be the very real need of the employer for good domestic help.

Despite its surface friendliness, however, the reciprocity on which the patron–client relationship is based is unbalanced and the friendship is therefore instrumental. The domestic is clearly more dependent upon her employer's benevolence and his or her capacity to grant goods and services, than the employer is upon her domestic work. This work, if not absolutely essential is, however, a great convenience, enabling the employer to maintain a certain lifestyle. Some employers may also see their own prestige enhanced because they are able to hire domestic help.

In seeking domestic work, women often look for patrons. While not all women need patronage of a specific sort, because they do not wish to be exploited they look for employers and work situations in which the instrumental, lop-sided friendship characteristic of the patron–client relationship can emerge. The following well illustrates the lop-sided friendship characteristic of the patron–client relationship.

> Mr. Z . . . got me a job with Jean A. There were sixteen of them, not all of them hers, and I had to do the work for them too. Mr. A did construction. He built highrises all around. . . . I lived in and got $150 per month (1972). They never raised my wages but Mrs. A used to buy me things. I would tell her I saw some nice sheets when I had been out shopping and she would get them for my room. Or I would buy a dress and she would pay for it. We got along real good. We used to talk together a lot. She would let me go out with her husband. She would say, "Hurry and get through these things and you can go out with Mr. A." I saw a lot of Toronto that way. They were real nice people. I went to Montreal with them. They used to take me everyplace. They used to tell me to bring my boyfriend over. Even now, we see them and she calls me up. "If you want to leave your husband, you can come here." She told me, "Stay, and I'll leave you something in my will." But I had a disagreement with one boy and I left (Excerpt from interview with a former West Indian domestic — Turrittin, 1975: 76)

Note how the employer, in this situation, attempted to level out the status difference between herself and her employee by making gestures to include the domestic in her family, and held out rewards to her contingent upon her becoming such a member, and how in turn the domestic was able to take advantage of this propensity by asking favours. The instrumental aspect of the patron–client relationship is apparent here — thus, even though the relationship between the informant and her employer was mutually satisfactory, she left domestic work when she no longer needed her employer's patronage.

More crucial than an employer's ability to grant material security to a domestic may be his or her ability to use influence on her behalf. Of course, an employer's help in meeting simple goals, such as how to get to the post office or how to get information about evening courses, is welcomed by a domestic, especially if she is new to Canada. But the employer's ability to link a domestic to certain institutional structures may be critical in enabling her to meet more basic goals.[4] For example, an employer may use his influence to help a domestic secure landed immigrant status, or a work permit if she is in the country illegally. The ways in which a number of West Indian women who first worked as domestics in Canada were successful in securing the patronage of potential or actual employers to reach tangible goals has been reported elsewhere (Turrittin, 1975).

An illustration of this widespread practice[5] is an instance in which the friendship of the employer was crucial in enabling a woman who came into Canada as a visitor to secure landed immigrant status. Although it has not been legal since 1973 to come into the country as a visitor and secure landed immigrant status from within, many women still do come as visitors, secure domestic jobs, and thus are illegal immigrants. A benevolent employer, who is either in the legal profession himself or who has a friend who is, may be very useful in acting on behalf of an employee in this situation.[6]

Through a woman I met on the plane coming up, I was put in contact with a widowed lawyer with 5 children who hired me as a domestic and paid me $150 per month. My employer did not ask my status. I had entered Canada as a visitor with Mr. J, but after six months had gone by I had gotten together the necessary credentials to get landed immigrant status. These included a letter from my employer (the lawyer) saying I had a job, a letter of reference from Montserrat, a letter from church at home (this was not essential — it depends on the immigration officer), a police certificate from home, a school record certificate, birth certificate. My boss went down to Immigration with me, but the immigration officer thought I was his client. My boss lied to immigration so that I could stay. He said I was a guest in his house. You had to have an address, and mine was the same as his. He said I had not been working for him but he had a job for me. He told the officer I had come up with his last housekeeper. He also swore I would be under his care until I was 21, and that he would be responsible for me. You can only get landed status when you are 21, but it was possible for me to have OHIP once I contacted Immigration. After three months my work permit came and once I was 21 I got my landed status promptly, along with medical forms. Some girls have to pay a lawyer $500 to help them with immigration. I was lucky. He paid me those six months. (Turrittin, 1975: 77)

Besides enabling a woman to become a landed immigrant, patrons can promote the mobility of domestics in a number of other ways. It is common for

West Indian domestics to take night school courses while doing domestic work. They can thus upgrade their educational credentials and develop occupational skills for which there is a demand in the wider labour market. In order to go to school, however, a woman needs the co-operation of her employer; some domestics even manage to work out arrangements to attend day school while continuing to live-in with their employers and do housework.

> They really don't need me where I am. There are three children. The girls are 20 and 18 and the boy 11, but they never help. Mrs. Q was shocked when I told her I would be going to school days, but I didn't quit. (Turrittin, 1975: 79)

The social interaction characteristic of domestics and their employers varies with the situation, and may include elements of both models elaborated here — servitude and the patron–client relationship. While servitude demeans both parties, patronage can be mutually advantageous. However, because of the lack of public scrutiny and control over the domestic work setting, even patronage may not always serve a domestic's best interests. Does the fact that an employer may use his or her influence on behalf of an employee, helping her meet such personal goals as furthering her education, for example, compensate or justify the low pay and long hours typical of domestic work?

AREAS OF NEGOTIATION AND STRATEGIES FOR REFORM

In some instances, the particular situation of domestic work — its privatized setting, the fact that domestic workers are not covered by protective labour legislation, etc. — offers certain short-term advantages to both domestic workers and their employers. In other situations, however, the interests of domestic workers and employers are quite distinct and opposed.

In working out a contract, one of the areas of negotiation between an employer and a domestic concerns whether the employer should make deductions from the employee's wages for the Canada Pension Plan, medical coverage and other types of benefits, and whether the employer should make contributions on behalf of the employee. In some instances, domestic workers perceive it as advantageous to circumvent tax laws and their employers comply, since it is not disadvantageous for them to do so. Many cleaning women, for example, ask their employers not to make deductions since they do not wish to declare their income for tax purposes. Women on welfare who are allowed to earn a certain maximum income while receiving mother's allowance may wish employers to under-report their income from domestic work.

In other instances, however, such as whether or not an employer should deduct wages paid for childcare from his income tax, the interests of the babysitter and the employer are at odds (Women's Bureau, 1976: 10). A babysitter, preferring not to declare her babysitting income, may ask her employer not to claim the $1000 per year deduction for each child allowable under present federal tax law. (An employer requesting such childcare deductions from the government must report the name and address of the babysitter on her tax form.) While it is advantageous in the short-run for a cleaning woman or babysitter to request her employer not to make such deductions, it is disadvantageous for the parents who work since they lose the tax deductibility. For domestic workers, the long-run disadvantage of not making such deductions is that they cannot claim pensions when they retire, nor can they demand compensation during periods of unemployment.

A number of attempts have been made by domestic workers to secure more control over their working conditions and pay, but these efforts have had little success. Leslie cites efforts to unionize by domestics in Canada in 1919; efforts to unionize domestic workers in Quebec in 1974 by Les Aides Familiales were underwritten by the Secretary of State, but the fact that each employee has a different employer is a major deterrent to collective action.

At present, the Montreal Household Workers Association is working to improve conditions of domestic workers, and domestic workers themselves, with the support of certain voluntary groups, such as the Council on the Status of Women, are putting pressure on the government to reform the worst excesses of the temporary work visa program as it applies to domestic workers. In response to these pressures, a former Minister of Manpower and Immigration, Ron Atkey, stated that efforts were being made to ensure that a contract signed by an employer with a foreign domestic set out working conditions such as her hours of work, pay for overtime, and medical coverage, and that the regulations prohibiting persons on temporary permits from attending classes will be changed so that women can take night school courses. Further, in Ontario, the Minister of Labour has indicated that "either a minimum monthly wage" be set for domestic workers "or an agreement will enforce those written contracts" (Toronto *Globe and Mail*, Dec. 3, 1979). Government officials, however, have not made any commitments in response to pressures by domestic workers to be given landed immigrant status.

As suggested in a report commissioned for the Council on the Status of Women, a greater degree of control could be exerted over the working situation of domestics. A number of independent nonprofit agencies could be created, not only to co-ordinate the demand for domestic help with supply, but to guarantee, by a series of spot checks, that contracts worked out according to standards suggested by the agency and entered into by both employers and domestics, using the agency's services, be maintained. Because this system contains the provision for public scrutiny of the domestic's work situation, the worst excesses which can develop for domestic workers could not long remain hidden. In addition, because such a system recognizes the private-dyadic nature of the contract between domestics and employers, it could promote the emergence of patron–client relationships. A model of such an agency is the Montreal Household Workers Association. Should such a network of agencies be developed however, a major problem would be to ensure that all employers and domestics make use of it. If the wage standard of the agency is too high, many employers will attempt to recruit domestic help outside its offices, while domestic workers who prefer the short-term advantages of tax-free unreported income will look on their own for jobs.

CONCLUSION

This paper has discussed the relationships which characterize interaction between domestic workers and their employers. Such work relationships are of interest because they differ significantly from those in the wider economy. It is the interstitial and private nature of household work in our market economy which permits the emergence of conditions of servitude and patron–client relationships. Moreover, the work relationships in which domestic workers and their employers are enmeshed are not likely to become anachronistic in the near future because, as has been argued, so many aspects of housework do not lend themselves to rationalization.

NOTES

1. The ways in which personal service workers were classified in the 1961 and 1971 Canadian Censuses are as follows:

1961

Service and Recreation occupations
Housekeepers, waiters, cooks and related workers
Lodging and boarding housekeepers

Babysitters	12,214
Maids and related service workers N.E.S.	120,392

Other Service Occupations

Barbers, Hairdressers, Manicurists	23,305
Launderers and dry cleaners	
Elevator tenders, building	
Funeral directors and embalmers	68
Janitors and cleaners	31,869

Housekeepers (except private households),
   matrons, cooks

Guides	145
Service workers N.E.S.	2,484

Source: Table 6. Labour Force, 15 years of age and over by occupation and sex for Canada, the Provinces and Territories, 1961 Cat. 94–503 (Vol. III — Part I)

1971

Personal Service Occupations	117,290
6141 Funeral directors, embalmers and related occupations	160
6143 Barbers, hairdressers and related occupations	35,620
6144 Guides	895
6145 Hostesses and stewards, except for food and beverage	4,060
6147 Babysitters	20,230
6149 Personal service occupations N.E.S.	56,325

Other Service Occupations

6190 Supervisors, other service occupations	1,620
6191 Janitors, charworkers and cleaners	54,795
6193 Elevator operating occupations	900
6198 Occupations in labouring and other elemental work, services	23,770
6199 Other service occupations, N.E.S.	950

Source: Table 3. Female Labour Force 15 years of age and over by detailed
occupation showing Marital Status by Age Group, for Canada 1971
Cat. 94–733 (Vol. III — Part 3)

2. The 1911 Canadian Census reports that 35 per cent of all "Domestic and
Personal Service" women workers over the age of 10 were immigrants
(Leslie, 1974: 95).

3. If an amendment to the Human Rights Code which has been introduced
before the Ontario provincial legislature is passed, all domestics, with the
exception of those involved in "personal care", will be covered by the
Human Rights Code. As of March 15, 1981, however, this legislation had
not been passed.

4. Effective January 1, 1981, domestics are covered by the Employment
Standards Act. Ontario Regulation 1013/80 protects domestics and
specifies that their wages be not less than $3/hour, that they receive two
weeks annual vacation with pay, that they not work on public holidays, and
that they have "not less than 36 consecutive hours off in each week from the
performance of any duties". The extension of legal protection to domestics
with this legislation is a significant event in the effort to alleviate the
conditions of servitude characteristic of domestic work. However changes in
the law may in many cases have relatively little effect on actual practices.
Further, three important categories of workers are not covered by the
legislation:
   (a) a domestic worker who works 24 or fewer hours per week for one
   employer;
   (b) a babysitter who spends more than three-quarters of her time on duties
   relating to the care of children, e.g., supervising, preparing meals for
   the children, and dressing; or
   (c) a companion who is employed to provide fellowship, care and protection
   to an aged, infirm or ill member of the household.

5. This ability to provide a link with institutional structures is an important
function of the patron, and patrons can be found providing this service in a
number of settings, e.g., in the educational system where students seek the
patronage of teachers to get into preferred classes, universities and
graduate schools, or in the performing arts, where "contacts" may be as
important as ability. Wolf writes: "(W)here the institutional framework of
society is far-flung and solidly entrenched . . . patronage will take the form
of sponsorship, in which the patron provides connections" (1966: 18).

6. The ability to enter into patron–client relationships may differ with
cultural and individual characteristics. If it is a culturally induced skill, it
may thus be more congenial to women from some ethnic backgrounds than
from others. Most West Indian women are adept at entering into
patron–client relationships. Whether women of other ethnic backgrounds
generally possess this social skill is a question worth empirical investigation.

REFERENCES

Arnopoulos, S.
1979   "Problems of Immigrant Women in the Canadian Labour Force,"
Canadian Advisory Council on the Status of Women, Ottawa: Supply
and Services.

Bled, Y.
1965 "La Condition des Domestiques Antillaises à Montréal," M.A. Thesis, University of Montreal.

Blumenfeld, E. and S.A. Mann
1979 "Domestic Labour and the Reproduction of Labour Power: Towards an Analysis of Women, the Family and Class." Paper prepared for the annual meeting of the Canadian Sociological and Anthropological Association, Saskatoon, Saskatchewan.

Boyd, M.
1977 "The Status of Immigrant Women in Canada," in *Women in Canada* Marylee Stephenson (ed.) Toronto: General Publishing Company, 228–244.

Farkas, E.
1978 "Exploiting Domestics," *The Last Post* 6(6): 17–19.

Greaves, I.
1930 "The Negro in Canada," *National Problems in Canada*, Montreal: McGill University Economic Studies, 16.

Henry, F.
1968 "The West Indian Domestic Scheme in Canada," *Social and Economic Studies* 17 (1): 83–91.

Leslie, G.
1974 "Domestic Service in Canada, 1880–1920," in *Women at Work, Ontario 1850–1930*, Toronto: Canadian Women's Educational Press, 71–125.

Memmi, A.
1965 *The Colonizer and the Colonized*. Boston: Beacon Press.

Ontario Human Rights Commission
Ontario Human Rights Code Toronto: Queen's Printer.

Park, R.E. and E.W. Burgess
1969 *Introduction to the Science of Sociology*, 3rd ed. M. Janowitz (ed.) Chicago: University of Chicago Press.

Rex, J.
1975 *Race, Colonialism and the City*. London: Routledge and Kegan Paul.

Saskatchewan Department of Labour Research and Planning Division
1977 "Domestic Service in Saskatchewan" (mimeo).

Turrittin, J.
1975 "Networks to Jobs: Case Studies of West Indian Women from Montserrat," M.A. Thesis, University of Toronto.

1976 "Networks and Mobility: The Case of West Indian Domestics from Montserrat," *Canadian Review of Sociology and Anthropology* 13 (3): 305–320.

Wolf, E.
1966 "Kinship, Friendship and Patron–Client Relations in Complex Societies," in M. Banton (ed.) *The Social Anthropology of Complex Societies*, A.S.A. Monograph No. 4, London: Tavistock.

Women's Bureau, Ontario Ministry of Labour
1976 "Overview of Domestic Workers in Ontario," mimeo.

Chapter 6

Initiation into Medicine: Neophyte Uncertainty and the Ritual Ordeal of Professionalization*

Jack Haas
Victor Marshall
William Shaffir

INTRODUCTION

A significant characteristic of professional socialization is the anxiety, trauma and uncertainty experienced by those being prepared for professional practice and responsibility. Student anxiety deserves close attention because it is central to the process of professionalization. The themes of student anxiety and uncertainty are found in studies of socialization into various professions (Bucher and Stelling, 1977; Lortie, 1968; Mechanic, 1962; Olesen and Whittaker, 1968; Orth, 1963), but especially medicine (Becker et al., 1961; Bloom, 1973; Coombs, 1978; Fox, 1957; Fredericks and Mundy, 1976; Merton et al., 1957; Simpson, 1972).

Hughes describes initiation into professional culture as a period that "seems to be more lively — more exciting and uncomfortable, more self-conscious . . . than the rest of life" (1956: 22). Renée Fox (1957) aptly refers to the neophyte's problem as one of "training for uncertainty." During this initiation, or conversion experience (Davis, 1968), students must deal with the variable, ambiguous and, sometimes, exaggerated expectations of their teachers. In becoming a professional, therefore, the student must learn to use impression-management skills to demonstrate competence and thereby legitimate his/her claim of trustworthiness in serious or fateful matters.

To demonstrate how professionalization becomes an ordeal for neophytes, we note its central feature: socializers create dramas intended to convince participants and legitimating audiences that the conversion experience is serious and successful. This belief is typically communicated many times through ritual mortification processes of suffering and degradation which convert neophytes into a new and select category of moral persons. The professionalization process (Haas and Shaffir, 1980; Kamens, 1977), like the deviance process (Goffman, 1963; Garfinkel, 1956), involves dramatic rituals which symbolize how the "called" are transformed into "the chosen."

Initiation into the profession includes processes of social control and personal change. Students must subordinate themselves to those who legitimate the process. During professionalization, socializers test and validate

*We wish to thank Berkeley Fleming and Sherryl Kleinman for very helpful comments on an earlier draft of this paper.

109

candidates as they move toward increasing claims of responsibility, trustworthiness, and competence. Aspiring and practising professionals and professions seek to convince legitimating audiences of their success in developing an appropriate competence (Blankenship, 1977). The ambiguity involved in evaluating professional competence requires a set of strategies whereby audiences are convinced. This is accomplished in a context of uncertainty by the adoption by students and occupational groups of "a professionalizing perspective" — they take on a "cloak of competence" (Haas and Shaffir, 1977).

This paper describes medical students' initiations into the professional culture and examines the ritual ordeal as it is initially perceived and experienced by a first-year class of neophytes at an innovative medical school.[1] We examine the sources of medical students' anxieties in the socialization experience, seeking to describe those that are general to such experiences and those that are peculiar to the innovative socialization setting we have observed.[2] We suggest that the traumatic and dramatic "culture shock" experienced by students in the early stages of their medical education is not unique to medical students but rather, is characteristic of professionalization generally. This feature of professionalization is highlighted in medical socialization, we suggest, because of the morally fateful "life and death" nature of medical work (Freidson, 1970: 4) and the Aesculapian authority (Siegler and Osmond, 1973) granted the physician.

BACKGROUND

This paper is part of a larger study of professional socialization, in which we observed, talked to, and interviewed 80 students enrolled at an internationally recognized innovative medical school in Hamilton, Canada, for a three-year period. We observed the students in the full range of their student experiences, including tutorials, the development of clinical skills on the wards of various hospitals and extra-curricular activities. Our observations commenced with the students' encounters with the school's admission process and continued beyond their graduation as physicians.

The data we present here were collected during the first year of research;[3] that is, when the students were enrolled in the first year of the M.D. program. During this period, we relied primarily on participant observation techniques, although some informal interviews were also conducted. Each of us followed one or two tutorial groups, each consisting of five students, in the full range of its activities and, in addition, tried to meet other students in the class in group and in individual settings.

The medical school's program spans three academic years, each of eleven months' duration. The training period is divided into five sequential phases, but is otherwise completely integrated. Except for elective periods, students are assigned randomly to tutorial groups of five students and one tutor for each ten-week block of time during Phases I to III. Similar small-group learning continues during Clinical Clerkship (Phase IV). There is little emphasis on large-group teaching methods, although a number of lectures and seminars are available. It is in the framework of the tutorial group and a "problem-solving" approach to learning that objectives are developed, problems presented, issues and solutions discussed, and where students and tutor evaluate each other.[4]

In contrast to traditional medical schools, the concept of a basic or "core" curriculum is de-emphasized. Students without science backgrounds are also admitted. There are no traditional examinations in the program. At the end of each unit of study, teachers rate and evaluate students' performances as satisfactory or unsatisfactory. The emphasis is on frequent assessment of the student and continuous feedback by tutors, peers, faculty and staff. The main evaluator is supposed to be the student, who, during the course of the evaluation process, presumably reflects on the strengths and weaknesses of his/her performance. Students are placed into clinical settings from the beginning, in the expectation that their problem-based learning will be rooted in situations resembling those of professional practice.

A NOVEL EVALUATION APPROACH: THE ABSENCE OF BENCHMARKS

Studies of medical socialization describe how students in a four-year traditional program face the problem of not being able to study all that is presented to them (Becker, et al., 1961; Bloom, 1973; Coombs, 1978; Simpson, 1972). Consequently, students collectively attempt to determine what is important to learn, which usually means on what they would be examined. As the students' immediate problem is to pass examinations and courses, they learn what is likely to be on their examinations. Faced with the problem of too much to know, students develop a short-term perspective — learning what they judge is important to the faculty.

In our study, we also observed an anxiety among students about their ability to absorb and integrate such a massive amount of material. The following student's remarks indicate the importance of the problem and the intensity of the anxiety:

> There is no way that you are going to be able to learn everything. I mean, there is just an incredible amount of information that is available. I mean, let's face it, there is a fantastic amount that is thrown at you and then the question is "what are you going to do with all of that, how are you going to tackle that?" . . . the greatest source of anxiety is that there is just a hell of a lot that you have to pick up and that can really make people very neurotic because you know you are trying to learn things, and you realize that there is more to know and so you spend more time learning things and when you learn more things you realize that there is even more to know, and so on. This place can really drive you crazy. (nine months)

Unlike the traditional medical school, McMaster de-emphasizes lectures and lacks a formal examination and grading system. Therefore, the problem of "too much to know" is compounded by the absence of tests and grades which typically serve as standards which students can use to assess their progress, particularly by comparing themselves with members of their cohort (Becker et al., 1968). Some students said they favoured the traditional educational methods to which they were accustomed. In their earlier educational experiences, they had experienced some security in passing tests and competing successfully with other students. After all, their earlier success at these methods was one of the important determinants of being selected out of a pool of 2400 applicants. Here, on the other hand, there are no clear benchmarks of progress. The relationship of uncertain progress and student anxiety is expressed by a student who says:

> I think a lot of people would like to have tests and grades and then they would be able to measure themselves and also they would feel confident they are done with an area and they could leave that behind. They've learned enough about that. That is one of the problems we have is never knowing if we learned enough. With tests and grades that problem might be better resolved. That is why people are anxious, they don't really get the feedback as to whether they do know enough. (five months)

Although students do not take conventional tests and strenuously compete for grades, teachers regularly and frequently evaluate them. In one type of evaluation, students do write-ups of problems which their tutors read and review. In another important, nontraditional form of evaluation, members of each tutorial assess each other's progress and contributions and analyse their own progress, competencies, and inadequacies. This innovative form of evaluation initially produces much anxiety, because few, if any, students have had to reveal so much of themselves in other educational contexts. Two students make this point by saying:

> The biggest difference for me, here, is that you have to reveal more of yourself. You can't hide yourself. You're open to scrutiny and you expose yourself in the tutorial as part of your education. (four months)

> You know, I think you have to have a lot of confidence in a group to go through what we're going through now [evaluation]. I mean you're opening yourself up to people's comments, to their criticisms and it's really like pulling down your pants. (five months)

The educational system in which these students previously were successful, afforded them a protective cloak of anonymity. At McMaster, students' personal evaluations are supposed to reflect candour, and include "confessions" of guilt, and re-dedication to their education and student colleagues. The following, based on observation of a tutorial group evaluation, illustrates how students manage this problematic situation:

> It was time for the students' evaluation and it was clear that no one knew exactly how to go about it. Tom [tutor] offered, "Oh why don't we bad-mouth the tutor and start from there?" Alex said, "I'd be willing to go first, what do we want to do? Do we want to all talk about each other or have Tom talk about us first or what?" Jerry said, "I've already filled in the evaluation form of myself. What I would like to do is go through it with you and tell you my own analysis and the scores that I gave myself and when I'm done then we could comment on my impressions and whatever evaluations you have, and then maybe I could revise these scores that I've given myself." (five months)

What we find noteworthy in this incident (and in other evaluation situations observed) is that students approach the evaluation situation with great caution. Students often try to do the evaluations in a setting familiar to them or to turn some of the session into a "social occasion." In the above excerpt, we can interpret Jerry's suggestion for the evaluation procedure as his attempt to retain a high degree of control over his own evaluation. We see him attempting to control the participants' definitions of the situation.

Students have little to gain by challenging self-praise; and little incentive to severely criticize their peers. While evaluations are supposed to be critical, they become teamwork efforts (Goffman, 1959) in which each student tacitly agrees to be "nice" in order to collectively produce a public sense that everything is going reasonably well. Ironically, this "gentleman's agreement" increases private doubts about progress because the individual compares himself to the common judgment that everyone is doing well. Tutorial evaluation is often a situation of pluralistic ignorance (Schanck, 1932: 102, 130–31; Mayer and Rosenblatt, 1975) whereby students avoid negative evaluation that breaks down the "gentleman's agreement" that everyone is doing well. In a situation of unclear standards and measures of progress and competence, we observe students and tutors avoiding a confrontation that disrupts the collective commitment to reducing evaluation threats and criticism. A situation develops where severe criticism might snowball throughout the institution, making all participants vulnerable to direct attack. Privately, students and others are criticized, but mainly through gossip, without disturbing the shared commitment to develop a harmonious situation. This, we contend, is the main reason students make primarily individualistic responses to the anxiety they experience in the early months of the students' training. They role play and attempt to control others' impressions by adopting a symbolic-interactional "cloak of competence" (Haas and Shaffir, 1977).

Group evaluation, then, provides only an imperfect indication of a student's mastery of medicine, with his own tutorial group taken as a reference group. Students face the additional problem of estimating the competence of their own tutorial group in relation to that of other tutorial groups.[5] This situation is aggravated by the prevailing norm that it is considered inappropriate to visit other tutorial groups for comparative purposes. Students therefore compare themselves and their group to others on the basis of rumour and informal conversation.

TOO MUCH IS UNKNOWABLE

As students progress, they are immediately confronted by the complexity of the subject matter of medicine. They learn that it is difficult to keep abreast of new discoveries and advances in the medical sciences, and, more significantly, that medicine is an imperfect science. Renée Fox aptly summarizes this important source of student anxiety when she characterizes medical student socialization as "training for uncertainty":

> Students were confronted with three basic types of uncertainty as they advanced from one phase of the curriculum to another: (1) uncertainties that stem from the incomplete mastery of the vast and growing body of medical concepts, information, and skills; (2) those that come from limitations in current medical knowledge and techniques; and (3) the

uncertainties that grow out of difficulties in distinguishing between personal ignorance or ineptitude and the open-ended, imperfect state of medical science technology, and art, (Fox, 1974: 202)

When discussions in tutorials turn into unsettled debates and when the accuracy and suitability of patient diagnoses and treatments are seen as problematic, students realize not only that there is too much to learn but that much will change, or remain unknown. A student expresses this awareness in Phase II when he says:

A lot of what we do, we know the consequences of but we don't know the processes involved. We don't know what interaction takes place. We just know the end result and we continue to use it because the end result seems favourable. One of the intangibles that we can't measure is how much a patient's desire to improve affects his improvement and how much of medicine or a particular technique helps. (five months)

The students become aware during Phase I, with its heavy emphasis on psychosocial aspects of health, that environmental and emotional factors are important, but vague and generally indeterminate variables that affect patient well-being. As at other medical schools (Becker et al., 1961; Coombs, 1978; Coombs and Boyle, 1971; Fox 1957), the ambiguity and complexity of medical science is made even more profound in their clinical experience. Clinical experience at McMaster begins, however, not in the third year, as is the case in so-called traditional medical schools, but in the first few weeks, and before many students feel adequately confident in their knowledge of medicine. In a clinical practice environment, students begin to appreciate the uneasy relationship between patient symptoms, diagnosis and treatment. They learn first-hand the imprecisions of medical observation and testing in accurately determining the cause(s) of a patient's condition. Simple matters like listening to heart sounds or blood pressures are not always confidently accomplished. The problematic nature of the physical observation of a patient is noted in the following discussion between a student and faculty clinician.

Harper [student] says, "You know, I've checked some people's ears, but I'm really not sure that I'm seeing what I'm supposed to be seeing. Sometimes when someone looks into the ear you say: 'Did you see this?' They'll say 'yes' even though they never saw it." The clinical preceptor says: "Don't feel too bad about this, because I'm telling you that even when I look into an ear I don't always see what I believe I'm supposed to." (three months)

Besides trying to master a vast and complex body of clinical information, students must learn the highly technical and specialized language of the profession. At this early stage of their training, the sheer inundation of a new language and a complex medical terminology confuses students, making it more difficult for them to understand medicine. They become uncertain about whether they will ever understand and become facile with the communication tools of the professional.

Learning the language is critical to students' symbolic participation and identification with the profession (Roth, 1957). For the students, facility with the medical terminology is a prerequisite for acceptance and recognition by faculty and peers, and demonstrates to important others that they have not only learned knowledge but can apply it.

ANXIETY FEEDING ANXIETY

A marked change comes over students as they try to achieve standards of learning in an educational system which lacks clear standards. We observed students working day and night, and through weekends, trying to "keep pace" and "cope with" their feelings of uncertainty and anxiety. A student describes how all-encompassing their work becomes when she says:

> I have to spend the weekends working or else I just fall too far behind. I find that you just don't take medicine, you live it. You're surrounded by it. You breathe it. You eat it and sleep it. (five months)

Ironically, and in contrast to the finding of Becker et al. (1961), their shared perspective incorporates an individualizing, rather than a collective, mode of action. Because of the pressures to appear and to become more competent, and the complexity and disputable nature of much of the material, including the fact that much could be found in books and articles, students in their first year work hard and in private. Unlike the traditional medical school, this school supports and encourages students to learn individually. This is part of the school's philosophy to develop independent doctors who will be motivated professionals for the rest of their lives. Faculty encourage students to define learning medicine as a life-long process. This early socialization is methodological preparation for later independent research and study (Neufeld and Barrows, 1974; Spaulding, 1969).

Teachers and students create collective support for independent work and, although some of the students' experiences are group and co-operative ones (tutorial and clinical experiences), much of the activity involves a private struggle to learn and absorb medicine. The pressure to grow competently in a three-year program creates in the students' minds a situation requiring maximum individual attention. They feel they should not only study hard, but alone.

Because the students isolate themselves from each other, they create a new source of anxiety and insecurity: loneliness. One student describes the process this way:

> I think we work so hard at it, we really become alienated. I think that one of the problems that most of us have is that we haven't been able to develop real friends here, because we're wrapped up in getting our work done. I think a lot of people feel this. You just don't feel like there is any time to relax, because you always got it hanging over your head. (nine months)

Many feel that they must put interpersonal relationships aside because of the pressures of their learning, and this becomes a related insecurity. The students are in a vicious cycle. They become over-anxious when not working hard, because they fear that they are not keeping up and learning enough. As they attempt to assuage that concern and work hard, they find themselves more and more separated and alienated from their fellow students and friends. The following excerpt reflects this feeling of isolation:

> ... one of the greatest and saddening features perhaps is the fact that there aren't too many people outside of medicine that I relate to and it's not a consequence so much of my own choice, but it's just the fact that outside of that school the world rarely exists, and I just don't have the time to explore it. That's a really big regret, the fact that people around me are really working very hard and mostly of their own neurosis that they do. ... They tend to really over-work. This puts you in a position where you, too, work very hard and you just get caught up in it. (ten months)

Students work hard in an attempt to assuage or relieve their anxiety but they also begin to take on a role and demeanour that provides them a protective "cloak of competence" from the threat of being defined as incompetent. Students begin in the tutorial to learn how to manage themselves in ways that give them control over the situation and lessen the possibility that mistakes or incompetence will be charged or revealed. We elaborate elsewhere on the theme of developing a professional cloak of competence as a way of coping with student anxiety (Haas and Shaffir, 1977, 1980).

THE PATIENT AS A SOURCE OF ANXIETY

McMaster medical students deal with patients at an earlier time than students in most other schools, and they have less of an introduction to medical science to guide them and allow them to enact a professional, physician-like role. They receive no clear guidelines about whether to emphasize the learner or student–physician role. Although students are introduced to patients as students, we observed a range of demeanour with patients that indicated students were not consistent in emphasizing the student or physician part of their role. While this innovation of the school provides students with practical clinical experiences, the ambiguity of their role and the variations in patient and staff expectations add to their anxiety.

Students begin by taking patient histories and eventually move on to doing physical examinations. We found that initially the physical examination was the most anxiety-producing aspect of their contact with patients. This supports Fox's finding:

> Certain aspects of the history and physical were particularly embarrassing and emotion-laden experiences for students; for example taking a sexual history; examining a woman's breast; doing a vaginal or pelvic examination, palpating a man's testicles or a person's abdomen; carrying out a rectal examination. These intimate and potentially erotic aspects of the clinical tasks they were learning to perform, along with "any very emotional reaction" by a patient, were likely to be disturbing to students. For, at this point in their training, most students were struggling to manage their own overabundance of concerned feelings and to achieve greater detachment as they undertook their still very new, physician-like role. (1974: 206)

We observed that students varied in their confidence about the problem of sexuality when examining patients. At one extreme was a student who attempted to alleviate the anxieties of her fellows by allowing herself to be examined:

> When we took the clinical in Phase I, we used to listen to each others' heart sounds and all four of the guys each week took off their shirts, allowed us to listen to them and palpate them. I thought it would be kind of inevitable that a girl would do it. But I knew that the guys were nervous about it so we started talking about it in tutorial. I decided that it is kind of foolish. I mean, it's only a human body, and I would volunteer because I didn't think the other girl should do it. So I volunteered to let them do a breast examination. I told Dr. James, I believe he's kind of a blue-nose. I think he was shocked by it. I told him it didn't bother me and I thought it would be a good experience for them. So I did it. I let them examine me, and I wasn't bothered at all. I'm sure they were bothered, at least initially, but after a time I noticed that they seemed to be able to deal with it more objectively. (four months)

For most of the students, however, examining patients of the opposite sex produces more anxiety:

> When Dr. Michelson (clinical skill preceptor), was out of the room, a medical student says: "It's happened again, another beautiful woman. I didn't do an examination. I walked in and I saw how beautiful she was and I just put my hands in my pockets." He put his hands in his pockets, demonstrating how he'd tried to act professionally. When Dr. Michelson returned, Joe [student] told him that Lawrence has said he was nervous because he had another beautiful patient. Dr. Michelson smiled and asked: "You didn't examine her then?" Lawrence replied: "No, I didn't have time. I guess I'll try and do it this evening." (four months)

> A student about to examine a simulated[6] patient says, "I hear that they really picked a beauty for this. Like she's really supposed to be a sharp babe. So I don't know how it's going to be in there." After the exam, he says with a smile, "She really is a sharp looking babe. I would've liked to do a lot more with her but, you know, under the circumstances, it would really have been improper." (five months)

Examining patients, particularly those of the opposite sex, is a shared student problem that is perceived with uncertainty and discomfort. This is particularly true of students in the early phases of their training where they have not yet learned how to control themselves or their patients.

Students' anxieties about examining patients' sexual parts remain, but they gradually limit and control these anxieties through carefully managed performances. Students try to conceal their nervousness and uncomfortableness, which they partly manage by adhering to the ritual of draping patients' sexual parts. Students affect a serious and professional posture with patients in order to turn a potentially erotic or embarrassing situation into a clinical one (Emerson, 1970). A successful performance is one in which the patient is comfortable, thereby allowing the student to relax.

Also, students feel they are expected to act as coolly and objectively as some of the practitioners they observe. Students criticize these doctors for being "insensitive" or "callous" to patients. As the students move toward an attitude of "detached concern" (Merton, 1957) they fear that they will not strike the appropriate balance of detachment and concern. In moments of idealism, students believe that they will not act impersonally toward their patients; at the same time, they recognize that the demands of socialization may corrupt them (Fox, 1974; Coombs and Boyle, 1971).

MANAGING THE MEDICAL STUDENT STATUS

An essentially unreported and neglected issue in studies of medical socialization is the problem medical students face adjusting to their new status. Although an extended period of socialization awaits, admission is virtually tantamount to membership because few fail to successfully negotiate the training period. Selection, therefore, becomes the crucial stage of status passage and with it emerge problems of status management (Glaser and Strauss, 1971). Acceptance into a most prestigious and respected profession brings with it an accompanying alteration in status in the eyes of others, and ultimately in the mind of the possessor.

Students often reported that their new status of medical student created difficulties for them in their relationships with significant others. They feel unchanged but others treat them as possessing a markedly enhanced status. A student describes the reactions of others and the problem they create when he says:

> It is a problem because people immediately think of you as something special, and you don't want them to think of you as something special. It gets to be a hassle. (five months)

Others treat students with new respect and deference, commensurate with their new master status (Hughes, 1945) which becomes their primary badge of identity and the major focus of interaction with them. A female student describes the centrality of the medical student identity to interaction when she reports about her Christmas vacation:

> It was incredible. Everybody was coming to me for advice. They'd tell me the symptoms and ask me what to do. My grandmother asked me to accompany her to the doctor and on the way back she told me what the doctor said and asked me what it meant. (five months)

Students find that, more and more, friends and family put them in the structural role of "doctor," rather than treat them interpersonally. They are treated like indigenous medical experts who are related to chiefly on the basis of their new identity and presumed expertise. Within the medical school complex they are typically treated as the chosen few. Outside the school, in affiliated hospitals and services, they receive varied reactions. Even within the medical school, their neophyte and subordinate status is reinforced on numerous occasions. More importantly, their own insecurity about how well they are learning medicine and how successfully they are wearing the privileges and prerequisites of their acclaimed status, have important anxiety producing effects despite the deferential and isolating or elevating reactions of others. They live with the tension that they are not all that is expected of them, bearing the burden of living up to standards that no one can accurately measure.

CONCLUSION

To the outsider, there is a striking contrast between the extremely anxious neophyte professional and the confident demeanour of the graduate practitioner. This marked difference has a "taken for granted" quality and, as Louis Wirth so incisively instructs us, the most important thing to know about a group is what it takes for granted (1964: XVII).

In this paper we examine the endemic nature of student anxiety in medical and professional socialization, seeking to understand the sources of uncertainty in traditional schools and, by contrast, in the innovative school we studied. We note that the perceived sources of uncertainty that characterize medical professionalization can be thought of as a ritual ordeal wherein it is assumed that a challenging, rigorous and anxiety-producing set of experiences will produce trustworthy, competent and confident practitioners.

First-year McMaster medical students experience all the anxieties reported in other studies of medical socialization. Beyond anxiety over mastery of knowledge, dealing with matters of life and death and other concerns common to medical education, we found anxiety engendered by the somewhat novel features of the McMaster program. These include the lack of evaluative benchmarks, the shortened training program, personalization of the evaluation process, and the introduction to direct patient contact very early in the program. Thus, while organizationally innovative, the McMaster program fails to reduce anxiety which inevitably accompanies medical socialization and, to the contrary, creates new sources of uncertainty and anxiety.

Lortie (1968) and others (Brim and Wheeler, 1966; Glaser and Strauss, 1971: 116–141; Marshall, 1978–79) have emphasized a distinction between solo, aggregate and collective status passages or socialization careers. Our data confirm the distinction between aggregate and collective status passages: co-presence with others does not of necessity lead to a highly co-ordinative and interactive stance toward the passage (Glaser and Strauss, 1971: 122; Marshall, 1978–79). While anxiety is experienced in both traditional and novel forms of socialization, there is variability as to whether it is experienced from an individual or group perspective (Becker et al., 1961; Lortie, 1968). In our observation, the first-year McMaster students generally reacted to anxiety in a much more individual way than that described in accounts of the more traditional, lecture and content-oriented schools. The organization of their program variegated their experiences and worked against their ability to compare themselves with others in their own tutorial group, or to compare their tutorial-related experiences with those of other groups (for a strikingly similar description see Bucher and Stelling's account of psychiatric residencies, 1977: especially 260–61).

We conclude that different organizational structures essentially serve the same purpose of dramatizing the ritual ordeal of students, legitimating the idea that important changes are taking place (Kamens, 1977; Lortie, 1968). However, organizational differences may also affect the outcomes of socialization. Thus, Lortie argues that "shared ordeal contributes to the development of a subculture of self-confidence, while its absence makes it less likely that such a subculture will emerge" (Lortie, 1968: 261). Ritual ordeal is not necessarily integrative, but it does help to develop a community of fate which is believed to be specially prepared to accept professional responsibility and *act* competently and confidently by learning and adapting a symbolic-interactional and ideological "cloak of competence." The ritual ordeal of professionalization requires initiation and testing, and anxiety is a common reaction accompanied by the professionalizing adaptation of conversion into the professional role.

NOTES

1. As a convenient shorthand we refer to traditional approaches to medical education in contrast to the so-called innovative approach observed in the school we studied. We realize that these approaches are ideal types. Each school shares some elements of the other (Popper, 1967) but the typical model we have in mind refers to the studies by Becker et al., 1961; Merton et al., 1957 and Bloom, 1973.
2. The school recently created a team of students and physicians to be available for confidential assistance. For a recent analysis of medical student stress similar to those we describe, see Coombs (1978: 111–135). For a discussion of anxiety at McMaster Medical School, see Hamilton (1976).
3. The data we report on the first year in medical school are identified by the month it was recorded. All names have been changed to protect the confidentialities and anonymity of the study participants.
4. For a fuller description of the program and philosophy, see Neufeld and Barrows, 1974.
5. Considered in reference group terms, this is a problem of defining oneself in relation to a reference group when the standing of the reference group is changing, by some criterion, with respect to other groups. This problem is well treated by Runciman (1966).
6. At McMaster, actors are employed to simulate patients in educational experiences.

REFERENCES

Becker, Howard S., et al.
1961   *Boys in White*. Chicago: University of Chicago Press.
Becker, Howard S., Blanche Geer, Everett C. Hughes and Anselm Strauss
1968   *Making the Grade: The Academic Side of College Life*. New York: John Wiley and Sons.
Blankenship, Ralph (ed.)
1977   *Colleagues in Organizations: The Social Construction of Professional Work*. New York: John Wiley and Sons.
Bloom, Samuel
1973   *Power and Dissent in the Medical School*. New York: The Free Press.
Brim, Orville G., Jr., and Stanton Wheeler
1966   *Socialization After Childhood*. New York: John Wiley and Sons.
Bucher, Rue and Joan Stelling
1977   *Becoming Professional*. Beverly Hills, California: Sage Publications.

Coombs, Robert H.
1978   *Mastering Medicine: Professional Socialization in Medical School*. New York: The Free Press.

Coombs, Robert H. and Blake P. Boyle
1971   "The Transition to Medical School: Expectations Versus Realities," in Robert H. Coombs and Clark E. Vincent (eds.) *Psychosocial Aspects of Medical Training*. Springfield, Ill.: Charles C. Thomas, 91–109.

Davis, Fred
1968   "Professional Socialization as Subjective Experience: The Process of Doctrinal Conversion Among Student Nurses," in Howard S. Becker et al. (eds.) *Institutions and the Person*. Chicago: Aldine Publishing Company, 235–251.

Emerson, Joan
1970   "Behavior in Private Places: Sustaining Definitions of Reality in Gynecological Examinations," Hans Peter Dreitzel (ed.) *Recent Sociology No. 2*. New York: Collier-Macmillan.

Fox, Renee
1957   "Training for Uncertainty," in Robert K. Merton, George G. Reader and Patricia L. Kendal (eds.) *The Student Physician*. Harvard University Press, 207–241.

1974   "Is There a 'New' Medical Student?" in Lawrence R. Tancred (ed.) *Ethics of Health Care*. Institute of Medicine: National Academy of Science, 197–227.

Fredericks, Marcel A. and Paul Mundy
1976   *The Making of a Physician*. Chicago: Loyola University Press.

Freidson, Eliot
1970   *The Profession of Medicine*. New York: Dodd, Mead.

Garfinkel, Harold
1956   "Conditions of Successful Degradation Ceremonies," in *American Journal of Sociology* 61 (March): 420–424.

Glaser, Barney G. and Anselm L. Strauss
1977   *Status Passage*. Chicago: Aldine-Atherton.

Goffman, Erving
1959   *The Presentation of Self in Everyday Life*. Garden City, N.Y.: Doubleday Anchor.

1963   *Stigma: Notes on the Management of Spoiled Identity*. Hammondsworth: Penguin Press.

Haas, Jack and William Shaffir
1977   "The Professionalization of Medical Students: Developing Competence and a Cloak of Competence," in *Symbolic Interaction* 1: 71–88.

1978   "Do New Ways of Professional Socialization Make a Difference? A Study of Professional Socialization." Paper presented at the 9th World Congress of Sociology, Uppsala, Sweden.

1980   "Innovative Professionalization and the Ritual Evaluation of Professionalizing Competence: The Symbolic Cloak of Professionalism." Unpublished manuscript, Department of Sociology, McMaster University.

1980   "Professionalizing Adaptations to Ritual Ordeals of Uncertainty." Unpublished manuscript.

Hamilton, John
1976   "The McMaster Curriculum: A Critique," in *British Medical Journal* 15 (May): 1191–1196.
Hughes, Everett C.
1945   "Dilemmas and Contradictions of Status," in *American Journal of Sociology* 50 (March): 253–259.
1956   "The Making of a Physician," in *Human Organization* 14: 21–25.
Kamens, David H.
1977   "Legitimating Myths and Educational Organization: The Relationship Between Organizational Ideology and Formal Structure," in *American Sociological Review* 42 (April): 208–219.
Marshall, Victor W.
1978-79   "No Exit: A Symbolic Interactionalist Perspective on Aging," in *International Journal on Aging and Human Development* Vol. 9, No. 4: 345–358.
Mayer, John E., and Aaron Rosenblatt
1975   "Encounters with Danger: Social Workers in the Ghetto." *Sociology of Work and Occupations* 2:227–45.
Mechanic, David
1962   *Students Under Stress: A Study in the Social Psychology of Adaptation.* New York: Free Press of Glencoe.
Merton, Robert K.
1957   "Some Preliminaries to a Sociology of Medical Education," in Robert K. Merton, George G. Reader and Patricia Kendall (eds.) *The Student Physician.* Cambridge, Mass.: Harvard University Press, 3–79.
Neufeld, Victor and Howard Barrows
1974   "The McMaster Philosophy: An Approach to Medical Education." *Journal of Medical Education* (4): 1040–1050.
Olesen, Virginia L. and Elvi W. Whittaker
1968   *The Silent Dialogue: A Study in the Social Psychology of Professional Socialization.* San Francisco: Jossey-Bass.
Orth, Charles D.
1963   *Social Structure and Learning Climate: The First Year at the Harvard Business School.* Boston: Division of Research, Graduate School of Business Administration, Harvard University.
Popper, Hans (ed.)
1967   *Trends in Medical Schools.* New York: Grune and Stratton.
Roth, Julius
1957   "Ritual and Magic and the Control of Contagion," in *American Sociological Review* 22: 310–314.
Runciman, W.G.
1966   *Relative Deprivation and Social Justice.* London: Routledge and Kegan Paul.
Shanck, Richard L.
1932   "A Study of a Community and its Groups and Institutions Conceived of as Behaviors of Individuals." *Psychological Monographs* 43, 2.
Siegler, Miriam and Humphry Osmond
1973   "Aesculapian Authority," in *Hastings Center Studies* 1: 41–52.
Simpson, Michael A.
1972   *Medical Education: A Critical Approach.* London: Butterworth.

Spaulding, W.B.
1969   "The Undergraduate Medical Curriculum (1969 Mode): McMaster University," in *Canadian Medical Association Journal* 100: 659–664.
Wirth, Louis
1964   *On Cities and Social Life*. Albert J. Reiss, Jr. (ed.) Chicago: University of Chicago Press.

Chapter 7

Chiropractors and Their Competitors*

M.J. Kelner
O. Hall
I. Coulter

Canada's health care system is made up of a whole web of occupations and organizations. Each of these occupies a recognizable niche in the larger social system and a good deal of consensus has arisen as to what each of them is legitimately expected to do. A rich body of understandings exists today as to "who is permitted to do what" in the name of health care. Such understandings, of course, do not arise easily; there is always a good deal of pushing and shoving among occupations as they strive to secure a monopoly over some aspect of health care, and to defend it against intruders who ignore boundary lines and trespass on occupied territory. It seems, however that the occupations that play a part in health care have, over time, worked out a set of accommodations, each to the others, that permits a *modus vivendi* for all.

Among the health occupations that our health system currently comprises, chiropractic occupies a unique and intriguing place. For most of its history, it has been the target of bitter attacks by other healing occupations. Its competitors have referred to it as a "cult." Medical associations have gone even further and described it as an "unscientific cult," declaring that it is unethical for individual medical practitioners to cultivate any relationship with it. Since medicine serves as the symbolic figurehead for most of the other health practitioners, it has affected the way each has responded to chiropractic.

This article focuses not only on the relationships of chiropractors with medical practitioners but also on those with other health practitioners. Some of these practitioners are closely allied with the medical profession, while others are genuinely marginal to it. The emphasis here is on the concrete details of relationships at the personal level. The data are derived from the findings of a much larger study* in which a national sample of 350 Canadian chiropractors was interviewed concerning a range of issues involved in the practice of chiropractic.

At the most elementary level, that of day-to-day contacts, there is interaction between chiropractors and the members of other health occupations groups. At one level they all share the same body of patients. Inevitably they also come to refer patients one to another (none can do *everything* for a patient) either formally or informally. At another level, in pursuing knowledge in their respective fields, the "seamless" framework of science brings them into contact. At a more personal level friendships develop. All of these relationships

*Reprinted with permission from Kelner, M.J., O. Hall, and I. Coulter, *Chiropractors: Do They Help?* (Toronto: Fitzhenry and Whiteside), 1980.

are of a different order from those imposed by law. They lack the formality and uniformity of the relationships between associations, and they are, in effect, spontaneous relationships which develop along many lines.

We will now turn to the relationships between chiropractors and members of other health occupations, particularly those which may be considered their competitors.

Chiropractic has been described as an "unscientific cult"[1] by various medical associations, whose members have been warned that it is unethical to cultivate any relationship with it. But this is a misuse of the term "cult."[2] Cult members turn inward upon themselves, putting distance between themselves and others. Relationships with nonmembers of the cult are singularly cool. As the following results will show, our survey of the contacts between chiropractic and competing occupations renders the label "cult" quite inappropriate.

Chiropractors' most significant professional relationship has always been with medical practitioners and their various associations. The medical associations, as figureheads for most other health practitioners, have in turn affected the response of the health care world in general to chiropractic.

Scores of occupations now play some part in health care. For the purposes of this survey seven have been selected from the mainstream of the medical system: dentists, medical doctors, nurses, pharmacists, physiotherapists, podiatrists and radiologists. A further five have been selected which are marginal to organized medicine: acupuncturists, herbalists, homeopaths, naturopaths and osteopaths. These last are relatively small groups, so small that the Canadian census does not provide separate statistical counts on them.

We queried chiropractors about their relationships with these groups along three lines: whether patient referrals and sharing were practised, whether they treated, or were treated by, members of the other occupations, and whether friendships existed between them. Table 7-1 shows the results of the first question.

Table 7–1

Percentage of Chiropractors Who Share Patients With And Report Referrals From, and To, Selected Health Practitioners
(n = 349)

	Referrals to	Referrals from	Share Patients With
Acupuncturists	28.4	10.3	18.0
Herbalists	0.3	10.6	7.0
Homeopaths	6.3	4.9	5.0
Naturopaths	19.8	16.9	13.0
Osteopaths	4.6	3.2	3.0
Dentists	77.9	50.7	*
Medical Doctors	97.4	84.5	78.0
Nurses	15.2	88.0	18.0
Pharmacists	47.9	54.2	*
Physiotherapists	24.1	17.5	21.0
Podiatrists	59.3	29.2	30.0
Radiologists	32.1	20.3	*

*Information not available.

The pattern that emerges is plain. There are relatively few contacts with the marginal healing occupations such as osteopathy, which is close to chiropractic in terms of techniques used. On the other hand, chiropractors universally report contact with the established health occupations, most particularly with doctors and nurses.

Almost all (97 per cent) of the chiropractors reported referring patients to doctors. This was reported by all age groups of chiropractors, though we gained the impression that the younger practitioners were seeking such contacts more vigorously than their elders.

It was not possible to verify these reported relationships by polling medical doctors, but data from the patients provides some confirmation. Asked why they had come to the chiropractor, 3.5 per cent of all patients said they had been referred by other health practitioners, mainly medical doctors. Of course the proportion of referrals would vary from one chiropractor to the next, but in any event *some* level of referrals to them from the core of the medical system clearly exists.

Table 7–2 shows the results of our second question, whether chiropractors treated or were treated by members of other health occupations.

Table 7–2

Percentage of Chiropractors Who Provide Treatments For, and Who Receive Treatments From, Selected Health Practitioners

(n=349)

	Gives Treatments to	Receives Treatments From
Acupuncturists	5.0	7.0
Herbalists	7.0	1.0
Homeopaths	4.0	1.0
Naturopaths	10.0	6.0
Osteopaths	2.0	0.0
Dentists	63.0	83.0
Medical Doctors	55.0	54.0
Nurses	94.0	8.0
Pharmacists	58.0	37.0 (patronize)
Physiotherapists	20.0	3.0
Podiatrists	17.0	7.0
Radiologists	5.0	19.0 (consult)

From this we can see that chiropractors provide services to, and accept them from, a large proportion of health care personnel — particularly the core of the medical system, i.e., medical doctors, nurses, dentists and pharmacists. They have very little to do, in this practical sense, with the marginal practitioners in acupuncture, osteopathy, and the like.

With regard to the chiropractor as patient, as well as consulting other chiropractors, they also take their health problems to the main core of the medical system. Over half of them report receiving treatment from medical doctors. Considering that chiropractors are mostly in the prime of life this is a substantial proportion. Moreover they report that their families use M.D.s to an even greater extent.

Clearly chiropractors are not isolated from the mainstream of health care with respect to either their dealings with their patients or their own use of health services; their work, as they report it, is embedded in the larger health care system.

From our third question, whether friendships existed between chiropractors and other selected occupational groups, the results were as follows:

Table 7–3

Percentage of Chiropractors Reporting Friendships With Selected Health Practitioners
(n = 349)

Acupuncturists	16.0
Herbalists	7.0
Homeopaths	5.0
Naturopaths	2.0
Dentists	33.0
MDs	72.0
Nurses	77.0
Pharmacists	54.0
Physiotherapists	16.0
Podiatrists	15.0
Radiologists	16.0

The friendship links correspond closely to the patterns of work relationships. Here again the contacts with doctors and nurses are those most frequently reported. Three-quarters of the chiropractors count at least one nurse and one doctor in their circles of friends. On the other hand friendships with the five marginal groups are only infrequently reported.

Far from being a self-centred cult, it appears that chiropractic has numerous relationships with the larger health system. Perhaps the term cult could more usefully be applied to the five marginal groups of practitioners, given that their reported relationships to chiropractic are so limited.

Regarding those five occupations, two points are worth noting. The two of these that have the closest relationships with chiropractors are the acupuncturists and the naturopaths. The M.D.s have claimed acupuncture as part of the medical scope of practice, but the working relationships are far from clear. However, the link of acupuncture with chiropractic, though limited, tends to bring medicine and chiropractic together in an indirect way. Naturopathy, on the other hand, is a bit of an orphan in this whole field. Its interest in diet and nutrition is hardly shared by M.D.s, but chiropractors give it considerable attention. So it may be more than coincidence that chiropractors report having closer relationships with acupuncture and naturopathy than they have with herbalists, or homeopaths, or osteopaths. Indeed some practitioners are both chiropractors and naturopaths.

As far as the medical associations are concerned, both those in Canada and the U.S. have traditionally refused, officially, to have any relationships with chiropractic. Under the code of ethics of the American Medical Association its members have been forbidden to associate with those who practise "unscientific" medicine. This policy statement is straight-forward enough, but it does not tally with the way medical practitioners behave. In actual practice patients come to them, at the behest of the chiropractors, to obtain laboratory tests and X-ray examinations, which chiropractors may not be able to provide. There is clear evidence that medical practitioners provide some of these services, while well aware that a chiropractor is also involved in treating the patient.

The matter was debated at a meeting of the American Medical Association in Chicago in December, 1978. At that meeting the 271 members of the House of Delegates discussed a resolution by which medical practitioners were specifically forbidden to perform laboratory or X-ray services for patients referred to them by chiropractors. "The house was uncompromising in its stand that chiropractic is an unscientific cult. But by an overwhelming voice vote, after heated debate on Tuesday, it approved a proposal to allow physicians as individuals to accept referrals from Chiropractors" (*Globe and Mail* Dec. 7, 1978). Subsequently "the American Medical Association's policy-making body has confirmed a decision allowing physicians to accept patients referred to them by chiropractors. Nevertheless it is still warning that chiropractic medicine [sic] is a hazardous healing system" (*New York Times*, Dec. 10, 1978). These statements reflect the contradiction that has existed between the official positions adopted by professional associations and the concrete day-to-day conduct of the members. The AMA has been unable to prevent its members from accepting referrals from chiropractors, and finds itself now proclaiming that the "acceptance of referrals does not constitute professional association" (*Globe and Mail*, Dec. 7, 1978). What is clear from this is that the rhetoric of the AMA, no matter how strident, at times fails to control the professional conduct of the members, which would appear to be attuned to what their clients demand of them.

The medical associations in Canada mirror their American counterparts, but in somewhat more subdued ways. Here too the conflict revolves around the same three main items of contention: the philosophy of chiropractic being viewed as a false doctrine; the validity of chiropractic knowledge and its adequacy; and the range of treatments to which chiropractic should be restricted.[3]

Not all of the medical associations stress these three items equally. There is conspicuous variation among provincial medical associations, and between them and the Canadian Medical Association. The CMA has launched its heaviest attacks on the philosophy of chiropractic. It has inveighed against it as a false doctrine. In its sharpest attacks it denounces chiropractic as sheer quackery. Chiropractic doctrines are regarded as so false and repulsive that doctors have been forbidden even to lecture to chiropractors, and meetings between their associations have been rejected.

It is not clear how far these official pronouncements of the CMA reflect the opinions of all of the members. Many individual doctors do have working relationships with chiropractors, and some of the votes on these matters at CMA meetings have been very close. Nevertheless the official rhetoric has remained intact over many years.

By contrast some of the provincial medical associations have adopted a more pragmatic approach to chiropractic. In provinces where chiropractic is financed by the provincial health plans, the medical associations have paid less attention to matters of doctrine and dogma and have gone in the direction of recognizing that doctors may properly refer patients to chiropractors. The emphasis in these provinces is focused on the scope of chiropractic practice. In these provinces a *modus vivendi* has been established, and although chiropractic does not receive a warm welcome, the era of outright conflict seems to have ended.

However, this does not apply in Quebec and Alberta, where the conflict rages along all three of the fronts noted earlier. Medical associations in those two provinces officially repudiate the philosophy of chiropractic, deny that chiropractic services can be of use to the patients of M.D.s, and attack the knowledge base of chiropractic which is viewed as both inadequate and misguided.

While medical associations in Canada have been more circumspect than their American counterparts in dealing with relationships with chiropractors, nevertheless there is some evidence that a similar contradiction exists in Canada between the official positions of the medical associations and the actual conduct of the members. In interviewing chiropractors for this study we found that at least some of them were involved with medical practitioners in telephone conversations regarding their mutual treatment of cases, conversations which were initiated by both sorts of practitioners.

We also came across situations where the chiropractor was able to secure laboratory tests through the help of physicians, who helped make arrangements with the laboratory concerned and facilitated the transmission of the results. In some cases hospitals were tacitly encouraging such arrangements, while in others they deplored the practice as unethical.

Our field workers discovered other situations where the chiropractor actually shared space, patients, and records with medical practitioners. In these cases an organic division of labour had developed so that the "team" consulted with each other in a systematic way. There were some cases where a community health centre was in operation, where the chiropractor was given an official status as a member in good standing of the team, given access to X-ray records and equipment, and reimbursed on the same basis as were the medical personnel.

Although the research activities of chiropractors are extremely limited in scope, here too there was evidence of collaboration. In one hospital an orthopaedic surgeon and a team of chiropractors had joined forces in a research enterprise to compare the effects of chiropractic adjustment and spinal surgery in the treatment of selected spinal problems. A single episode of this type may not appear very significant. However, during a conference under the sponsorship of the US Department of Health, Education and Welfare in 1975 a number of medical specialists in neurology, orthopaedics, and biomechanics, were brought together with osteopaths, radiologists, statisticians and chiropractors to discuss possible research in the problem areas to which chiropractors direct their therapies.[4] For our present purposes the results of such research are less significant than the form of association it imposes on the chiropractors and the medical practitioners.

Perhaps it is to be expected that a health profession, once firmly established, should battle vigorously any novel systems of treatment that parallel its efforts. Most established professions show this tendency.[5] The legal profession attempts to construct a single system of courts to administer law. Religious professions have traditionally sought to become national religions, to become "established" churches. The military profession seeks a monopoly in society on the merchandizing of death. Educationalists strive to establish total systems of education over which only their members will preside. So it should not come as a surprise that the medical profession should strive so mightily to achieve and retain a monopoly over the dispensation of health services, and therefore try to eliminate chiropractic.

The survival and expansion of chiropractic, in spite of hostile opposition, has been the most striking finding of this study. Not only has it become embedded in the fabric of health services; it also now has legal recognition in almost every state and province. It shares, at least in part, in the funds that governments dispense for health services. It has developed working relationships, though not warm partnerships, with other health practitioners. Chiropractors make use of their services, and they in turn make use of chiropractic services. Where chiropractors meet their competitors in the actual work place there inevitably spring up sympathetic relationships, so that competitors in time become fellow workers, and on occasion friends.

To understand why the medical profession has failed to eliminate chiropractic from the health care field we must turn to the ally of both, the patient. He is the fundamental factor in all this, because it is he who makes the decision to consult one or another sort of practitioner. Despite medical pronouncements and legal edicts it is fundamentally the client, the patient, who has made chiropractic legitimate. The efforts to declare it either illegal or illegitimate have foundered in the face of the choice made by the patient. And his influence extends far beyond indicating a preference for chiropractic over alternative forms of treatment. Once he has made that choice he pulls the medical practitioner in the same direction, because each time he goes to his doctor for a test or an X-ray required by his chiropractor, he strengthens the bond. In the course of time the doctor takes for granted these relationships. It is at this point that the American doctors have decided to ignore the protestations of their own national association, and to declare that they are now proceeding publicly to accept a continuing referral relationship with chiropractors. In this case neither physicians nor chiropractors initiated the relationship; the patient can claim responsibility for working out the plot.

The process by which an alternative system of dealing with illness becomes embedded in the larger health system is highly complex. In time it interrelates with other health occupations in intricate ways. Once this process is started it is hard to stop. Its roots become entangled with those of other occupations in an almost organic way.

Remembering our earlier emphasis on technique, knowledge and social interaction, it is now apparent that the technical expertise of chiropractors has found a wide range of niches in the total health care enterprise. It is becoming apparent that the search for new knowledge about the spine, the back, about pain and distress is evolving in the direction of systematic research in which chiropractors are being drawn into new relationships. This, together with technical relationships, is largely responsible for the expanding web of sociability that has started to emerge. These factors have gnawed at the edifice of hostility and isolation that characterized an earlier stage of chiropractic.

Historically speaking, the animosity felt by the medical profession toward chiropractors is not a unique occurrence. The history of medicine on this continent has been one of ubiquitous conflict.[6] Some of it has been directed at the state itself; most steps toward government control have been fought vigorously. Some has been directed at insurance schemes which introduced a third party into the doctor–patient relationship. And a very large part of the conflict has emerged within medicine itself. In the not so recent past medicine on this continent was polarized in two hostile camps, the allopaths and the homeopaths. Though these groups are no longer politically recognizable their history was written in the names of hospitals, which were either homeopathic or allopathic. These two groups fought bitterly over the use of drugs for treatment, at a time when exceedingly little was known about pharmacology. Indeed it was the reported excesses in drug dispensing that led to the emergence of another group, the osteopaths, who, in their efforts to heal, totally rejected the drugs then current. In the course of time the drug-prescribing practitioners turned their attacks on the osteopaths, who, like the chiropractors, had gradually developed a set of training institutions. Eventually the graduates of the osteopathic colleges, and their patients, sought access to hospital facilities, particularly those under government control. The various state licensing bodies finally reversed their policies, and osteopaths were admitted to hospital staffs. They were also granted licensure for regular practice, and their training colleges were recognized as proper places for the preparation of practitioners.

Much of the impetus for acceptance of osteopathy and chiropractic became evident during World War II, when the families of service personnel demanded that the government pay not only their medical bills but also those for osteopathic and chiropractic treatments. Under the conditions of war these demands were honoured. Whereas the US government had intended only to honour the requests of those who were making notable war sacrifices, the eventual result was to extend a degree of legitimacy to both osteopathy and chiropractic. Although the American Medical Association has finally relented in its attacks on osteopathy, those on chiropractic have continued unabated.

At the time of writing, the struggle has entered a historic new phase both in the US and Canada. Chiropractors have launched legal suits to test in the courts the validity of their demands to be recognized as health practitioners. The transfer of the struggle to the courts changes the nature of the contest. The weapons are different. The rhetoric and invective of earlier days are not appropriate in the courtroom. In their place the parties must substitute rational argument. And there is now an umpire to monitor the struggle. To a degree this means that the two parties are struggling over principles rather than venting sheer hostility on each other.

This development may soften the official relationships between chiropractic and the medical associations. Whatever the results, they will be reflected sooner or later in the relationships of practitioners at the individual and associational levels. They may finally be drawn into a common pattern. In those circumstances it would become much easier for the governments concerned to draw up legislation concerning the scope of practice for each.

The point of departure for our section on the Chiropractor in Society is the recognition that no occupational group can be an island unto itself. Once launched, an occupation becomes part of a social order. Willingly or not, it becomes subject to the legal order of the society. Either freely or under compulsion, its members form associations that are fundamentally similar to those of other occupations, and they become a part of the complex division of labour that is the hallmark of modern society.

NOTES

1. American Medical Association, "No Double Standard for Patient Care," *Journal of the American Medical Association*, 1968, 206: 2091–2092.
   American Medical Association, "Chiropractic Condemned," *Journal of the American Medical Association*, 1969, 208: 352.
2. For a thorough discussion of the term, see H.M. Johnson, *Sociology: A Systematic Introduction*, N.Y.: Harcourt, Brace and World, 1960, 437–439.
3. See for example: D.G. Bates, "History of Chiropractic Demonstrates its Opposition to Scientific Medicine," *Canadian Medical Association Journal*, 1973, 108: 532–533.
   D.G. Bates, "Chiropractic Theory Has Nullified Legal Attempts to Limit Treatment," *Canadian Medical Association Journal*, 1973, 108: 792–796.
4. M. Goldstein (ed.) *The Research Status of Spinal Manipulative Therapy*, Report of a workshop held at the National Institutes of Health, February, 1975. National Institute of Neurological and Communicative Disorders and Stroke Monograph No. 15, Department of Health, Education and Welfare publication (N.I.H.) 76–998, Washington, D.C.
5. T.J. Johnson, *Professions and Power*, London: The Macmillan Press, 1972, 57–59 and E. Freidson, *Profession of Medicine*, N.Y.: Harper and Row Publishers, 1972, 361–364.
6. D.H. Calhoun, *Professional Lives in America: Structure and Aspiration*, New Haven: Yale University Press, 1968.

Chapter 8

Police Definitions of the Situation: Evaluation of a Diploma Program in Law Enforcement and Community Relations*

Robert A. Stebbins
Colin Flynn

For over one hundred years, members of the Newfoundland Constabulary who currently serve as the St. John's municipal police force have received their primary training from its senior members. Today, advanced training is available, which comes from an external source: the Diploma Program in Law Enforcement and Community Relations sponsored by the Extension Division of Memorial University and the Department of Justice of the Government of Newfoundland and Labrador.[1] The program consists of twelve courses offered at two per term over a three-year period. Its major aims are to provide police officers with:

(a) the professional knowledge base and skills required in the pursuit and maintenance of high standards of law enforcement and community relations;
(b) an understanding of the social, psychological, and cultural forces which impinge upon the life of communities, the enforcement of laws, and the role and status of the police in the community;
(c) a generic training in preparation for advanced study in specialized areas of law enforcement and community relations.

This paper presents a summary of two sets of observations, which constitute an evaluation of the effectiveness of part of the program.[2] Its first two aims focus, in effect, on the interaction between policemen as they carry out their occupational roles and various citizens of the community with whom, in this capacity, they come in contact. It is here among other places, that the architects of this Diploma Program seek improvement. Put differently, the program is, in one of its aspects, an attempt to alter the way St. John's policemen orient themselves toward or define occupational situations in which they deal with the public. It seeks to change personal outlook or perspective rather than add to factual knowledge. Thus, the way chosen to evaluate it, in addition to course examinations, is to determine whether the policemen's definitions of occupational situations concerning the public have changed with the training received in the courses.

*Reprinted with permission from *Canadian Journal of Criminology*, Vol. 17, No. 4 (October 1975).

THE DEFINITION OF THE SITUATION

Briefly and simply put, the definition of the situation is the meaning human beings attach to the social, physical, and psychological events of the immediate present, a meaning that guides their subsequent behaviour there. The theory of the definition of the situation and some of its empirical applications are considered in greater detail elsewhere.[3] In these sources phases of the definition of the situation, predispositions, types of definitions, situational boundaries and types of goals are discussed. In this paper only those aspects of the theory are presented that bear strictly on the evaluation of the Diploma Program.

Though simplified a good deal here, the following model indicates, in general, the location of the definition of the situation in relation to the initial reaction of individual policemen to their encounters with one or more citizens:

(a) First, the policeman enters the situation or happens on the event with one or more goals in mind (e.g., to keep order, to make an arrest).
(b) Then, he perceives what is happening. That is, he sees and hears and perhaps even smells and feels what is taking place.
(c) Then, he interprets or gives meaning to these perceptions. That is, he defines the situation or event.
(d) Finally, he performs his duties on the basis of this definition, at least until reinterpretation occurs.

The policeman, like those in other roles, learns through training and experience, standard definitions which he applies to routine situations. Occasionally, however, he finds himself in unusual circumstances, for which his training and experience have provided only a partial definition at best. Under these conditions, he must construct or improvise to some extent a nonstandard interpretation. The policeman's definitions of both standard and nonstandard situations comprise answers to many or all of the following questions (generalize operationalizations of the definitions of the situation):

Policeman's perception of citizens
(1) Identification of the citizens present and their behaviour. Who are these people and what are they doing?
(2) Perception of citizens' evaluations of the situation. What does this situation or event mean to them?
(3) Perception of citizens' goals while in the situation. What do they intend to do?
(4) Perception of citizens' plans of action (strategies for reaching the goals). How are they going to reach their goals?
(5) Perception of citizens' justifications for having such goals and pursuing them in the ways planned. How do they justify their goals and plans?

Policeman in the looking glass
(6) Perception of self by citizens. Who do these people think I am?
(7) Perception of evaluation imputed to self by citizens. What do these people think they and their behaviour mean to me?
(8) Perception of goals imputed to self by citizens. What do these people think I intend to do about them and their behaviour?

(9)   Perception of plans of action imputed to self by citizens. How do these people think I will reach the goals?

(10)   Perception of justifications of goals and plans imputed to self by citizens. How do these people think I will justify my goals and plans?

Policeman's reactions (to perceptions 1 through 10)

(11)   Policeman's evaluation of the situation. What does this situation mean to me?

(12)   Policeman's plans of action. How will I reach my goals?

(13)   Policeman's justification of his goals and plans. How do I justify these goals and plans?

METHODOLOGY

The effects reported here were observed during the summers of 1972 and 1973 in the occupational behaviour of members of the first and second classes of the program. Except for four men whom we were able to observe both after their first year and after their second year of classes, all were observed after their first year only. Regardless of when they were observed these officers made up, in essence, the experimental group of the study. This group's definitions of work situations involving the public and those of a matched comparison or control group were examined through a combination of observation and interviewing within an ex-post-facto experimental field design.[4]

The first class comprises 14 officers and the second class 15. Of these 29 men only 20 were assigned, at the times of observation, to jobs within the Constabulary that brought them into a substantial degree of contact with the citizens of the community. So, over the two periods of evaluation, these 20 were observed and compared with 20 of their nonstudent colleagues. The members of the comparison group were matched with the students on the following variables: education, age, rank, years of service, section in the force (type of job), and rural–urban background.[5]

Methodologically, the evaluation proceeded as an exploratory study, the principal aim of which was to generate grounded theory in the form of categories, dimensions, and testable hypotheses. In this respect, we strove for flexibility in our data collection and otherwise generally followed the advice offered by Glaser and Strauss.[6] Still, it is clear that this evaluation is no example of ordinary exploratory research. From the beginning data collection, though flexible, took place within the confines of the theory of the definition of the situation and an ex-post-facto experimental design, both of which are indispensable aspects of this evaluation of the Diploma Program. The larger focus of the project, in other words, called for certain empirical and theoretical controls. But, since no data have ever been *systematically* gathered within the framework of the theory of the definition of the situation on how policemen, in Newfoundland or elsewhere, define their encounters with the public, our wisest decision was for a flexible approach to data collection within the framework of that theory and the experimental design. Plenty of time remains in the future for movement toward precision in data collection. In the meantime, no unwarranted assumptions have been made about how St. John's policemen define situations involving citizens, simply to achieve, from the start, the precision we will eventually achieve — with greater validity — anyway.[7]

Two to three days were spent with each officer during which the observer noted every encounter with the public, classified it, recorded its major characteristics, and subsequently conducted an unstructured interview about it based on the 13 questions. The interviews, which lasted from 30 to 45 minutes per encounter, took place immediately following the occurrence of the encounter. This helped ensure accurate recall. Only a portion of the incidents recorded were discussed in the interviews. The selection of particular incidents depended partly on the requirement that for each officer the widest possible range of citizen encounters be assessed. Moreover, as the number of encounters considered in this manner increased, the amount of new information about how any one policeman defined them decreased. Discussion of an average of five, whatever the types, tended to constitute the point of diminishing returns. The students were observed in and interviewed about 69 encounters with the public. Those in the comparison group were observed in and interviewed about 64 such situations. Altogether, the 40 policemen were interviewed 133 times over the two summers.

IDENTIFICATION OF CITIZENS AND THEIR BEHAVIOUR

Although policemen in the two groups differ little, if any, in their identification of the people they were observed confronting and of the behaviour those people were believed to be engaging in (Question 1), knowledge of how this is done is critical to an understanding of other aspects of their definitions of these sorts of situations. For this is the St. John's policeman's taxonomy of a significant portion of his working world, which must be described before considering the effects of the Diploma Program.

The majority of policemen in every community interact in some way with its nonpolice members whom we will call *citizens*. Policemen in St. John's, and probably those elsewhere, tend to identify the citizens with whom they come in contact during the course of their work in two broad ways: by *community* criteria and by *police* criteria. Our research turned up three community criteria: age category (child, teen-ager, young adult, middle-aged adult, old adult); sex (male, female); socio-economic status (poor, average income, rich).[8]

Two police criteria were found: *legal reputation* and *occupational goals*. In terms of their legal reputation, most citizens confronted are presumed to be *law-abiding* up to the time of contact, if for no other reason than that, formally or informally, they are unknown to the police in connection with any unlawful behaviour. Ex-offenders, regarded by the police as rehabilitated, are included in this category. A handful of citizens, occasionally constituting whole families, are known to the police, and possibly the neighbourhood in which they live as *troublemakers*. Troublemakers have, at best, been convicted of only minor offences, such as driving while drunk or disorderly conduct. But they have been associated, in some fashion, with illegal behaviour in their part of the city for so long that the police immediately suspect their involvement when a crime of any sort is reported there. *Known offenders* are citizens who have been convicted of at least one major crime and who have so far failed to demonstrate to the police that they are sufficiently rehabilitated to warrant recategorizing them as law-abiding citizens.

Perhaps the most complex form of identification of citizens is made in terms of the goals that bring an officer to the problematic situation. So far, our research has produced five major occupational goals pursued by St. John's policemen: to make an arrest or consider making one, to investigate a case, to keep order, to answer a complaint, and to dispense information.

Each goal, however, is pursued somewhat differently, depending on the kind of citizen behaviour or activity toward which the policeman's effort is directed. Thus, citizens are further identified in connection with the behaviour. Turning to the goal of making an arrest, the officer is concerned with one type of individual, the offender, labelled according to the crime he commits; namely drunkard, traffic violator, burglar, thief, vandal, and so forth.

The goal of investigating a case is associated with the largest number of different citizen activities. St. John's policemen were observed investigating traffic accidents, burglaries, robberies, embezzlements, frauds (cheques only), fires, assaults, murders, drug offences, and sudden deaths. Citizens in these situations are further identified in terms of their perceived role in the incident being investigated. So generally, they are seen as *offenders* (both principals and accessories before and after the fact), *victims, witnesses, informants,* or *experts*. Specifically, they are identified as, for example, a burglar, a victim of assault, a witness to a traffic accident, an informant in a narcotics case, an expert who performs an autopsy.

Keeping order, as a goal, has been observed, so far in the evaluation, to bring policemen into contact with citizens who have created traffic hazards (e.g., double-parked truck), gotten into fights or family quarrels, and accumulated in large crowds that must, for some reason, be dispersed. When answering a complaint is the goal, interaction takes place with one, possibly two, categories of citizens: *complainers* and *culprits*. St. John's policemen deal with complainers and culprits (if they can be found) who are connected with assorted forms of disorderly conduct, such as excessive noise late at night, or connected with property damage, usually caused by vandals. Dispensing information results in brief exchanges with relatively new citizens in the community or tourists who are seeking directions to some point in the city or requesting miscellaneous data, such as how many boats enter the harbour daily.

Policemen were observed over the two years pursuing all these goals. But making arrests and investigating cases were by far the most common, and our attention is confined to these in this report. The citizens typically encountered here are middle-class males, all ages, law-abiding or known offenders, and offenders or victims.

When keeping order does occur, it is usually handled by officers manning the police van, while dispensing information normally falls to the man on the beat. Such physical constraints as seating for only two officers in the van and minimal citizen contact while on the beat, prevented the observer from obtaining much useful information on the way officers pursue these goals.

EFFECTS OF THE DIPLOMA PROGRAM

The effects of the Diploma Program on its participants, are reported under the headings of the two main goals of St. John's policemen: investigation and arresting. Their definitions of investigation situations are presented for encounters with law-abiding citizens who have become offenders, known offenders and troublemakers, and citizens as victims. Police definitions of arrest situations involving known offenders and troublemakers are the same as investigative situations containing these people. Within these two main goals the effects observed are presented in the sequence of the thirteen questions listed earlier.

THE GOAL OF INVESTIGATION

LAW-ABIDING CITIZENS AS OFFENDERS

(1) While investigating cases, policemen encounter citizens in a variety of potentially illegal incidents from traffic accidents to rape and murder. There are two main categories of such incidents from the stand-point of an investigating officer: *minor offences*, including traffic accidents, minor property damage, and public disturbances; and *major offences* including rape, assault, car theft, fire, and all other offences involving bodily harm or potential bodily harm. In all such incidents both student and comparison groups assume the citizen–offender is guilty of the offence, even when the case has yet to be presented in court. As noted later, such assumptions influence the ways policemen perceive a citizen and in turn how they believe he perceives them. The citizen referred to throughout this section is of the heretofore law-abiding variety; the situation of the troublemaker and known offender being defined differently.

(2) Minor offences, prosecution for which results in no significant loss of freedom, are seen by both the university and the comparison groups as meaning little to these citizens. Policemen believe a citizen knows such incidents can be handled by civil law or settled out of court, with little if any police influence exercised over his fate. Comments, such as "They saw it more of a joke than anything" or "didn't mean too much" indicate awareness of this perceived lack of concern and disinterest for the police officer's intervention in the case.

When investigating major offences both university and comparison groups perceive the citizen–offender as anxious about his involvement in such events and their consequences for him.

The policemen commented:

He seemed a bit worried when questioned.
She didn't like the idea and was scared.
He was scared.
[He was] fearful he would be locked up.
[He had a] fear of having to go to jail.

(3–5) Police perceptions of citizens' goals in the encounter, their plans of actions, and their justification of those plans and goals are most readily treated as a unit. This is how individual officers tended to answer probes concerning these matters. Generally, policemen of both the student and the comparison groups see the citizens whom they encounter as intending to co-operate with them in a manner appropriate to the situation, which citizens justify from their respect for law and police power to inflict penalties. When investigating a case, this generalization is most likely to hold when a minor offence is the object of scrutiny. Reasons for such co-operation reflect an assumption officers make about a citizen's actions — they co-operate because they have no fear of losing their freedom as a result of this sort of encounter. Co-operation, the police believe, is seen by citizens as placing them in a more favourable light with the investigating officer, hopefully leading to dismissal or reduction of the original charge. In the words of a couple of patrolmen:

[He intended] to give a story to make the young fellow look bad, because he felt he was right and the young fellow was wrong.

They intended to give details to the police to convince us whom they considered responsible, because they felt they were not at fault.

When major offences are being investigated co-operation is present under some conditions and absent under others. Citizens who are seen by police officers of both student and comparison groups as worried about their involvement in the incident, are also seen as co-operating with them. They do so in hope of beating the rap and its associated penalty. They are perceived as fearful of losing their freedom and as attempting anything to avoid arrest. Official suspicion of these citizens' intentions, actions and justifications are reflected in the following comments:

[He planned] to co-operate a bit in order to beat the rap.

[He planned] to co-operate to some extent in order to avoid arrest.

[He wanted to] try and explain the situation and try to get to where he was going because he wanted to get home.

At other times policemen of both groups perceive offenders as unco-operative, offenders who are not only worried about their involvement in major incidents, but also fear the officer and his authority. The policemen believe these offenders justify such behaviour out of a fear that co-operation will lead them into deeper trouble and only hinder their chances of avoiding the potential charge. As the officers put it:

[She intended] to play it by ear and tell a story to fit the situation, because she lives in a poor situation.

[He wanted] to try and get out of it, because he feared his mother and the police.

He feared us and did not wish to co-operate.

(6) Because they are generally uninformed when on the job, the policemen observed tend to see themselves reflected in the eyes of citizens as policemen. But, when one is an officer of the law, there are other, more subtle views of oneself available through the eyes of the public. The students, in contrast to their colleagues in the comparison group, say they are sometimes defined as mediator in a dispute, as competent protector of the public welfare, or as humane individual concerned for the unfortunate members of the community. Further evidence of the existence of these reflected images is found in the

response to questions 7 through 13. Members of the comparison group could see no other image of themselves than their normal role of officer of the law, which is enforcing laws they are told to enforce.

(7–10) Concerning the goal of investigation, the first major difference between the police student and his counterpart in the comparison group comes out in his perceptions of the intentions, actions, and justifications for those actions as seen through the eyes of citizens. Still, when it comes to minor offences, both groups see themselves in much the same way, through the looking glass of the citizen, as policemen doing their job. In a few of these incidents, the offender does see the student officer, according to the latter, as playing the role of mediator in a dispute; it is his intention to listen to all sides and make an objective assessment on the basis of the known facts.

The students see themselves through the eyes of citizens involved in major offences as intended to act with all haste to prevent any serious injury or property damage, and as attempting to alleviate any misfortune that may have befallen either the citizens (offenders and victims) or the general public. The justifications perceived to be attributed for such actions harmonize with their intentions, which are to aid and comfort those needing it. They commented:

> He knew we would continue investigation into the incident because a crime was committed and he knew lives could have been lost.
> He knew I would check it out because a serious crime had been committed.

Such intentions, actions and justification are seen by the students to be imputed to them by all citizens, whether defined as co-operative or unco-operative.

When it comes to major offences, those of the comparison group see intentions, actions, and justifications attributed to them by citizens that are similar to those of minor offences. They see themselves as intending to arrest and detain for some sort of actual or potential violation of the law. They see their plans justified as part of their job of maintaining law and order and bringing to justice those who challenge this goal:

> [He knew] we would arrest him, because he thought we had a right to do so.
> They knew we would arrest and convey to the lockup.
> She thought I would have her summoned to court.
> [He thought] I would interview him and take a statement and then convey him back to work.

(11) The differences in the definitions of situations held by the student group and those held by the comparison group are still more noticeable in their reactions to the various perceptions described above. Let us turn first, however, to the similarities that were observed. Minor incidents that are investigated, are dismissed with little concern by both groups. A number of other incidents, of more serious nature, are looked on by both with open-mindedness and understanding. Neither group is willing to accept, without question, the word of a complainer or victim against an offender or

culprit unless such accusations are substantiated by concrete facts. In the policemen's words:

> The cab driver is just as saucy as the drunk, so it wasn't all his fault.
>
> It seems one is picking on someone [the offender] to prove someone else is right.
>
> The evidence did not warrant that I take action against this boy, even though many claimed he was the culprit.

Whether the offender is considered co-operative or unco-operative, those in the Diploma Program show a deep concern for the consequences of the situation for both the offender and the community as a whole, while hoping for a successful, though harmless, conclusion to it. This group also expresses genuine concern, when the situation warrants it, for the physical and mental well-being of offenders. Some of these officers remarked:

> We were not satisfied that everything was alright and no harm had been done.
>
> There was not sufficient evidence to indicate the boy did start the fire, but there was evidence he had been with others who had done it and thus, should be strongly reprimanded for his actions. If necessary, he should be taken to a psychiatrist and given help.
>
> I felt the boy, age 17, was home at the time and knew how the fire started. He is very backward and appears to be retarded.

The comparison group, which becomes entangled in incidents of as great an intensity and importance as the police students, exhibits little concern for either the well-being of offenders or the well-being of the community. Comments, such as the following, are typical:

> It meant absolutely nothing.
>
> Another routine incident.
>
> It meant nothing.

(12) Most officers stated they follow the usual police procedures in dealing with the majority of offences. As mentioned, minor ones are treated with open-mindedness and understanding. The incidents, in which the students show concern for the physical and mental well-being of the citizen and the community, produce plans of actions in accord with this evaluation. These policemen say they plan to provide for the offenders' more serious needs and to protect the community by cutting down on the frequency of such incidents in the future. In their words:

> After finding two stolen cars in the area and seeing several car parts around, this man was the logical suspect, and was interviewed to see if any information could be obtained.
>
> If the boy is involved, I shall request a psychiatric examination of him.
>
> Parents of the boys were to be informed as to what I knew about them.

(13) Those incidents considered routine and acted on as routine are

justified by the student policemen for that reason — they are routine and demand routine handling. Those actions reflecting interest in the well-being of the offender and community are also justified in a related manner.

The boys involved were only 5 years old, but by informing their parents this may stop their acts. And, if not, maybe they need psychiatric help.
If the boy is mentally ill, then he is not aware of the seriousness of what he did.

KNOWN OFFENDERS AND TROUBLEMAKERS

(1) When the police are investigating a case involving troublemakers or known offenders, it is usually a major offence. Conviction for such offences threaten these people with loss of freedom through imprisonment or with ostracism from the community or with both. These threats, along with previous encounters with the law, account for their hostility toward the investigating officer. On the other side, reactions to the troublemakers and known offenders are coloured by a policeman's previous experiences with them and his perceptions of the hostility projected toward him. So, police definitions of situations concerning these citizens, including investigative situations, are bound to differ from those concerning other types of citizens.

(2) Both student and comparison groups perceive the disrespect and hostility of troublemakers and known offenders. Moreover, the troublemaker and known offender are viewed as fearing the law and as suspicious of the investigating officer and his motives. In the policemen's words:

He was suspected of theft and a bit reluctant to talk.
The person arrested seemed to be concerned to some extent, but he did not have any comment on the situation and was reluctant to make a statement or submit himself to any test.
They felt the police were always after them and would do anything to get them convicted of a crime.
He was scared because he didn't want to lose his freedom. He didn't like to get caught.

(3–5) Troublemakers and known offenders are seen by both groups as intending to be unco-operative in a way appropriate to the situation out of disrespect and hostility for law and policemen. They may even be seen planning to lie and in other ways to deceive the officer who is before them.

(6) Previous experience with the law has left offenders and troublemakers, as these officers see it, with certain unflattering stock views of the policeman and his role in the social order. He is seen as a ruthless, though simultaneously engaging person, who attempts to seduce these offenders into conferring responsibility for a crime, because another conviction enhances his image both with his peers and with his superiors. Both groups also see an inhumanity attributed to themselves in their dealings with known offenders and troublemakers, including the view that they would turn such people in for the least transgression of the law.

(7–10) In harmony with the perceptions in Number 6 is the perceived attribution that investigating officers of both groups will put extra effort into an investigation in order to obtain a conviction of a known offender or troublemaker, thereby ensuring his return to prison. Investigating policemen also see themselves through the eyes of these deviants as very strict and impersonal in their inquiries and as attempting to hide any favourable information that might help them. Two policemen stated their views on this issue in the following manner:

> The person mostly knew I was suspicious of the story he was telling, but felt I was only trying to get him into trouble.
> He knew I would charge him with one offence, but he wasn't going to let me pin the others on him.

(11) Because both groups of policemen have set images of the known offender and the troublemaker, and they believe, he of them, their evaluations of encounters with him are much stronger than one normally finds. Both groups show considerable concern for the seriousness of their offences, both for the community and for the unsuspecting victim. They are also concerned about the dangerousness of such people. Neither group shows much interest in them personally or in their plight, nor do they attempt to rationalize their behaviour. The image of the known offender as dangerous and thoughtless prevails:

> A serious offence had been committed, and an all out effort should be made to apprehend the accused.
> [It] meant a lot because he had a gun and wouldn't shy away from using it.
> [It] meant the guy was in the process of making a nuisance of himself. When the guy is drinking he is a very destructive person.

(12) Consonant with their evaluation of these situations, policemen of both groups plan to proceed in the normal police manner, such as "apprehend" or "take to court." Their orientation toward troublemakers and known offenders is manifested in their failure to take any positive steps toward understanding their actions, or even toward making helpful suggestions.

(13) The justification of these actions are in line with them. Officers of both groups believe the citizen and the community need protection. If this means treating such deviants in the manner just described, then this is what should be done. As two of the men put it:

> It is the police officer's duty to investigate and more important to protect life and property.
> His arrest would cut down on house breaks.

CITIZENS AS VICTIMS

(1) As with the goal of investigating an offender's role in a case, policemen divide the investigation of a victim's role into minor and major offences. Because investigation, at this point, involves only the innocent, they are more deeply concerned, humane, and open-minded in their orientation.

(2) Policemen of both groups believe that minor incidents mean little, if anything, to victims. The incidents are seldom more than an inconvenience, for there is no real threat. Any property damage incurred is repaired by a third party, such as an insurance company or individual.

> She was not too concerned, because she was not at fault. She was more concerned with the missed appointment.
>
> [It] just meant the police had come along, and he was quite pleased they had arrived.
>
> To him it simply meant he was right and had the right-of-way.
>
> [They were] only obeying the law — they were required to report anything over $200.

Student policemen dealing with offences of more serious nature, see the victim as pleased with their arrival, but members of the comparison group are more rigid. They are narrower in their perceptions of citizen evaluations of their encounters with police. These men believe that citizens are suspicious of their motives in questioning them, even when they themselves have called the police. Indeed, these observations suggest a lack of confidence among victims in the policeman's ability to adequately handle the situation.

(3–5) Like law-abiding citizens, victims, in minor incidents, are seen by both student and comparison groups as intending to co-operate, because they are innocent and because co-operation will, therefore, help their case. In the words of some of the officers:

> He co-operated by giving details not mentioned by the older fellow, because he felt he was not at fault.
>
> She intended to give the necessary information, because she is not at fault.
>
> He intended to give information and co-operate, because he wanted the guy apprehended.
>
> He decided to tell it as it happened, because the actions of the other driver justified his responses.

Student policemen dealing with victims of major offences also see them as intending to co-operate, an orientation that appears to carry with it a feeling of confidence in the policemen's ability to adequately handle the situation and to protect the individual from further harassment.

Because members of the comparison group feel that victims are suspicious of their investigations, they also feel such people will be unco-operative when involved in a serious crime. Where these policemen do see a victim as intending to co-operate, they believe he justifies his actions with some ulterior motive, such as to avoid direct questioning or to make himself look better. Consistent with earlier observations is the implication here that victim suspiciousness and lack of co-operation is, at bottom, an absence of confidence in the officer's ability to investigate the complaint and thereby to afford protection. These policemen described their perceptions in the following way:

> He would try to find out on his own and forward any information he

received. However, he was unconcerned about the incident and would probably make no effort to assist.

At first she did not co-operate because she was afraid of me and her parents, but later told all.

He was going to be helpful, but since he was the owner of the money, he would give information that would benefit himself.

(6) As with other kinds of citizens, the officers believe that victims see them as performing the normal duties of policemen qua policemen. Additionally, the students see themselves pictured in minor offences as neutral mediators of disputes between two opposing parties. They see themselves reflected in more serious offences as protectors of the public interest and safety and as upholders of the law who can competently handle the situation.

Such views are rare among the comparison group, where one is struck by their reflected image as an ordinary and sometimes incompetent police officer. As seen in our observations bearing on questions 11 through 13, this sort of image influences the responses of these men to the victims of serious crime.

(7–10) The fundamental differences between the student and comparison groups in their interaction with victims begin to appear in their perceptions of victims' pictures of their intentions, actions and justifications for those actions. In minor offences, the police students believe that victims see them as intending to give needed help, while competently providing the expertise to correct the injustice. They see themselves through the citizens' eyes as being on their side:

He thought his actions were correct, and I would make the right decision.

She felt I would be able to help if necessary, and I was on her side.

He knew I would take the information, and thought we would do something about it.

He thought we would find the guy responsible and solve his problem for him.

[They believed I would] investigate the matter and interview the person responsible and take the necessary action.

She knew I would take information and try and help.

The students see themselves as even more welcome to the victim when the offence is major. It is from such perceptions that they infer a confidence in their abilities existing among the citizens they encounter. There are, at times, situations in which the students see attributed to themselves the plan of following normal police practice and justifying that action through their duty as police officers. This perception, however, is far more common in the comparison group.

Thus, the students, in contrast with their fellows in the comparison group, perceive a more favourable reflection of their occupational performance in connection with investigations of victims' involvement in major crimes. The former who seem to be viewing these people in a new light as a result of a year or two years special training, approach them differently. As pointed out in the next section, victims are approached by the students with more open-mindedness, greater understanding, and more concern for their well-being than comparison group policemen manifest. Such a propitious introduction to relations with an officer seems to encourage the victim who would like to see relations remain congenial, to indicate, in some way, a degree of respect for him and his ability. For the officer, these indications suggest he has, so far in this encounter, performed competently in his role. The opposite effect is produced among those in the comparison group. They receive indications from the victims they confront, which owing to their less flexible approach (see next section), suggest they are relatively incompetent.

Police self-images, of course, are formed from sources other than citizens; namely, colleagues, friends, and family members. Still, initially sour relations between a citizen and a policeman (which are likely to be initiated by the latter, because he typically initiates the relations in general) are especially critical. That is, they have a way of ramifying to everyone's disadvantage: the policeman winds up with an unfavourable reflection of self, the victim with an uneasy feeling that his interests are being unsatisfactorily looked after. The policeman is definitely better off without the unfavourable reflection. The victim and even the community are better off without the feeling of police inadequacy.

(11-13) With respect to these questions, members of both groups have little to say about minor incidents, since they are usually routine and require no special attention by an investigating officer. Whether or not the victim sees such incidents as important, the policemen are relatively unmoved by his reaction and maintain their routine orientation.

Our observations on the investigation of serious cases from the victim's side are largely the same for these questions as the corresponding observations presented earlier about law-abiding offenders. The students approach victims with more open-mindedness, greater understanding, and more concern for their well-being than those in the comparison group.

THE GOAL OF ARREST

LAW-ABIDING CITIZENS AS OFFENDERS

(1) As with the goal of investigating a case involving a law-abiding citizen as offender, the goal of arresting him can be further divided into the categories of minor and major offences. Because this goal requires the policeman to take a decisive step — either arrest or ticket — one usually finds a somewhat firmer interpretation of such incidents.

(2) Generally, members of both groups of policemen see law-abiding citizens as worried about the possibility of arrest and its consequences. Our observations do suggest that those in the comparison group are more inclined than their student counterparts to perceive the offender as unconcerned about arrest and its consequences, even when the offence is serious:

It meant nothing.
It meant nothing at all.
Not that much. He was caught by the police and had to take the consequences.

I did not see the individual as concerned about the incident or the damage he had caused.

(3–5) A general theme in our observations is the perception by both groups of citizens' intent to co-operate. This is true, whatever the officer's goal (investigation or arrest) or kind of citizen encountered, excluding troublemakers and known offenders. With a couple of idiosyncratic exceptions, the justifications perceived are the same.

Our observations also suggest, however, that there are times when even the students, when arresting as when investigating, see law-abiding citizens as intending to be unco-operative. This occurs with serious offences, where such behaviour is seen as being justified by the belief that co-operation can only cause the offender further trouble by giving officials more evidence with which to convict him.

(6–3) The remainder of the questions that guided data collection with respect to the arrest of law-abiding citizens yielded no new information. That is, both the police students and their counterparts in the comparison group tended to respond to the observer's probes with the same answers they gave when he asked about these parts of their definitions of investigation situations.

A SPECIAL COMPARISON

Comparison of the responses of two men who were members of the comparison group in the 1972 study and became members of the student group in the 1973 study, reveals certain critical differences in their approach to offenders after a year in the program. When their goal is investigation of a minor offence, perpetrated by a law-abiding offender, both men, as members of the comparison group in 1972, stated that most of the time these incidents were routine to them and that the offender holds the same view. The only thought given to him was that occasionally he might be seen as co-operative in order to serve better his own interests. At the end of their first year in the program, these two officers, even when it comes to investigating serious offences, now express greater concern for the offender and his plight. They also display more confidence in their own ability to handle the situation.

Their arrests of law-abiding offenders place these men in a still more favourable light. The serious incidents in which they were observed in 1973 show that they now try to understand the situation and to protect the offender from further harm to himself, often, paradoxically, by arresting him. No such concern was expressed in similar encounters during the previous year, even when events warranted such a response. In both 1972 and 1973, however, they showed a degree of concern for the protection of personal and community property. In 1972 justifications for such protection were based on one's duty as a police officer, while in the second year these men saw their actions as helping the community as well as expressing their duty.

CONCLUSIONS

We believe our observations support the conclusion that the Diploma Program in Law Enforcement and Community Relations is reaching aims (a) and (b) presented at the beginning of this paper. Of course, we are unable to say how much more extensive the differences might be between those policemen who have completed the full three years of the program and other policemen who, on all other relevant dimensions are equal, but who lack such training. Based on their experience of one to two years in the program the students observed have manifested some clear and significant differences, which alone, would justify its existence.

Two methodological problems have been solved with the second year of observation, which adds strength to our conviction that the program is reaching aims (a) and (b). First, the initially small experimental and control groups were more than doubled in size in the second year. Second, the experimental logic of the design was initially weakened through nonrandom recruitment of the first class of students to the program. That is, those who showed sufficient interest in the program and ability as policemen were likely to be chosen to fill the initial class, rather than giving everyone in the Constabulary an equal chance at being selected. Thus, it was possible that most officers in the first class because of their high interest in their work and their exceptional ability as policemen, would have distinguished themselves from their colleagues in the ways we have seen without the instruction.

To correct this weakness, the second summer of observation concentrated not only on the first class at the close of its second year, but also on the second class at the close of its first year. The second class, though also nonrandomly selected, is comprised of officers who volunteered for the program. Further, it then became possible to observe the two policemen who were part of the comparison group during the first summer of observation and who became part of the student group during the second summer.

Our main conclusion is further strengthened through careful selection of the comparison group. Only men considered by both the police administration and the researchers to be among the best in their particular assignments were chosen. This procedure, it was felt, would counteract the tendency of the administration during the first year to select only those of high ability to enter the program.

Finally, although it may be possible for some students actually to feign the routine expression of what they have learned in these courses, the occurrence of such deception appears improbable. If these students have made the exceptional effort required to learn the instructional material to the extent that they can turn its expression on and off at will during the evaluation or at any other time, then it is safe to conclude that they genuinely wish to apply it wherever appropriate. Any student who is unable to accept the perspective fostered by this program, but who might wish to feign that perspective for personal reasons, would be very unlikely to assimilate the rather complex ideas imparted there. Learning would be noticeably inhibited by his countervailing value system. He would likely fail the course examinations. And without that knowledge, he could not possibly pretend to have it while encountering citizens on the job.

NOTES

1. The program was specially designed for the Newfoundland Constabulary by

Dogan D. Akman who was, at the time, Assistant Professor, Department of Social Work, Memorial University, in collaboration with John Browne, Deputy Assistant Chief, Newfoundland Constabulary. A description of it may be obtained from the Extension Division, Memorial University.

2. The evaluation was directed by the first author, formerly of Memorial University and now in the Department of Sociology, The University of Texas at Arlington. Neither author taught in the program. Had funds been available, the evaluation would have been continued, in order to clarify certain questions that have arisen concerning particular aspects of police definitions of the situation.

3. See Robert A. Stebbins, "A Theory of the Definition of the Situation," *Canadian Review of Sociology and Anthropology*, 4, 1967, 148–164; "Studying the Definition of the Situation," *Canadian Review of Sociology and Anthropology*, 6, 1969, 193–211; "The Meaning of Disorderly Behavior: Teachers' Definitions of a Classroom Situation," *Sociology of Education*, 44, 1971, 217–236; "A Sociological Theory of Motivation," *Behavioral Sciences Tape Library* (3-hour cassette), Fort Lee, N.J.: Sigma Information, 1974. *Teachers and Meaning: Definitions of Classroom Situations*, Leiden, Holland: E.J. Brill, 1975.

4. The ex-post-facto experimental design is described by Ernest Greenwood, *Experimental Sociology*, New York: King's Crown Press, 1945, 32–33. Several illustrations appear in F. Stuart Chapin, *Experimental Designs in Sociological Research*, rev. ed. New York: Harper & Bros. 1955, chaps 5 and 10.

5. See the tables in the Appendices in Colin Flynn and Robert A. Stebbins, "Evaluation of the Diploma Program in Law Enforcement and Community Relations," Reports No. 1 and No. 2, St. John's, Newfoundland: Extension Division, Memorial University, 1973 and 1974.

6. Barney G. Glaser and Anselm L. Strauss. *The Discovery of Grounded Theory*, Chicago: Aldine, 1967.

7. The concept of the definition of the situation serves as a "sensitizing concept," whose function it is to suggest directions along which to look in research and to give us a sense of what is relevant there. Precise reference and clear-cut identification are not intended. See Herbert Blumer, *Symbolic Interactionism*, Englewood Cliffs, N.J.: Prentice-Hall, 1969, 147–148.

8. It may come as a surprise to those unacquainted with the population characteristics of St. John's that citizens have not been found to be identified by race. No wonder, the city is almost entirely a community of Caucasians. In 1961, only 9 of the 63,633 people in St. John's were black. Another 11 were either American Indian or Eskimo, while 137 were Chinese. Today, metropolitan St. John's has a population of 132,000, but the proportion of white to nonwhite people appears to remain much as before.

REFERENCES

Emerson, Joan P.
1970 "Nothing Unusual Is Happening," in Tamotsu Shibutani (ed.) *Human Nature and Collective Behavior*. Englewood Cliffs, N.J.: Prentice-Hall, 208–222.

Gerber, Irwin
1969 "Bereavement and the Acceptance of Professional Services," in Community Mental Health Journal 5: 487–495.

Hayano, David M.
1978   "Strategies for the Management of Luck and Action in an Urban Poker Parlor," in *Urban Life* 6: 475–488.

Martin, Wilfred B.W.
1976   *The Negotiated Order of the School*. Toronto: Macmillan.

Scheff, Thomas J.
1969   "Negotiating Reality: Notes on Power in the Assessment of Responsibility," in *Social Problems* 16: 3–17.

Siporin, Max
1972   "Situational Assessment and Intervention," in *Social Casework* 53: 91–109.

Stebbins, Robert A.
1970   "Career: The Subjective Approach," in *Sociological Quarterly* 11: 32–49.

1971   "The Meaning of Disorderly Behavior: Teacher's Definitions of a Classroom Situation," in *Sociology of Education* 44: 217–236.

1975   *Teachers and Meaning: Definitions of Classroom Situations*. Leiden, Holland: E.J. Brill.

Young, T.R. and P. Beardsley
1968   "The Sociology of Classroom Teaching," *Journal of Educational Thought* 2: 175–186.

Waller, Willard
1932   *The Sociology of Teaching*. New York: John Wiley.

Chapter 9

The Administrative Revolution in the Canadian Office: An Overview*

Graham S. Lowe

> The construction of the modern office grows constantly more like the construction of the factory. Work has been standardized, long rows of desks of uniform design and equipment now occupy the offices of our large commercial and financial institutions. With the increasing division of labour each operation becomes more simple. The field in which each member of the staff operates is narrower. (*Monetary Times*, 1 October 1920, p. 10)

The turn of the century marked a watershed in Canada's socio-economic development. The forces of industrialization and urbanization propelled the country into the twentieth century. By the onset of the Depression, corporate capitalism was well entrenched, as evidenced by the presence of large corporations and factories which employed thousands of workers in growing urban centres.[1] While the factory and the joint-stock corporation are widely recognized as the hallmarks of this emerging industrial era, equally important was the development of the modern office with its expanding corps of clerical workers. As the above editorial from the *Monetary Times* attests, by 1920 a transformation was underway in many major Canadian offices. Today it is obvious that capitalism could not function without huge office bureaucracies staffed by an army of subordinate clerical workers. But how and why did this form of administration originate? What brought about the proliferation of clerical jobs? More fundamentally, how was this combination of changes — which we shall refer to as the administrative revolution — shaped by the development of corporate capitalism in Canada after 1900? The intent of this paper is to examine these questions in detail.

There was no sharp dividing line between the old-style office of the nineteenth century and the modern twentieth-century office (see Lockwood, 1966: 36). Yet we can locate the origins of the administrative revolution roughly between 1911 and 1931. We shall argue that during these years, leading corporate and government offices underwent far-reaching changes which established the framework for the modern office and created a new stratum of subordinate clerical workers. Documentary evidence presented below will show how the administrative revolution was a direct result of the organizational and economic forces of corporate capitalism. We shall first trace

*This paper is based on the author's doctoral dissertation. Financial support provided by the Canada Council is gratefully acknowledged.

the growth and development of clerical occupations and corresponding changes in office organization and the clerical labour process. The second part of the paper will offer a theoretical discussion of how the rise of corporate capitalism precipitated the transformation of administration so graphically described above by the *Monetary Times*. The concept of administrative control will be used to help us explain both the expanding administrative functions of the office, as the scope of managerial powers increased, and the subsequent rationalization of the clerical labour process.

THE ADMINISTRATIVE REVOLUTION: MAJOR OCCUPATIONAL AND ORGANIZATIONAL DIMENSIONS

The rise of corporate capitalism pushed the office into the centre of the economic stage. The small, informal office of the nineteenth century was characterized by unsystematic administrative procedures. At the hub of the old counting house was the bookkeeper. A generalist, he learnt his craft through apprenticeship and carried the office systems in his head. In sharp contrast, the modern office which emerged during the early decades of the twentieth century was a large bureaucratic organization, staffed by countless rows of clerks who performed specialized tasks with mechanistic routine. The mass of low-level clerical jobs necessitated by economic progress resembled in many respects jobs found in factory work (Hoos, 1961: 79; Lockwood, 1966: 92–94; Shepard, 1971: 8). Jobs within the expanding office bureaucracies became increasingly standardized and specialized, subjected to the constraints of rigid hierarchy and formalized work relations. The implications of these changes for clerks were severe, for as Dreyfuss (1938: 113) observes, "the bookkeeper in a large firm is no longer in a position to know whether 'the books are in good shape.' "

A persistent metaphor in social science is Adam Smith's notion of an "invisible hand" regulating the capitalist market place. However, in the era of corporate capitalism, hidden market mechanisms were replaced by elaborate administrative systems devised by managers whose newly-acquired expertise emphasized organizational efficiency and the regimentation of labour as the route to higher profits (see Chandler, 1978). Administrative co-ordination through the modern business enterprise became the most effective means of regulating economic activities. New technologies, expanding markets, increased competition, and the greater production, marketing and consumption of goods and services created the economic environment in which these changes in the office took place. Paper work became the life-blood of administration. And as Simon (1952: 185) suggests, the actual job of carrying out the objectives of an organization is delegated to those workers at the bottom of the administrative hierarchy. Clerical employment soared, leading Mills (1956: 189) to refer to the twentieth-century office as "the 'Unseen Hand' made visible as a row of clerks."

With this background, we can now itemize the main features of the administrative revolution in Canadian offices.[2] The organizational and occupational changes which we shall examine occurred gradually. Moreover, their development was uneven in the sense that not all offices, even within large organizations, experienced the full impact of the administrative revolution. We can nonetheless assert that by the Depression, five characteristics could be found in central offices of leading firms and major government departments across the country. Here, then, is what gave shape to the administrative revolution between 1911 and 1931: (a) a huge increase in the clerical sector of the labour force; (b) a dramatic shift in the clerical sex ratio toward female employees; (c) a concentration of new clerical jobs in the leading industries of corporate capitalism; (d) a relative decline in the socio-economic position of the clerk; and (e) the rationalization of office work by an emergent group of "scientifically oriented," efficiency-conscious office managers. We shall now describe the administrative revolution by examining each of these characteristics in turn.

THE GROWTH OF CLERICAL OCCUPATIONS

The proportion of clerical workers in a country's labour force is a good index of both the internal bureaucratization of enterprises and the general level of industrialization (Bendix, 1974: 211). It is thus not surprising to find that rapid clerical growth paralleled the ascendancy of corporate capitalism in Canada after 1900. Table 9–1 shows that the number of clerks increased from 33,017 in 1891 to 1,310,910 in 1971. In other words, the proportion of the total labour force engaged in clerical occupations shot from 2 per cent to 15.2 per cent. Now the largest single occupational group in Canada, clerks have been at the forefront of the expansion of the white-collar labour force throughout the century.

As Table 9–2 indicates, the clerical growth rate peaked between 1911 and 1921. While this was followed by another decade of intensified expansion between 1941 and 1951, the earlier period is most significant because it demarcates the administrative revolution. The 1911 to 1921 boom in clerical jobs cannot be attributed to either population or labour force growth, both of which were much more pronounced during the preceding decade. The lag in clerical growth during the 1920s does not mean that the administrative revolution was losing its force. Rather, it was in this decade that the growing army of clerks was moulded into an efficient corps of administrative functionaries. Clerical procedures were increasingly rationalized and mechanized to consolidate and control the burgeoning office staffs. By the 1930s, the foundations of the modern office had thus been laid.

THE FEMINIZATION OF CLERICAL WORK

Nowhere has the feminization trend in the labour force been more pronounced during this century than in clerical occupations. Strictly male-dominated at the turn of the century, by 1941 the majority of clerical jobs were held by women (see Table 9–1). The rate of feminization in the office was highest from 1891 to 1921. Increases exceeded 166 per cent in each decade, almost ten times that for the total female labour force (Lowe, 1980). There was an absolute increase in the number of female clerks over this period from 4,710 to 90,577, with the female share of clerical jobs reaching 22.1 per cent by 1921 (Table 9–1). This signals the emergence of a trend which resulted in the concentration of 30.5 per cent of all female workers in clerical occupations by 1971.

The segregation of women into a small number of relatively unrewarding

Table 9-1

Total Labour Force, Clerical Workers and Female Clerical Workers, Canada, 1891–1971*

	Total Labour Force	Total Clerical	Clerical Workers as a Percentage of Total Labour Force	Female Clerical	Females as a Percentage of Total Clerical	Female Clerks as a Percentage of Total Female Labour Force
1891	1,659,335	33,017	2.0%	4,710	14.3%	2.3%
1901	1,782,832	57,231	3.2	12,660	22.1	5.3
1911	2,723,634	103,543	3.8	33,723	32.6	9.1
1921	3,164,348	216,691	6.8	90,577	41.8	18.5
1931	3,917,612	260,674	6.7	117,637	45.1	17.7
1941	4,195,951	303,655	7.2	152,216	50.1	18.3
1951	5,214,913	563,083	10.8	319,183	56.7	27.4
1961	6,342,289	818,912	12.9	503,660	61.5	28.6
1971	8,626,930	1,310,910	15.2	903,395	68.9	30.5

*Data adjusted to 1951 Census occupation classification.

Sources: Canada D.B.S., Census Branch, *Occupational Trends in Canada, 1891–1931* (Ottawa, 1939), Table 5.

Meltz, *Manpower in Canada* (Ottawa: Queen's Printer, 1969), Section I, Tables A-1, A-2 and A-3.

1971 Census of Canada, Volume 3, Part 2, Table 2.

Table 9–2

Percentage Increase Each Decade, Population, Labour Force and Clerical
Occupations, Canada, 1891–1971*

	Population	Labour Force	Clerical Occupations
1891-1901	11.1%	10.4%	73.3%
1901-1911	34.2	52.8	80.9
1911-1921	21.9	16.2	109.3
1921-1931	18.1	23.8	20.3
1931-1941	10.9	7.0	16.5
1941-1951	21.8	26.1	85.4
1951-1961	30.2	22.4	45.4
1961-1971	18.3	33.6	60.1

*Data adjusted to 1951 Census occupation classification.
Sources: Computed from the following:
  D.B.S., Census Branch, Occupational Trends in Canada, 1891–1931, Table 5.
  Meltz, Manpower in Canada, Section I, Table A-1.
  1971 Census of Canada, Vol. 3, Part 2, Table 2.
  Canada Year Book, 1974 (Ottawa: Information Canada, 1974), Table 4.1, p. 160.

occupations has remained fairly stable since 1900 (Armstrong and Armstrong, 1978: 20). This is especially true of clerical work, where the share of clerical jobs held by females steadily increased over this century. Segregation characterized certain key office jobs even in the early stages of the administrative revolution. In stenography and typing, for example, the "female" label became firmly affixed as the proportion of jobs held by women rose from 80 per cent to 95 per cent between 1901 and 1931 (Lowe, 1980). What this represents is a more basic trend in office employment: the creation of many new specialized, routine jobs in the lower reaches of administrative hierarchies. It was into these jobs that women were increasingly recruited. The multiplication of such tasks brought about a shift in demand from male to female workers. In this way, the feminization trend largely accounts for the remarkable growth of clerical occupations, especially during the 1911 to 1921 period.[3]

THE CHANGING INDUSTRIAL DISTRIBUTION OF CLERICAL WORKERS

There is a direct connection between shifts in the industrial employment patterns of clerks and the advance of corporate capitalism. In brief, clerks became concentrated in manufacturing and in major service industries. As Table 9–3 reveals, the most rapid expansion of clerical jobs between 1911 and 1931 occurred in manufacturing, the sector most directly connected with the entrenchment of corporate capitalism. Facilitating the creation of a manufacturing base in the economy was the development of a wide range of services, especially in trade, finance and transportation and communication. By combining these four sectors – manufacturing, transportation and communication, trade and finance – we can account for over 85 per cent of total clerical growth between 1911 and 1931. It was during this period that the most dramatic shifts in the industrial distribution of clerical employment occurred.

Table 9–3

*Increases in Clerical Occupations by Major Industry Groups, Canada,
1911–1931* *

	Net Increase, No. of Clerks	%
Manufacturing	51,743	34.5
Transportation & Communication	21,165	14.1
Trade	23,412	15.6
Finance	31,333	20.9
Community & Business Service	12,688	8.5
Government	6,496	4.4
Construction	3,004	2.0
Sum of all increases	149,841	100.0

*Data adjusted to 1951 Census industry and occupation classifications.
Sources: Computed from the following:
      1901 Census of Canada, Census and Statistics, Bulletin I, *Wage-Earners by Occupations* (Ottawa: King's Printer, 1907) Table II.
      1901 Census of Canada, Census and Statistics, Bulletin XI, *Occupations of the People* (Ottawa: King's Printer, 1910), Table II.
      1911 Census of Canada, Volume VI, Tables I, III and IV.
      1911 Census of Canada, Volume IV, Table IV.
      D.B.S., Census Branch, *Occupational Trends in Canada, 1891–1931*, Table 5.
      Meltz, *Manpower in Canada*, Section II, Tables D-1, D-2, and D-3.
      Unpublished D.B.S. working tables for the censuses of 1901, 1911 and 1921, showing occupations by industries, using 1951 census occupation classification.

Most of the new clerical jobs created in manufacturing and service industries between 1911 and 1931 were fundamentally different from the craft-like bookkeeping jobs typical of the nineteenth-century office. Traditional clerical tasks were fragmented and routinized. Employers thus offered lower salaries, expecting less job commitment from workers. Women were considered more suitable for this new stratum of clerical jobs than men. Lower female wage rates, the higher career aspirations of male clerks and stereotypes of women as better able to perform monotonous, routine work underlay this shift in clerical labour demand. Consequently, we find that by 1931 manufacturing, trade and finance each accounted for over 20 per cent of all female clerical employment (Lowe, 1980). These three sectors had over 40 per cent of their clerical positions occupied by women by 1931 (Lowe, 1979: 190). The most dramatic shift in sex composition occurred in the finance industry. Women were a rarity in banks, insurance companies and other financial institutions in 1900, yet within years they came to occupy almost 50 per cent of the clerical posts in such firms (Lowe, 1979: 184). In short, the industrial concentration pattern of female clerical employment highlights the massive restructuring of administration.

THE RELATIVE DECLINE OF CLERICAL EARNINGS

Accompanying the rapid growth of clerical jobs was the erosion of the clerk's socio-economic position. This is to be expected, given the de-skilling of the clerical labour process and the influx of lower paid females into offices. Table

9–4 traces the earnings pattern for clerical workers, broken down by sex, from 1901 to 1971. Examining the total clerical group, we find that wages entered into a steady decline from after 1921, cutting below the labour force average wage by 1951.[4] Influencing this general trend was the rise in blue-collar wages over the century, and the expansion of the potential clerical supply through the spread of public education.

Table 9–4

Average Clerical Earnings Expressed as a Percentage of Average Earnings for the Total Labour Force, Canada, by Sex, 1901–1971*

	1901	1911	1921	1931	1941	1951	1961	1971
Total	116%	113	125	119	106	95	87	77
Male	128%	128	118	125	112	102	92	89
Female	145%	147	137	148	149	127	117	106

*Data adjusted to 1951 Census occupation classification.
Sources: Computed from the following:
   1901 Census of Canada, Census and Statistics Bulletin I, *Wage Earners by Occupations*, Table II.
   1911 Census of Canada, Unpublished working tables for wage earners, Statistics Canada microfilm roll number 11002.
   1931 Census of Canada, Volume 5, Table 33.
   1971 Census of Canada, Volume III, Part 6, Table 14.
   D.B.S., *Manufacturing Industries of Canada*, Section A, Summary for Canada, 1961, p. 16.
   Statistics Canada, *1971 Annual Census of Manufacturers*, Summary Statistics, Preliminary, July 1973, p. 3.
   Meltz, *Manpower in Canada*, Section V, Table A-1.
   M.C. Urquhart and K.A.H. Buckley, *Historical Statistics of Canada* (Toronto: Macmillan, 1965), p. 99.

The feminization process created two fairly distinct clerical labour pools, one male and the other female. It is noteworthy, then, that the wages for both groups have declined relative to the total labour force since 1901. As Table 9–4 indicates, male clerical wages dropped from 25 per cent above the labour force average in 1931 to 11 per cent below the average by 1971. Likewise, female clerks, while better off than women in other job ghettos, have been rapidly losing ground. From a wage advantage of between 48 per cent and 49 per cent from 1931 to 1941, female clerical salaries fell to only 6 per cent above the female labour force average by 1971. In making the comparisons between male and female clerical wage trends, we must bear in mind that female clerks earned 53 per cent of their male counterparts in 1901, inching up slightly to 58 per cent by 1971 (Lowe, 1980).[5]

To summarize, the decline of clerical wages relative to the rest of the labour force reflects, more than anything, the erosion of skill levels and responsibilities associated with the old-style office and the resulting inundation of clerical ranks by relatively cheaper female workers. The advance of office rationalization, when combined with the general clerical wage trends, provides evidence of gradual clerical proletarianization. Indeed, the women who now operate modern office machines are considered the most proletarianized sector of the white-collar work force (*Work in America*, 1973: 38; Rinehart, 1975: 92; Glenn and Feldberg, 1977). Clearly, the roots of proletarianization can be traced back to the administrative revolution in the early decades of the twentieth century.

THE RATIONALIZATION OF THE OFFICE

The transition from nineteenth-century small-scale entrepreneurial capitalism to twentieth-century corporate capitalism involved a number of fundamental organizational changes. Foremost among these was the growing predominance of bureaucracy, for it was the form of work organization best suited to capitalism (see Weber, 1958; 1964). As Bendix (1974: 2) argues, industrialization is "the process by which large numbers of employees are concentrated in a single enterprise and become dependent upon the directing and co-ordinating activities of entrepreneurs and managers." Accompanying the rise of bureaucracy was the emergence of a new occupational group, the expert salaried manager. The growing size and complexity of enterprises compelled owners to delegate daily operating responsibility to hired managers. Administration thus became a specialized activity after 1900, as managers sought the most efficient ways to achieve organizational goals (see Chandler, 1978; Nelson, 1975). The major strategy utilized by managers was organizational rationalization. Consequently, rigid hierarchies with clear lines of authority were developed, new accounting procedures were implemented to control production and labour costs, traditional labour skills were broken down as the division of labour became more specialized, and workers' control over the productive process passed to management with increasing standardization and mechanization of tasks. Braverman (1974: 107) claims that the key to all modern management is "the control over work through the control over decisions that are made in the course of work." This principle applied equally to office and factory.

When William H. Leffingwell (1917) published the first book on scientific office management in 1917, he found a receptive audience among many American and Canadian office managers. By the early 1920s, there is evidence that large offices were being rationalized according to the dictates of scientific management in order to increase administrative efficiency.[6] In fact, after 1910 major business publications such as the *Monetary Times, Industrial Canada* and the *Journal of the Canadian Bankers' Association* devoted increasing coverage to a variety of managerial reforms designed to rationalize work procedures. Even as early as 1905, Canadian manufacturers were cautioned to control rising office overhead (*Industrial Canada*, July 1905: 843). In the finance sector, the Bank of Nova Scotia pioneered a system for measuring the efficiency of branch staff (Bank of Nova Scotia Archives, n.d.). Not until 1910, however, did the new science of management really catch hold in Canadian industry. Canadian businessmen, as well as senior government administrators, were attracted to the ideology of efficiency which, inspired by F.W. Taylor's program of scientific factory management, pervaded the Progressive Era in America (see Haber, 1964). Taylor himself published accounts of his scientific management system in *Industrial Canada* (March, April, May 1913) during 1913. It is thus not surprising to find that employers such as the Canadian Pacific Railway, the federal civil service in Ottawa, the government of Quebec, Massey-Harris and Canadian Cereal and Flour Mills Ltd. rationalized their operations by hiring American efficiency experts.

The most advanced scientific office management practices during the 1920s were found in the insurance industry. Sun Life Assurance Company led the way when it appointed a personnel manager at its Montreal head office in 1920. Scientific methods of staff recruitment and training were implemented, departmental structures were reorganized to improve internal co-ordination and integration, the latest in office machines were introduced, and standardized job classifications and salary scales were developed (Lowe, 1979). The formation of the Life Office Management Association in 1924 by Canadian and American life insurance companies is a good indication of the advancing administrative revolution in the industry. The aim of the organization was to collectively develop innovative methods of "correct organization and administration of . . . clerical activities" (Life Office Management Association, 1924: 8).

Mechanized clerical procedures were perhaps the most visible feature of office rationalization. As we have indicated above, tasks such as typing and operating other office machines were defined as "women's work" from their inception. The close interconnection between feminization and the mechanization of office work clearly demonstrates how the rationalization of the clerical labour process was fundamental to the administrative revolution. Interestingly, early stenographers performed craft-like jobs — evidenced by their range of skills, responsibilities and high level of job control — and consequently attained considerable socio-economic status (Lowe, 1980). However, by World War I, dictation and typing, the two core elements of the job, were being separated. Dictation machines facilitated the organization of central typing pools. Combining technical innovation with organizational rationalization, these pools gave rise to the "office machine age" (Mills, 1956: 195). Many large Canadian offices had typing pools by the mid-1920s. Employees resisted the pool concept, but management found that centralized typing operations were easier to control and more efficient because machines could be kept in continuous use.

The Hollerith punch card system, the forerunner to the electronic computer, fully established the "office machine age." The female operators of these machines performed repetitive, minutely subdivided and machine-paced tasks. In short, their jobs resembled those found in many mass-production factories (Shepard, 1971: 63). A revolution in office technology was underway, marked by the inclusion of the job title of "office machine operator" in the 1921 Census. The application of Hollerith office technology was fairly extensive. International Business Machines, the main supplier, had 105 Canadian offices among its customers by the early 1930s (Lowe, 1980). The new class of office machine operators which emerged in the 1920s is an enduring feature of the administrative revolution, as any observer of the contemporary office will quickly recognize.

To briefly recap, we have documented how specific organizational and occupational changes in the office between 1910 and 1930 represented a transformation in administration. Considering the rapid growth of clerical occupations in key industries, the influx of women into routine office jobs, the deteriorating economic position of the clerk, and the rationalization of office organization and procedures, there can be little doubt that fundamental changes occurred in early twentieth-century Canadian offices. All of these changes are directly related, we have suggested, to the process of capitalist development. The exact nature of this link will be the subject of the second part of this paper.

ADMINISTRATIVE CONTROL AND THE TRANSFORMATION OF THE OFFICE

A prominent theme in our discussion thus far has been that the changing nature of administration — and what this entailed for clerical workers — was a result of the development of corporate capitalism. Now we must probe the complexities of this relationship more carefully. Was it simply that a large, rationalized office staff was an inevitable by-product of the logic of capitalist development? Clearly, to argue that economic factors alone were responsible for the transformation in administration would be simplistic, ignoring major organizational variables which we have already identified as instrumental in these changes. Certain characteristics of large-scale organizations — such as their intricate division of labour, numerous departmental sub-units and sheer size — must also be considered as decisive in the growth and transformation of administrative activities. There is no need to engage in debate over whether economic or organizational factors are more critical once we recognize that corporate capitalism provided the environment which nurtured the spread of bureaucracy. We are nonetheless concerned with how organizational and economic forces interacted during the early twentieth-century to precipitate a revolution in the means of administration. In this respect, the concept of administrative control will be used to integrate economic and organizational factors into a comprehensive explanation of this phenomenon.

Briefly, we have argued that the modern office is the administrative centre of corporate capitalism. Through the office, managers attempt to exercise greater control and co-ordination over internal operations and employees as well as larger environmental factors affecting the organization. However, in order for the office to function effectively in this role, increasing control had to be exercised over office administration. The notion of administrative control thus has a dual meaning. In the first sense, control can help us explain the growth of clerical occupations. The second can account for the rationalization of the office and the clerical labour process. In short, we are suggesting that in order for administrative control to be exercised *through* the office, managers also had to apply the same principles of control *over* the office.

Let us set this argument out in more detail before exploring its theoretical underpinnings. The concept of administrative control encompasses the organizational, occupational and economic dimensions of the administrative revolution. But exactly how did these variables interact to transform the means of administration? On the economic plane, the rise of corporate capitalism after 1900 brought rapid expansion to Canada's manufacturing and service industries. It was in these industries, we have noted, that the escalating demands for the processing, analysis and storage of information created a boom in clerical employment. The central organizational feature of the administrative revolution was the rise of the office bureaucracy. Driven by the competitive forces of the marketplace, capitalists carried out mergers and consolidations. The resulting corporate entities had their equivalent in the public sector in the form of large government bureaucracies. Whether the organizations were public or private, or engaged in services or manufacturing, the office became the nerve centre of management. For it was through the office that the daily operations of large-scale organizations were run. This brings us to the main occupational dynamic underlying the administrative revolution. The modern corporation — and in a similar fashion, the public bureaucracy — delegates operating authority to expert salaried managers. This new semi-professional group became increasingly concerned over aspects of organizational design, the work process and other nontechnical factors which may have hindered the achievement of overall goals, be they profit maximization or efficient public service.

As the role of the office became enlarged to include co-ordination of internal activities and regulation of environmental factors impinging upon the organization's future, strains and inefficiencies resulted. In short, the office itself became stricken with bureaucratic maladies. Soaring clerical costs threatened to undermine profits or, in the case of public bureaucracies, cost efficiency. By the First World War, office managers were beginning to recognize the advantages of office rationalization. It was the managerial drive for higher efficiency in clerical operations and greater regimentation of the office labour force which underlay the rationalization of the clerk's job.

Two trends thus converged, precipitating a transformation in office work. First, more clerks were required to process the flood of information. Second, managers increasingly came to rely upon the office as the support system for their power and authority. The office was the key instrument in all managerial decision making. Together, these factors magnified the scope of office procedures. Inefficiencies in clerical routines — resulting from organizational weaknesses as well as from the underlying tensions of worker resistance to their subordination — were exacerbated. This launched a managerial drive for control over the clerical labour process. The result was a highly rationalized office in which deskilled jobs were defined as suitable women's work. What this suggests is that three factors, linked by the concept of administrative control, underlay the administrative revolution: (a) the rapid growth of manufacturing and service industries; (b) the growing predominance of large-scale bureaucratic work organizations; and (c) the operation of these organizations by a cadre of salaried managers concerned with the efficient co-ordination of work activities and the regulation of workers. It is now useful for us to analyse how each of these factors contributed to the administrative revolution.

THE DYNAMICS OF CORPORATE CAPITALISM

There can be little doubt that the rise of corporate capitalism paralleled the changes we have already documented in administration between 1911 and 1931. Manufacturing, the cornerstone of an industrial economy, underwent tremendous expansion after 1900. Between 1880 and 1929, the number of manufacturing establishments was reduced from 50,000 to 22,000 through mergers and acquisitions (Firestone, 1953: 160). At the same time, the gross value of production soared from 700 million to 3,116 million (constant) dollars (Firestone, 1953: 160). The wheat boom in western Canada during the first decade of the twentieth century provided the primary stimulus for this rapid industrialization (Buckley, 1974: 4; Brown and Cook, 1976: 83–84). The First World War also was crucial, precipitating faster, more far-reaching expansion of industry than would have occurred under normal conditions. Much of the new industry established was accounted for by U.S. direct investment. The number of U.S. manufacturing branch plants increased from 100 in 1900 to 1,350 by the end of 1934 (Marshall, et al., 1976: 18). By 1918, we find that "the foundation for a modern industrial economy had been laid" (Firestone, 1953: 152). In fact, corporate capitalism was so well established by 1929 that, in that year, investment in manufacturing achieved a peak which would not be surpassed until the 1950s (Firestone, 1953: 156).

A direct measure of the growing demand for clerical workers in manufacturing is the changing ratio of administrative to production workers. As the economy expanded and factories grew, more office staff was required to administer the rising production. We thus find that the number of administrative employees (mainly clerical, but also including supervisory workers) for every one hundred workers in manufacturing increased from 8.6 in 1911 to 16.9 by 1931 (International Labour Office, 1937: 513). What this demonstrates is the direct connection between the advance of industrialization and the development of large central offices.

Service industries also underwent remarkable growth in response to the demands of an emerging industrial economy. Similarly, this sparked an enlargement of office staff. The development of white-collar bureaucracies was, in fact, most apparent in the service sector. For example, the insurance business grew by 850 per cent between 1909 and 1929, yet the number of companies only increased by one, to 41 (Poapst, 1950: 14). Sun Life Assurance began acquiring other insurance firms in 1890, when its head office staff numbered 20. Between 1910 and 1930, a total of 13 acquisitions was made, bringing the number of head office staff to 2,856 employees (see Neufeld, 1972; Sun Life Archives, Personnel File no. 2). Likewise, in transportation we find the same type of concentration of capital and employment. The railways, for instance, became the nation's largest employers, with Canadian National and Canadian Pacific having a combined work force of 129,000 in 1931 (Rountree, 1936: 12). Another indicator of economic expansion is the rise of a huge civil service bureaucracy. Total employment — much of it clerical — in all three levels of government soared from 17,000 in 1901 to 108,000 by 1931 (Bank of Montreal, 1956: 128).

In sum, the rise of manufacturing and service industries established a modern capitalist economy in Canada by the 1930s. Fundamental to this economic development was the concentration of employment into large bureaucracies. It is indeed significant that, during the period we are studying, there were two major waves of corporate mergers and acquisitions, one from 1909 to 1913 and another more pronounced wave from 1925 to 1929 (Weldon, 1966: 233). This combination of industrialization and bureaucratization set the stage for the rise of modern administration.

BUREAUCRACY AND THE MODERN OFFICE

How, though, did the characteristics of bureaucracy influence the evolution of administration? As the office became the administrative centre of the economy, unsystematic, *ad hoc* office procedures were replaced by comprehensive administrative systems designed to provide an orderly flow of information. Only in this way could management exercise control over both external and internal factors affecting the achievement of organizational goals. Clerks became the functionaries of these new administrative systems. The basic function of the office is to facilitate the making and execution of managerial decisions (see Simon, 1976: Gulick, 1937). As Kaufman (1968: 61) argues, all administration is designed "to 'carry out,' to 'execute' or 'implement' policy decisions, or to co-ordinate activity in order to accomplish some common purpose, or simply to achieve co-operation in pursuit of shared goals." However, this is a Weberian view of administration and, as such, presents an image of bureaucracy which cannot fully account for the changes encompassed in the administrative revolution.

Weber assumes that bureaucracy is the most efficient form of organization under capitalism (Weber, 1958: 1964). His ideal-typical bureaucracy rests on the notion that all forms of administration tend toward full rationality and efficiency. Although Weber never concisely defines bureaucracy, he stresses that formal rules and regulations are its foundation. Rules inject order and stability into organizational life, specifying the division of labour, the delegation of responsibilities and the hierarchy of authority. The advantages of this in terms of administration include "precision, speed, unambiguity, knowledge of the files, continuity, discretion, unity, strict subordination, reduction of friction and of material and personal costs" (Weber, 1958: 214).

There are two related problems with the Weberian concept of bureaucracy. In the first place, Weber's critics claim that he avoids the problem of administrative efficiency which underlies the facade of formalized rules and hierarchical structure (see Albrow, 1970; Blau, 1963; Merton, 1952). Examples of how bureaucracy creates conditions which tend to undermine the achievement of organizational goals are especially found in the subdivision of tasks and the multiplication of departmental sub-units. Administrative theory after Weber focused on how managers could achieve greater co-ordination and integration within large-scale organizations. As Gulick (1937) argues, the increasing subdivision and delegation of work tends to create confusion. Even as early as 1900, managers recognized that task specialization was only a cost-saving technique if accompanied by administrative measures which integrated the tasks into an efficient, unified whole (Litterer, 1963: 370).

Secondly, the Weberian concept of bureaucracy posits internal organizational dynamics as determinant in administrative change. For example, office rationalization involving "the development of greater standardization, consistency and co-ordination" (Theodorson and Theodorson, 1969: 335) is essentially viewed as inherent in the process of bureaucratization. What this overlooks is that rationalization must be consciously planned by management. Furthermore, given the conflict of interests existing between management and workers under capitalism, one can expect that the very fact of the workers' subordination will generate resistance to organizational change. This is especially true with respect to how hierarchy and the division of labour tend to downgrade work by eliminating the control workers traditionally exercised over their jobs. As such, the bureaucracy is fraught with potential inefficiencies because tactics designed to tighten management's grip over the work process are resisted by workers.

This perspective draws on Marx's insights regarding class relations, viewing the thrust for administrative control as coming not from organizational imperatives but rather from decisions made on behalf of capital. Capitalism's competitive context, its need to grow and survive, and its antagonistic class relations create organizational strains which are remedied through the rationalization of production (see Braverman, 1974; Palmer, 1975). This leads Marglin (1971) to claim that capital accumulation, not technical efficiency, underlay the origins of hierarchy. Simply put, managers are in a better position to regulate the creation and allocation of profits once they have usurped the control of production from workers.

Yet neither the Marxian nor the Weberian view alone can fully address the question of how and why the administrative revolution took place. It is therefore useful to combine aspects of both. The Marxian perspective helps us to see how modern management largely entails the transfer of control over the productive process from workers to managers. The results, plainly evident in the twentieth-century office and factory, are devastating: job fragmentation, rigid hierarchies, and the coercive discipline and surveillance of workers — what Braverman (1974) refers to as the degradation of labour. But it is also reasonable to assert that inefficiency stemming from organizational problems often has sparked rationalization. How else would one explain the dramatic transformations in government offices, executed by foremost American scientific management experts, during the 1920s? The issue of organizational inefficiency suggests, then, that a modified Weberian view is also useful. The problems of large-scale organization reflect the tendency for co-ordination and integration to break down with increased division of labour and structural differentiation. These are organizational problems, although one could argue that the rise of modern bureaucracy was itself fundamentally a by-product of capitalist development. What this misses, however, is that against the background of capitalist development, managerial initiatives were also directed against problems resulting directly from the expansion of bureaucracy.

By combining the economic and class perspectives of Marxism with the organizational emphasis of the Weberian tradition, we can thus account for the growth of clerical jobs and the transformation of office procedures in both public and private bureaucracies. This is achieved by defining administrative control as encompassing strategies to deal with the economic forces of competition and capital accumulation, means of regulating labour and diminishing class conflict, and systems to improve the co-ordination and integration of organizational operations. To more fully understand how administrative control was exercised through the office, and its impact on clerical workers, we must consider the origins and functions of modern management.

MODERN MANAGEMENT AND THE OFFICE

The rise of modern management was a crucial aspect of the administrative revolution, for only through the actions of this new semi-professional group were changes brought about in the office. The office began to assume its contemporary functions in the closing decades of the nineteenth century. Litterer (1963) documents how specialized staff functions originated with the advent of cost clerks and production control clerks in factories (see Nelson, 1975). Cost accounting — toward which Canadian manufacturers turned their attention after the turn of the century — and other scientific approaches to factory management were the administrative sequel to mechanized production (Landes, 1969). The office thus began to dominate the factory, becoming the "visible hand" of management. As Braverman (1974: 301) notes, management functions themselves became labour processes as administrative tasks were increasingly subdivided and delegated to a growing clerical work force.

The most prominent managerial strategy for dealing with organizational problems and regulating workers' activities was Taylorism. Frederick W. Taylor's science of management, widely disseminated by the start of the First World War, involved three basic axioms: (a) the dissociation of the labour process from the skills of the workers; (b) the separation of the conception and execution of a task; and (c) the application of management's resulting knowledge of the labour process to control each step in production (see Braverman, 1974; Copley, 1923; Urwick, 1957; Nelson, 1975). The cumulative effect of these initiatives leads Rinehart (1978: 6) to observe that "today, most workers are locked into jobs that require little knowledge and skill and that are defined and controlled from the upper echelons of complex organizations."

Two points can be made regarding the impact of the managerial thrust for control of the office. First, especially in manufacturing we find a direct link between the extension of managerial control and clerical growth. For example, Rushing (1967) and Melman (1951) both suggest that the disproportionate increase in administrative staff relative to production workers in U.S. manufacturing reflected the enlargement of management control functions. And second, as the scope of office operations expanded, managers in both manufacturing and service industries found it necessary to apply principles of rationalization, which originated in the factory, to clerical work.

"Management, the brain of the organization," to use a physiological analogy, "conveys its impulses through the clerical systems which constitute the nervous mechanism of the company" (Murdoch and Dale, 1961: 2). This underlines how clerical work furnished the means of integrating the components of an organization. Even in white-collar industries, such as insurance or banking, special departments were established to facilitate managerial control over administrative practices. As one insurance executive asserts, "office administration is not a job by itself. We are in the insurance business, and office administration, scientific office administration, is merely one of the tools to help us carry on the insurance business more efficiently" (Life Office Management Association, 1927: 188). By the First World War, office managers in both Canada and the U.S., already aware of the importance of systematic administration, were being told that Taylorism and other scientific factory management schemes could be easily adapted to the office (Hagedorn, 1955: 167; Leffingwell, 1917:5). The logic of office rationalization is clearly expressed by the father of scientific management, W.H. Leffingwell (1917: 35, 111, 109):

> Effective management implies control. The terms are in a sense interchangeable, as management without control is inconceivable, and both terms imply the exercise of a directing influence. . . . The clerical function may then be correctly regarded as the linking or connecting function, which alone makes possible the efficient performance of hundreds of individual operations involved in the "sub-assembly" cycles of the business machine as a whole. . . . If (management) co-ordination requires clerical mechanisms and cannot function without them, it follows that the problem of management through them constitutes a major function and is unquestionably vital to the conduct of business.

This statement encapsulates the essential nature of the modern office. Without clerical procedures as efficient, predictable and regimented as the factory assembly line, managerial control over external and internal factors affecting organizational goals would be diminished. An efficient bureaucracy, whether its goals are public service at the lowest cost or capitalist growth and profits, requires systematic administration. The entrenchment of these changes in major Canadian offices is precisely the concern of the editorial in the *Monetary Times* cited at the opening of the paper.

CONCLUSIONS

The purpose of this paper has been to analyse the administrative revolution which occurred in major Canadian offices between 1911 and 1931. By the onset of the Depression, the central features of the contemporary office were well in place. Increasingly, the typical clerk was a woman who performed a specialized job, often machine-paced, in a highly regimented bureaucratic setting. As in any kind of large-scale social change, the transition from the old nineteenth-century counting house to the modern twentieth-century office was not a smooth, all-encompassing process. The changes described above in the nature of clerical work as well as in office organization and management took place in a more or less halting, uneven fashion. Evidence suggests, though, that alterations in the means of administration were sufficiently sweeping and well rooted by the 1930s to characterize them as a "revolution."

Theoretically, our task has been to unite into a comprehensive explanation the broad occupational, economic and organizational forces associated with the rise of modern administration. This has been achieved by using the concept of administrative control. We have shown that control was the central feature in both the growth of the office and its rationalization by management. Yet in drawing on the theories of Marx and Weber to develop this explanation, we have merely glossed over many of the knotty theoretical problems involved in any attempt to merge these contrasting perspectives. Still, the relevance of this approach to explaining changes in the labour process during particular stages of capitalist development is clear. A one-sided theory, whether emphasizing economic forces, as Marxists are wont to do, or positing organizational imperatives as determinate, as do Weberians, cannot possibly account for the intricate causal nexus underlying the rise of the modern office. No doubt the same would be true in studies of the expansion and rationalization of other work settings.

NOTES

1. Following Clement (1975: 71–80), we have used the concepts of entre-preneurial capitalism and corporate capitalism as a way of highlighting major socio-economic changes in Canadian society during the early 20th century.
2. Our evidence is limited to the Canadian office; however, there is good reason to believe that the argument we present can also explain the development of modern administration in other advanced capitalist countries (see Chandler, 1978; Lockwood, 1966; Braverman, 1974; Mills, 1956; Lederer, 1937).
3. The First World War, which occurred in this decade, influenced the formation of the contemporary office in two important respects. In the first place, the tremendous demands of the war economy for goods and services sparked rapid industrial expansion. This in turn produced a boom in clerical employment, as office staffs swelled. And second, severe labour force disruptions, as many male workers enlisted, accelerated the shift toward female clerical employment (see Lowe, 1980).
4. This wage pattern seems to be standard in advanced capitalist societies. Research in the U.S. by Braverman (1974) and Burns (1954) and in Britain by Lockwood (1966) documents how the growth of the white-collar sector of the labour force has been marked by a relative decline in clerical wages.
5. This is consistent with broad labour force trends. In 1971, the average income of women doing paid work was about half that of men (Armstrong and Armstrong, 1975: 371).
6. While Taylorism was undoubtedly the label most commonly attached to attempts to rationalize the labour process, it was only one strategy in the broad "thrust for efficiency" which took root after 1900 (see Palmer, 1975). The term scientific management includes, then, a variety of systematic programs initiated by management to inject order and efficiency into the organization and execution of work.

REFERENCES

Albrow, Martin
1970   *Bureaucracy*. London: Macmillan.

Armstrong, Hugh and Pat Armstrong
1975   "The Segregated Participation of Women in the Canadian Labour Force, 1941–71," *Canadian Review of Sociology and Anthropology* 12: 370–84.
1978   *The Double Ghetto: Canadian Women and Their Segregated Work*. Toronto: McClelland and Stewart.

Bank of Montreal
1956   *The Service Industries*. Study No. 17, Royal Commission on Canada's Economic Prospects.

Bank of Nova Scotia Archives
n.d.   "The Bank of Nova Scotia, 1832–1932, One Hundredth Anniversary."
        Toronto.

Bendix, Reinhart
1974   *Work and Authority in Industry*. Berkeley: University of California
        Press.

Blau, Peter M.
1963   *The Dynamics of Bureaucracy*, revised ed. Chicago: University of
        Chicago Press.

Braverman, Harry
1974   *Labor and Monopoly Capital: the Degradation of Work in the Twentieth
        Century*. New York: Monthly Review Press.

Brown, Robert Craig and Ramsay Cook
1976   *Canada 1896–1921: A Nation Transformed*. Toronto: McClelland and
        Stewart.

Buckley, Kenneth
1974   *Capital Formation in Canada, 1896–1930*. Toronto: McClelland and
        Stewart.

Burns, Robert K.
1954   "The Comparative Economic Position of Manual and White-Collar
        Employees," in *Journal of Business* 27: 257–67.

Canada
        Censuses, 1891–1971 (published and unpublished data).
1907   Wage-Earners by Occupations. 1901 Census, Bulletin I. Ottawa: King's
        Printer.
1939   Occupational Trends in Canada, 1891–1931. Special Bulletin, D.B.S.
        Census Branch. Ottawa: King's Printer.
1961   *Manufacturing Industries of Canada*. Ottawa: D.B.S.
1973   *1971 Annual Census of Manufacturers, Summary Statistics, Prelimi-
        nary*. Ottawa: Statistics Canada.
1974   *Canada Year Book*. Ottawa: Information Canada.

Chandler, Alfred D., Jr.
1977   *The Visible Hand: The Managerial Revolution in American Business*.
        Cambridge, Mass.: Harvard University Press.

Clement, Wallace
1975   *The Canadian Corporate Elite*. Toronto: McClelland and Stewart.

Copley, F.B.
1923   *Frederick W. Taylor, Father of Scientific Management*, 2 Vols. New
        York: Harper and Row.

Dreyfuss, Carl
1938   *Occupation and Ideology of the Salaried Employee*, 2 Vols. trans. Eva
        Abramovitch. New York: Works Progress Administration and the
        Department of Social Science, Columbia University.

Firestone, O.J.
1953   "Canada's Economic Development, 1867–1952," paper prepared for the
        Third Conference of the International Association for Research in
        Income and Wealth, Castelgandolfo, Italy.

Glenn, Evelyn Nakano and Roslyn L. Feldberg
1977   "Degraded and Deskilled: The Proletarianization of Clerical Work," in
        Social Problems 25: 52–64.

Gulick, Luther
1937   "Notes on the Theory of Organization," in *Papers on the Science of Administration*. Luther Gulick and L. Urwick (eds.) New York: Institute of Public Administration.

Haber, Samuel
1964   *Efficiency and Uplift: Scientific Management in the Progressive Era, 1890-1920*. Chicago: University of Chicago Press.

Hagedorn, Homer J.
1955   "The Management Consultant as Transmitter of Business Techniques," in *Explorations in Entrepreneurial History* 7: 164-173.

Hoos, Ida R.
1961   *Automation in the Office*. Washington: Public Affairs Press.

Industrial Canada
International Labour Office
1937   "The Use of Office Machinery and Its Influence on Conditions of Work for Staff," in *International Labour Review* 36: 486-516.

Journal of The Canadian Bankers' Association
Kaufman, Herbert
1968   "The Administrative Function," in *International Encyclopedia of the Social Sciences* Vol. 1, David Sills (ed.) New York: Macmillan Co. and the Free Press.

Landes, David
1969   *The Unbound Prometheus: Technological Change and Industrial Development in Western Europe from 1750 to the Present*. Cambridge: Cambridge University Press.

Lederer, Emil
1937   *The Problem of the Modern Salaried Employee: Its Theoretical and Statistical Basis*. Trans. E.E. Warburg. New York: State Department of Social Welfare and the Department of Social Science, Columbia University.

Leffingwell, William Henry
1917   *Scientific Office Management*. Chicago: A.W. Shaw.

Life Office Management Association
Proceedings of Annual Conferences.

Litterer, Joseph A.
1963   "Systematic Management: Design for Organizational Recoupling in American Manufacturing Firms," in *Business History Review* 37: 369-391.

Lockwood, David
1966   *The Blackcoated Worker*. London: Allen and Unwin.

Lowe, Graham S.
1979   "The Administrative Revolution: The Growth of Clerical Occupations and the Development of the Modern Office in Canada, 1911-1931." Unpublished Ph.D. thesis, University of Toronto, Toronto.

1980   "Women, Work and the Office: The Feminization of Clerical Occupations in Canada", 1901-1931, in *Canadian Journal of Sociology* 5 (forthcoming).

Marglin, Stephen A.
1971   "What Do Bosses Do?: The Origins and Functions of Hierarchy in Capitalist Production." Harvard Institute of Economic Research, Discussion Paper No. 222.

172   *Work in the Canadian Context*

Marshall, Herbert, F.A. Southard and K.W. Taylor
1976   *Canadian–American Industry*. Toronto: McClelland and Stewart.

Melman, Stewart
1951   "The Rise of Administrative Overhead in the Manufacturing Industries of the United States, 1899–1947," in *Oxford Economic Papers*, New Series 3: 62–112.

Meltz, Noah M.
1969   *Manpower in Canada, 1931–1961*. Ottawa: Queen's Printer.

Merton, Robert K.
1952   "Bureaucratic Structure and Personality," in *Reader in Bureaucracy*. R.K. Merton et al. (eds.) New York: Free Press.

Mills, C. Wright
1956   *White Collar: The American Middle Classes*. New York: Oxford University Press.

Monetary Times
Murdoch, Allan A. and J. Rodney Dale
1961   *The Clerical Function: A Survey of Modern Clerical Systems and Methods*. London: Sir Isaac Pitman and Sons.

Nelson, Daniel
1975   *Managers and Workers: Origins of the New Factory System in the United States, 1880–1920*. Madison: University of Wisconsin Press.

Neufeld, E.P.
1972   *The Financial System of Canada*. Toronto: Macmillan.

Palmer, Bryan
1975   "Class, Conception and Conflict: The Thrust for Efficiency, Managerial Views of Labour and the Working Class Rebellion, 1903–22," in *Radical Review of Political Economics* 7: 31–49.

Poapst, James
1950   "The Growth of the Life Insurance Industry in Canada, 1909–47." Unpublished M. Comm. thesis, McGill University, Montreal.

Rinehart, James W.
1975   *The Tyranny of Work*. Don Mills: Longman Canada.
1978   "Contradictions of Work-Related Attitudes and Behaviour: An Interpretation," in *Canadian Review of Sociology and Anthropology* 15: 1–15.

Rountree, Meredith G.
1936   *The Railway Worker: A Study of the Employment and Unemployment Problems of the Canadian Railways*. Toronto: Oxford University Press.

Rushing, William A.
1967   "The Effects of Industry Size and Division of Labour on Administration," in *Administrative Science Quarterly* 12: 273–295.

Shepard, Jon M.
1971   *Automation and Alienation: A Study of Office and Factory Workers*. Cambridge, Mass.: M.I.T. Press.

Simon, Herbert A.
1952   "Decision-Making and Administrative Organization," in *Reader in Bureaucracy*. R.K. Merton et al. (eds.) New York: Free Press.

1976   *Administrative Behaviour*, 3rd ed. New York: Free Press.
Sun Life Assurance Co. Archives, Montreal
Urquhart, M.C. and K.A.H. Buckley

1965   *Historical Statistics of Canada.* Toronto: Macmillan.

Weber, Max
1958   *From Max Weber: Essays in Sociology.* Trans. and ed. H.H. Gerth and C.W. Mills. New York: Oxford University Press.
1964   *The Theory of Social and Economic Organization.* New York: Free Press.

Weldon, J.C.
1966   "Consolidation in Canadian Industry, 1900–1948," in *Restrictive Trade Practices in Canada,* L.A. Skeoch. (ed.) Toronto: McClelland and Stewart.

Work in America
1973   Report of a Special Task Force to the U.S. Secretary of Health, Education and Welfare prepared by the W.E. Upjohn Institute for Employment Research. Cambridge, Mass.: M.I.T. Press.

Theodorson, George A. and Achilles G. Theodorson
1969   *A Modern Dictionary of Sociology.* New York: Thomas Y. Crowell.

Urwick, Lyndall P.
1957   *The Life and Work of Frederick Winslow Taylor.* London: Urwick, Orr and Partners.

Chapter 10

The Changing Occupational Structure of the Canadian Timber Industry*

Roy T. Bowles
Mary-Ann Haney

This is an essay in the historical sociology of Canadian society. It addresses the question of how occupations in the forest industries have changed as a consequence of changes in the nature of those industries. This question is placed within a broader framework of the impact of resource staple development on patterns in Canadian society. The concrete objective will be to show that each type of forest exploitation in central Canada gave rise to a particular set of occupations.

One of the central features of Canadian economic development has been heavy reliance on the extraction and export of raw materials, frequently called "staples." Export staples are raw materials which are produced in one country or region for shipment to, and marketing in, another. Staple products which were important in early Canadian development include cod fish, furs, forest products, and wheat. Wheat and forest products have continuing importance, but minerals, petroleum, and hydroelectric power are now also important. A group of scholars working within a common framework known as "the staples approach to the Canadian economic history" have traced the consequences of resource exploitation for Canadian society. The themes most commonly emphasized are that (1) growth in the staples industries has been the most important factor in the growth of the Canadian economy as a whole (Watkins, 1967); and (2) national patterns of transportation, communication, and

---

*Because this essay attempts to capture in limited space some sociologically significant consequences of one hundred and fifty years of historical development many simplifications have been necessary. Developments in British Columbia and Atlantic Canada have not been discussed. The manufacture of pine "deals" has been ignored. The period following World War II, which was characterized by mechanization and technological change with important consequences, has not been examined. The seasonal nature of work, part-time work, sub-contracting, and payment in piece rates which are important to understanding forest work have not been considered. Discussion of "phases" of the timber industry may imply clear sequential ordering when in reality there was substantial overlapping.

The conceptual perspective applied to the timber industries is developed in more general terms in Bowles and Craib, "Canada: Economy, Opportunity and Class" (1979) which the reader may consult for more complete discussion and bibliography. The works of A.R.M. Lower have been used heavily, because he has provided a comprehensive overview of Canadian forest industries and because the structure of his analysis is amenable to links with discussions of occupation and class.

175

political structure have been shaped by the requirements of the staple trades (see esp. Innis, 1973). This paper contends that the staples approach is equally important in furthering an understanding of the daily contexts in which people live and work (Bowles, 1980).

The general framework can be stated briefly. Exploitation of a particular resource in a given environment requires a suitable technology (i.e., tools, machines, and knowledge of process). Given a particular technology, certain tasks must be performed and occupations are created to complete related sets of tasks. The diverse activities necessary to the trade or industry must be co-ordinated, and the particular problems of co-ordination generate typical forms of economic organization. Occupations arise to perform the co-ordination tasks within these organizations. Changes in the staple product or the technology used in exploiting it bring changes in the tasks to be performed, and hence in the occupations associated with the staple trade. This basic perspective will be illustrated by showing how changes in the forest industries brought changes in the associated occupations.

Lower outlines the basic changes which occurred in the forest industries of central Canada between 1800 and the 1930s.

> Canadian forests have been exploited in different ways at different times in response to varying pressures of demand and supply, and to influence of geography and the development of industrial technique. At first, demand created the square-timber export industry on the one hand, and the local sawmill on the other. Then the canal and the railroad expanded the area of exploitation and enabled the sawmill to follow up its retreating raw material. When a new source of demand arose in the United States, which accentuated these processes and either created or took advantage of the innumerable mechanical inventions that aided exploitation, the square-timber industry in time gave way to the great export sawn-lumber industry. This industry now tends to be masked in its turn by the rise of another method of forest exploitation, that of the pulp-and-paper industry. (Lower, 1968: 43)

This paper will briefly outline the technological and economic patterns associated with the square timber trade, local saw-milling, industrial saw-milling, and the pulp and paper industry. It will then examine the structure of occupatibns associated with each of these phases of forest exploitation. In this synoptic overview it will not be possible to discuss systematically the historical developments within each phase, or to examine the many variations in pattern which were present. Occupations will be treated in broad categories of social class. The classes or class fragments which it will be useful to distinguish for the following discussion are: (1) large-scale capitalists, (2) small-scale capitalists, and (3) proletariat. Large-scale capitalists own and control major concentrations of property. They employ the labour power of many members of the proletariat to perform the actual tasks of production. Their own work consists of directing the organizations which co-ordinate the labour and property used to accomplish the tasks of production. Typically, they do not engage in the physical activity of production itself. Small-scale capitalists own and control small businesses which they operate themselves. Compared to major capitalists they employ relatively few hired workers and own relatively small amounts of productive property. Frequently, they participate in the physical activity of production itself and exercise control through direct personal supervision rather than through elaborate organizations. The proletariat consists of those people who gain income through the sale of their labour (Bowles and Craib, 1979).

THE SQUARE TIMBER TRADE

The first major forest industry in Canada was the square timber trade. The product of this industry was pine logs hewn square, and markets were in the United Kingdom. Trees were cut and squared in the watersheds of the St. Lawrence and its tributaries, floated downstream to Quebec City, and hauled by ship across the Atlantic. This trade lasted from early in the nineteenth century until early in the twentieth century.

The square timber trade developed in response to British demand. Prior to the nineteenth century, Britain had obtained most of the timber she needed from the Baltic countries. The Napoleonic wars spurred demand for timber, particularly to maintain the fleet of wooden ships. In 1808, Napoleon successfully imposed an embargo against shipments from the Baltic to Britain. British policies were then directed toward procuring this strategic commodity from the vast but previously untapped forests of British North America. British market preferences and practices dictated that the principal product would be the squared log, rather than the entire log or sawn lumber. Logs were sawn into boards in Britain. The ups and downs of the industry in Canada depended largely on swings in the British economy, high points being associated with industrial expansion and railroad construction and low points associated with recession (Lower, 1971: Lower, 1973).

The most prominent occupations in the square timber trade were timber merchants, timber makers, woodsmen and raftsmen. The timber merchant was a large-scale capitalist who was involved in purchasing logs and organizing their shipment from Quebec to Britain. He filled a slot within the mercantile system and could be seen as "just another example of the world wide species the British 'factor,' whose job was to buy and ship home local products on as good terms as possible" (Lower, 1971: 45).

In the early stages of the trade, much of the actual timber production was organized by small-scale capitalists. In the process of clearing his land, a farmer could cut timber and raft it to Quebec. Such small timber producers progressively declined in importance and the trade became more concentrated. The demand for larger quantities of timber, the expansion of cutting areas up the Ottawa and away from prime agricultural areas, and the ability of a large firm to spread risks over a large number of cutting and rafting operations probably accounted for this concentration. By 1850, most production was in the hands of "timbermakers" who "were for the most part substantial men, managing many camps and bringing down many rafts" (Lower, 1971: 39–46).

Timber was cut during the winter. Company representatives selected a defined cutting area and established a camp or "shanty," consisting of rough buildings to shelter men, animals, and provisions. Camps varied in size, apparently getting larger as production became concentrated in large organizations. Lower's description of a two gang camp provides a coherent picture of the actual work process.

After the shanty had been built and supplies safely housed therein, roads would be cut to strategic positions in trees suitable for making timber, and the work of felling and squaring would begin. The men were divided into gangs of three, sometimes four each. A two-gang camp . . . would, with road-cutters, haulers, and others, total about fifteen men. The gang consisted of liner, scorer, and hewer. . . .

Felling . . . the tree required skill, for the cut had to be made so that the trunk would fall just where it had been planned, onto a bedding of small trees to prevent its breaking and to keep it a little off the ground. When the trunk had been topped and limbed, the liner took a strip of bark off both sides and along each of these strips drew a line indicating the size of the square to be made. The scorer then mounted the trunk and about every thirty inches notched in towards the line. He then split out from notch to notch, as closely as possible to the mark. The hewer with his broadax followed and hewed to the line. . . . An artist in his way, the hewer would leave a surface almost as smooth as if planed. Two sides flattened, the tree was canted over and squared up on the other two sides. (Lower, 1973: 200–201)

The squared logs were cut into lengths and skidded over snow and ice by horses or oxen to the nearest stream. With the spring thaw, they were floated down small streams as loose logs to larger rivers, such as the Ottawa or the St. Lawrence. On the large waterways, workmen using a variety of techniques, including holes and pins, twisted saplings serving as ropes, and loading layers of logs so that weight and friction prevented logs from floating apart, formed the individual logs into rafts which could withstand the buffeting of waves and rapids as they made their way hundreds of miles to Quebec City. Given that the average raft contained 80,000 cubic feet of wood and that it was constructed completely of products found in the forest, it must be recognized that raft construction involved tremendous energy and skill.

Rafts were guided through currents and rapids by means of oars and sweeps. They were coaxed across lakes and calm waters by crude sails or by the tedious process of dropping an anchor in front of the raft and cranking forward by means of a windlass.

CLASSES IN THE SQUARE TIMBER TRADE

The timber merchant was a commercial capitalist. His work consisted of organizing and financing the purchase of timber in Canada, its shipment to Britain by sea, and its sale. To accomplish these tasks, he needed an organization of workers to keep records, negotiate specific transactions and handle timber.

The timbermaker was also a capitalist but his major concern was the production of timber in the Canadian forest and its transport to Quebec. His own work tasks were organization and co-ordination. It was necessary for him to locate and secure permits to timber limits, to plan a cutting and rafting schedule, to recruit the men required to perform the physical work as such, and to organize the financing necessary to pay expenses from the beginning of a campaign until the sale of timber in Quebec. It is clear that to achieve all of these tasks he needed a large organization of reliable subordinates to keep records, to supervise the execution of work and to co-ordinate the flow of men, provisions, and lumber.*

Some of the men who worked in the woods or on the rivers spent only part of the year in the timber industry and the remainder on their farms. Part of the cutting and rafting was performed by small-scale entrepreneurs acting as sub-contractors. In the large firms which came to dominate the trade, however, most workers were employees and significant groups of workers found their sole employment in the timber trade. Thus, the timber trade gave rise to a pre-industrial proletariat or a "forest proletariat" (Careless, 1972: 30; Cross, 1960). This forest proletariat worked in direct contact with the forces of nature: the severe climate of the winters, the rigorous terrain in which the trees were located, the massive trees themselves, and the force of spring floods and large rivers. They made some use of horses and oxen as sources of power. Most work, however, was accomplished with human energy and relatively simple hand tools, such as the axe and the cant hook. At least during the period of the winter campaign and the river drive, the forest proletariat lived and worked in small, isolated, and temporary communities made up almost exclusively of adult males. Living conditions met minimum needs of food and shelter but provided little diversity in activities. For men who worked year after year in the forests, contact with permanent settlements made up of families was seasonal and short term.

LOCAL SAW-MILLING BEFORE 1850

Local saw-milling deserves discussion, because the occupational structure associated with it differs dramatically from that associated with other aspects of the forest industries. Saw-mills, like blacksmith shops and grist mills, were established as part of the craft manufacturing operations to serve the local needs of new and growing settlements. The technology used was simple. The earliest tool for making boards was the whip saw operated by two men, one standing above the log and the other below. The "muley-saws" driven by early local water wheels had the same vertical action. Power from the water wheel speeded the sawing, but much of the movement of logs and lumber was accomplished by human energy aided by relatively simple tools. Lower characterizes the role of the saw-mill in the economy of the community:

> Getting out logs was part of the regular winter program of every farmer who had some pine on his lot. These would be hauled to the mill and in the spring its one upright saw would begin to creak and the logs would slowly change into boards. The men who had hauled logs took home what lumber they wanted, paying the saw-mill owner on a share basis. If there was a surplus, it went to the neighbours who had no pine and was probably paid for in kind. When the community's needs had been supplied the mill shut down and its proprietor went on with other tasks. (Lower, 1936: 41)

---

*The occupations of workers who performed organizational tasks in preindustrial firms, which operated with a structure different from the modern joint-stock corporation, have not been subjected to much systematic study.

The earliest small saw-mills used local trees harvested by local people to produce a commodity for local consumption. There was a phase, in Canada and elsewhere, when markets beyond the local area were served. Lumber produced in the craft-manufacturing style by many local mills was assembled into large lots for shipment to more distant markets. (Lower, 1968: 59–60). By about 1830, there was a growing demand for sawn lumber in the United States. In the early stages of this export trade, and in the agricultural areas of southern Ontario, there was a compatibility between the timber industry and farming. Farmers cut logs on their own land during the winter and sold them to local mills, thus acquiring capital needed for the development of their farms (Jones, 1977: 20, Lower, 1936: 42).

CLASSES IN LOCAL SAW-MILLING

The people most directly involved in local saw-milling, farmers and mill operators, were small-scale capitalists who combined their own labour with their own productive property to produce marketable commodities. Some millers later expanded into industrial operations, but local saw-milling itself did not become a specialized industry. For both farmers and millers, lumber production was but one aspect of a diversified operation. While some hired labour was engaged on farms and in mills, there was no distinct proletariat associated with local saw-milling as there had been in the square timber trade, and would be in industrial saw-milling. In contrast to the remote and isolated living conditions of workers in the square timber trade, workers involved in local saw-milling were members of communities which were made up of all age groups and both sexes and which had continuing institutions such as churches, schools, and associations.

INDUSTRIAL SAW-MILLING

Lower speaks of the "great export sawn-lumber industry" (1968: 43). "Industrial saw-milling" will be used here because this phase of forest exploitation involved the extensive application of inanimate power within a factory system for the transformation of raw materials (trees) into finished products (boards). Industrial saw-milling developed in the mid-nineteenth century in response to an expanding demand for sawn lumber, and was made possible by improved technology for energy production and machine operation. It was aided by the improved transportation. The growing American demand for Canadian timber resulted from the exhaustion of timber supplies in parts of the United States, the growth of urban centres in the north east, and the settlement of the American midwest. Developing canal systems and railroads made it possible to transport Canadian lumber to these markets cheaply, and also made it possible to reach Canadian timber stands which had previously been inaccessible (Head, 1975: 87–88).

Technological improvements in the saw-milling process made it possible to expand the size and productivity of mills. The water wheel which had powered local saw-mills was replaced by the iron turbine wheel, which could more efficiently capture the force of falling water and could be used in places where water powers were greater. Steam engines permitted mills to be established in places where there was no water power, and hence increased the territory available to the industry (Lower, 1968: 47). Improvements in saws, in lumber handling, in log handling, and in co-ordination are succinctly captured by Lower.

> The first and greatest effort was to increase the speed at which logs could be cut up and this was accomplished by a succession of inventions, beginning with the substitution in the seventeenth century of the windmill and the waterwheel for the old English whip saw and going on through such devices as putting two saws and then many saws (that is, making a "gang-saw") into the saw frame, to the circular saw, the "gang-circular," the band-saw and the "gang-band." But lumber being such a bulky commodity each new type of saw embarrassed its operator by cutting so much that the mill became choked. Hence a whole series of inventions designed to "clear the saw," such as edging saws, butting saws, rollers for shoving away the boards, "live" rollers, rotated by mechanical power, tracks instead of roads leading out into the piling yards, finally tracks with powered vehicles upon them, and so on.

> In this battle between saw and products, every victory of the accessory expedients in taking away the boards as fast as the saw would cut them was met by a new device for speeding up the work of the saw. From this urge arose the log-track with its endless chain for taking the logs out of the water and drawing them up to the saw, . . . [the] ram which comes up alongside the log carriage and turns over the log ready for another cut, and the mechanical carriage which feeds the log back and forth to the saw, a cut in each direction. That mill has been most successful which has succeeded in best co-ordinating all these various factors to the one end of getting the logs through the saw and out into the piling grounds as boards and by-products as quickly as possible (Lower, 1968: 46–47).

The reader will recognize in this description of technological changes the classic features of industrialization or mechanization: increased use of inanimate power, the development of machines for handling materials, the linking of many different machines in a sequence to complete several phases of the manufacturing process and the more efficient applications of energy.

CLASSES IN INDUSTRIAL SAW-MILLING

Certain occupations common to the square timber trade continued into the industrial saw-milling industry. A forest proletariat continued to work in the woods and on the river performing the tasks necessary to getting trees out of the forest and to the mill. But highly skilled artisans who hewed the logs square disappeared, and the sophisticated techniques of rafting were no longer necessary as loose logs could be floated to the mill. While camps became larger and acquired more amenities, the forest proletariat continued to live in isolated communities made up exclusively of adult males.

Two new occupational or class groups, industrial capitalists and an industrial proletariat, came into being with the advent of large-scale saw-milling. The entrepreneur who owned and operated a large saw-mill was an industrial capitalist. His principal objective was to transform raw materials into finished products, and in the process to make a profit. He must organize or bring together the pieces of technology to construct an operating factory and bring to this factory the labour and raw materials necessary for the manufacture of end products. Large-scale industrial entrepreneurs had not existed in previous phases of the lumber trade.

Saw-mill workers made up the first industrial proletariat associated with Canadian forest exploitation. They made their living by exchanging their labour for a wage. Allowing for seasonal shutdowns, they worked full time in the mills. While the forest proletariat worked in close contact with natural forces using simple tools and their own energy, the industrial proletariat of the saw-mills worked in a factory environment and used their energy and judgment to tend machines driven by sophisticated sources of inanimate power.

While some saw-mills were designed to be easily movable and even large mills were sometimes dismantled and transported to a new location, the large mills were stationary factories. As a consequence, saw-mill workers were more likely than woods workers to live in permanent communities consisting of men, women, and children. If a mill was built in an established settlement it brought occupational diversity. If it was built in an unsettled area, a new single-industry community was created.

THE PULP AND PAPER INDUSTRY

The pulp and paper industry had its beginnings in the late nineteenth century with the development of processes for the manufacture of paper from wood. The core outcome of the technological developments necessary to pulp and paper manufacturing was "the successful isolation of the cellulose component of wood and its introduction into the manufacture of paper in place of the traditional materials: rags, straw and grasses" (Burley, 1970: 332). The innovations specific to pulp and paper making were inter-related with a set of processes which together are called "the new industrialism." These include the development and application of hydro-electric power, the more sophisticated application of chemical processes to transform raw materials into usable constituents, and in general more systematic application of physical science principles in manufacturing processes (Easterbrook and Aitken, 1971: 517–20).

The growth in the size and distribution of newspapers in North America, which resulted in part from increased advertising of consumer products, created a rapidly expanding demand for newsprint. By the end of World War I, the pulp and paper industry was rapidly turning Canadian trees into American newspapers. Improved transportation, especially the expanding railroad network, made it possible to bring manufacturing inputs to pulp mills and to deliver paper to markets.

The large permanent industrial mill was the central feature of the pulp and paper industry, but the cutting and transport of logs was still essential. Work in the woods to cut trees for pulp making was both like and different from woods work in the earlier forest industries. As in previous phases, men lived in isolated camps near the cutting areas and harvested trees according to a plan designed by company officials. Until World War II human energy, hand saws, axes and horses were used to accomplish the various tasks. Where possible, wood was floated from forest to mill.

In general, however, cutting pulp wood required less skill than woods work in earlier forest exploitation. In cutting trees for saw milling, care was required to avoid damage that might reduce the yield of boards. In the square timber trade, the skills of hewing and rafting were vital. In pulp wood cutting, the objective was simply to get logs to the mill where they could be reduced to wood fibres. In a typical campaign, an area would be divided into strips and each strip assigned to a wood cutter. He would clear a road through the centre of his strip, fell trees on either side, cut them into lengths of four feet, and pile these logs for transport (Canadian Pulp and Paper Association, 1954: 36–47). Because trees were smaller, processing in the woods more limited, and damage less critical, the pulp-wood cutter required less skill than his counterpart in earlier forest industries.

The following description provides sufficient information about the processes occurring at the pulp and paper mill to guide discussion.

Groundwood pulp is produced by the abrasive action of large revolving grindstones. After being carefully cleaned [of bark] the pulpwood logs are fed (mostly in four-foot lengths) into large grinders and forced under considerable pressure against the face of revolving pulpstones. Water in large amounts must be used to prevent charring. Since a tremendous amount of power is consumed in this operation, it is necessary to find a cheap source of energy for newsprint manufacture. . . .

Sulphite pulp, produced by chemical process, is combined with groundwood in the ratio of one to four in the finished newsprint. This product is obtained by subjecting the wood to the action of a solution of calcium bisulphite. The logs are first chipped and deposited in large steel tanks. A solution of calcium bisulphite is then introduced and the chips are cooked for several hours under steam pressure. This cooking results in the dissolving out of approximately half of the volume of wood; only the cellulose fiber remains at the end of the process. . . .

After the groundwood and sulphite pulp are prepared they are carefully screened and mixed in the required proportions. Color and filler are added, and the stock is diluted by the additions of water to a consistency of 99.5 per cent water. Since it is used extensively not only in cleaning and pulping processes but in conveying the pulp stock through the paper machine, a plentiful supply of fresh water is essential to the operation of a paper mill.

The final manufacturing process is accomplished on the Fourdrinier machine, a huge rectangular machine some 250 feet in length and varying in width from 12 to 25 feet. The diluted stock fed in at one end flows on to a rapidly moving copper screen belt. The water is removed by gravity and suction, and the matted sheet of wet pulp passed rapidly over a long series of steam-heated rollers, emerging at the dry end as a continuous sheet of paper. It is then cut to the desired width, rewound in rolls weighing approximately 1,400 pounds each, and covered with heavy wrapping paper ready for shipment by rail or water. (Guthrie, 1941: 51–52)

WORK AND CLASSES IN THE PULP AND PAPER INDUSTRY

The operation of large pulp and paper mills required a large number of permanent industrial workers, that is, an industrial proletariat. The new technology involved had consequences for the nature of work. Pulp and paper making represented a major change in manufacturing processes. In saw-milling, wood from trees is changed to wood in the form of boards. In pulp and paper making, wood in the form of trees is mechanically and chemically broken down and then reconstituted as something quite different — as paper. Because of the processes used, workers spend relatively little time in the direct handling of either wood or paper. Relatively more time is spent servicing and maintaining machines, in supplying machines with the materials required in processing, and in monitoring the operation of the machines. In effect, the worker becomes an appendage of, or hand servant for, the machine.

Occupations concerned with quality control, e.g., cullers and graders, had existed in all phases of the timber industry. The application of complex processes for transforming wood into paper led to an increase in the numbers and importance of these occupations. This is illustrated by a 1929 description of the Pine Falls Mill.

> The control of this plant is in the hands of a staff of specially trained, highly capable, operating engineers, assisted by a chemical laboratory, whose staff control, especially, the manufacture of chemical (sulphite) pulp. The chemists also keep a close check upon the paper making qualities of the pulp provided hour by hour from the grinding room and the storage tanks of the sulphite plant. Scientific control from beginning to end marks the operation of this modern mill. (Shipley, 1929: 71–72)

A pulp and paper mill was a large, expensive, permanent establishment. Its operation required large amounts of energy (usually supplied by hydro-electric power), large amounts of fresh water, and large supplies of wood. As a consequence, mills gave rise to permanent communities, but these were often single-enterprise communities located deep in the resource hinterland, and away from settled areas. Hence, while the industrial proletariat working in pulp and paper mills lived in settled communities made up to some extent of families, these communities were very sensitive to the economic ups and downs of a single resource industry. The workers who lived in these communities, though not as isolated from major institutions of the society as stereotypes often imply, were certainly not as closely connected to central institutional processes of the society as were those who worked in the local saw-milling industry of southern Ontario.

The joint-stock corporation was the form of business organization within which most pulp and paper manufacturing was organized. Mills were very costly, and many were established during the period when the joint-stock corporation was becoming the common form of organizing enterprises. The rapid expansion of productive capacity in the 1920s, followed by the reduction of demand in the 1930s, led to many mergers and produced even greater consolidation of control by a few large corporations (Nelles, 1974: 43–64).

The prominence of the joint-stock corporation had consequences for occupational patterns. A corporation typically operates with a hierarchical structure of authority, a staff for record keeping, and specialized personnel engaged in such tasks as corporate planning and product development. The white-collar employees so characteristic of the mid-twentieth-century —

clerks, middle- and lower-level managers, and technical specialists — are found in the large corporations. The pulp and paper industry added to the occupations of the forest industry that set of occupations necessary to the operation of large corporations. (While many of these occupations are "middle class" in everyday language, they are more adequately understood as proletarian in the nature of their relationship to employers.)

The capitalists most centrally associated with the pulp and paper industry were, and are, the directors and chief executive officers of the corporations which owned pulp and paper companies. Their occupational tasks, narrowly defined, were the management of corporations. They were, like the saw-mill owners, industrial capitalists whose concrete objective was to bring together capital, resources and labour for the purpose of creating products to be sold for a profit. The significance of this group, in comparison to the entrepreneurs of the square timber trade and early industrial saw-milling, is that they were operating in the framework of modern corporate capitalism. They used the structure of the modern corporation to bring together massive resources, only a portion of which they directly owned, and to control these resources for ends they thought appropriate.

In review, the pulp and paper industry introduced new and more complex technology, and was developed in the organizational form of the modern corporation. These changes created new types of working conditions for the industrial proletariat, resulted in more "middle-class" occupations, and gave rise to the modern type of corporate capitalist. The forest proletariat continued their role of getting trees from forest to mill.

CONCLUSION

Like so many things made by Canadian industries, this paper is only a partially finished product. Many of the sweeping generalizations advanced would better be regarded as hypotheses to be explored through more systematic analysis of quantitative data about occupations and more specific applications in actual work contexts. It is hoped, however, that the perspective suggested will be fruitful in further study.

The general premise of the paper is that the staples approach to Canadian society can make an important contribution to understanding more specific aspects of Canadian social structure. To clarify this premise, the history of forest industries in central Canada has been examined in broad terms. Each phase of forest exploitation — square timber trade, early local saw-milling, industrial saw-milling, and the pulp and paper industry — gave rise to a particular set of occupations and had consequences for the contexts in which the people who filled those occupations worked and lived.

The square timber trade was characterized by commercial capitalists; capitalists organizing the extraction of a primary resource, and a forest proletariat. The most important of those engaged in local saw-milling were small-scale capitalists (farmers and local mill operators), for whom lumber production was but one phase of diversified operations. Industrial saw-milling brought mechanization to the timber industry. It had a continuing place for the forest proletariat, but also gave rise to an industrial proletariat and a group of industrial capitalists. The pulp and paper industry was dominated by industrial capitalists, but they more systematically used the joint-stock corporation as a means of control than had those engaged in saw-milling. A forest proletariat continued to harvest trees. An industrial proletariat worked in the mills but, because of the sophisticated technology, their work was dominated by the nature of the machine processes employed. The daily requirements for running the large corporate structures produced a corps of white-collar workers, many of whom had a proletarian relationship to employers. To state the major point briefly, changes in the technological processes by which the Canadian forest industries were exploited brought about changes in the occupations and class positions of workers associated with this particular staple product.

REFERENCES

Bowles, Roy T.
1980   "Deloro and the World: The Local Manifestation of the Ontario Mineral Industry." Paper presented at the annual meetings of the Canadian Historical Association.

Bowles, Roy T. and Prudence Craib
1979   "Canada: Economy, Opportunity and Class," in John Allan Fry (ed.) *Canada: Economy and Social Reality*. Toronto: Butterworths, 51–77.

Burley, K.H.
1972   *The Development of Canada's Staples*. Toronto: McClelland and Stewart.

Calvin, D.D.
1945   *A Saga of the St. Lawrence: Timber Shipping Through the Generations*. Toronto: Ryerson Press.

Canadian Pulp and Paper Association
1954   *The Pulpwood Harvest*. Montreal.

Canadian Pulp and Paper Association
1955   *From Watershed to Watermark: The Pulp and Paper Industry of Canada*. Montreal.

Careless, J.M.S.
1967   *The Union of the Canadas*. Toronto: McClelland and Stewart.

Cross, Michael S.
1960   "The Lumber Community of Upper Canada, 1815–1867," in *Ontario History* 52: 213–33.

Easterbrook, W.T. and Hugh G.J. Aitken.
1956   *Canadian Economic History*. Toronto: Macmillan.

Easterbrook, W.T. and M.H. Watkins (eds.)
1971   *Approaches to Canadian Economic History*. Toronto: McClelland and
1967   Stewart.

Edwards, Nina
1947   "The Establishment of Papermaking in Upper Canada," in *Ontario History* 39: 63–75.

Fraser, Joshua
1883   *Shanty, Forest and River: Life in the Backwoods of Canada*. Montreal.

Gillis, Peter
1974 "The Ottawa Lumber Barons and the Conservation Movement," in *Journal of Canadian Studies* 9: 14–30.

Greening, W.E.
1970 "The Lumber Industry in the Ottawa Valley and the American Market in the Nineteenth Century," in *Ontario History* 62 (March): 134–36.
1965 Paper Makers in Canada. Cornwall, Ont.: International Brotherhood of Papermakers.

Guthrie, John A.
1941 *The Newsprint Paper Industry: An Economic Analysis*. Cambridge: Harvard University Press.

Head, C. Grant
1975 "An Introduction to Forest Exploitation in Nineteenth Century Ontario," in J. David Wood (ed.) *Perspectives on Landscape and Settlement in Nineteenth Century Ontario*. Toronto: McClelland and Stewart, 73–112.

Hughson, John W. and C.J. Bond Courtney
1965 *Hurling Down the Pine*, 2nd ed. Old Chelsea, Que.: The Historical Society of the Gatineau.

Innis, Harold A.
1973 *The Fur Trade in Canada*. Toronto: University of Toronto Press.

Lower, A.R.M.
1971 "The Trade in Square Timber," in W.T. Easterbrook and M.H. Watkins (eds.) *Approaches to Canadian Economic History*. Toronto: McClelland and Stewart, 28–73.
1936 *Settlement and the Forest Frontier in Eastern Canada*. Toronto: Macmillan.
1968 *The North American Assault on the Canadian Forest*. New York: Greenwood Press.
1973 *Great Britain's Woodyard*. Toronto: McGill–Queen's University Press.

MacKay, Donald
1978 *The Lumberjacks*. Toronto: McGraw-Hill Ryerson.

Nelles, H.V.
1974 *The Politics of Development*. Toronto: Macmillan.

Watkins, M.H.
1967 "A Staple Theory of Economic Growth," in W.T. Easterbrook and M.H. Watkins (eds.) *Approaches to Canadian Economic History*. Toronto: McClelland and Stewart.

Shipley, J.W.
1929 *Pulp and Paper-Making in Canada*. Toronto: Longmans, Green and Co.

Weigman, Carl
1953 *Trees to News*. Toronto: McClelland and Stewart.

Chapter 11

The Subordination of Labour in Canadian Mining*

Wallace Clement

The past century has witnessed two fundamental changes in Canadian mining's class relations. Around the turn of the century there was the transformation from petty commodity to capitalist relations of production, representing the formal subordination of labour. More recently there has been the real subordination of labour accomplished by transformations within the capitalist mode of production. Both resulted in radical reorganizations of the social relations of production and were carried out with the infusion of large amounts of capital and technology. The first change, from owner-operated mining to capitalist control, was accomplished by capitalist ownership of mining sites. The second change is characterized by mechanization of underground operations and automation of surface plants, reducing the amount of direct labour required and the autonomy of the remaining mine workers, thus increasing the direct control of capital over the labour process.

This paper will analyse the impact of technology on the nature of work in mining, focusing on the implications for the number of workers required and their skill levels. In the analysis of the first change from petty commodity to capitalist production, we will briefly examine mining historically, while in the second change we will concentrate on recent transformations in the underground and surface operations of Inco Limited, Canada's largest mining company.[1]

INTRODUCTION

Property relations involve a series of rights which determine control over various aspects of production.[2] Independent commodity producers control, for example, access to the means of production, their own labour power, the products of their labour, and the way they organize the labour process. With the subordination of petty commodity production by capitalist relations these rights are eroded. A transformation results under capitalist relations, as Guglielmo Carchedi has argued, from the formal subordination of labour to real subordination. Formal subordination of labour means that only the products of labour are appropriated by capital while the prior technological conditions of production remain intact; that is to say, "At first, capital subordinates labour on the basis of the technical conditions in which it historically finds it."[3] Real subordination means the labourer is stripped of control over the products of his labour but also of control over the way his labour power is utilized in the social organization of work. Workers are

*Reprinted with permission from *Labour/Le Travailleur*, 5 (Spring 1980): 133–48.

transformed into "collective labourers" and subjected to a detailed division of labour.[4] This process is accomplished, Marx argued, by the "decomposition of handicrafts, by specialization of the instruments of labour, by the formation of detail labourers, and by grouping and combining the latter into a single mechanism."[5] Thus workers are stripped of the rights of property associated with petty commodity production only partially eroded with the formal subordination of labour and are left with only detailed labour to perform. Capital appropriates all the rights of property and uses technology to subject the labour process to minute units devoid of previously acquired skills.

In Canadian mining the formal subordination of labour occurred very rapidly, cutting short the independent commodity producer's premier place within the industry.[6] Formal subordination was accomplished primarily by capitalists gaining control over access to mining property by having the state transform mining areas from common property available to anyone to private property which the capitalists could appropriate.[7] The real subordination of labour in mining has, however, been a longer process. Control over the labour process within the mines has been accomplished primarily by the introduction of capital-intensive technology and training methods which dramatically reduce workers' autonomy and bring them directly under the control and supervision of capital. While mechanization has been the principal expression of capitalization underground, in surface operations the change has been toward greater automation; that is, interdependent control systems which involve both electronic machines directing other machines to perform pre-determined tasks, thus minimizing workers' intervention, and the centralization of reporting control information. Mechanization and automation have altered the skill levels of mining workers and made possible their loss of control over the production process. In both settings capitalization has decreased the amount of "bull-work" or heavy labour performed but it has also decreased the requirement for craftsmen and tradesmen within the mining industry. The mechanization of mines and automation of surface plants has been an important dimension of management's strategy to contain labour in what has always been a militant fraction of the working class. Additional strategies not to be discussed in detail here have included internalization of mine production centres and diversification of profit centres.

In response to the militancy of Canadian labour, cyclical shortages of labour and threats to its control over the international nickel market, Inco embarked on a multi-pronged strategy to enhance its profitability in the late 1960s. Its program of internationalization meant the development of laterite ores in Indonesia (at a cost of $850 million) and Guatemala ($235 million). Its diversification program included purchases of ESB Limited, the world's largest battery manufacturer ($241 million), as well as investments in a rubber company, a machinery company, an energy company, and an investment company, all designed to reduce its dependence on the metal mines industry (hence on the workers in that industry).

The thrust of this paper, however, is to explore the implications of capitalization for workers within the mining industry as they are expressed in new types of technology and the re-organization of work. The forces of production are related to the relations of production in such a way that capital dominates labour and uses technology and the organization of work to reinforce its control to facilitate capital accumulation. Production is both a technical and social process in which the social dominates the technical. Decisions governing the introduction of technology are determined by profitability (a social imperative for capitalists) and require being able to induce workers to accept them. It will be argued that the relation between the social and technical aspects of production presented here explains the development of class relations within Canadian mining.

PETTY COMMODITY TO CAPITALIST RELATIONS

In Canada the historical moment of petty commodity production in mining was relatively brief. Part of the reason for its rapid demise was the existence elsewhere of capitalist mining which rapidly penetrated this activity in Canada, sometimes directly through branch plants and sometimes mediated by indigenous capitalists expanding their activities. The relationship between capital and technology is at the heart of the transition from petty commodity production and the realization of capital's success was made possible by favourable state policies. It is important to establish the relationship between capital and technology. Large amounts of capital are required to develop and, more importantly, to implement sophisticated technology in large-scale capitalist production. Since only the largest capitalists have access to such large capital pools, either internally generated or from outside financial sources, large capital tends to monopolize the benefits of technological advance. This advance tends at the same time to undercut the relative productivity of earlier forms of production. Further prerequisites to capitalism are control over the factors of production (in this case, mine sites) and the availability of labour unable to seek out its own means of production. Both of these conditions were met by the destruction of petty commodity mining and aided by state policies.

The gold rushes on the west coast between 1863 and 1898 were the heyday of petty commodity production in Canadian mining. Land for mining was readily available and only rudimentary technology was required for production, primarily in the form of "hand-picking." Miners typically worked in pairs. Once they located a pay-streak in a creek bed they would remove gravel along the shore and dig a shaft to the source of the gold-bearing ore. Drifts (parallel shafts underground) would then be made along the vein of ore by using picks and shovels. The ore would then be hoisted to the surface by hand. It was placed into sluice boxes to wash out the gold. Sluicing required access to large quantities of water and provided the first area for capitalist penetration, since capitalists were often able to gain control over water supplies.

The major toe-hold of capitalist penetration occurred, however, through the development of a speculative market in mine stakes and the emergence of a mining exchange to auction claims. This market made it possible for capitalists to concentrate many claims under their ownership. The high cost and scarcity of labour in the area, however, prevented the widespread use of wage labourers. Instead a "lay system" was created. It was a transitional form of production between petty commodity relations and capitalist relations of production. Formal subordination occurred in the sense that capitalists owned the claims but let them out to miners who worked the claims using the same techniques as before. The miners covered all the costs of production while the owner paid the royalties and received half the gross output of the mines, the other half going to the miners. During the height of the gold boom of 1897–98 in the Klondike region, the lay system accounted for three-quarters of all claims.[8]

After the construction of railways into the region, heavy equipment was introduced in the form of mechanical dredges. These dredges allowed capital to eliminate the lay system and create one based on wage labour. As a result of the dredges the cost of moving a cubic foot of gravel was cut in half between 1899 and 1903, thus the premium on labour was reduced. The introduction of mechanical dredges in 1900 meant that three men could perform the labour of 156 men using hand methods. Each dredge cost $300,000 in 1905 thus making possible the monopolization of production by a few large firms.[9]

The removal of ore from alluvial soils along creek beds by placer mining encouraged petty commodity production, but such primitive techniques could not withstand competition with capital-intensive ones. Lode mining, in which ore is removed from hard-rock underground, encouraged capitalist relations from the outset because of the high capital costs involved. Initially lode mines did not use wage labour. Throughout the mining industry — in coal, copper, nickel, zinc, and silver mines — a contract system of employment developed. Miners were paid either by the amount of ore removed (tribute-work) or ground cut (tutwork). In a sense, they sold the products of the mines to the mine owners. Miners worked in pairs or small groups and organized their own production. Coal cutters, for example, were paid by the box of coal and hired their own loaders and checkweightmen. The mine owners furnished the tools, but the miners had to pay for their own blasting powder.[10] Although the contract system common throughout mining gradually gave way to wage labour supplemented by bonus payments for output above a minimum amount of production, the miners continued to retain a good deal of autonomy in their organization of work underground.

These systems combined elements of both petty commodity and capitalist production but the direction of the relations of production was clear. The capitalists owned the mines and their products; the workers worked "for themselves," yet did not own the means of production. Today many remnants of these earlier systems persist in mining. There is still a bonus system distinct from hourly wages, as well as a "loose" supervisory system, and miners still control the organization and pace of their work. Recent developments, to be discussed shortly, are beginning to strip away these remnants and complete the real subordination of labour in mining.

Particular technology is not necessarily capitalist; it becomes so only under certain social relations. A sluice box (used to separate rock from minerals by passing water over ore) is, for example, as easily the equipment of petty commodity producers as the capital of a capitalist. It is reasonable to assume, however, that once the equipment or machinery (such as a mechanical dredge) reaches a certain scale and cost, requiring more than a handful of men to operate and hundreds of thousands of dollars, then it cannot be utilized under petty commodity class relations. It must either become the common property of all those using it, as in co-operative ownership, an unusual development under capitalist dominated social relations, or more probably it will become the property of capitalists who in turn employ the labour power of others to operate it. The experience of capitalism has been that petty commodity relations are unable to sustain the competition of capitalist relations and are thus eliminated, most of the actors becoming absorbed into the proletariat. They then offer only their labour power for sale, rather than the commodities they produce.

Social labour is created when workers are drawn together to produce as a unit, whereas individual labour occurs primarily in craft settings. Technology has the potential to socialize labour but control over that technology by capital distorts this potential by directing it towards particular ends — capital expansion through profitability — and not necessarily towards the benefit of workers or of society. Advanced capitalism socializes the means of production but not the relations of production. The means of production are organized for the purpose of capital expansion.

TRANSFORMATIONS WITHIN CAPITALIST RELATIONS

There has always been a formal subordination of labour in Canada's nickel mines but the real subordination of labour has involved a fairly lengthy process. This section will examine the way capital has penetrated the organization of work in nickel mines and undercut the relative autonomy of miners. These are processes still under way, and by analysing mines and surface operations at different stages of capitalization it is possible to understand the direction of the forces at work.

Until the late 1960s there were few changes in the labour process or the level of technology in Inco's mines. Miners worked in small crews performing an entire cycle of work: drilling, blasting, removing the ore, timbering, etc. There was a minimal amount of supervision: most miners saw a shift boss (or supervisor) only once a shift for a few minutes. Prior to large-scale mechanization the only significant technological innovations were the development of pneumatic drills to replace hand hammering or screw-drills and slushers to replace shovellers to move ore within the work place. Slushers reduced the amount of "bull-work" and were simple mechanical blade-like devices, operated by a member of the mining team, which scraped ore along the stope into an ore pass. Neither the pneumatic drills nor slushers seriously re-organized the social relations of production.

Since 1965 Inco has introduced over 500 pieces of trackless diesel equipment into its Canadian mines.[11] There are now four basic types of mines: traditional hand mines, captured-equipment mines, ramp mines, and open-pit mines. Traditional hand mines continue with essentially the same level of technology and organization of work that has been in place since the turn of the century. Captured-equipment mines have introduced scooptrams (diesel-powered, front-end loaders) into traditional stopes (or work areas). The effect has been to enlarge these work areas somewhat, but the basic organization of production is retained. In captured stopes the scooptrams are disassembled on the surface and taken into the work areas where they are reassembled and maintained. They replace slushers in traditional mines and increase the miner's capacity to move ore. They are integrated into the traditional mining cycle and a scooptram operator (in captured-equipment stopes) is also responsible for other phases of mining together with the driller and stope leader. Ramp mines have revolutionized the organization of work underground. In them, there is a ramp built from the surface so heavy diesel equipment can be driven throughout the mine. Ramp mines are of two types: either blast-hole mines (like Creighton No. 3) where huge slices of ore are blasted at one time after months of long-hole drilling or enlarged stope mines (like Levack West) where different phases of the mining cycle are performed by specialized crews rotating through the giant stopes. In both types the number of work areas in a mine is dramatically reduced and the scale of the work place enlarged. Rather than being responsible for an entire cycle of work, each miner is essentially a machine operator and continuously performs one aspect of the work process (drilling, blasting, removing ore, bolting and screening, or sand-fill). The final type of mine, and the one which has induced much of the mechanization underground, is the open-pit mine. Here heavy diesel equipment is used in a surface mine and each person has a specialized task involving the operation of a particular piece of equipment. The major limitation of open-pit mining is the depth below surface it can practically go before true underground procedures must be used (only about 11 per cent of ore removed from nickel mines in Canada is from open pits).

A sense of the difference between types of mines is provided by a comparison of two mines standing side by side near Sudbury. Levack Mine was opened in 1900 and continues to use traditional mining methods. Employing 1000 workers, the mine's capacity is 5000 tons of ore a day. Levack West, a ramp mine, has been operating since 1974, and the 185 workers are able to produce 3800 tons per day. It has 47 pieces of diesel equipment for only 50 men per shift working underground, and 32 maintenance workers. Repairs are made to the diesel equipment in a huge maintenance bay built right into the rock underground. Each worker at Levack produces an average of 5 tons of ore per day; at Levack West the average is 21 tons per day.

In Inco's Sudbury mines, the cost of labour as a proportion of the overall production cost varies from less than 40 per cent in the most mechanized mines to over 70 per cent in the least mechanized. Increasing mechanization is being introduced into the mines, requiring less labour and less skilled miners to operate the equipment. The output of ore in the metal mining industry as a whole increased by 114 per cent between 1964 and 1973 and its value increased by 158 per cent, while the labour force grew by only 15 per cent. Obviously fewer workers using more equipment can produce more ore than they could using traditional methods.

The major types of trackless mining equipment introduced include diesel ore-moving machines such as scooptrams and load-haul-dumps (or ore carriers). A scooptram can move fifteen times the amount of ore per man shift as a slusher. Multi-boom jumbo drills, in which a driller stands on a platform and uses levers to control three drills are more common, together with another new form of drill, adopted from the petroleum industry, the in-the-hole drill which drills 6½-inch holes two hundred feet in preparation for large-scale blast-hole mining (such as the Creighton No. 3 ramp mine). Compared to conventional drilling, in-the-hole drills reduce the drilling cost per ton from 55 to 24 cents. Raise borers have also been introduced. These machines make eight-foot diameter raises between levels underground; these raises are used for service passages, ore passes and ventilation. Traditionally this task has been performed by the most skilled miners, driving openings between the 200 foot levels. Raise borers drill 6½-inch holes from one level until they break through below and then draw up huge bits 8 feet in diameter to carve out an opening. In 1968 there were only 10 raise borers in the world; by 1975 there were 200 (but only 25 in North America). In 1977 Inco had 14 of these machines and they had drilled 37 *miles* of raises in the Sudbury area alone. Each of the tasks now performed by these types of equipment was once done by skilled miners. Indeed, drilling, slushing, and driving raises were the three most skilled tasks underground. These same activities are now performed by machine operators who can be trained in a few weeks to perform tasks skilled miners took years to perfect.

The more equipment used underground, the more likely a miner will perform only one aspect of the mining cycle, the quicker he can be trained to perform his appointed task, and the greater the scale of the work area. From management's perspective, more mechanization means less reliance on the skills or individual initiative of the miner. Traditionally miners have trained one another in a *de facto* apprenticeship system. As a new miner was introduced into a mining crew he acquired the knowledge of the necessary skills from those he worked alongside. After a period of about two years as a driller working with a stope leader, the miner would move into another work area as a stope leader and train another driller. Both of these miners would be responsible for the entire cycle of work as outlined earlier. With the introduction of mechanized mining, management has appropriated the training process and designed it around each piece of equipment. This training will be discussed shortly.

Supervision in the mines is ambiguous in a number of respects. On the one hand, it has traditionally been very tough. Supervisors have exercised very arbitrary and at times ruthless power over workers in the past. On the other hand, miners have enjoyed a great deal of autonomy and seldom seen their supervisors. They organized and paced their own work. In addition to this basic ambiguity, the nature of supervision has been changing in response to mechanization and to larger work areas. The transformation of the mines from many small production stopes, numbering upwards of 100 in traditional mines, into a few large areas means that supervisors can keep a closer watch over workers and that workers themselves have less discretion in organizing or pacing their own work, since they are confined to the operation of one machine and one task.

Supervisors (or shift bosses as they are called by the miners) are themselves in an ambiguous position in the hierarchy of the mines. They are directly on the firing line between workers and management. In all of the shaft mines they are expected to cover a very large area with many distinct work places — all on foot; in ramp mines supervisors have access to vehicles that can move quickly from one area to another and the workers themselves are concentrated into a few work sites. In the shaft mines the supervisor is pressured by management to insure production but cannot directly oversee the men's work. Moreover, a greater differentiation takes place among the miners themselves as a result of centralized production. Not only do they become specialized in one task, but the stope leader who used to work alongside his driller in a partnership now becomes a stope boss who gives direction to several machine operators rather than performing the tasks himself.

In place of close supervision, mines have traditionally used a system of production "incentives" or a bonus system. During the formative period and through the years, the bonus became an institution integral to mining. It came to be called an "invisible supervisor" by the workers which induced miners to maximize production. This bonus is outside the wage structure negotiated by the union and is controlled by management. In theory the bonus is a simple incentive or inducement to reward miners for producing more ore or doing more development work quickly. In practice it is much more complex. It is a source of pride for many miners since it sets them apart from most workers in other industries and among miners it is a measure of skill and dedication to their trade; it is also a justification for taking the risk of working underground. To the unions it is a source of danger, luring miners to work unsafely and taking jobs away from other miners. To the companies it is a means of social control, the carrot that reduces the amount of supervision needed. In the minds of many, it is "what makes the miners go."

About one-half of all those working underground are on bonus. Underground the miner still commands a great deal of control and the company relies on the miner's ability, not just his hard work. Tradition in the mines has had it that anyone who can affect the rate of production is on bonus. This system is still evident in all underground operations of Inco, but there are important variations as a result of mechanization. The most notable is Levack West, mentioned earlier as a ramp mine, where the entire mine is on a single contract rather than a bonus geared to a crew of miners in a single work area. Other mines have had the bonus system adjusted with mechanization as the rates of production needed to attain bonus have been revised upwards, mainly because the machine operator has less control over the rate of production and is deemed not to require as much inducement simply to keep his machine operating. When the machine sets the pace and supervision is direct, the bonus loses its original "invisible" control purpose.

Given the great distance between work crews and management, the bonus system is used to fill the gap. As tasks are subdivided and the co-ordinating role of management takes on greater importance as a result of mechanization, there is a trend away from this system. Supervisors have greater mobility and workers less control over their rate of production, leading some managers to conclude that the bonus is no longer necessary. The relationship between the bonus and the skill of the traditional miner is very close. There is not simply a correspondence between hard work and more money; technique has a lot to do with whether or not the miner will end up the month with no bonus or 500 dollars. This has at least been true in traditional mining. What is currently in dispute within Inco is whether or not the bonus is anachronistic in mechanized mines; that is, now that the real subordination of labour has been accomplished. Levack West may well be indicating the direction for the future:

the open-pit mines, the most mechanized form of mining, have already abandoned the bonus.

The way technology has been introduced and the interests it serves have been controlled by capital, not by labour. Work has been re-organized *for* the miners, not *by* them. To be sure, it has reduced the amount of "bull-work" within the mines but at the expense of miners' jobs, not to create better ones. With the increase in mechanization it has been possible for management to penetrate — to a greater extent than in the past — the miner's control over the pace of his work and the skills he brings to bear. Management's strategy in introducing technology has been to decrease its reliance on the skills of the miners and to minimize the number and quality of workers needed, thus increasing their control over the work process and maximizing their profits from the benefits of technology. The miners have lost in many ways — in their ability to demand a bonus as a result of their control over the pace of work, in their knowledge of mining practices, in their numbers and, all too often, in their health and safety.[12] Technology is not neutral in the struggle between capital and labour because it has been employed from the outset to meet the needs of capital, not those of labour. It has been used to accomplish the real subordination of labour and to embellish the command of capital. Technological development does, however, offer the potential to humanize the labour process but only if it is adapted in a way most beneficial to those most directly affected — the miners.

Dramatic changes in the organization of work underground are matched by those on the surface in the mills, smelters, and refineries. Surface mining operations have traditionally combined "bull-work" and craft production. They have been labour-intensive even though highly mechanized, since workers perform a great deal of detail labour, much of it directly determining the quality of production. Workers usually control the machinery they work with rather than being controlled by it. With automation, the "bull-work" is eliminated but so is craft production. It is replaced by dial watching and patrol duty. The tasks are no longer those of controlling machinery; instead, workers monitor equipment and make repairs when necessary.

Automation has been introduced into the milling and refinery operations of Inco on a large scale but only certain aspects of the smelting operations have experienced automation.[13] The Copper Cliff Mill, built in 1930, has only one-half the capacity of the Clarabelle Mill, built in 1971 for $80 million, but employs 322 people compared to 235 for the new mill. Mills have always been quite capital intensive with the older mill having an operator to maintenance ratio of 1.3 to 1. The newer automated mill, however, actually has more maintenance workers than operators, with a ratio of 0.8 to 1.

Developments in refining are even more significant than in the mills. The Port Colborne Nickel Refinery, built in 1918 and using a labour-intensive electrolytic process, produced an average of 60,000 pounds of nickel a year per employee while the Copper Cliff Nickel Refinery, built in 1973 for $140 million and using an automated high-pressure carbonyl process, produces six times as much per employee or 360,000 pounds per year. With one-quarter the number of employees, the CCNR produces 50 per cent more nickel than the PCNR. The more labour intensive refinery has an operator to maintenance ratio of 1.8 to 1 compared to the automated plant where the ratio is 0.9 to 1. It should come as no surprise that in 1978 the PCNR was mothballed, aside from a few speciality items, and the CCNR has assumed virtually all the nickel refinery duties for the Ontario division.

Because it experienced mechanization much earlier than underground, surface supervision has always been much more direct. Workers are located in centralized operations. After automation, however, the nature of supervision changes again. With fewer workers, spread over a broader area, there is again a different form of supervision. Management does not need workers to perform constant operations; instead they need people to service equipment, to watch for problems, and to be available for maintenance. Contact is ensured by instrumentation to monitor the equipment and through radio contact with individual workers. Workers no longer have a direct hand in production and have virtually no control over the rate of production. The real subordination of labour reaches its ultimate; capital can directly control production by controlling instrumentation.

Mechanization underground and automation of surface operations have dramatically reduced Inco's labour requirements. Since 1972 the size of union locals at Inco have shrunk from 2800 to 750 at Local 6200 at Port Colborne; from 18,500 to 11,100 at Local 6500 in Sudbury; and from 2910 to 2250 at Local 6166 in Thompson. There has been an overall decline of hourly-paid workers by 42 per cent. Not only has there been a drastic reduction in the number of workers required, there has also been a decline in the quality of labour required by new labour processes. As the full implications of capitalization work themselves through the entire Canadian operations of Inco, it can be anticipated that even fewer and lower skilled workers will be required.

IMPLICATIONS OF MECHANIZATION AND AUTOMATION FOR SKILLS AND TRAINING

Changes in the use of equipment in mining have been accompanied by another form of technology — "people technology" as Inco managers refer to it — a form of training intended to meet the changed skill requirements brought about by greater capitalization and designed to give management even greater control over the labour process. The first major application of the MTS program (modular training) was at the highly-automated Copper Cliff Nickel Refinery in 1972. As a result of operators being required to do maintenance work (at operators' rates), there were over 1000 grievances filed in the first year. Arbitration ruled for an expansion of operators' tasks without an increase in pay. Modular training gives management the tools for pushing operators into more maintenance work, and for an expansion of tasks contained in each job. The tasks themselves are simplified and regularized with the minute division of labour and standardization inherent in modular training. Since March 1977 Inco has pursued a policy of extending modular training across its entire Ontario division, both underground and on the surface.

Modular training means that each operation is broken down into its parts and these parts become interchangeable and can be arranged in a variety of ways. At the same time performance rates and standards allow management to control precisely the performance of workers. Every process and piece of equipment is documented in a systematic way and inventoried. Production is rationalized and each task subdivided into minute parts, whether it is an operating or maintenance task. A training manual is produced for each piece of equipment and is administered largely by self-learning.

The system is not yet entirely in place but according to the MTS report outlining the program for Inco, "many operators will learn (or be asked to learn) to do things that do not fall within their present duties."[14] Maintenance workers will have more manuals than production workers but production workers will be trained on more than one manual. The unit is the equipment, not the person. In a trade there is a common core of skills. Principles and techniques are learned and these are then adapted to the situation. The training is broad. In modular training, however, the situation is determined by specific equipment; training is more immediate and "practical" (from the company's, not the workers' perspective). The result for the workers is a limit on the marketability of their skills with modular training, hence reducing their mobility between companies and industries, unlike the wide applicability of skills learned by tradesmen.

MTS is a reaction to technology and is only applicable to highly-mechanized and automated tasks. It gives management leverage in utilizing and policing the time it takes workers to perform pre-determined and measured tasks. A person can be trained for a number of tasks and these tasks are then codes attached to him. Inco is moving ahead rapidly in the area of "people technology" just as it has in other forms of technology.

While management has been attempting to narrow the jobs its employees perform in the mining industry, workers have been attempting to broaden their skills. This is expressed in a program known as "miner-as-a-trade." The intent is to certify miners as in trades such as plumbers and mechanics that require "tickets" to practice. Miners have been certified in several European countries since 1951 but the first program in North America began in January 1975 in Manitoba. The apprenticeship is over a three-year period and requires eight weeks of school a year with the rest of the time spent working in specified areas. The mining companies were reluctant to become involved but the program was implemented by the New Democratic government because of union pressure. "Grandfather" tickets were issued to about 300 experienced miners with four or more years of mining in 1975 but the program was not made compulsory, denying the essential exclusive quality of traditional apprenticeship practices. Miners in Ontario have not yet been successful in having the program implemented.

"Miner-as-a-trade" in its present form is not going to revolutionize the industry. At present it is a mere drop in the bucket. In 1977 the first graduates completed the course; there were only six of them. There are only about 20 people currently enrolled in the apprenticeship program in Inco's Thompson operation. As long as it is not a prerequisite to being a miner, there is little possibility that "miner-as-a-trade" will counteract the tendencies of fragmented labour inherent in mechanization and MTS as Inco is implementing them.

Contrary to the popular opinion that increased technology leads to greater skill requirements, the overall effects of automation and mechanization in combination with modular training have been the opposite. In part this is attributable to workers having less control over the functioning of machinery but it is also the result of simultaneous changes in the organization of work and the way workers are trained. In a classic study, James Bright of the Harvard School of Business identified this trend in 1958, arguing that "we tend to confuse the maintenance and design problems or exceptional operator jobs with the most common situation: namely that *growing automaticity tends to simplify operator duties.*"[15] Capitalization clearly results in de-skilling within mining if, following Bright, we define skill as a "blending of several things — manual dexterity, knowledge of the art, knowledge of the theory, and comprehension and decision-making ability based upon experience."[16] While there has not been an increase in skill for production work, there has been in designing equipment and, in some cases, maintenance. In Canadian mining most of the equipment design takes place outside the country, thus reducing many of the potential benefits for the skilled component of the Canadian labour force in manufacturing.[17]

Moreover, maintenance work is itself being subjected to modular training practices which threaten the traditional tradesmen who have performed these activities. Elaborate educational systems and apprenticeships have traditionally been developed to transmit their skills, giving these workers considerable power, a power reflected not only in their higher wages but in their leadership position within the working class. Much of the tradesmen's leverage came from their freedom to change employers because of general skill shortages. Recent developments such as MTS, however, threaten to eliminate the company's need for their skills and hence their power. Individuals no longer have traditional training and become tied instead to specific equipment and specific companies. Tradesmen become more expendable as companies develop means to transmit rapidly aspects of their trades to unskilled workers. Increased capitalization will certainly demand a great deal of maintenance work, but these tasks are being performed by workers trained to maintain specific equipment rather than by tradesmen. This will probably lead to a fall in the value of the labour power of maintenance workers and a diminishing of apprenticeships.

For the most part, management has been successful in implementing changes in the techniques of production and training. They serve the twin goals of increasing the ability of capital to accumulate and of management to control the workers. These strategies have been costly; tremendous amounts of money have been invested in capital equipment and training programs. But in the long term management feels these investments will increase their power at the expense of workers. There is every reason to believe they are right, particularly since unions, at least at Inco, have been unsuccessful in resisting these developments.

CONCLUSION

Two aspects of class transformation have briefly been explored in the case of Canadian mining. The first was the transformation from petty commodity to capitalist production. It was argued that the autonomous organization of work, craft skills, and bonus system meant that all the characteristics of this form were not completely destroyed with the formal subordination of labour. These remnants are, however, disappearing with the real subordination of labour. The most obvious change in the property relations of mining occurred with the destruction of the petty commodity form, but there have also been significant changes within capitalism itself. As a result of mechanization, the autonomous organization of work and the bonus system are threatened.

The quality of labour required to operate and maintain a traditional electrolytic refinery differs from that required for an automated carbonyl process refinery. This is not a mere mechanical relationship. On the one side capitalists seek to minimize their variable costs in the form of labour and maximize their fixed costs in capital, thus reducing the amount of labour required. On the other side labour struggles against its own elimination and against changes in the demands made by capitalists. The forces and relations of production are dynamically related, each having implications for the other. The fundamental relation is, however, a social one: capital controls labour in order to maximize profitability and uses the technical division of labour as a means to accomplish this end.

As a consequence of capitalization, management strategies toward workers have changed. Underground there has been a strong tendency to move away from the traditional "responsible autonomy" of mining crews towards greater direct control. On the surface direct control has always been more prevalent but with automation, new strategies have been devised. Automated plants like Clarabelle Mill and the Copper Cliff Nickel Refinery have different labour requirements than do labour-intensive operations. Workers are required more for patrol and maintenance than for detailed labour. As a result, there is at least the appearance and ideology of a "responsible autonomy" strategy on the part of management. In fact, workers and first-line supervisors find that what they are responsible for is accountability, not decision-making. They have virtually no control over the actual work process, this having been programmed into the equipment.

The effect of capitalization is to decrease dramatically the need for both skilled and unskilled labour. They are replaced by "semi-skilled" labour. Both heavy manual labour and craft skill give way to machine tenders and those patrolling equipment programmed to perform pre-designed tasks. This is not an automatic process — labour resists management strategies because many jobs are lost and the strongest faction of the working class, the tradesmen, are directly threatened. The consequence of the overall trend is towards a homogenization of the working class in mining. The net effect may well be a stronger, more unified class in a political and ideological sense since the impact of these processes tends to decrease traditional divisions within the working class between operations and maintenance, labourers and craft workers, and even surface and underground workers.

Class struggle focuses on control over the production process and the distribution of the expanding surplus which technology makes possible. Having broken the power of the craftsmen and eliminated most labourers, capital can afford to increase the wages of the remaining workers and still appropriate the lion's share of the surplus. Struggles for control rather than those for wages are much more threatening to capital. The forces outlined may well open the possibility for broad-based action by workers to appropriate the means of production.

It is not the introduction of technology *per se* or the technical division of labour that have caused the negative effects of technology, but the social relations of production and the way technology is used as a strategy by management to minimize control by workers. As Marx observed for the initial industrial revolution, "It took both time and experience before the workpeople learned to distinguish between machinery and its employment by capital, and to direct their attacks, not against the material instruments of production, but against the mode in which they are used."[18] It is no longer possible (or even desirable) to return to petty commodity production in mining. The forces of production have become "socialized" by giant multinational corporations. The only progressive direction would be to socialize the relations of production; that is, create a system of property relations whereby the means of production become the common property of those working them and providing rights and claims to the consumers of the products. It may first be necessary to nationalize the mines and processing facilities by turning them into a state property, but this would have little bearing on the relations of production. If there are to be equitable and just relations of production and a guarantee of the safest working conditions, it will be necessary for those most directly affected to control the conditions and organization of their work.

NOTES

1. This paper draws upon a thread of argument contained within my larger study, *Hardrock Mining: Industrial Relations and Technological Change at Inco* (Toronto 1980) which documents changes in the technology of mining and the labour process only touched upon here. The purpose of this paper is not to provide a history of mining, or even a survey of the labour process in that industry. Rather, it is to make a specific argument about changes in the labour requirements within the industry as it progresses through various relations of production.

2. For a discussion of this point, see Wallace Clement, "Class and Property Relations: A Preliminary Exploration of the Rights of Property and the Obligations of Labour," a paper presented to the International Structural Analysis Colloquium on "The State and the Economy," University of Toronto, 6–9 December 1979.

3. Karl Marx, *Capital*, I (New York 1967): 310.

4. See Guglielmo Carchedi, "Reproduction of Social Classes at the Level of Production Relations," *Economy and Society*, 4 (1975): 14–16, and his *On the Economic Identification of Social Classes* (London 1977): 53–55.

5. Marx, *Capital*, 1, 364.

6. See Wallace Clement, "Class Transformations in Mining: A Critique of H.A. Innis," in Mel Watkins, ed., *The Legacy of Harold Innis* (Toronto 1980).

7. See Harold A. Innis's documentation of the development of mining exchanges and state regulations providing long-term leases on large mining areas requiring heavy capitalization in the Yukon at the turn of the century in *Settlement and the Mining Frontier* (Toronto 1936): 226–27.

8. Ibid., 207.

9. Ibid., 223–224.

10. Greg Kealey, ed., *Canada Investigates Industrialism* (Toronto 1973): 404–442.
11. All information in this section on Inco's operations comes from the management of its surface operations and mines, union officials, mining workers, or trade journals. For a thorough overview, see Clement, *Hardrock Mining*.
12. For an analysis of the relationship between health and safety and mechanization, see Clement, *Hardrock Mining*, ch. 7.
13. In the Sudbury operations of Inco the milling operations on one side of the Copper Cliff Smelter and the refining operations on the other have been automated. Between these automated operations stands the labour-intensive smelter with 1650 hourly workers and 200 staff. It is without doubt destined for automation, likely requiring the construction of an entirely new building. It is interesting to note that this smelter is the base for the 1250-foot "super-stack" which daily disperses 3600 tons of sulphur dioxide into the atmosphere. A great public outcry over this pollution has occurred and the Ontario government has rescinded its order to cut emissions, effectively licensing the company to continue polluting at its present level until 1982. One must wonder whether Inco is fostering the outcry to strengthen its case with the state for subsidies to build a new plant, legitimized by sulphur dioxide reductions but having the effect of reducing the demand for labour.
14. Management Training Systems, *Inco Consolidated Report*, Ontario Division (April 1976): 10.
15. James Bright, *Automation and Management* (Boston 1958): 183, emphasis in original.
16. Ibid., 187.
17. See John N.H. Britton and James M. Gilmour, *The Weakest Link: A Technological Perspective on Canadian Industrial Underdevelopment*. Science Council of Canada Background Study, No. 43 (Ottawa 1978): 94.
18. Marx, *Capital*, I, 429.

Chapter 12

The Occupational Structure of Earnings in Canada, 1931 to 1971*

David Stager
Noah M. Meltz

INTRODUCTION

The long-run changes in relative earnings among occupations in Canada are of interest for several reasons. First, one often encounters the notion that a constant relationship exists among occupational earnings in the long run; and that fairness requires this relationship to be maintained. This view seemed to underly the provision in Canada's Anti-Inflation Program of 1975–1978 for maintaining "historical relationships" among occupational earnings. It is also found in arguments used in collective bargaining by groups such as teachers, police, and firemen. Second, comparable historical data on occupational earnings are required to study supply responses to changes in relative wages, especially for professions with long training programs. Manpower planning studies, for example, often ignore the effects that changes in relative earnings will have on the supply side of labour markets. A third reason is to emphasize the occupation variable in analyses based on human capital theory. Occupation was used in earlier periods as a proxy for education when data on earnings by education were not available. More recently, education sometimes is treated as a proxy for occupation and this latter variable is omitted. Moreover, studies on historical wage relationships should show the extent to which cross-sectional earnings differentials can be used to estimate expected longitudinal differentials required in rate of return calculations. Occupation also is central to studies of economic rents due to licensing through craft unions, apprenticed trades, and protected professions.

Several studies have examined occupational wage or earnings structures observed at specific times but few studies have focused on changes in the structure over time. Furthermore, most historical studies have been based on average hourly earnings in the United States, have usually covered a period prior to 1960, and have tended to deal only with the skilled/unskilled wage differential.

Terms such as wage structure, relative earnings, wage differentials, are used in studies of labour income. The central term in this article is "relative earnings" which is defined as the average annual earnings of workers in a specific occupation as a percentage of the average annual earnings for the total

---

*This article is based on a study undertaken for the Anti-Inflation Board, Canada, in 1976–77. The authors are indebted to the Board for permission to use material from their final report, *The Occupational Structure of Earnings in Canada, 1931–1975*. The views expressed here, however, are not necessarily those of the Board.

wage and salary earners in the labour force. One can therefore speak of a decline in the relative earnings of a specific occupation even though the absolute earnings of all occupations have increased.

The findings of earlier studies on occupational wage structures were generally similar for the United States, Canada, and the United Kingdom; namely a long-run narrowing of the relative wage differential between skilled and unskilled occupations.[1] This appears to have occurred in most industrial countries since 1900, with most of the narrowing occurring in the years 1915 to 1920 and 1940 to 1950. The narrowing of the earnings structure in the United States during 1900–1920 was followed by widening in 1920–1932, with little change occurring in the depression of the 1930s. There was a pronounced narrowing during the 1940s, particularly during World War II, with a return to stability in the 1950s and 1960s. There is some evidence, however, of widening toward the end of the 1960s. This detailed pattern is generally the same for Canada and the United Kingdom, with two exceptions: there is some evidence of stability in the 1920s (rather than widening) and of widening in the 1950s and 1960s. In short, the pattern of behaviour in the occupational relative earnings structure appears to be one of long-run narrowing with shorter-run cyclical movements: these consist of narrowing during the world wars and widening in the prosperity of the 1920s and 1960s.

This paper differs from previous studies in that it examines relative earnings for a large number of specific occupations over a rather long period. The next section of the paper discusses the problems encountered in obtaining suitable earnings data for such comparisons. Then the major patterns in the behaviour of relative earnings are presented, followed by a discussion of changes in main determinants of occupational differences in relative earnings.

A lack of comparable earnings data has been a serious limitation on historical studies of relative earnings by occupation. The only comprehensive Canadian source of earnings data for detailed occupations has been the decennial population census but each census since 1931 has employed a new occupational classification system.[2] The problem of comparability is particularly serious between the 1971 and 1961 censuses: of the 486 occupation classes in the 1971 census, only nine classes are precisely comparable with the 1961 classes.[3] A major task of this study was to identify other occupations in earlier censuses for which the 1971 census data would be at least closely comparable. For the period 1931 to 1961 there were over 100 occupations which Meltz in his 1969 study determined to be comparable among censuses. One then needed to identify which of these had remained comparable with the 1971 classes, and which of the 1971 classes could be considered comparable at least with the 1961 classes. A total of 52 occupations were identified which were comparable between 1961 and 1971; of these only 23 were comparable across the complete period of 1931 to 1971. These occupations were concentrated in professional and protective services.

Earnings data more closely approximate the total compensation of workers than do wage data, but no available measures of labour compensation include estimates of fringe benefits by occupation. This is a serious deficiency because the existence of large inter-industry differences in fringe benefits suggests that similar differences probably exist among occupations. Wage and

Figure 12–1

Relative Earnings in the Selected Occupations Compared Decade by Decade

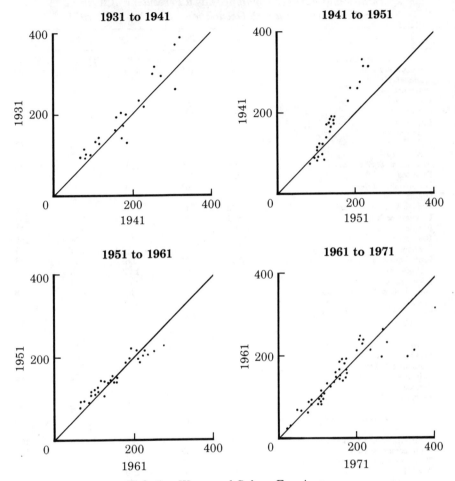

Relative Wage and Salary Earnings

Source: *Canadian Journal of Economics* XII, 2 (May 1979): 312–15.

salary earnings are used because earnings from self-employment were not collected until 1961.

OBSERVATIONS

Consider first the general pattern of change in relative earnings by single decades. Figure 12–1 shows these inter-decade changes in terms of scatter diagrams. Each point on a diagram represents an occupation from the list in Table 12–1. For example, the uppermost point in the 1931 to 1941 diagram is for lawyers: their relative earnings were 379 in 1931 and 321 in 1941. Just

Table 12-1

Average Annual Wage and Salary Earnings in Selected Occupations
(Males and Females Combined) as a Percentage of Average
Annual Earnings for all Occupations, Canada, 1931–1971

	1931	1941	1951	1961	1971
All Occupations[1] (Actual)	$847	$867	$1,860	$3,170	$5,337
(Percent of Total)	100	100	100	100	100
Managerial					
Postmasters				80	97
Professional					
Architects	306	256	197	209	230
Engineers					
Chemical			211	240	202
Civil			202	224	211
Electrical	288	273	205	231	207
Physicians & Surgeons	365	310	215	207	338
Dentists	226	219	220	191	324
Nurses, graduate	108	81	93	88	92
Optometrists				189	258
Judges & Magistrates[2]	662	618		317	392
Lawyers & Notaries	379	321	211	228	264
Physicists				232	211
Biologists				178	155
Economists				208	197
Professors & Teachers	132	117	106	133	138
Professors	292	251	186	215	
Teachers	126	111	101	127	
Dieticians & Nutritionists				96	108
Clerical					
Secretaries, Stenographers & Typists	99	84	89	81	71
Commercial & Financial					
Newsboys				16	17
Service Station Attendants			88	65	45
Insurance Salesmen & Agents				162	151
Salesmen, securities				182	169
Service					
Personal					
Bartenders				82	74
Barbers & Hairdressers	90	70	77	64	56
Protective & Other					
Fire-fighting Occupations	195	184	140	140	167
Policemen & Detectives	184	159	134	136	163
Transportation & Communication					
Air Pilots, Navigators & Flight Engineers	255	307	228	264	262
Locomotive Engineers & Firemen	214	223	179	175	166
Deck Officers, ship				164	174
Engineering Officers, ship				142	156
Engine & Boiler-Room Crew, ship				97	102
Bus Drivers		136	127	111	104
Taxi Drivers & Chauffeurs		84	90	77	76
Subway & Street Railway Operators	156	155	138	145	155
Telegraph Operators	172	174	140	125	127
Mail Carriers	132	115	112	103	103
Fishing, Hunting, Trapping					
Fishermen				48	62
Manufacturing & Mechanical					
Flour & Grain Milling	124	108	104	93	101
Fish canning, curing & packing				35	33
Metal Rolling	126	186	148	153	145
Tool & Die Making	131	171	150	141	151

Table 12-1 — Continued

*Average Annual Wage and Salary Earnings in Selected Occupations
(Males and Females Combined) as a Percentage of Average
Annual Earnings for all Occupations, Canada, 1931–1971*

	1931	1941	1951	1961	1971
Motor Vehicle Mechanics & Repairmen			113	103	109
Radio & T.V. Service Repairmen				106	106
Typesetters & Compositors			132	129	121
Power Station Operators		175	142	152	172
Motion Picture Projectionists	194	170	140	119	121
Construction					
Brick & Stone Masons & Concrete Finishing	95	91	113	94	111
Plasterers	89	80	116	98	112
Inspecting, Testing, etc., Construction, except Electrical		171	137	133	133

[1]Excludes Armed Forces
[2]Median earnings cannot be calculated for 1951
Sources: Noah M. Meltz, *Manpower in Canada, 1931–1961*, 246–249.
        1971 Census of Canada, Volume III, Part 6, No. 94–765, Table 15.

below the lawyers' dot is the one for physicians since their relative earnings were 365 in 1931 and 310 in 1941. Points lying above the diagonal line represent occupations which experienced a decline in relative earnings over the decade. Most occupations had a decline in relative earnings in 1931–41 and again in 1941–51. The diagram for this latter decade illustrates a pronounced narrowing of relative earnings: occupations with lower earnings increased their relative earnings while those with higher earnings experienced substantial decreases in relative terms. In the 1951–61 decade there was a slight widening in relative earnings. This seems to have continued into the 1961–71 decade, with an increase in relative earnings for the majority of occupations and particularly larger increases in the higher-earnings occupations.

The most striking feature in the behaviour of relative earnings for specific occupations is that there are three distinct patterns for the 1931–1971 period. These are presented in Figure 12–2. The first pattern is a U-shape. A decline in relative earnings during 1931–41 and 1941–51 was followed by increases during 1951–61 and 1961–71. This group of occupations includes several professions (architects, lawyers, judges and magistrates, professors and teachers, and physicians)[4] and some occupations which are largely in municipal service (firemen, policemen, and operators of subways and street railways).

A second prominent pattern is a long-run decline in relative earnings, with a decline in at least three of the four decades. The occupations in this group are not so easily categorized: these are the lower-wage, semi-skilled (barbers and typists), several in transportation and communication (bus

drivers, taxi drivers, mail carriers, and locomotive engineers), and others —
flour milling, movie projectionists, and electrical engineers. Finally, there was
a third pattern where relative earnings changed direction each decade. These
included airline pilots, metal rolling, some construction trades (plasterers,
masons) and some health professions (dentists and nurses).

Notwithstanding this diversity of changes in occupational wage relationships, there do appear to be some cases of long-run consistency in relative
earnings. Pairs of occupations such as firemen and policemen, plasterers and
masons, and bus drivers and locomotive engineers, (which in each case are
within the same broad industry group) have experienced similar changes in
their relative earnings. Short-run variations have also occurred, however,
even among pairs of similar occupations such as these.

ANALYSIS OF THE DATA

Regression analysis was used to examine specific factors underlying the
patterns of change in relative earnings. Due to the small number of
observations, separate calculations could not be made for each occupation.
Instead, the data for all occupations were combined and examined for the
effects of four variables which are commonly associated with occupational
earning differentials: age, education, industry and region. Since these
occupations are not a representative sample of the total labour force the results
cannot be generalized to apply to the entire labour force.

Age is included as a proxy for years of working experience. The mean ages
for each occupation and for the total labour force were computed from the
five-year age classes in the census. Education represents the acquisition of
human capital which is expected to increase earnings. The mean number of
years of schooling completed was also calculated from schooling categories but
these do not include information on various post-secondary educational or
training programs. This measure also obviously omits variation in quality of
education. Because earnings data by schooling level are not available in the
1931 census, the regression analysis covers only the period since 1941.

Since earnings in an occupation vary by industry, a change in the
industrial distribution of an occupation could affect relative earnings. The
industry variable used is the percentage of the occupation's labour force which
was in government service[5] because it is sometimes suggested that government's own wage and salary levels are a major influence in the general
wage structure, both through market forces and through comparisons cited in
collective bargaining.

Earnings also vary by region or province. Since Ontario is the province
with the largest labour force, the regional variable was defined as the
percentage of each occupation's labour force which was in Ontario.

Long-term changes in relative earnings were examined first by considering what happened in each census year on a cross-section basis and then
whether major changes had taken place in these cross-section results. Separate
equations were estimated for males and for females in each of the four census
years using data for 28 occupations for males and 15 occupations for females.[6]

In all years and for both males and females education was a highly

Figure 12–2

Patterns of Change in Relative Wage and Salary Earnings in Selected Occupations, 1931 to 1971

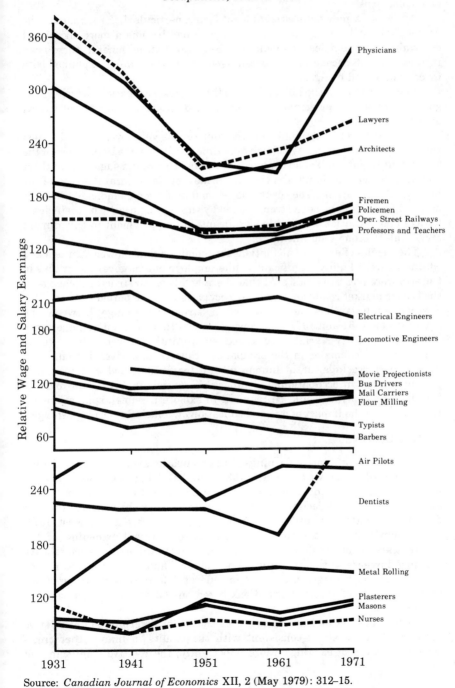

significant factor. The effect was stronger for females, perhaps due to the concentration of women in professional and clerical occupations where education is a more important determinant of relative earnings than in blue-collar jobs.

Age was a somewhat less significant factor, particularly for females in the decade 1951 to 1961. By 1971, however, age had become a more significant determinant for females. It should also be noted that, in general, there is an increase in each decade in the percentage of relative earnings explained both by education and by age.

The proportion of the labour force in the selected occupations which was in government service or employed in Ontario did not have a significant impact on relative earnings.

The initial set of estimates for the four census years were pooled to test whether there had been any change over time in the relative importance of the significant variables. If such changes were found this would suggest that there had been structural changes in the labour markets for several if not all of the individual occupations. The results based on data for males indicated that the original findings have been strengthened by this aggregation. The coefficients for age and education are highly significant, but employment in government service also becomes significant.

The results of similar calculations for females again showed that age and education were highly significant, while employment in government and in Ontario were not. This indicated that there had been no structural change in the labour market conditions for these occupations in the period 1941 to 1961. Further analysis, however, indicated a structural change between the equations for 1961 and 1971. The conclusion was that the relative importance of the explanatory variables changed significantly between those years, namely that for females in the occupations concerned, a given increment in work experience (age) or in human capital (education) had a significantly greater impact on occupational earnings differentials in 1971 than in 1961. Still further analysis would be required to explore possible explanations for this change in the impact of age and education on females' relative earnings.

CONCLUSIONS

Differences among relative earnings of the occupations included in this study have generally narrowed between 1931 and 1971, but there were diverse patterns within this general picture. While some occupations have experienced an almost continuous decline in relative earnings, others have moved through a U-shaped pattern of decline to 1951 and an increase to at least 1971. Consequently it appears that there has been a recent widening of the differentials — at least for the occupations included here — as relative earnings increase in the higher-wage occupations and fall in the lower-wage occupations. Such long-run changes in differentials raise some reservations concerning rate of return calculations based on the assumption of constant differentials.

That education and age emerged as the major determinants of relative earnings differentials is consistent with the results in many other cross-sectional studies of earnings. More importantly, the relative significance of education and age showed very little change for males across four decades despite major changes in the general and relative levels of education in the labour force. Conversely, the effect of age (as a proxy for experience) on relative earnings for females did vary across the decades.

The data presented in this paper have implications for policy concerning wage and price controls. If a version of these were to be re-introduced in Canada, our findings suggest that it would be a mistake to adjudicate wage changes under such a program by reference only to past earnings relationships among occupations. While some imperfections in labour markets may require a policy of intervention, normal market forces are clearly operating and must be considered when such policies are formulated. Occupational labour markets need to be examined separately, with particular attention paid to institutional and technological changes occurring in each occupation. Such changes include a long list of factors influencing labour market behaviour: unionization and professional licensing, immigration and emigration, changes in an economy's industrial structure, legislation on labour conditions, and innovations in production methods and products.

NOTES

1. The studies reviewed here are listed in the bibliography of the authors' A.I.B. report.
2. Some earnings data by occupations are available from as early as the first decennial census but the first systematic occupational classification was introduced in 1931. Occupational titles are the most detailed category in occupational classification systems. Titles are combined to form classes which in turn are combined to form groups. For example, in the current classification, 44 titles (such as city solicitor, patent attorney, and lawyer) are combined to form the occupational class, Lawyers and Notaries (code 2343). Then there are 3 such classes combined to form the minor group, Occupations in law and jurisprudence (code 234); 5 minor groups combine to form the major group, Occupations in social sciences and related fields (code 23); 25 such major groups constitute the total labour force.
3. The nine occupations are: postmasters, dentists, nurses-in-training, optometrists, service station attendants, commissioned officers, other ranks-armed forces, bartenders, bus drivers.
4. Physicians showed a slight variation from this pattern, with a small decline during 1951–61. This was followed by an unusually large increase in 1961–71 which emphasized the U-shape.
5. The industrial class is "public administration"; this includes the three levels of government but excludes the public sector industries such as schools and hospitals which are classed as community services.
6. The equations and coefficients estimated for this section are fully reported in the authors' published report to the Anti-Inflation Board but have been omitted from this article in order to reach a wider range of readers.

REFERENCES

Meltz, Noah M.
1965 *Changes in the Occupational Composition of the Canadian Labour Force, 1931–1961*. Ottawa: Queen's Printer.

1969   *Manpower in Canada, 1931–1961*. Ottawa: Queen's Printer.
Meltz, Noah M. and David Stager
1979   *The Occupational Structure of Earnings in Canada, 1931 to 1975.*
Ottawa: Anti-Inflation Board.

Chapter 13

The Clergy's Decline: A Historical Perspective on the Declining Power of Anglican and United Church Clergy

Juanne Nancarrow Clarke

SECULARIZATION

One bellwether of religion in modern life is the role of the clergy. In a society which is dominated by supernatural explanations of everyday events, it is likely that the clergy, the major conveyors of this perspective, will have considerable sway. In contrast, a society dominated by an acquiescence to empirical definitions of reality is probably more significantly influenced by scientists. Our society, it is almost a cliché to say, is a secular society. God is believed dead. Classic sociologists foretold that this would be the result of a secularizing process begun a century ago. Moreover, the envisioned trend was one of the primary concerns of the most eminent of these first sociologists, Durkheim, Weber, Simmel, and Marx (Nisbet, 1966). Weber viewed it as an increase in rationalization, while Durkheim stated that it was an aspect of a move away from what he called mechanical to organic solidarity in society. Simmel saw it as a diminution in piety and Marx as an aspect of the change from a capitalist to a communist economic system.

Just as there were differences in the understanding of secularization held by the classical theoreticians of society, so too, are there differences in the meanings of the concept among contemporary sociologists. Moreover the contemporary analyses are not solely theoretical. They also involve empirical examination of secularization in modern society. The term secular derives from the Latin *saeculum* which means "a generation or an age." By the time of the Vulgate the term had already been redefined in practice to refer to either an enormous length of time or to an irreligious world, a world controlled by the devil. Today, according to Shiner, there are six competing meanings in sociological literature given to the term secularization: (1) the decline of religion; (2) conformity with this world; (3) disengagement of society from religion; (4) transposition of religious beliefs and institutions; (5) desacralization of the world; and (6) a movement from a "sacred" to a "secular" society (1967).

The decline of religion refers to the process whereby accepted religious symbols, doctrines and institutions lose their prestige and influence. Secularization of this sort would culminate in a society without religion. Increased conformity with the world occurs when the religiously informed society turns its attention from the supernatural and becomes increasingly involved in this world. The disengagement of society from religion is the result of the movement of a society separating itself from the religious understanding which has previously informed it. Religion becomes confined to private life alone. The transposition of religious beliefs and institutions attributes secularization to the transformation of knowledge, and institutional arrangements into phenomena of purely human creation. The desacralization of the world implies that secularization is evident in the increased reliance on reason and causality as explanations of human actions. The movement from a "sacred" to a "secular" society is the trend toward a society in which all calculations are based on rational and pragmatic considerations.

This work examines one aspect of the trend described above. It is concerned with the estimation of whether religious institutions through their chief functionaries have lost power in society over time. It is the first definition of secularization which is the most appropriate for this paper, because it is the loss of the influence of clergy which is under examination. If we define secularization as the decline in prestige of accepted symbols of doctrines and institutions, then the role played by the occupation which is chiefly responsible for the religious interpretation and the promulgation of the symbols and doctrines, and the perpetuation of the institutions, is of great significance. Thus, a fruitful way to analyse secularization empirically is as a function of the relative influence of the clergy over a period of time.

OPERATIONALIZATION OF SECULARIZATION

Johnson proposed an explanation for the power of a profession (1972). It lies, he argued, in the occupation's ability to define the needs of its clients. The capacity to impose its own viewpoint, the necessity of its services, is at the heart of professional power. In a modern, industrialized society characterized by a complex division of labour, members of different occupational groups may be socially distant from, and may not understand the work of one another. In Johnson's estimation, there are three major criteria which determine the puissance of the occupation: esoteric knowledge, social power or prestige, and the heterogeneity of the consumer and homogeneity of the professional group.

To the extent that the client is unable to understand the knowledge held by the specialist, that it is not available to him, and that the client has a need for such knowledge, it can be considered esoteric. Similarly, the greater the social distance between the client and the occupational group in terms of status, and the less the client is able to partake of the prestige of the occupational group, the more power will be in the hands of the occupational group. Finally, the more homogeneous the professional group as compared with the heterogeneity of the consumer group, the more likely is the occupational group able to hold the power of social control. "Where the consumers are a large and heterogeneous group, any attempt by the occupation to extend technically-based authority to a broad social control of practice is likely to be more successful than in contexts where there is a single client or small group of powerful clients" (1972: 51).

DATA USED

It is our intention in this paper to evaluate the existence of secularization through an examination of the power of clerical occupations over approximately one century in Ontario and, in some instances, in Canada. Ontario has been chosen because it is the most industrialized and modernized of the provinces in Canada, and is thus often considered to be in the forefront with regard to social change. When data are available for the whole of Canada but not for Ontario alone, the Canadian data have been included. Certain caution in interpretation is warranted because, as is often the case with historical data, they are at times incomplete. But the purpose of the work is not to test hypotheses, or to search for universal causal laws, but, in an exploratory fashion, using one model, to examine a trend over time. Moreover, historical sociology, while not predominant in the field, does have a long and venerable tradition in the discipline. Indeed, all of the classic scholars, mentioned earlier, were engaged in historical research. In addition, any attempt to estimate or describe social change must have recourse to data for a period of time (Zaret, 1978).

Information regarding historical trends in esoteric knowledge, in social power and in heterogeneity and homogeneity, will be drawn from several sources. Movements in esoteric knowledge will be examined through an investigation of the curricula and the entrance requirements of representative schools of theology along with the changing demands for qualification for practice as a cleric; social power — prestige — is distinguished from power in an eloquent manner by Kemper (1974), and deserves mention here. "Since, for the most part, those who hold power find it costly to exercise, it is convenient to transform the power into status, so that the rewards, benefits and compliance are given voluntarily" (1974: 852). Thus social power can be seen as the prestige and other benefits of position that voluntarily adhere to the position. An evaluation of the status of religious functionaries over time will involve an examination of (1) the decrease of membership in the elite of personnel from this occupational group as reflected in *Who's Who in Canada* and in other Canadian biographies of the elite; (2) the social class backgrounds of those who have entered and continue to enter into the field; and (3) the relative prestige and income of members of the group.

The final variable to be examined is the extent of heterogeneity or homogeneity among members of the clergy and among their clients or parishioners. Legislation regarding the powers of various kinds of religious functionaries will be used to estimate the extent of their heterogeneity and homogeneity. Census materials and legislation regarding numbers of alternative religious client groups will be examined.

ESOTERIC KNOWLEDGE

To evaluate whether or not the knowledge held by the clergy is less esoteric at the present time than it was in the past, we systematically read and coded calendars, one from every decade, from the schools of theology which train the clergy in the two largest Protestant denominations in Ontario, the Anglican Church College, Trinity, and the United Church College, Emmanuel. The third denomination with a major proportion of the population of Ontario is the Roman Catholic Church. Information regarding the training of the Roman Catholic priest was not included because each order of the priesthood trains its priests individually. Since there are a number of orders in Ontario, a general statement of Roman Catholic trends would not have been possible. Telephone conversations and written correspondence with representatives of all three denominations provide additional information.

(a) Entrance Requirements

At the beginning of the century, students who wished to study theology at Emmanuel College, the United Church college, had to be candidates for the ministry. This sort of exclusivity does not exist today. At the turn of the century the calendar for Emmanuel College (then called Victoria University) included the following statement asking for the guarantee of religious commitment from students: "All applicants must be graduates in Arts and of *at least two years standing in some branch of the Christian Church*" (*Victoria University Calendar*, 1900–1901). In 1975–1976, the College Calendar suggested a much less stringent criterion as an entrance requirement. Emmanuel "offers candidates for the ministry a course that fulfills the academic requirements for ordination within the United Church of Canada and welcomes students, *regardless of affiliation or belief* who are interested in theology as a field of study" (*Emmanuel College Calendar*, 1975–76: 3) (emphasis mine). A similar trend is evident at Trinity College, the college which trains clergy for the Anglican Church. But, in the 1960–1962 Calendar, no mention is made of the religious intention or of the religious affiliation of those who wished to study at Trinity. In fact, in the statement of purpose of the 1960–62 Calendar, we read the following:

> It aims to teach the basic theological disciplines in their historical context and development. The ideal is that of a liberal education on the theological level, free from partisan bias and preconception. The members of the teaching staff, representing a wide variety of churchmanship, are concerned first and foremost with the quest for truth, which is the motivation of all disinterested scholarship. Students are invited to enter upon their training sharing in this spirit. (*Trinity College Calendar*, 1960–1962: 7)

Entrance to both Emmanuel and Trinity College has become less restricted over time. In this way, each defines the knowledge that they offer as less esoteric, i.e., as more broadly accessible, than it did in its past.

(b) Curricula

The curricula of the theological schools have expanded. At the turn of the century, the curriculum of Emmanuel included the theological disciplines of apologetics, theology, exegesis, history and practical theology only (*Victoria University Calendar*, 1899–1900). The curriculum has been broadened to include theology, philosophy, history, homilectics, pedagogy, public speaking, hymnology, field work, common worship, Christian mission, and sociology (*Emmanuel College Calendar*, 1947–1948). The curriculum of Trinity (1890–1893) included apologetics, practical theology, elocution, rhetoric, Old Testament, New Testament, dogmatic theology, church history, history and philosophy of religion, moral and pastoral theology and Christian missions. This is a more inclusive list of subjects. They are now not as narrowly theological as they were at the earlier time. Several are social–psychological in their orientation. Pastoral theology, for instance, combines an explanation of theology with an explanation of ways to make theology meaningful to the parishioners.

Additionally, as of 1969, Emmanuel and Trinity College joined with five other divinity colleges, (representing the United, Anglican, Presbyterian and Roman Catholic churches), into the Toronto School of Theology. The students from all of these denominations are now free to study theology with those of other denominations. *But, and this is the crucial point, this has occurred at the same time that entrance requirements have been broadened.*

CONCLUSION

Entrance is now available to those who do not pass the stringent requirement of having spent at least two years in a Christian church. The curricula have changed over time. At first the subjects which were included were more narrowly theological. Presently, subjects in the arts and the humanities are also included. Thus, while the churches are training their clergy to speak about ever widening areas of life, they are insisting on fewer restrictions regarding who can become clergymen.

SOCIAL POWER

Several indicators of social power will be examined in this section. First, an evaluation of the relative incidence of clerical occupations in the elite in Canada during approximately one century will draw from a sample of various Canadian biographies of the elite, including *Who's Who in Canada* (Green). Second, will be a discussion of the socio-economic backgrounds of clergy, from available data sources. Third, a report on the earnings of the clergy will be examined. And fourth, the prestige of the occupation will be investigated.

The first indicator of social power is the representation of the occupational group in *Who's Who in Canada*. The persons in these volumes are taken to be representative of the elite in Canada (Tepperman, 1977; Porter, 1965). As well, there is another class of positions including the Members of Parliament (federal), federal and provincial cabinet members, judges of the Supreme Court of Canada and Superior courts of the provinces, Dominion Department Heads, all Canadian Ambassadors and Ministers plenipotentiary, all Ambassadors and Ministers accredited to this country, heads of universities and colleges, bishops and chief ecclesiastics of the religious denominations in Canada and authors and artists whose works are well known.

The data from *Who's Who* were collected over a period of approximately one-half century. Included were the following years: 1922, 1925, 1928, 1931, 1937, 1941, 1944, 1947, 1951, 1955, 1959, 1963, 1967, 1971, 1974. These years were chosen as a systematic sample of all of the years available. The earlier years were available from a similar volume with a different title, *Canadian Men and Women of the Time*. The years from 1898 to 1912 were drawn from this source. Additionally, a still earlier volume, again with comparable goals and editorial policy, *A Dictionary of Canadian Biography*, was used for the years from 1871 to 1880 (Brown). Data on the occupations were collected from each of the selected volumes, so that approximately fifty randomly selected persons/occupations per volume are included in the sample. The occupations were coded into the following categories: business, clergy, medicine, law, military, arts, academic, engineering, government, other and not available. Division into occupational categories was made after a preliminary reading of a sample of occupations mentioned in the reference books. All those occupations mentioned with any frequency were grouped together into the categories which are described above. Finally, each volume was coded by one individual and then recoded by a partner. Discrepancies in occupational coding by partners were discussed, and the final assignment of codes made with the advice of a third party. Very few discrepancies were noted. Reliability was thus attended to. Table 13–1 presents some of the data which were collected in this manner.

If we divide the time into three periods, an early (1871 to 1898), a middle (1912 to 1941) and a late period (1943 to 1974), and compare the proportions of each of these occupations in these periods, we can see from Table 13–1 that among those included in *Who's Who*, the proportion of those who are members of the clergy declines. This is true of all of the occupations mentioned above, other than engineering and business. The business category has grown over the years to a far greater extent than any of the other categories, from 20 per cent to 63 per cent. The percentage of the elite who are members of the clergy has declined from 15 per cent in the first period to a current 3 per cent. In other words, the proportion of the elite which is clergy is presently one-fifth (or 20 per cent) of what it was in the earliest historical period.

Table 13–1

Representation in ***Who's Who in Canada*** *of Clergy, 1871–1974*

Occupation	YEAR[1] 1871 to 1898	1912 to 1941	1943 to 1974	Total
Business	43(20%)	165(45%)	259(63%)	467(47%)
Clergy	31(15%)	18(5%)	13(3%)	18(5%)
Medicine	18(8%)	14(4%)	6(1.5%)	38(4%)
Law	36(17%)	53(15%)	47(11%)	136(14%)
Military	5(2%)	8(2%)	1(.2%)	14(1%)
Art	13(6%)	20(6%)	4(1%)	37(1%)
Academic	22(10%)	35(10%)	26(6%)	83(8%)
Engineer	2(1%)	19(5%)	15(4%)	36(4%)
Government	29(14%)	23(6%)	25(6%)	77(8%)
TOTAL	213(100%)	363(100%)	411(100%)	987(100%)

[1]The division is made this way for three reasons: (i) it divides the data approximately into thirds; (ii) it follows the years of the available volumes in the first category; (iii) it divides the time period into approximate thirds.

SOCIO-ECONOMIC BACKGROUND OF THE CLERGY

While data for clergy which are directly useful are not available, there is some information which we can use. In a study of Anglican clergy (i.e., Episcopalian) in the United States, Bonn and Doyle (1974) described the father's occupations of the sample as follows: 9 per cent of the clergy had fathers who were clergy, 16 per cent had fathers who were classified as managers, 21 per cent had professional fathers, 27 per cent of the fathers were in technical occupations and 6 per cent were self-employed. Further, 38 per cent of the Episcopalian clergy had fathers who had at least a college-level education. That 46 per cent of the clergy had fathers who were professional or managerial in occupational background (including fathers who were clergy) suggests that this particular sample of Episcopalian clergy is, in comparison with the whole population, drawn from the upper occupational levels. Episcopalian church members are, however, as a whole, drawn from a relatively high occupational background (Lazerwitz, 1961: 568).

PRESTIGE OF CLERGY

The Pineo-Porter occupational prestige scale is a scale that replicates the second stage of the American National Opinion Research Centre (NORC) study which ranks two hundred occupations in the U.S.A. (Pineo–Porter, 1967). Adjustments were made by the Pineo–Porter study to ensure that the occupations were representative of the Canadian labour force. In addition, the Canadian study was bilingual as the occupations were translated into French. A total of 793 persons ranked three to four hundred occupational titles. The average Canadian prestige ranking for the Catholic priest was 72.8. The average prestige ranking for the Catholic priest in English Canada was 71.5, while his average prestige ranking among the French sample was 77.2. The Protestant minister's Canadian average level of prestige was 67.8. In English Canada this occupational prestige for Protestant ministers is 71.7, while it is 53.7 among the French. It is interesting to note that the average Canadian rank for a physician is 87.2. The English-Canadian average and the French-Canadian average are very similar, 87.5 and 86.1 respectively. Today, for both French and English Canadians, then, it appears that the physician is given a higher rank than either the Catholic priest or the Protestant minister.

CLERGY INCOMES

Systematic data regarding the socio-economic backgrounds of clergy from the Anglican and United clergy in Canada are not available. However, it is the policy of both the local diocese of the Anglican church and the local presbytery of the United Church to give financial assistance to persons from their respective geographic areas in their training for the clergy. It is also common for the "home congregation" to give additional help to a person in training for the clergy both financially and in goods and services. The importance of this is that it makes the training accessible to anyone who wants to be a member of the clergy and who is approved as a candidate by his church.

According to a National Council of Churches (NCC) study (1974), the annual cash income of ministers in local (American) churches averaged $7,703 in 1974 (Kiely, 1974). When combined with housing, car allowances and utilities payments, the average median salary increased to $10,348. According to the same study, this salary is about half of what an attorney, accountant, or personnel director made on average. The same study also showed that ministers' salaries have increased thirty-four percent over the decade from

1964 to 1974. This was slightly below an estimated inflation rate of 41 per cent. Thus, the income of the clergy has not quite kept up with the rate of inflation.

Denominations vary widely in the average incomes paid to their clergy. Christian Reformed leads with an average salary of $12,250. The Episcopal Church is next at $11,869, and the American Lutheran third with an average of $11,692. In Table 13–2, an ordered list of selected churches is given.

Table 13–2

Average Salary of American Church Clergy in Descending Order (1974)

Church	Salary
Lutheran Church of America	$11,328
United Methodist	10,915
Presbyterian, U.S.	10,886
Lutheran Church — Missouri Synod	10,777
Evangelical Covenant	10,370
United Church of Christ	10,357
Christian Church (Disciples of Christ)	10,031
American Baptist	9,688
Church of the Brethren	9,600
Open Bible Standard	8,500
Friends United Meeting	8,250
Church of God	8,125
Wesleyan Church	7,641
Assemblies of God	7,091

Canadian salaries are similar to American salaries on average (Kiely, 1974). They do, however, vary widely across the country, and even among churches in the same geographic area. The most complete figures are for the Lutheran Church of the Missouri Synod, Ontario district. The average salary of the Lutheran minister was $11,500 ($1,000 more than the comparable American denomination). This includes a number of benefits including a car, a replacement allowance, a mileage rate, a pension and auto insurance, and housing or a housing allowance. Other benefits included automobile loans of up to $800 at one percent interest, disability insurance, surgical care and moving expenses. The Presbyterian Church offered a minimum salary of $6,400, not including housing or other benefits. The United Church offered a basic minimum salary of $7,500. The Anglican Church of Canada took part in the NCC study, but its pay scales vary so much from diocese to diocese that an average is almost meaningless. The minimum paid in Huron Diocese was $4,900 with an $1,800 allowance and a parsonage or a housing allowance. The minimum salary of a minister ordained prior to 1958 is $6,500 plus travel allowance. The diocese also pays 20 per cent of Ontario Hospitalization Insurance and a travel allowance (Kiely, 1974).

CONCLUSION

The proportion of clergy in the elite has declined over the past century. We do not, however, have data which would provide an adequate historical picture of the incomes of clergy, or on their socio-economic backgrounds over time.

Anecdotal evidence from Canadian fiction and biographies suggests that the prestige of the cleric, and with the prestige, the socio-economic status of the cleric, was similar to that of the physician. Now of course, relatively speaking, the physician has a greater income, and greater prestige (Ruderman, 1974 and Blishen, 1967).

HETEROGENEITY AND HOMOGENEITY

When an occupational group loses power in a society, members of the occupational group, coincidentally, are likely to be differentiated and lacking in cohesion. They are likely to have to compete among themselves for clients for their services. They are unlikely to be able to form a solid, unified body to negotiate for their economic and social position. On the other hand, when the consumers of an occupational group over time become increasingly homogeneous in ethnicity, social status or other similar demographic conditions, they gain power. They can then call upon one another to form a solidarity, to withdraw services, money or other support from the occupational group.

Differences among clerical occupations have proliferated, along with denominational proliferation, over the past century. As Table 13–3 indicates, there are presently 27 census categories of religious denominations. Each of these is served by clergy with somewhat different training, ideology and methods of practice. The Ontario government presently allows all of these clergy to practise their work in the way that they and their respective denominations see fit. All are subject to the same legislation. All receive approximately similar remuneration. While their practices are diverse, all have the same relationship to the state. Three, with significantly greater numbers than the others, the Roman Catholic Church, which includes 33.3 per cent of the population of Ontario, the United Church, with 21.8 per cent, and the Anglican Church, with 15.8 per cent, are the focus of this section of the paper.

HISTORY OF LEGISLATION REGARDING RELIGION AND RELIGIOUS FUNCTIONARIES

Today, the people of Ontario have many denominations to choose from. This was not always the case. In the early days of our history, the first European settlers and explorers spoke French and practised the Roman Catholic religion. The Roman clergy were leaders in the governing of the first settlers, the schools and the hospitals. The Roman Catholic Church was the largest landowner, and was entitled to a tithe on crops (Crysdale, 1977: 422). After the conquest by the British, legislation was passed in the form of the Quebec Act of 1774, which guaranteed French Catholics their religion, their language and their well-established customs (LeBlanc and Edinborough, 1968).

And in Nova Scotia in 1758, the first provincial assembly passed a statute enacting that:

> the sacred rites and ceremonies of divine worship according to the liturgy of the Church established by the laws of England shall be deemed fixed, and the place wherein such liturgy shall be used shall be respected and known by the name of the Church of England as by law established (Millman quoted in Grant, 1963: 5).

Table 13-3

Percentage Distribution of the Population by Religious Denomination for Provinces, 1971.

Denomination	Can. (%)	Nfld. (%)	PEI (%)	N.S. (%)	N.B. (%)	Que. (%)	Ont. (%)	Man. (%)	Sask. (%)	Alta. (%)	B.C. (%)	Yuk. (%)	N.W.T. (%)
Adventist	0.1	0.1	0.1	0.2	0.1	—	0.1	0.1	0.2	0.3	0.3	0.1	—
Anglican	11.8	27.7	6.2	17.2	10.9	3.0	15.8	12.4	9.4	10.5	17.7	25.3	36.4
Baptist	3.1	0.2	5.7	12.7	14.0	0.6	3.7	1.9	1.6	3.1	3.0	4.8	1.1
Brethren in Christ	0.1	0.1	0.2	—	—	—	0.2	—	0.1	0.1	0.1	—	—
Buddhist	0.1	—	—	—	—	—	0.1	0.1	—	0.1	0.3	0.1	—
Christian & Missionary Alliance	0.1	—	—	—	—	—	0.1	0.1	0.5	0.3	0.3	—	0.1
Christian Reformed	0.4	—	0.2	0.1	—	—	0.7	0.2	—	0.8	0.5	0.1	0.1
Churches of Christ Disciples	0.1	—	0.8	0.1	0.1	—	0.1	0.1	0.2	0.1	0.1	0.1	0.1
Church of the Nazarene	0.1	—	0.5	0.1	0.1	—	0.1	—	0.1	0.2	0.1	0.2	0.1
Confucian	—	—	—	—	—	—	—	—	0.2	—	—	0.1	—
Doukhobor	—	—	—	—	—	—	—	—	—	—	0.3	—	—
Free Methodist	0.1	—	—	—	—	—	0.2	0.1	0.1	0.1	0.1	0.1	—
Greek Orthodox	1.5	—	—	0.2	0.1	1.0	1.7	2.6	2.9	2.9	0.9	0.9	0.5
Hutterite	0.1	—	—	—	—	—	—	0.5	0.2	0.4	—	—	—
Jehovah's Witnesses	0.8	0.4	0.4	0.6	0.4	0.3	0.9	0.9	1.1	1.1	1.9	3.2	1.5
Jewish	1.3	—	—	0.3	0.1	1.8	1.6	1.9	0.2	0.4	0.4	0.1	0.1
Lutheran	3.6	0.1	0.1	1.6	0.3	0.4	3.9	6.9	10.3	9.2	6.2	6.0	2.1
Mennonite	0.8	—	—	—	—	—	0.5	6.0	2.8	0.9	1.2	0.3	0.1
Mormon	0.3	—	0.1	0.1	—	—	0.2	0.1	0.3	1.9	0.6	0.4	0.3
Pentecostal	1.0	5.5	0.9	0.9	2.7	0.1	1.0	1.0	1.3	1.4	1.6	1.1	2.0
Plymouth Brethren	—	—	—	—	—	—	—	—	—	—	0.1	—	—
Presbyterian	4.0	0.6	11.7	5.1	2.1	0.9	7.0	3.1	2.2	3.5	4.6	3.8	1.3
Roman Catholic	46.2	36.6	45.9	36.3	52.2	86.7	33.3	24.6	27.9	24.0	18.7	25.4	41.3
Salvation Army	0.6	7.9	0.3	0.6	0.3	0.1	0.6	0.3	0.4	0.3	0.5	0.2	0.1
Ukrainian Catholic	1.1	—	—	0.1	0.1	0.4	0.7	5.8	3.7	2.5	0.5	0.5	0.3
Unitarian	0.1	—	—	—	0.1	—	0.1	0.1	0.1	0.1	0.2	0.2	0.1
United Church	17.5	19.5	24.9	20.6	13.4	2.9	21.8	26.0	29.6	28.1	24.6	16.9	8.6
Others	1.2	0.8	1.0	0.7	0.8	0.3	1.4	1.1	1.3	2.0	2.6	2.5	0.8
No Religion	4.3	0.4	1.0	2.4	1.9	1.3	4.5	4.3	3.7	6.7	13.1	8.8	2.9
TOTAL [approx.]	100.0	100.0	100.0	100.0	100.0	100.0	100.0	100.0	100.0	100.0	100.0	100.0	100.0

Thus, the Church of England was given a legal monopoly. Some legal provision was given, however, to Protestants "dissenting from the Church of England to have free liberty of conscience and to build meeting houses for public worship, and to enjoy exemption from taxes levied from the established church" (LeBlanc and Edinborough, 1968: 26). Later, by 1783, Roman Catholicism was granted the right to establish churches.

The Church of England in Canada spread across Canada from the Maritimes (except in Quebec) as a state Church, as it had been in Britain. The majority of persons in Upper Canada were Church of England. And, insofar as it was possible to speak of a class structure in Canada, the upper classes were generally Church of England. As well, the personnel of government at all levels from governor to the executive council, to the administration, civil and military officers and the judiciary were usually Church of England (LeBlanc and Edinborough, 1968).

Usually the interpretation of Protestant was taken to be Church of England. Apparently there was doubt and debate about whether reference to Protestants was necessarily reference to members of the Church of England (Carrington, 1963). Only the Church of England clergy could perform legal marriages in Upper Canada. At the time of this provision, there were only two clergymen from this denomination. And, by themselves, they were unable to perform the number of marriages that were desired. And so it was changed to include clergy of other denominations, if they were designated as "suitable" by one of the two Church of England clergy. As well, in Upper Canada, only the clergy from the Church of England were originally able to hold property, for example, church lands, cemeteries, pensions and missionary funds. Other clergy, called "non-conformists," were able to hold property only as individuals.

The Anglican clergy do not presently hold these powers. Today, all of the religious denominations in Ontario have a similar relationship to the state. But there are two major points during the history of the province when the relationship between the church and the state was problematic: (1) the clergy reserves settlement and (2) the determination of the distinction between public and religious schooling. Both of these issues were settled through legislation. Both were, at the time, the subject of fierce polemics.

(a) Clergy Reserves

After the British conquered the French, Canada became a colony. As a British colony, it operated under the Church of England. The Canada Act in 1791 divided the colony into Upper and Lower Canada with separate governors and assemblies and two commissaries appointed by the Bishop. It also put aside land to strengthen the English church and clergy. The clergy reserve land settlement was the source of sixty years of bitter struggle. Sir John Colborne supervised the creation and endowment from the clergy reserves of forty-four rectories in various parts of the province. Each was held the responsibility of a clergyman from the Church of England. Many of the Canadian people were opposed to the British dominance of the land. They argued that it ought to be secularized and given back to the government, and thus to all of the people. By 1831, a move toward reverting Church lands was begun (Carrington, 1963). In this procedure, the Church of England lost some of its monolithic position.

(b) Roman Catholic Separate Schools

Today, the secular Ministry of Education, rather than a religious denomination, officially controls all education, public and separate, in the Province of
Ontario. Teachers in the separate religious schools, most of which are Roman
Catholic in Ontario, are given the same training and pass through the same
accreditation procedures as those in public schools. The hierarchy of the
Catholic Church does not have the legal right to control education. The Board
of Trustees is composed of religious and lay members who are elected by and
from among the separate school tax supporters. Roman Catholic Bishops have
no formal place in the educational system. The financial support for the schools
is not in proportion to the number of Catholics in the population but, rather, to
the actual tax monies paid by separate school supporters. The school district
boundaries are legislated by the government of the province, rather than by
the Catholic parish districts (Westhues, 1976: 142). Thus, while the Catholic
public schools, through the separate school system, are allowed to support
themselves as separate institutions, their power to determine their fate in
terms of school districts, divisions and teacher training is limited. More
importantly, they are deprived of some crucial powers of religious education
which are seen as legitimate by the Church itself.

CONCLUSIONS

Today, the Roman Catholic schools are only one alternative among many
religious and secular schools supported by the state. From the educational
domination of the Church of England to the support of their chief competitor,
the Roman Catholic church, it was a short move to religious equality for all
denominations in the Ontario separate school system. The Clergy Reserves Act
was settled in a manner that deprived the clergy of the Church of England in
Canada of some of the power that had formerly been theirs. The issue of the
secularization of education was settled so that the Church of England lost
power and had to share it with the Roman Catholic Church. Now, all religious
denominations have the right to their own educational systems, once approved
by the secular governmental authorities in the Ministry of Education. The
Roman Catholic Church lost a good deal of its power to determine schooling for
Catholics in the province of Ontario. The movement of the clerical profession
has been toward decreased homogeneity. On the other hand, the religious
denominations are increasingly homogeneous as numbers of new denominations, sects and cults develop, each to serve its own increasingly homogeneous
clientele.

This paper has argued that secularization has occurred in the province of
Ontario over the past century. This has been seen through the declining power
of the profession which is chiefly responsible for the promulgation of religion —
the clergy. Specifically, it has been demonstrated that clerics have lost power
with respect to the three measures articulated by Johnson: esoteric knowledge,
social status and homogeneity (1972).

However, Johnson's (1972) theory regarding the power of the professions is
just that, a theory. In this work, the purpose has not been to evaluate the
theory but to use it. Thus, Johnson's propositions have been assumed to be
essentially correct. They have been used as indicators of the power of the

clergy. While this may seem an unwise procedure, the propositions appear to be valid. The hypotheses which were derived from Johnson's work are exploratory in nature. The data that were gathered to test these propositions were descriptive data. Hypothesis testing of the precise nature dictated by statistical theory was not possible. Moreover, because of the historical nature of the questions asked and because of the need for data for approximately one century, there are areas of research, namely with regard to the income and prestige of clergy over time, where there are gaps in the data. Nevertheless, the available data have tended to support the propositions, and further research in the area seems warranted.

REFERENCES

Blishen, Bernard
1967   "A Socio-Economic Index for Occupations in Canada," in *Canadian Review of Sociology and Anthropology* Vol. 4: 41–53.
1969   *Doctors and Doctrines: The Ideology of Medical Care in Canada.* Toronto: University of Toronto Press.

Blishen, Bernard and Hugh A. McRoberts
1976   "A Revised Socio-Economic Idea for Occupation in Canada," in *Canadian Review of Sociology and Anthropology* Vol. 13 (February): 71–79.

Bonn, Robert L. and Ruth T. Doyle
1974   "Secularly Employed Clergymen: A Study in Occupational Role Recomposition," in *Journal for the Scientific Study of Religion* Vol. 13: 328–343.

Brown, George D., et al. (eds.)
1976   *Dictionary of Canadian Biography.* Vol. IX (1861–1870, 1871–1880). Toronto: University of Toronto Press.
       Calendar of Emmanuel College (Victoria University). 1899–1978.
       Calendar of Trinity College. 1853–1978.

Carrington, Philip
1963   *The Anglican Church in Canada.* Toronto: Collins.

Clark, S.D.
1948   *Church and Sect in Canada.* Toronto: University of Toronto Press.

Crysdale, Stewart
1977   "Some Problematic Aspects of Religion in Canada," in *Sociology Canada.* Christopher Beattie and Stewart Crysdale (eds.) Toronto: Butterworths.
1966   "Earnings of Physicians in Canada," *Supplement to Health Care Series No. 211.* Ottawa: Department of National Health and Welfare.

Grant, John W.
1967   *The Experience of Church Union.* London: Butterworths. The first century of Confederation.
1972   *The Church in the Canadian Era.* New York: McGraw Hill.

Greene, B.M. (ed.)
1925–26   *Who's Who in Canada.* Toronto: International Press.

Johnson, T.J.
1972   *Professions and Power.* London: Macmillan.

Kiely, John
1974   *Kitchener–Waterloo Record*. (Sat., Sept. 7): 60.

Lazerwitz, Bernard
1961   "A Comparison of Major United States Religious Groups," in *Journal of the American Statistical Association* Vol. 56: 568–579.

Le Blanc, Philip and Arnold Edinborough
1968   *One Church: Two Nations*. Don Mills: Longman.

Middleton, Jesse E. et al.
1927   *The Municipality of Toronto: A History*. (3 volumes). Toronto: Dominion Publishing.

Millman, T.R.
1966   "Tradition of the Anglican Church in Canada," in *The Churches and the Canadian Experience. A Faith and Order Study of the Christian Tradition*. J.W. Grant. (ed.) Toronto: Ryerson Press.

Nisbet, Robert A.
1966   *The Sociological Tradition*. New York: Basic Books.

Pineo, Peter C. and John Porter
1973   "Occupational Prestige in Canada," *Social Stratification in Canada*. J. Curtis and W. Scott. (eds.) Toronto: Prentice Hall, 55–68.

Porter, John
1965   *The Vertical Mosaic*. Toronto: University of Toronto Press.
       Principals' Reports of Queen's University. 1923, 1933, 1943, 1953, 1963, 1973.

Roberts, Sir Charles G.D. and Arthur Turnell (ed.)
1936–37   *The Canadian Who's Who*. Toronto: Trans Canada Press, Vol. II.

Ruderman, A.P.
1973   *The Community Health Centre in Canada*. Ottawa: The Queen's Printer, Vol. II.

Shiner, Larry E.
1967   "The Concept of Secularization in Empirical Research," in *Scientific Study of Religion* 6, No. 2: 207–220.

Sessons, Charles Bruce
1959   *Church and State in Canadian Education*. Toronto: Ryerson Press.

Tepperman, Lorne.
1977   "Effects of the Demographic Transition upon Access to the Toronto Elite," in *The Canadian Review of Sociology and Anthropology*. Vol. 14, No. 3: 285–293.

Westhues, Kenneth
1976   "Public vs. Sectarian Legitimation," in *The Canadian Review of Sociology and Anthropology*. Vol. 13. No. 2: 137–151.

Zaret, David
       "Sociological Theory and Historical Scholarship," *The American Sociologist* Vol. 13 (May): 114–121.

Chapter 14

The Fishermen of Newfoundland

R. Parsler

THE HISTORICAL BACKGROUND

The fishing grounds off Newfoundland are the richest in the world, and are the basis of the oldest North American industry worked by white Europeans. The indigenous people of the island, the Beothuck Indians, were a small and peaceful tribe who, although they fished from the coast in summer, had little or no effect either upon the fish stock or upon the efforts of Europeans to exploit the fishing grounds. This exploitation was, therefore, unhindered by the native people of Newfoundland.

The first authenticated discovery of Newfoundland by Europeans seems to be that of the Norsemen over a thousand years ago. They had already colonized Iceland and Greenland and made these lands the base for further exploration to the west. Bjorni, Leif Ericson, and Thorvald discovered and explored the coasts of Labrador and Newfoundland, while Karlsefrei started a short-lived colony in Newfoundland. Woodcock describes the authentication of this discovery from the evidence of the Norsemen's sagas and from later archaeological evidence:

> In Vinland, where Leif found wild grapes and felled timber for use in Greenland, the dew was sweet to the taste, there were bigger salmon than the Norsemen had ever seen before, and, as the sagas remarked, "there was such abundance that it seemed as though cattle would need no winter fodder, since the grass hardly withered in winter, while the days and nights were more equally divided than in Greenland or Iceland." It is now virtually certain that Vinland was Newfoundland, since it was here at L'Anse aux Meadows, that Helge Ingstad in 1961 and later years discovered the remains of a Norse settlement of eight houses and four boatsheds; this must have been the place where Leif wintered and to which his brother Thorvald returned in the following year. (Woodcock, 1980: 11)

It does not seem that there were further European settlements for a period of some five hundred years although it is possible, but unrecorded, that small fleets of boats visited the Newfoundland fishing grounds in summer, returning with their catch in the early fall.

The basis of European interest in the fishing grounds was profit. Winter protein was scarce and expensive in Europe, and dried salt cod fetched luxury prices. With the voyage of John Cabot from Bristol to Newfoundland in 1497, the reports of the rich fishing grounds grew in credence and importance. The prospect of good profits became more obvious.

> The sea is full of fish which are taken not only with the net, but also with a basket in which a stone is put so that the basket may plunge into the

water — and the Englishman, his parties say that they can bring so many fish that the kingdom will have no more business with Iceland and that from this country there will be a very great trade in the fish they call stock-fish. (Cited in Perlin, 1930: 163)

From this time onward, the fishing of Newfoundland waters by Europeans was regular and growing. The land of Newfoundland had, however, not yet been claimed by any country and interest in permanent settlement seemed slight. It does appear that, at least in the St. John's area, even in those early days, the English had some kind of ascendency over other nationalities using the same waters. This is verified by a letter written in 1578 by Anthony Parkhurst, a Bristol merchant who had made four voyages to Newfoundland:

There were generally more than 100 sail of Spaniards taking cod, and from 20–30 killing whales; 50 sail of Portuguese; 150 sail of French and Bretons, mostly very small; but of English only 50 sail. Nevertheless the English are commonly lords of the harbours where they fish and use all strangers' help in fishing, if need require, according to an old custom of the country; which they do willingly, so that you take nothing from them more than a boat or two of salt, in respect of your protection of them against rovers or other violent intruders, who do often put them from good harbours. (Cited in Perlin, 1930: 165)

There is little doubt from this that the English, on whatever basis, had a good protection racket on the strength of which they had the first cut at the best fishing. These informal procedures were important in later history as they were legitimated in various ways. The first English captain to arrive for the season in Newfoundland was in fact dubbed "Fishing Admiral" for the season, and his word was law among the fishing fleets, and in the Island.

The method of fishing at this time was from galleries jutting from the ships' side, using weighted lines. The men doing the fishing were the "servants" of those putting up the capital for the trip, whether it was the owner-captain or a merchant from England's western counties.

In 1584, Sir Humphrey Gilbert, making for the American mainland with the intention of founding a colony, sailed off-course, entered St. John's harbour in Newfoundland and took possession of the island in the name of Queen Elizabeth I. From that time until the present, the stage was set for constant bickering and violence between the seasonal, visiting fishermen on the one side and the Newfoundland settlers on the other. The seasonal fishermen had the most power, since they were backed by the capital of the West of England merchants who, by and large, had the favour of royalty.

After the establishment of the American colonies, a profitable fish trade began between the new colonial settlements and Newfoundland. The English merchants became uneasy at this growing trade and tried to enforce the powers of the Fishing Admirals against the settlers. The First Western Charter in 1634 gave legality to this repression, and the possessions of the existing settlers were to be at the command of the Fishing Admirals. Further settlement was prohibited, and existing settlers were to be shipped back to England or to the West Indies.

In spite of this repressive legislation some settlement endured. The strict letter of the law was difficult to enforce in two ways. The first was that those rich enough found the Fishing Admirals easy to bribe, and these prospered as merchants in St. John's. The second was that because the coastline of Newfoundland is long, wild, and has many coves difficult of access even from the sea, those who were poor found it relatively easy to settle in small communities in places where it was unlikely that they would be harrassed, either by the guns of the Royal Navy or by the visiting fishing fleets. Under these conditions, it is not surprising that few details are known about the unofficial squatters' settlements until quite late in the eighteenth century. The historical legend that has grown up has been largely to the effect that any settlers under those conditions were either deserters, criminals fleeing from justice, or social deviants of some kind. This legend is certainly grounded in popular folklore in which the early inhabitants are portrayed in stories and songs as being reformed pirates, privateers and the like (Nemec, 1973: 23). To some extent, Nemec puts this legend into perspective:

> . . . most future inhabitants probably visited the Island to begin with as fishermen–servants in the employ of either adventurers or planters. After spending possibly several summers and perhaps even a winter or two on the Island, they may have decided to permanently settle — the naval authorities may have been relatively ineffectual in preventing deserters and fugitives from residing in the smaller, less accessible settlements, they were fairly successful in rounding up any such individuals who were foolish enough to reside in the major outports. This was due in large part to the cooperation elicited from the "merchants and principal inhabitants," a common interest group which sought to prevent lawlessness, especially crimes against property, by either informing the authorities about fugitives and criminals or simply apprehending them themselves. (Nemec, 1973: 23)

The number of settlers slowly grew until, at the end of the Seven Years War in 1815, there were about 40,000 people in the Island. In 1824, the English Parliament founded the Supreme Court in St. John's and, for the first time, the settlers were subject to reasonably fair trials by properly appointed judges, and were free from the arbitrary dictates of the fishing admirals. With this act, Newfoundland became a full colony of Britain.

During this time, the French attempt to conquer Newfoundland affected the military and political events on the Island, but *whether dominated by the French or the English*, the working lives of the ordinary people were little affected. They were driven by the need to subsist from whatever they could wrest from the sea and the largely inhospitable land. The social structure of their communities and the organization of their work was dominated by this economic necessity rather than by large-scale political events.

THE LIVES OF THE FISHERMEN

The lives of the people remained essentially the same until the middle of the present century. This continuity of structure was ensured by the isolation of the outport communities which resulted in a peasant fishing society of an extremely decentralized character. "St. John's was the only town of any size, a nest of merchants, and most of the people lived in the hundreds of tiny hamlets or outports, sited on inlets or coves along the island's highly indented shores and each inhabited by a hundred or even a few score people. . . . The square wooden houses of the outports, painted dull red with a foul-smelling mixture of ochre and codfish oil, were scattered along the steep rocky paths, for there were usually no roads and most of these places could be reached only by water" (Woodcock, 1980: 82). By necessity, these communities were almost entirely self-sufficient, the fishing boats were built of local materials, the lobster pots and cod traps were made in the community, and the chief product and staple diet of the people was salt fish.

> The characteristic Newfoundland dishes are poor man's food, like *brewse* or *brewis*, a kind of stew made of dried salt cod and bread or ship's biscuit, with a bit of salt pork for flavour, simmered on the hob. (Woodcock, 1980: 83)

Apart from food from the sea there were moose in the woods, and wildfowl. Potatoes, cabbage and turnips were grown in gardens in the scanty soil. A few pigs, sheep for wool, and one or two cows for milk were likely to be the only livestock. Rum was usually the only alcohol available and this, in the early days at least, could apparently prove to be disastrous to a small community.

> On arriving at Richard's Harbour about a league further on, I found that one of the scourges of this coast, a floating grog-shop, had been sojourning at Muddy Hole last week, and had kept "all hands" during the time of its stay, in a state of intoxication. And it was likely now that they had not a stick to burn, or a fish for the kettle; and as the floating nuisance had only left the place the day before, it was not unlikely that the fumes of the evaporating poisons thus supplied had not yet evaporated. (Wix, 1836: 121)

When rum was available, this state of affairs was apparently not confined to the males of the community:

> The arrival of a trading schooner among the people affords an invariable occasion for all parties (with only one or two exceptions and those I regret to say, *not* among the females!) to get into a hopeless state of intoxication. Women, and among them positively girls of fourteen, may be seen under the plea of it's helping them in their work, habitually taking their "morning" of raw spirits before breakfast. I have seen this drain repeated a second time before a seven o'clock breakfast. (Wix, 1830: 169–70)

Hard work was, however, essential for survival of these outport communities, and the fishing season meant long hours of hard labour for both men and women, even in the later days of motorized boats.

> Down to the land-wash probably by midnight or one o'clock in the morning with your lunch-pail and oilskins. There the two or three other fishermen in your boat join you. You launch your small rodney or dory and row out to your motor boat . . . you cast off and head towards the fishing grounds three or five or eight miles out from land on the bosom of the Atlantic Ocean. . . . The fish are not very plentiful on this spot of

fishing ground, so you take aboard your grapnel and try another spot you know. . . . On the broad expanse of water off Brig Cove there are some ninety spots of ground . . . and if you are a good fisherman you can commence at the first and find your way to each one until the ninetieth is reached, and then go back over the distance again, locating each one as you go. . . . However, you have got your load or part load or what there is for you today . . . it is three or four o'clock when you reach the collar again, and now you must get your fish up from the boat to the stage-head for dressing. By the time the fish are all pewed up from the boat, gutted, headed, split, washed from the knife, and salted away, it is five or six o'clock . . . but your day is not yet over. After a "mug-up" in the house you have at least a dozen chores to do, a dozen matters to attend to. But at last, by nine or ten or eleven o'clock, you are snugly in bed, having earned the rest of the righteous. (Smallwood, 1930: 8–9)

Thus the day of the inshore fisherman would be spent from May until the end of October, or later if the weather was good.

The women of the community would often help with the cleaning and salting of the fish. They would also "make" the fish, that is, dry the fish by spreading it out on the "flakes" every morning and gathering it in piles in the evening. When the fish was sufficiently dried, it was taken to the local merchant to be exchanged for provisions. The better quality fish was then taken and sold in European markets, while the poorer quality went to the West Indies.

The women would also work in the gardens where they grew mainly potatoes, cabbages, carrots and turnips. If farm animals were kept, it was usually the women who cared for them, made the hay for their winter fodder and stored it. Of course, all this was in addition to household chores and caring for the children.

In the winter the men cut wood for fires for the building of houses, boats, and the equipment for making the dried salt fish. They also hunted for whatever game was available.

Up until the later nineteenth and early twentieth centuries, and sometimes not even then, many of the outports had no schools and no medical care. These conditions changed only gradually after socially conscious leaders, such as William Coker and Wilfred Grenfell, began their work. All in all, the outport communities remained isolated to such an extent that their culture was derived intact from their distant English or Irish past. The people still spoke dialects of seventeenth century Devon and Ireland, and each community was very insular, regarding people from other communities as foreigners. They developed and treasured the quality of independence and, as A.P. Herbert wrote, developed a reputation for being "the best tempered, best mannered people walking" (Woodcock, 1980: 90).

Until well after the start of this century, the outport society was not a money economy. English merchants had established a truck system whereby goods, including salt for processing the fish, were brought from Britain and bartered for the fish the settlers produced. There would normally be a local merchant to whom the fishermen took their fish and he, in turn, passed it to a merchant in St. John's or another larger centre in exchange for the goods brought in from abroad. The merchants manipulated the truck system in four

234 Work in the Canadian Context

ways to the detriment of the fishermen. First, they would underestimate the quality of the fish brought to them. Second, they would underestimate the value of that quality. Third, they would overestimate the value of the goods exchanged for the fish and, fourth, they would encourage the men to take rum. All in all, the fishermen were perpetually in debt. The worst conditions were among the few scattered settlements in Labrador, where the fishermen "existed in a kind of perpetual bondage, complicated by alcoholism encouraged by the merchants who used drink to drive the liveyerees deeper into debt. Tuberculosis was rampant among them and their children often died from malnutrition" (Woodcock, 1980: 84).

The merchants and the clergy were the top of the social strata of the outports, and the same merchant families would often continue to dominate a community for many generations. Since the fishermen were rarely in credit, the merchant had the services of as many fishermen as he could get to work for him. The relationship was complex and while there is no doubt that it had a severely exploitive side, it was also paternalistic.

On the paternalistic side of their relationship, the merchant provided "his" fishermen and their families with sufficient foodstuffs and necessities to maintain them through the winter — in both good fishing years and bad. Due to the ongoing credit and debit aspect of their relations, cash was not usually exchanged. In "good" years the fishermen simply accrued credit; in "bad" years they went into debt. On the extractive–exploitive side of their relationship, the merchant was able to set the price of fish so that his fishermen–client rarely accumulated capital, and therefore rarely became economically independent of him. Indeed, it was not unusual for families to enter into long-term credit or debt bondage with the merchant. And even as late as 1933, an official Royal Commission Report described inshore fishermen as "little more than serfs with no hope of independence," and the overall organization of the Island's fisheries as "largely feudal" (Nemec, 1973: 18).

If by "class" is meant ownership of the means of production or not, then there is no doubt that in these small communities the merchants were the bourgeois owners of the means of production. The fishermen, whether or not they "owned" their boats and fishing equipment, were, by virtue of their situation in the labour market and their constant indebtedness to the merchants, a proletariat with nothing to sell but their labour.

As Dillon points out, another view is that

The merchant's family constituted the local "upper class." Besides taking the fish and giving out supplies in return, the merchants usually dispensed road-work and other forms of government employment. Because of their position in the community, they demanded certain tokens of respect from the ordinary fisherman. The story is told locally of a man who went to see a merchant about a job he hoped to get, working on the road. He entered the office wearing his cap. He was told to go out and come in again and to take off his cap when he entered. (Dillon, 1968: 78, cited in Nemec, 1973b: 18–19). This implies not only that the bourgeois/proletarian relationship existed in an "objective" manner, but also that the situation was a fully "subjectively" conscious one.

According to Dillon, the simple bourgeoisie/proletariat relation was complicated when the merchant who was "upper class," shared this position with those fishermen who owned capital equipment (such as a cod trap) and could afford to hire fishermen to work for them. "The latter very often were unmarried. They usually lived with the family of their crew['s] skipper and worked with them in the garden or at any number of subsistence and productive tasks. Their room and board was paid from their share of the catch" (Nemec, 1973b: 19). This is apparently similar to the situation in the eighteenth century, as the list of Seary et al. describes:

> Masters, men who do not engage as Servants during the fishing season; Men servants, men who engage as Servants in the fishing season; Mistresses, wives of masters and women who have houses and employ Servants; Women servants, women not of the foregoing description; Children, all boys and girls under 15 years of age; and Dieters, men who remain on the Island during the winter (living upon their summer wages) without engaging as winter servants. (Cited in Nemec, 1973b: 19).

Taking this into account, together with the fact that the priest, various government officials and latterly the school teacher all played their part in this society, their relative strengths in the market place and the "class" structure is best described by Giddens in his model of class relationships:

> The effect of closure in terms of intergenerational movement is to provide for the *reproduction* of common life experience over the generations; and this homogenization of experience is reinforced to the degree to which the individual's movement within the labour market is confined to occupations which generate a similar range of material outcomes. In general we may state that the structuration of classes is facilitated *to the degree to which mobility closure exists in relation to any specified form of market capacity*. There are three sorts of market capacity which can be said to be normally of importance in this respect: ownership of property in the means of production; possession of educational or technical qualifications; and possession of manual labour power. In so far as it is the case that these tend to be tied to closed patterns of inter- and intragenerational mobility, this yields the foundation of *a basic three-class system* in capitalist society: an "upper," "middle" and "lower" or "working" class. (Giddens, 1973: 107)

NEWFOUNDLAND FISHERMEN TODAY

The world depression of the twenties and thirties had dire effects upon Newfoundland's economy. Taxes could not be raised to meet debts which had been incurred, and a commission was appointed by the British Colonial Office. This state of affairs lasted through the Second World War until 1949 when a referendum was held, asking the population whether they wished to continue as they were, to become independent or to join the Canadian Confederation. By the small majority of 7,000, Newfoundland entered Canada and change began to occur quickly. Newfoundland had its social and economic isolation penetrated by the events of the Second World War, and now it was plunged headlong into rapid integration with the Canadian social and economic systems.

The rapid changes were guided by the new Liberal premier, J.R. Smallwood, who was to remain premier for twenty-two years. One of the main planks of Smallwood's policies was to get the people of Newfoundland away from the traditional fishing/subsistence economy into the modern world of big industry. Brox comments: "In many ways, Newfoundland reminds one of the truly underdeveloped or dualistic countries which are found in the Middle East, where the Arab herdsman tends his goats in the same way as in biblical times within view of electronically controlled oil wells" (1972: 6). Put another way, Smallwood was guiding the country away from the situation where every man could build his own house and his own boat to one where he was encouraged to burn his boat and turn to a job in industry.

Overton, writing about nationalism in Newfoundland, comments on the profundity of the changes at this time:

> An attempt [was made] to prepare for and promote economic develop-
> ment by means of creating an economic, administrative and cultural
> infrastructure of the kind appropriate to an advanced capitalist society.
> The concentration was on the provision of transportation facilities (the
> Trans-Canada Highway and "Roads to Resources"), rural electrification,
> the creation of cheap hydro-electric power for industrialists, and the
> development of a modern communications system. An administrative
> bureaucracy and technocracy were formed, and educational facilities
> were provided to train the new bureaucracy and the less-skilled workers
> that were also needed. In addition, the period saw the development of the
> mass media, new institutions catering to the arts, and other leisure-time
> activities (camping and tourism). In fact, *all* the facets of the modern
> state and of modern capitalist society, including unions, where appropri-
> ate, were developed in preparation for a potential workforce made
> available by such means as the resettlement of isolated fishing
> communities in "growth" centres. Industrial development initially took
> the form of small-scale import-substitute industry; however, by the late
> 1950s, most of these enterprises had failed. Later developments
> concentrated on large-scale industrial schemes, especially those exploit-
> ing resources. (Overton, 1979: 223)

The following table shows that in twenty years Newfoundland had changed from being a country of isolated communities to one where a great deal of centralization and communication was possible.

Technological change in the fishing industry had occurred since the thirties which saw the demise of the schooners. Dories became popular in the thirties, and were then slowly replaced by long-liners with inboard engines and stern net gear. Large steel trawlers with good crew amenities and the ability to stay at sea for some time are now the rule for the off-shore fishery.

The following table shows the current trends in type of boat employed:

The type of nets favoured changed drastically from the old style. Cotton nets and traps changed to trawls and jiggers. Now the nets used on longliners are nylon and monofilament gillnets. The traditional trap and net industry in

Table 14-1

Selected Statistics on Newfoundland, 1950-1975

	Paved Road (miles)	Telephones (per 1000 population)	Registered Motor Vehicles	Population (1,000s)
1950	121	6.1	16,375	361
1955	130	8.1	39,766	415
1960	380	12.6	61,952	458
1965	1009	17.6	92,885	493
1970	1337	26.0	118,641	522
1975	2605	36.1	173,642	558

Source: Historical Statistics of Newfoundland and Labrador, Supplement, Volume 2 (1) (St. John's, 1977) cited in Overton, 1979: 223.

Table 14-2

Numbers and Types of Fishing Vessels

	1956	1965	1975	1976
Trawler	12	45	77	81
Draggers	18	10	—	—
Danish Seiners	8	—	—	—
Pune Seiners	4	3	9	8
Long Liners:				
Over 25 tons	28	32	285	265
10 to 25 tons	13	139	316	292
Boats:				
Sail and row	4,683	6,817	330	250
Gas and diesel	7,083	11,573	10,063	8,700

Source: Adapted from Table K-8, *Historical Statistics of Newfoundland and Labrador*, Vol. II (2) August 1979. Government of Newfoundland and Labrador.

Newfoundland became threatened by more efficient foreign-made gear. For example,

> The Inshore Fishing Gear Experiments Project was instituted to purchase and introduce new designs of fishing gear to the inshore fishermen of the province. This gear consists of Japanese cod, herring, mackerel and caplin traps and Japanese scallop and clam dredges. . . . Fishermen using the gear have advised the Authority that their earnings have, in some instances, doubled and tripled the earnings of their fellow fishermen who were using conventional fishing gear. (*Daily News*, 1972: Feb. 28: 24)

After Confederation, one of the largest changes in the fishery was the switch from dried salted fish to frozen fish. This led to a drastic reorganization of the family lives of inshore fishermen. The following table shows the trend of exports of salted cod:

Table 14-3

Year	Export of Salted Cod Amount of Export (metric tons)
1804	30,131
1900	55,933
1949	43,211
1955	36,815
1965	13,374
1975	2,277
1977	5,519

Source: Adapted from Table K–6, *Historical Statistics of Newfoundland and Labrador*, August 1979, Vol. II (2). Government of Newfoundland and Labrador.

The traditional kind of salt fish "making" had led to a whole family involvement for the inshore fisherman and, in the past, for the families of the skippers of off-shore schooners. Now, the advent of the quick freeze fish plant, and the customers' preference for this product, meant that the family involvement in the product had gone, and there was complete dependence on the local fish freezing plant. If there were no local freezing plant, then there was little prospect of successful fishing continuing. The following table shows the trend in the production of three kinds of frozen fish:

Table 14-4

Quantity of Fish Products by Type
(Metric Tons)

	1956	1965	1975	1977
Frozen, round or dressed	241	1,922	3,777	23,474
Frozen fillets	15,561	15,695	36,052	41,230
Frozen Blocks and Stubs	12,515	31,538	12,307	29,992

Source: Adapted from Table K–3, *Historical Statistics of Newfoundland and Labrador*, August 1979, Vol. II (2). Government of Newfoundland and Labrador.

The trend was toward the centralization of fish production with all the usual emphasis on low-cost large-scale production, increasing division of labour, and increasing administrative bureaucracy. Such an organization was the antithesis of the kinship-based small-scale community production of the old days.

When these technological trends are taken together with the vast resettlement program necessitated for efficient bureaucratic management of welfare funds, then the traditional life of the fisherman seems to have seen its last days. The resettlement program was intended to bring an end to the poverty of subsistence fishing in isolated outports and to provide secure industrial jobs for the men in towns which had good education, medical and housing facilities. What actually happened was that hundreds of distinctive micro-cultures based upon close kinship patterns and hundreds of years of comfortable tradition were replaced by "new town" living with no kin network, and very often no job and complete dependence on the state for welfare payments. There were certainly advantages in having the modern amenities of electricity, relatively good medical and educational services, but the change was for many from a meaningful independent existence to one of helplessness and anonymity in the face of a "rational" bureaucracy.

> The Government's obsession with rapid industrialization left it with few resources and few ideas for improving the fishery. To the extent that it had a policy, it was one of industrializing the fishery, too, through transforming it from an inshore to a deep sea operation, and from locally cured salt fish to centrally processed frozen fish. Such policies meant a shift from a labour-intensive to a more capital-intensive industry, with the elimination of thousands of jobs. Young people were educated for skilled and professional jobs; isolated villages were resettled into larger centres to provide pools of industrial labour; roads and electricity were put in place to open up the Island to industry; the inshore fishery was dismissed as archaic and allowed to decline. ... As industries failed, however, the new work force rapidly became a largely unemployed work force. ... Many rural Newfoundlanders ... had become too educated, too urbanized, too consumer-oriented, and, more recently, too dependent upon subsistence and social security payments (unemployment insurance and welfare benefits) to think of returning to the inshore fishery, the merits of which they had forgotten. (*The Report of the People's Commission on Unemployment*, Newfoundland and Labrador, 1978: 66)

Some of the most isolated communities were in the small islands off the shores of main Newfoundland. A number of these people felt that they would have had to move away

> ... because of limitations of island life and their unfulfilled aspirations for themselves and their children. However, 45% felt they had been forced out. The reason for these feelings became evident as they described the cut-back in services and pressures applied by clergymen and neighbours in addition to government officials. These pressures were indeed real. Schools were closed, medical services, as scanty as they were, were curtailed, mail service was reduced and likewise supply boats. This eventually forced some store-keepers to close, since there were just no supplies. The fishing product plant closed down as government stated that it was just not feasible to keep it operating. Likewise, the inshore fishery was played down province-wide and people were given the definite impression that there was just no chance of earning a decent living in an isolated community. Several people showed great bitterness in this area for they now know of similar places that withstood the pressures of the resettlement program, refused to move and thus had services greatly improved by government after a few years. (Dunne and Flaherty, 1979: 22–23. Unpublished paper, Memorial University)

The employment figures for the fishery indicate the effect of the above trends:

Table 14–5

Fisheries Employment

	Full time (over 10 mos./yr.)	Part-time (5–10 mos./yr.)	Casual (less than 5 mos./yr.)
1969	1,958	8,560	7,252
1970	1,855	7,282	8,628
1971	1,024	5,024	9,913
1972	712	4,105	9,635
1973	903	3,996	10,414
1974	607	4,521	7,665
1975	405	3,811	11,586
1976	621	3,718	11,012

Source: Adapted from Table K–7, *Historical Statistics of Newfoundland and Labrador*, Vol. II (2), August 1979. Government of Newfoundland and Labrador.

This clearly indicates the trend toward considering fishing, at least as in-shore fishing part-time or casual employment to be supplemented by unemployment pay or welfare benefits. The overall number of workers employed also shows a decline.

Recently, "foreign" fishermen have more and more been the source of complaint from native Newfoundlanders. The boats and equipment of foreign fleets are becoming larger and more efficient, to the extent that the fish stock appears to be severely depleted, thus leaving a smaller share for inshore fishermen. For example, while the efficiency of factory ships and their ability to keep several trawlers fishing without wasting time are a source of grudging admiration, they are obviously feared. "We can look and admire but we cannot afford her. That is a privilege that belongs to state socialism" (*Daily News*, 1968: 20 March: 4).

There has thus been no change in the basic structure of the conflict which has characterized the Newfoundland fishing industry from earliest times. The persistent question remains; how are the interests of the undercapitalized native fisherman to be reconciled with the interests of foreign fishermen who have adequate capital equipment, and who are free to roam the world in search of their fish?

REFERENCES

Alexander, David
1977 *The Decay of Trade: An Economic History of the Newfoundland Saltfish Trade 1935–1965*. St. John's: Institute of Social and Economic Research, Memorial University.

Brox, Ottar
1962 *Newfoundland Fishermen in the Age of Industry: A Sociology of Economic Dualism*. St. John's: Institute of Social and Economic Research, Memorial University.

Brym, Robert J. and R. James Sacouman, (eds.)
1979 *Underdevelopment and Social Movements in Atlantic Canada*. Toronto: New Hogtown Press.

Dillon, Virginia
1968 *The Anglo-Irish Element in the Speech of the Southern Shore of Newfoundland*. Unpublished M.A. thesis, Department of English, Memorial University, St. John's.

Dunne, Catherine P., and Alice Flaherty
1979 *Survey of the Socio-Economic Effects of Resettlement*. Unpublished paper, Department of Sociology, Memorial University, St. John's.

Giddens, Anthony
1973 *The Class Structure of the Advanced Societies*. London: Hutchinson University Library.

Nemec, Thomas F.
1973a *"Trepassey 1505–1840 A.D.: The Emergence of an Anglo-Irish Newfoundland Outport"* in *Newfoundland Quarterly* Vol. 69, No. 4 (March).

1973b *"Trepassey 1840–1900: An Ethnohistorical Reconstruction of Anglo-Irish Outport Society"* in *Newfoundland Quarterly* Vol. 70, No. 1 (June).

Overton, James
1979 "Neo-Nationalism in Newfoundland," in Brym et al., op. cit.

Seary, E., G.M. Story and Wm. J. Kirwin
1968 *The Avalon Peninsula of Newfoundland: An Ethnolinguistic Study*. Ottawa: National Museum of Canada, Bulletin No. 219, Anthropological Series No. 81, 1968.

Smallwood, J.R.
1930 *The Book of Newfoundland*, Vol. 1. St. John's. Newfoundland Book Publishers. Albert B. Perlin "An Outline of Newfoundland History," 162–194.

1978 *The Report of the People's Commission on Unemployment* "Now that we've burned our boats. . ." Ottawa.

Wix, Edward
1836 *Six Months of a Newfoundland Missionary's Journal, from February to August, 1835*. London: Smith and Elder.

Woodcock, George
1980 *The Canadians*. London: The Athlone Press.

Part III

Conflicts of Interest

Individual and Collective Strategies for Coping with the Work Situation

PERSPECTIVES ON CHANGE

Among students of modern society, two perspectives have been dominant: functionalism and a conflict approach. Functionalism views society as a system of interdependent parts, and each part is analysed in terms of the contribution it makes to the whole. In this view, change in one part of the system is responded to by appropriate adaptations in other parts, so that an approximate equilibrium is maintained. Such an equilibrium can nevertheless accommodate some change. An essential ingredient of the functionalist perspective is the belief that, for a society to survive, members must share a set of key values.

By contrast, a conflict perspective focuses on the different, and frequently opposed, interests of various groups in society. These groups vie with each other to maintain and improve their respective positions. Access to power is unequally divided; the elite few who control the greatest share are favourably placed for maintaining and improving their relative standing. Dominant values are seen as justifying the status quo.

In the broadest sense, a functionalist perspective stresses continuity, and tends to imbue current relative standings with a positive moral connotation. Change is incorporated into continuity and viewed as "progress" toward a more perfectly integrated society. What has clearly emerged as a theme throughout this collection of articles, however, is that powerful groups have often succeeded in appropriating change to expand their interests at the expense of the greatest number, i.e., of the workers. Continuity then, represents the entrenchment of a state of affairs in which benefits are disproportionately allocated, thus reinforcing existing inequalities within society.

The two perspectives referred to can be used to shed light on the constant interplay between continuity and change. The sub-title of this book is intended to draw attention, not only to this interplay, but also to the ways in which, in the Canadian context, change has tended to preserve continuity. For example, despite massive technological change,

243

Canada basically remains a hinterland economy, and although in absolute terms the standard of living has risen for the population as a whole, disparities among groups have persisted, and even widened in some cases.

The groups and individuals who see themselves as chronically short-changed in the distribution of benefits do not necessarily accept their position passively. The articles in this part of the book examine, in the context of work, the kinds of strategies employed in the quest for more equitable participation in societal rewards. In each instance, the articles deal with populations who are structurally disadvantaged, and with the ways in which they seek to overcome these disadvantages. The strategies themselves will be examined when we discuss the articles individually.

The industrial workers who are the subject of the papers by **MacKinnon** and **Knight** perform routine, monotonous work with minimal autonomy over the content of tasks and the manner in which they are carried out. Relatively high material rewards are bought at the cost of foregoing intrinsic satisfaction in the work itself. **Tataryn's** workers in high-risk industries are disadvantaged in the fundamental sense of facing the possibility of a reduced life span, and the likelihood of injury or serious health impairment. Historically, the manpower for industries like mining and construction was recruited from among the powerless, such as new immigrants, who were unable to assert their own interests (safety) over those of primary concern to employers (profits).

Native People, southern European immigrants such as the Portuguese, and women all possess ascribed characteristics which are disesteemed in our society. In order to gain access to employment, Native People must adopt new cultural values and overcome negative stereotypes. Most Portuguese immigrants come from a rural background, and have little formal education and work training. Together, these characteristics confer a low "entrance status" on them. Women have traditionally been excluded from lucrative and prestigious work, the exclusion being based on the justification that their salient roles are domestic ones. In each case, the attempts of such minorities to improve their relative standing must confront groups whose interests have become established in the social structure.

Unions have constituted an organized response by those who suffered from structural inequalities between employees and owner/managers. The Quebec union members discussed by **Smith** are disadvantaged not only by dint of their class position, but because they live in a region that historically has not shared fully in Canada's affluence. This means that their benefits have lagged behind those of workers in some other provinces, for example Ontario. **Baker** and **Robeson**'s female subjects, too, must cope with twin burdens: powerless-

ness in the work setting, and a weak position in unions where men are a numerical majority and dominate the leadership. As a consequence, issues which are interpreted as being of sole concern to women (such as paid maternity leave or the provision of childcare facilities) tend to be given short shrift in the bargaining process.

Our discussion so far has centred on the behaviour of groups as they vie for advantages in the work world. Underlying this behaviour are justificatory beliefs, ideas and views of the world — in other words, ideologies. Ideology denotes

> *. . . a system of interdependent ideas (beliefs, traditions, principles, and myths) held by a social group or society, which reflects, rationalizes, and defends its particular social, moral, religious, political and economic institutional interests and commitments. Ideologies serve as logical and philosophical justification for a group's patterns of behavior, as well as its attitudes, goals and general life situation. (Theodorson and Theodorson, 1969: 195–196)*

It will be apparent to the reader that the importance of ideology is implicit in many articles of this book. In this part, we have included those which explicitly address the various functions ideologies serve in the realm of work and industrial relations.

A brief discussion of each article now follows, using the same format as that adopted earlier in the book.

INDUSTRIAL WORKERS: AT WHAT POINT DO THEY BECOME ALIENATED?

*First, the methodology employed by **MacKinnon** merits attention. His is the only article in this anthology to be based on a sophisticated replication of a large-scale study, which seeks to establish which of two competing theoretical viewpoints has the greatest explanatory value. The question addressed is: at what point do industrial workers become alienated? Do they start work already anticipating that it will not provide intrinsic satisfaction, but merely serve as a means to the end of earning material rewards (the instrumentalism argument), or does the nature of the work itself cause it to be seen as intrinsically meaningless? In this view, minimal autonomy over the work process would produce a high degree of alienation (the technologism argument). Alienation can be defined as "a feeling of noninvolvement in and estrangement from one's society and culture. The values and social norms shared by others seem meaningless to the alienated individual" (Theodorson and Theodorson, 1969: 9).*

*The technologism argument gains support from studies such as Blauner's (1964) who found that the overall work experience affects whether, and to what extent, workers are alienated. **MacKinnon**, too, finds support for technologism and, by extension, for the Marxist* *argument that work experiences are the major determinant of attitudes. Alienation was highest among the least skilled of* **MacKinnon's** *respondents, and lowest among the most skilled. This support is qualified by the finding that respondents' social characteristics, such as age, education and geographic origin (rural or urban) independently affect orientations toward work. Those who have lived in Oshawa for a relatively short time, who are young, better educated than most G.M. workers, and also better educated than their own fathers, tend to have negative attitudes toward work, regardless of their skill level.*

MacKinnon's study traces the manifold connections between attitudes and behaviour. Beliefs by management about what shapes worker attitudes affect managerial behaviour. Acceptance of the instrumentalist view that workers do not seek intrinsic satisfaction from the job, but merely material rewards to be enjoyed elsewhere, removes from management the onus for making the work experience more meaningful. On the other hand, if the argument for technologism is accepted (i.e., that alienation stems from conditions in the job environment) then responsibility for reducing, if not eliminating, this alienation rests squarely with management. In other words, the debate whether the origin of workers' attitudes can best be explained by instrumentalism or technologism is not just academic hairsplitting, but has pragmatic consequences for managerial decisions.

INDUSTRIAL WORKERS AND THEIR DREAMS: MOVING UP OR GETTING OUT?

Knight's *study provides an example of another methodological approach. He uses secondary data, that is, data gathered by other investigators for their own purposes. Because of the expense involved in survey research, secondary data, such as census information, are frequently adapted for uses other than those for which they were originally intended.*

Whereas **MacKinnon's** *focus is on the process by which workers become alienated,* **Knight** *is concerned to discover whether workers harbour aspirations for individual mobility and, if so, how much mobility is envisaged. An interesting paradox emerges from* **Knight's** *findings concerning the aspirations of workers with differing levels of skill. On the one hand, semi-skilled workers are least likely to express aspirations for upward mobility within the corporation. This lack of aspirations would seem to be realistic considering the limited education and low skill level of these workers, and given the increasing importance corporations place on formal qualifications.*

On the other hand, the aspirations semi-skilled workers do have are far from realistic. **Knight** *demonstrates that, in the face of diminishing opportunities for advancement within industry, the very workers who are least likely to advance cling to the dream of "entrepreneurial individualism," that is, of going into business for themselves, even* *though this is becoming increasingly unattainable. Ironically, the persistence of the chimera performs the latent function of keeping class conflict in check. The "Walter Mitty" dreams of **Knight's** workers blunt their dissatisfaction, and make them less inclined to take action directed at bringing about fundamental social change.*

*A number of articles in this collection, notably those by **Marchak, Lowe, Bowles** and **Haney,** and **Clement** have shown that the quality of work life has been negatively affected by the ways in which technology has been used in a capitalist economy. The two articles just discussed attempt to measure more directly how workers with differing skill levels feel about their jobs. Students should be aware, however, that although these particular articles deal with industrial workers, the relationship between what people do, their job orientation and how they cope with disaffections arising from their work, has relevance for all occupations.*

OCCUPATIONAL HEALTH: WHO DECIDES ON "ACCEPTABLE" RISKS AND WHO TAKES THEM?

In our introduction, we noted that work and work-related issues must be looked at in a social context. A recent societal trend has been the emergence of a new militancy on the part of disadvantaged groups. That certain occupations put health, and even life, in jeopardy has long been known. What has not been generally known is the magnitude of the problem. Furthermore, the workers exposed to these risks for the most part used to accept employers' avowals that everything possible had been done to minimize hazards, and that the hazards that remained could not be eliminated.

Clearly, as long as a state of affairs is considered inevitable, it is not defined as a social problem. Occupational health and safety became a social problem when "authoritative" statements about "acceptable" risks began to be challenged. There was growing awareness that those who assessed the risks and those who had to take them were different groups with different priorities.

***Tataryn** talks about a "risk triangle" that consists of corporations, their workers and government agencies. The tasks of these agencies are to investigate what risks exist, and to establish and enforce standards of occupational health which are also acceptable to the society at large. Politicians and industrialists rely on scientists for guidance in establishing these standards. Belief in the sanctity of scientific evidence concerning acceptable risk levels has provided ongoing justification for minimal intervention in the face of ravaging industrial disease and death. It is remarkable that this ideology of scientific infallibility has withstood changing and contradictory findings. A dramatic example is provided by the number of asbestos fibres per cubic centimetre of air considered tolerable: between 1938 and 1976, this number was reduced* *from 30 to .1. A reduction of this magnitude can hardly be explained solely in terms of advances in scientific knowledge.*

It would seem that neither government agencies nor corporations rush headlong into the expensive task of protecting workers. Rather, they tend to respond to the pressure generated by media attention and public outcry. It should be borne in mind here that the media both reflect and create public concern. **Tataryn's book,** *Dying for a Living, on which his article is based, is a case in point. It resulted from an investigation of industrial hazards, an investigation* **Tataryn** *carried out while he was a CBC producer. Immediately following publication of the book, the Ontario government ordered a review of the supposedly therapeutic practice of having miners inhale aluminium dust. The practice was subsequently suspended, as it had already been in other industrialized countries.*

Two further points are worth noting about **Tataryn's** *article. First, it is an example of applied research, that is, research undertaken to establish the exact nature of a perceived problem, and to provide recommendations for ameliorating it. Secondly, the article demonstrates that a researcher can be intensely engaged in the issues at stake without allowing this to subvert standards of scientific enquiry.*

AFFIRMATIVE ACTION: EQUALITY OF CONDITION THROUGH INEQUALITY OF TREATMENT

An important place in Canadian ideology is given to the concept of a cultural mosaic, which implies that membership in a particular racial or ethnic group does not affect success within Canadian society at large. As Porter (1965) forcibly argued, however, race and ethnicity have had, and continue to have, profound consequences for the life chances of individuals. **Jain** *demonstrates that, in the case of Indians, a combination of negative factors serves to restrict their life chances in general, and their employment opportunities in particular. Membership in a disesteemed racial group, a low level of educational attainment, geographic remoteness and employer discrimination jointly and severally entrap Indians in a vicious circle. Such a circle can be charted as follows: unemployment and marginal employment — poverty — apathy and withdrawal — educational failure — more unemployment and marginal employment.*

The subtitle of this part of the book refers to individual and collective strategies for coping. However, it needs to be emphasized that a group can be so tightly entrapped that neither individual nor group efforts are sufficient to permit escape. Jain's article is specifically concerned with exploring how such entrapment can be broken by official action.

It is evident that legislating equality of opportunity for minority groups is a thorny undertaking. Since societal values in this area are contradictory, and since legislation must seek to accommodate these contradictions, it follows that the policies themselves are likely to be equivocal. This equivocation characterizes not only the scope of policies — the extent to which legislation should influence employment practices as regards recruitment, pay and promotion — but also their implementation and enforcement. A further source of confusion stems from the paradox that, to redress the inequality which particularistic considerations have created for minority groups such as Native People and women, unequal treatment in a positive direction is required, at least temporarily. Affirmative action programs are one means of bringing about equality of condition through inequality of treatment. In this specific sense, then, particularism must persist rather than be eliminated.

COPING AT THE LOWER RUNGS: INFORMAL NETWORKS IN LIEU OF FORMAL EDUCATION

A network can be defined as consisting of individuals who are linked by certain common characteristics, and who activate these links when they consider it useful to do so. Networks may be based on such characteristics as ethnicity, gender, social class, or on the sharing of significant experiences — for example, having been to the same school or to the same prison.

The importance of networks for success has been extensively studied at various levels of the occupational hierarchy. Kanter (1977) has shown that mobility within a large corporation is positively influenced by integration into the "right" networks, which frequently exclude such minorities as women. In her study of the elite structure of Toronto, Kelner (1969) noted that the perpetuation of Anglo-Saxon dominance is facilitated by linkages which ease the way for insiders, while handicapping outsiders. Thus, corporate ventures may be arranged within the privacy of clubs from which non Anglo-Saxons are excluded. Focusing on a lower societal level, Herman's study of Macedonians in Toronto's restaurant industry (1978) documents the importance of personal contacts for economic success. West Indian domestics, as discussed by **Turrittin** *in her article in this anthology, frequently use personal networks, both to obtain their entry jobs, and then to locate more attractive positions.*

Anderson *looks at the role of informal ethnic networks in making work available to Portuguese immigrants, and argues that, for these immigrants, access to "networks of contact" is a more reliable predictor of success than the level of education they have attained. It will be recalled that* **Stager** *and* **Meltz**, *in their longitudinal analysis of occupational earnings, stress the positive relationship at all levels of the work force between education and earnings. In fact, their findings show that the impact of education strengthened in the four decades from 1931* *to 1971. Similar positive relationships between education and earnings have been supported by the findings of numerous studies.*

How then can the lack *of this relationship be explained in the case of Portuguese immigrants?* **Anderson** *suggests, first, that below a certain education level, small increments in years of schooling may have only a minimal effect on earnings. This explanation gains some support from the large-scale investigation by Jencks et al. (1979) which established that the relationship between education and occupational status (and hence earnings) is strengthened at critical junctures. For example, the first and last years of high school, and of university, have a greater impact than any intervening year. Secondly,* **Anderson** *speculates that cultural differences may come into play, in that immigrants from minimally industrialized regions may have had no opportunity to obtain more than rudimentary schooling in their country of origin. In the face of such a structural constraint, low educational attainment may tell us very little about personal motivation or intellectual ability. Since more than rudimentary schooling is available to mainstream Canadians, education does mediate between personal qualities and occupational success to a far greater extent than it does for Portuguese immigrants and others from a similar background.*

SUCCESSFUL WOMEN: CONQUERING INNER CONFLICTS AND
EXTERNAL OBSTACLES

A theme that echoes throughout this book is the disjunction between the ideology of equality of opportunity in Canadian society, and the reality of structural barriers which make certain groups "less equal." However, individual members of such groups do overcome these barriers and attain success. This feat has somewhat paradoxical consequences. On the one hand, these achievers provide validation for the ideology without immediately changing the fundamental status quo. On the other hand, the successful minority group members provide role models whom others will seek to emulate. Thus an upward spiral is initiated.

Women in general, and particularly women in the work force, have constituted, and still constitute, a "less equal" minority. Their participation in the labour force has been substantially confined to sectors characterized by low pay, low prestige, minimal autonomy and few channels for advancement. Many of these work settings are female "ghettoes" (Armstrong & Armstrong, 1978) in that they are numerically dominated by women. **Symons**'s *study shows that some women do pass through the needle's eye, and move into traditionally male-dominated work spheres, becoming corporate executives and successful entrepreneurs.*

The paper examines three perspectives which have been used to explain women's subordinate status in the work world. In exploring these perspectives, students should note that any given one raises certain sets of questions, but leaves others unasked. Thus, the temperamental model that focuses on feminine attitudes and personal qualities which supposedly render women unsuited for the rigours of managerial tasks tells us nothing about the nature of the work setting itself. **Symons** *found that, in practice, each of the three models has some utility in explaining how her respondents overcame obstacles to success. In virtually every case an exceptionally fortunate configuration of circumstances was present — in terms of being at the right place at the right time, having a powerful sponsor and possessing the appropriate personal qualities. Another key factor was that these managerial women experienced relatively low conflict between occupational and domestic roles, due to the fact that they were not married, had no children, or had been able to establish an equitable division of domestic labour. Further, most of the married women commented upon the positive support their husbands provided.*

Because of the small number of respondents and the nonrandom nature of the sample, caution must be exercised in generalizing **Symons**'s *findings to all successful career women. The chief value of studies like this lies in the rich detail they provide about people's lives, and in the questions they generate to be explored by further research.*

It can be seen from the three articles we have just examined that the quest of "special people" for a better life may involve a variety of strategies. Affirmative action as discussed by **Jain** *involves official intervention, aimed at improving the lot of a disadvantaged collectivity. The informal ways in which a group "takes care of its own" through helping networks are explored by* **Anderson**. *Networks are also one means which* **Symons**'s *ambitious women have used in their pursuit of occupational advancement, and in paving the way for other women.*

LABOUR RELATIONS IN QUEBEC: THE ROUTE TO RADICALISM

When discussing the article on chiropractors, we referred to professionalization as one strategy occupational groups may employ to achieve collective upward mobility. Unionization is another tool workers have used to achieve a "better deal" in terms of pay, fringe benefits and working conditions. Haug and Sussman note the similarities in the two processes:

> *Unionization and professionalization are two processes by which members of an occupation seek to achieve collective upward mobility. Such combined efforts as job advancement are the analogue, on a group scale, of individuals striving for a better job — one with higher pay, pleasanter working conditions, more freedom from supervision and higher community status. Where individual upward mobility is blocked or hindered, occupational incumbents often turn to collective efforts with the same generalized goals of increased earnings, autonomy and prestige. In short, individuals unlikely to get better work tend to join with others similarly situated to make their work better. (1971: 525)*

Historically, unionization was the strategy adopted by blue-collar workers. In addition to improving material benefits, it was hoped that membership in an organization established for them and controlled by them would allow workers to retain dignity in work settings which were often ungratifying and impersonal.

In Britain, union goals found political expression through the Labour Party, but in North America the ruthlessness with which unions that posed an overt challenge to the capitalist system were smashed (for example the Knights of Labour and the Industrial Workers of the World) convinced mainstream union leaders that political involvement should be eschewed. Under the aegis of Samuel Gompers and his successors, the North American labour movement abandoned any attempts to topple the capitalist system and concentrated on "more, more now." Though less clear-cut than in the United States, the emphasis of the Canadian labour movement has generally been on pragmatic business unionism. With the influence of the Catholic church, Quebec unions were more docile than their counterparts in the rest of Canada, as evidenced, for example, by their lower propensity to strike.

Smith analyses the factors which played a part in the radicalization of the Quebec labour movement, manifested by more strikes and an increasingly Marxist rhetoric. Smith cautions, first, that ideologies enunciated by leaders need not be shared by the rank and file; secondly, he notes that the greater strike propensity of workers in Quebec, relative to those in Canada generally and in Ontario particularly, must be explained with reference to Quebec's distinctive industrial relations institutions, which are described in the article. Thus, while MacKinnon alerts us to the ramifications of ideology for action, Smith makes clear that ideology may be a necessary, but is not a sufficient, cause of the direction industrial conduct takes.

The elegance of Smith's method of analysis should be noted. He scrutinizes various explanations of changes in Quebec's industrial relations, and systematically eliminates each on the grounds that it does not account for all the events to be considered. For example, the argument that francophone workers, angered by the failure of the Quiet Revolution to eliminate the economic dominance of Anglophones, became more prone to strike cannot explain why the most bitter strikes (such as the 1972 Common Front Strike) were directed against francophone employers.

We noted that exploratory studies such as Symons's may act as a spur to further research. Similarly, the difficulty Smith encounters in finding a parsimonious explanation for recent Quebec labour history provides an impetus for continuing investigation.

THE WOMAN WORKER: HOW DOES SHE FARE IN UNIONS?

The values and attitudes held within social systems at large and within their constituent parts continually reinforce each other. In other words, in a society such as ours in which there is marked racism and sexism, it would be unrealistic to expect these to be absent in institutional sectors such as education, work settings or labour unions. In turn, the prejudice and discrimination that exist in the various institutions keep alive these forces in society generally.

Historically, neither ethnic minorities nor women have fared well in unions. Krauter and Davis note that, in 1918, the Trades and Labour Congress refused an application for a charter by the Order of Sleeping Car Porters, organized by black porters of the Canadian National Railway (1978: 53). The Chinese and Japanese were perceived as a threat to existing wage levels, in that they were often forced to accept low pay, and job discrimination against them was unequivocally supported:

> *Instead of using its collective power to bring about higher minimum wages for all workers, whatever their racial origin, organized labour chose to view the mere presence of Chinese and Japanese as a threat. (Krauter and Davis, 1977: 76)*

What circumstances have influenced the fate of women in trade unions? **Baker** *and* **Robeson** *review the literature addressing this question, and pinpoint four types of explanations which have currency. Three of these types focus primarily on ways in which women's position has been subject to influences external to unions. For example, until recently, most union members have been blue-collar workers, and it has been widely argued that such workers tend to see women's place as inferior. If negative feelings about oneself arise from low status in the occupational hierarchy (see* The Hidden Injuries of Class, *1973), it may be important to have others beneath one in the pecking order. The difficulties of unionizing women also reflect external influences. According to societal ideology, a woman's salient roles are those of wife and mother. Participation in the work force is regarded as temporary, even though many women must work all their lives. These ideological constraints, together with the pragmatic ones of having to cope with two jobs (at the workplace and in the home), have minimized the time and effort women have devoted to union activities. This can be linked to* **Symons**'s *findings that these constraints operate at higher occupational levels; executive women, too, have to juggle occupational and domestic responsibilities.*

In Men and Women of the Corporation, Kanter *noted that under-representation in management depresses women's power as a group, and tends to exert a negative influence on the power of individual female managers. This state of affairs is duplicated in unions — women's relative powerlessness means that their special concerns receive low priority. It is ironic, if hardly surprising, that institutions such as unions, that were founded to espouse the rights of the disadvantaged, themselves practise discrimination.*

REFERENCES

Armstrong, P. and H. Armstrong
1978   *The Double Ghetto*. Toronto: McClelland and Stewart.

Blauner, R.
1964   *Alienation and Freedom*. Chicago: University of Chicago Press.

Haug, M.R. and M.B. Sussman
1971   "Professionalization and Unionism." *American Behavioral Scientist*. 14: 525–540.

Herman, H.V.
1978   *Men in White Aprons*. Toronto: Peter Martin Associates.

Jencks, C. et al.
1979   *Who Gets Ahead? The Determinants of Economic Success in America*. New York: Basic Books.

Kanter, R.M.
1977   *Men and Women of the Corporation*. New York: Basic Books.

Kelner, M.
1970   "Ethnic Penetration into Toronto's Elite Structure." *Canadian Review of Sociology and Anthropology*. 7(2): 128–137.

Krauter, J.F. and M. Davis
1978   *Minority Canadians: Ethnic Groups*. Toronto: Methuen.

Porter, J.
1965   *The Vertical Mosaic*. Toronto: University of Toronto Press.

Sennett, R. and J. Cobb
1973   *The Hidden Injuries of Class*. New York: Knopf.

Theodorson, G.A. and A.G. Theodorson
1969   *Dictionary of Sociology*. New York: Thos. Y. Crowell.

Chapter 15

The Industrial Worker and the Job: Alienated or Instrumentalized?*

Malcolm H. MacKinnon

INTRODUCTION

In recent years, debate surrounding the nature of the relationship between the manual worker and the job has coalesced into rival camps. The "technological implications"[1] approach affirms that the material conditions of labour and the quality of work life produced represent the most important factors shaping the link between worker and job. When interaction between man and machine results in a denial of freedom and control, a condition of alienated labour prevails, adversely affecting attitudes toward firm and job. The prototypical experience here arises from assembly-line technology and the job-related consequences produced. Minute division of labour, narrow span of control and a monotonous and repetitive task cycle contribute to feelings of frustration and resentment.[2] By contrast, task roles not subject to fragmentation, featuring a wide span of control with novel and nonrepetitive task rhythms, engender sentiments of pride, dignity and accomplishment — an outcome producing a favourable appraisal of work and company. In short, job-related attitudes and behaviour are shaped by working conditions, by technology and the material conditions of labour it creates. These, in turn, produce task roles featuring varying degrees of freedom and control so that when discretion and autonomy are restricted, the worker becomes estranged from the job and the employing organization.

Opposed to this view stand the authors of instrumental theory.[3] The contemporary industrial worker, it is averred, expresses minimum concern for the task roles he is required to perform. Overwhelmingly, expectations focus not on working conditions but on material rewards such as wages and overall standards of living. Moreover, these priorities are not affected by on-the-job experience, but emerge from the conditions of life in society at large. Industrial labour is seen as a neutral activity evoking passions of neither love nor hatred, but simply as the means necessary to achieve economic ends. Equally alien to the mentality of the instrumental worker is the spontaneous joy of craftsmanship and the humiliation and despair of degraded labour. Severance of the psychic bond between man and work is accomplished by way of substitution — the intervention of economic priorities strips work of its emotional foliage, reducing it to a cipher. Derived from these premises is the conclusion that job-related attitudes and behaviour are not influenced by

*This article was previously published in the *British Journal of Sociology*, Vol. 31, No. 1 (March 1980) under the title "Work Instrumentalism Reconsidered." Reprinted with permission.

working conditions, but are formed prior to actual contact with the workplace. Thus, the worker is viewed as harbouring an antecedent commitment to instrumentality.

Substantial support for both "technologism" and "instrumentalism" can be found in the literature. In part at least, this polarization[4] can be attributed to the connection established by both theories to a more embracing set of issues, namely the political role assumed by the working class in the advanced capitalist state. Instrumentalism aligns itself with the "end of ideology"[5] thesis whereby the worker abandons commitment to a radical belief system, is co-opted and thus neutralized by capitalist institutions. This co-optation is manifested by the acquisition of instrumentality, the "cash-nexus" if you will, and the subsequent devaluation of work activity. Money, and the standard of living it can purchase become focal, and capacity to consume now is judged the criterion by which dignity and self-worth are attained. Class consciousness is replaced by commodity consciousness, and the need felt to democratize the decision-making apparatus controlling work and society withers away. Technologism, by contrast, is closely allied with Marxist tradition which affirms the centrality of work-based experience, that degradation on-the-job operates like a catalyst sensitizing the worker to conditions of exploitation in wider society.[6] This unified vision of existence is seen as a necessary condition for revolutionary activity but, if the operative dismisses the importance of work and seeks fulfillment through other means — means posing no intrinsic threat to capitalism — revolutionary potential is derailed.

While these issues remain central to sociological discourse, their resolution cannot be realized within the modest boundaries of this study. The task here is to retest instrumental theory and thereby establish whether its basic propositions can be sustained. Equally important are the claims made by technologism which will also be subject to empirical review. An attempt will be made to resolve the core dispute between the theories. Does work experience shape job-related attitudes and behaviour (technologism) or are they produced by events external to the work environment (instrumentalism)? Resolution of this controversy will allow us to identify the work orientations held by contemporary industrial workers. This end can be most effectively achieved by conducting an initial review and critique of instrumental theory.

The following framework is used to organize subject matter: (1) Instrumental theory is critically reviewed, (2) a description of the research setting and design used to test instrumentalism and technologism is then provided (3) the test implications used to achieve this end are introduced, and their results are tabled and discussed; (4) next the scope of investigation is broadened to include newly revealed issues, and finally key themes and test results are summarized.

INSTRUMENTALITY AND THE INDUSTRIAL WORKER: REVIEW AND CRITIQUE

As noted, this view of the industrial worker is most closely associated with the work of Goldthorpe and his associates. The theory is formulated from research material collected in England, more specifically Luton, an industrial town located in Bedfordshire about thirty miles north of London. For reasons to be clarified shortly, Luton is projected as a setting within which one is likely to find a significant number of instrumental workers. For the time being, however, conditions responsible for this orientation require disclosure. Who are instrumental workers and how do they undergo the conversion process?

Historically, the emergence of the instrumental worker is attributed to the economic decline of specific industries and the traditional working class communities they spawned. Typical British examples include docking,[7] coal mining[8] and fishing,[9] while in Canada a similar claim can be made for logging.[10] Coincident with this ongoing process of decay is the recent growth and development of the mass industrial enterprise, a system of production giving rise to a new type of community which contrasts sharply with the old traditional neighbourhood. As expected, workers abandon areas that are stagnating and migrate to those undergoing economic growth and expansion. The very rapidity with which this process of migration unfolds, results in the creation of a community whose members are strangers, the corollary being that an isolated and privatized existence ensues.[11] In the traditional neighbourhood, social interaction is both intimate and extensive so that identity, social status and esteem are extensions of the local value system.[12] In the new community, by contrast, interpersonal networks are attenuated and impersonal so that a shared system of values does not develop. Under these circumstances, material possessions form the base from which the individual's social worth is estimated. Personal identity becomes an extension of purchasing power; the greater the number and quality of commodities consumed and displayed, the greater the prestige conferred. Conspicuous consumption, a concern for material reward, represents an adaptive response to prevailing circumstances.

As Goldthorpe states:

> In terms of social values, the transition from the traditional to the new working class may be seen as a change from "solidaristic collectivism" towards what we would term a more "instrumental orientation" to work, trade unionism and politics alike. And in terms of social relationships a parallel movement may be suggested: away from "communal sociability" towards a more privatized form of existence, in which the economic advancement of the individual and his family becomes of greater importance than membership in a closely knit local community.[13]

Against this backdrop, the instrumental view towards labour assumes theoretical clarity. Those who have experienced geographic mobility, moving to Luton from another location, are identified as more instrumental than nonmobiles, the native inhabitants. While theoretically less important than geographic mobility, three additional sources are identified as causes of an instrumental attachment to the job. These are downward inter-generational (social) and career (occupational) mobility,[14] along with age. An individual experiences downward social mobility when failing to match occupational attainment of the father. If father holds a white collar job and offspring is a semi-skilled worker, then downward social mobility is observed. Similar thinking prevails in the instance of downward career mobility, except the crucial point of comparison now hinges on prior occupational standing of the respondent. When this indicates tenancy of a white collar position, in contrast to current status marked by a lower level of occupational prestige, downward career mobility has taken place. Age represents the fourth and final cause. Younger workers, by virtue of the economic pressures generated by this stage in the life cycle — the care of children and purchase of a home — are more likely to adopt instrumental values.[15] Because these factors precede contact with job presently held, the worker is viewed as having an antecedent commitment to instrumentality.

Implicit within this argument is the notion that instrumental workers maintain a psychic detachment from working conditions. They are characterized as entering present employment motivationally predisposed by a calculating stance, one responsible for the exchange of work featuring intrinsic gratification for an alternative imbued with drudgery but, and this is the important point, paying higher wages. Energized by instrumentality, the worker constructs a "rational" estimate of his current situation, weighs the alternatives, then directs behaviour toward economic ends.

> The primary meaning of work is as a means to an end, or ends, external to the work situation; that is, work is regarded as a means to acquiring the income necessary to support a valued way of life of which work itself is not an integral part. Work is therefore experienced as mere "labour" in the sense of an expenditure of effort which is made for extrinsic rather than intrinsic rewards.[16]

To this point, only the causes of an instrumental view towards labour have been discussed and identified; it is now time to specify the consequences. How is an instrumental orientation to the job expressed? Above all this is revealed by an extrinsic rather than an intrinsic job attachment.[17] To be attached extrinsically is to emphasize wages, security and prestige, whereas an intrinsic affiliation is revealed by a concern for the structure of work activity. Does it utilize inherent skill? Does it create opportunity for growth and development by encouraging the worker to exercise autonomy and discretion? Work instrumentalism is also expressed by attitudes toward workmates. They are tenuously expressed because work is viewed solely in economic terms, not a pastime from which one expects to obtain social stimulation. This pecuniary orientation also includes the union and the legitimate range of activities it can pursue. Predictably, the focus rests on securing a maximum in wages and benefits for the worker while foregoing a more activist and ideologically inspired political role. These attitudes are behaviourally revealed by a low level of participation in union affairs.[18] Work instrumentalism in its final form is an avoidance response to company sponsored clubs and activities.[19] Like the union, its mandate is cast in economic terms, to provide the worker with income and security in exchange for his labour power. Perception of the obligation between management and labour is so confined.

As an orientation, work instrumentalism is thus conceived in multi-dimensional terms. The impetus for economic security is revealed in various ways, each analytically distinct but related to the other. This means that when a worker expresses an extrinsic attachment to the job, he is also likely to be indifferent toward workmates, exhibit personal detachment from union affairs and social activities sponsored by the company. Thus, work instrumentalism is comprised of several distinct factors which interrelate because they are manifestations of the same phenomenon. The four causal variables previously described influence the degree to which work instrumentalism is experienced. Goldthorpe's causal model is presented in Table 15–1.

Table 15–1

Goldthorpe's Causal Model of Work Instrumentalism

Independent Variables	Dependent Variables
Social Factors	*Work Instrumentalism*
1. Geographic mobility	1. Extrinsic job attachment
2. Intergenerational mobility	2. Frequency of attendance at union meetings
3. Career mobility	3. Workgroup affiliation
4. Age	4. Frequency of attendance at company sponsored social activities

Perhaps the most glaring inadequacy arising out of Goldthorpe's study is that his findings are inconsistent with the theory devised. In other words, the theory goes beyond the evidence manifested by his data. Previously stated was the meaning assigned to the four dependent variables, that they are all slightly different expressions of work instrumentalism. This being the case, they should significantly correlate with each other.

By contrast, Goldthorpe's results reveal statistical independence, a result in direct conflict with the theory.[20] And yet despite this contradiction, Goldthorpe refuses to abandon his unitary interpretation and proceeds to create an instrumentalism score or single variable from independent items, from items bearing no relationship to each other. By analogy, this is equivalent to the submission of a basket of mixed fruit accompanied by the injunction that it contains only oranges. The credibility of the model continues to erode when other findings are examined. An attempt is made to establish a link between three of the four background variables and the instrumentalism score[21] but, again, supporting evidence is not forthcoming. Geographic mobility, because it is logically consistent with the historical scenario, should above all relate to the instrumentalism score. That it does not, undermines confidence in the historical account as an appropriate explanation for the origin of instrumental values. Some evidence linking downward career and social mobility with the instrumentalism score is produced, but the importance of such results is exaggerated.[22] An even more damning indictment surfaces when Goldthorpe's findings reveal work instrumentalism to be significantly affected by job conditions. Despite continued theoretical pronouncements to the contrary, semi-skilled workers are significantly more likely to be instrumental than the skilled.[23] Although acknowledged in a subterranean fashion, this result in no way causes the author to revise the theory's basic claims. The research is still touted as uncovering a new system of working class values likely to become even more pervasive in the future.

This serious gap between data and theory underlies much of current criticism, a hiatus which highlights the necessity to retest instrumentalism.

RESEARCH SETTING AND DESIGN

An adequate test of instrumental theory requires that particular attention be paid to the setting and research design featured by Goldthorpe's original effort. Particularly important is the necessity for this study to locate a setting and establish a design matching the original. Setting poses a difficult problem because it is virtually impossible to locate urban centres that are identical unless, of course, one returns to the original research site. But even in this instance, lapse of time introduces changes beyond experimental control and, realistically, the most to be hoped for is that the setting ultimately selected be a reasonable approximation of its counterpart. Before the reader can assess the eventual choice, however, disclosure of Luton's salient characteristics is required.

Luton is a relatively prosperous industrial centre, one that has recently experienced general economic expansion and growth. A high proportion of the town's labour force is thus made up of geographically mobile workers who presumably moved to the area in search of higher living standards. Community life is largely centred on private home ownership, which is conducive to the privatized form of existence pursued by instrumental workers. Industrial firms are noted for relatively high wages and generous packages of benefits. Harmony, stability and mutual accord characterize labour–management relations.[24]

The locale selected to retest the theory is Oshawa, a city located in south-central Ontario. It is a prosperous industrial centre dominated by General Motors which manufactures parts, automobiles and trucks. Its population has more than doubled in the past 25 years, increasing from 50,000 in 1951 to 110,000 in 1976, the year of data collection. Without wishing to impugn the fecundity of the inhabitants, an increase of this magnitude suggests input from external sources — more specifically from migration. In short, geographic mobility can be held responsible for much of this growth. Residential patterns suggest home ownership rather than apartment dwelling to be the dominant way of life.[25] G.M. is the largest source of local employment; a company offering relatively high wages and a comprehensive benefit package. Business unionism, a practical concern for wages, benefits and security, colours labour–management relations; differences are negotiated within a framework mutually conceived and endorsed to control or "cool out" the more overt and disruptive forms of industrial unrest. While by no means identical, these characteristics generally mirror those found in Luton.

Goldthorpe's sample is drawn from three of Luton's leading industrial firms: (1) Automobile manufacturing, (2) a ball-bearing enterprise, and (3) chemical production. Sample eligibility is restricted to men with the following characteristics:

(1) between the ages of 21 and 46;
(2) married and living with their wives;
(3) regularly earning 17 £ per week gross (October 1962);
(4) resident in Luton or in immediate adjacent housing areas.[26]

It is then stratified by level of skill. The skilled group comprises toolmakers, millwrights and other maintenance categories, men who have successfully completed an apprenticeship program. Setters make up the intermediate group, those whose task proficiency results from practical experience. A semi-skilled classification includes assemblers, machinists and process workers whose job training minimally requires a few hours and maximally a few days. The skilled number 56 workers, intermediate 23 and semi-skilled 150. Final sample size is 229.

The sampling frame for this study is drawn entirely from the G.M. workforce.[27] It is stratified by skill, creating a continuum of occupational powerlessness.[28] Assemblers experience this powerlessness to the highest degree. A support group of stock men, lift-truck operators, truck drivers and inspectors are intermediate on this continuum. Tradesmen, including tool and dye makers, electricians, mechanics, millwrights and tinsmiths, are low. Stratifying the sample by level of skill creates opportunity to test the effect of working conditions on job-related behaviour and attitudes.

The sampling frame comprises 2,317 individuals.[29] Stratified by skill, 1,330 are assemblers, 629 support and 358 craftsmen. Random selection of subsamples totalling 120 respondents for each group produces a sample size of 360. From this, 220 questionnaires were returned, a completion rate approaching 70 percent.[30]

A few caveats are required in relation to the nature of this sample. Recall that one-fifth of the eligibles were excluded for ethnic reasons, one-fifth on the basis of job title and a further third because of residence beyond city limits. These features impose limits on the degree to which the findings can be generalized to the wider population. Furthermore, the random selection of subsamples produces proportions under-representing assemblers and over-representing craftsmen. Problems of generalizability arise here when two variables relate, but the magnitude of the correlation varies among the three technological groups. This could be resolved by the use of weighting procedures but the basic problem remains, that the sample cannot be generalized to a wider universe. Responsibility for this arises from theoretical considerations, the necessity to stratify the sample by level of skill. Learning the subtle art of compromise is finely tuned by the grim realities of sample design. Ineptitude of function in one area is the companion of adequacy in another. Generalizability is the sample weakness of this study, the manipulation of the skill variable its strength. Indeed, Goldthorpe's research can be similarly described.

EXAMINATION OF RESULTS

Does a causal relationship exist between the independent and dependent variables listed in Table 15–1[31]? This is the core issue, one that the retest of Goldthorpe's theory is designed to resolve. Already established is the similarity between the two studies in absolute terms, that workers in Oshawa, like those in Luton, possess the background characteristics necessary to produce instrumental values and that both groups substantially subscribe to these values. These findings can mean one of two things: (1) That the data support instrumental theory. (2) That workers adhere to such views but do so for reasons other than those proposed by the theory. A final decision can only be tabled after the causes of these beliefs and the covariation among them is established. Theoretical insight is gained by examining one variable's relationship to another. For, although our results reveal support for instrumental values in absolute terms, this says nothing about the origin and meaning of these ideas.

Table 15–2

Matrix of Items Representing Work Instrumentalism

Variable Label	1.	2.	3.
1. Instrumental attachment		.01	−.01
2. Frequency of attendance at union meetings			.12*
3. Workgroup affiliation			

All coefficients Pearson product-moment.
*S < .05

Editors' Note: Pearson's r measures the degree of association between two variables; it can vary from 1 to 0 to −1. When r = 0 no relationship exists between the two variables. This situation is observed in Table 15–2 where the correlation between attending union meetings and an instrumental attachment is .01. An r of this size means that union attendance does not help predict whether or not people hold instrumental values. When r = 1 a perfect positive relationship exists between two variables and when r = − 1 a perfect negative relationship. This means that the score on the independent variable completely predicts the score on the dependent variable. However, perfect relationships are never found in sociology. More typical is the positive association (r = .< 11) between work alienation and self-estrangement found in Table 15–4. The correlation means that as work alienation increases so does self-estrangement. By contrast Table 15–4 shows a negative correlation between work alienation and evaluation of the company. Thus as a person's level of work alienation increases, his or her evaluation of the company decreases (i.e., becomes more negative).

For instance, the meaning assigned by Goldthorpe to the four dependent variables in Table 15–1 is that they are slight variations of a common theme, of an underlying phenomenon labelled work instrumentalism. If correct, the variables in question should express unidimensionality; they should relate to each other in a statistically significant way to sustain such an interpretation. Table 15–2 tests[32] this interpretation, but the results offer little support for it. A weak relationship between frequency of attendance at union meetings and affiliation with workmates is revealed, but more striking is the absence of a significant connection between job attachment and the other two variables. An extrinsic view of labour should represent the conceptual pivot around which a more general posture to the job takes shape, a view which receives no support from the data.

Table 15–3

Background Causes of Work Instrumentalism Controlling for Skill Level

Background Causes	Components of Work Instrumentalism	Simple Coefficient	First Order Partial
1. Downward social mobility	1. Frequency of attendance at union meetings	.14**	.13
2. Downward career mobility	2. Instrumental attachment to job	−.20*	−.01
3. Age	3. Instrumental attachment to job	.21*	.00

All coefficients Pearson product-moment.
* S < .001
** S < .05

What are the sources of instrumental ideas? Are they caused by the social characteristics identified by the theory? Table 15–3 subjects Goldthorpe's causal model to test by introducing level of skill as an experimental control. The reason behind this procedure is to determine if instrumental values arise independent of the work environment. This can be done by checking the simple coefficient (skill uncontrolled) against the first-order partial (skill controlled). When the introduction of a control variable results in substantial change in the coefficient, the conclusion is that the original relationship is being influenced by the control. If instrumental theory is correct, therefore, controlling for level of skill should not affect the original relationship.

With four independent and three dependent variables, the possibility exists for a maximum of 9 significant relationships, but only three arise.* The experience of downward social mobility[33] is moderately associated with infrequent involvement in union affairs and the relationship is independent of job conditions. Although this finding reflects expectation, a more acceptable interpretation of its meaning is available, one having nothing to do with instrumental theory.[34] The connection between career mobility[35] and work instrumentalism[36] runs in the opposite direction to the one predicted, in that loss of occupational prestige results in less, rather than more instrumentality. Results for age agree with the theory — older workers are less, rather than more, instrumental. Completely unexpected, however, are first-order partials showing job conditions entirely responsible for the original relationships. These results provide no support for instrumental theory.

---

*Table 15–3 refers only to three of the independent variables, since the fourth, geographic mobility, shows no significant relationship to components of work instrumentalism.

Figure 15–1

Work-Based Determinants and Correlates of Work Instrumentalism

Determinants   **Correlates**

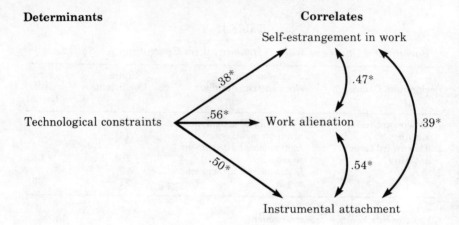

All coefficients Pearson product-moment corrected for attenuation where applicable.
*S < .001

Because the introduction of skill as an experimental control generates significant impact, it is reasonable to assume that job conditions are responsible for instrumental values, or an instrumental work attachment. Theoretically, technologism would also endorse this claim. A crucial test will now be devised to assess the merit of these contrasting positions. Does an instrumental posture to the job arise in response to social conditions — the position advocated by instrumental theory — or is it a mere reflection of working conditions, as technologism maintains? The question can be decided by examining the effect of skill on a perceived sense of alienation and estrangement from work.[37] Now if an instrumental work attachment is inserted into this system as a dependent variable, under the assumption that instrumental theory is correct, the following results are expected: (1) Skill level does not affect an instrumental attachment. (2) The instrumental attachment should not significantly co-vary with alienation and self-estrangement because its origins exist beyond the workplace.

Examination of the results in Figure 15–1 leads to the acceptance of technologism and the rejection of instrumentalism. The material conditions of labour, level of skill, quality of work life, occupational powerlessness, technological constraints — call it what you will — determine alienation, self-estrangement and instrumentality. More specifically assemblers, those most profoundly touched by occupational powerlessness, are most instrumental, whereas craftsmen, least affected by this condition, are least instrumental. Based on this rather compelling evidence, work instrumentalism can now be

Table 15–4

Correlates of Work Instrumentalism and Alienation

Variable Label	Work Instrumentalism	Work Alienation Uncorrected	Corrected
1. Self-estrangement in work	.39*	.41*	.47
2. Evaluation of company	−.25*	−.38*	−.43
3. Technological constraints	.50*	.49*	.56
4. Size of community of birth	−.25*	−.17**	−.20
5. Age	−.21*	−.33*	−.37
6. Years worked in G.M.	−.20*	−.32*	−.36
7. Type dwelling: (1) House (2) Apt	.22*	.26*	.30
8. Valuation of technological conditions at work	−.33*	−.31*	−.35
9. Valuation of work as a social activity	−.13***	−.25*	−.29

All coefficients Pearson product-moment corrected for attenuation where applicable.
  *S < .001
 **S < .01
***S < .05

understood as an additional form or manifestation of work alienation — a perceived form of disenchantment with actual job conditions — and its causes rooted in the material conditions of labour.

Because work instrumentalism and alienation are varying expressions of a common underlying phenomenon, they should relate to a third variable in an equivalent fashion, a prediction confirmed by Table 15–4. Instrumental workers, like those affected by work alienation,[38] are significantly more likely to perceive work as self-estranging. Like their alienated counterparts, instrumental workers have a poor opinion of the company; they are mostly assemblers originating from smaller communities who now reside in apartments: they are most likely to be young, to have worked in G.M. for a relatively short period of time and to have low valuation of job technology and work activity in general.

The confounding effects generated by skill level in Table 15–3 can now be understood. Those subject to the experience of downward career mobility "appear" less, rather than more instrumental, simply because the greatest proportion are craftsmen located in task settings with low levels of occupational powerlessness.[39] In short, craftsmen are less alienated than support and assemblers. Similar reasoning can be used to explain the diminished instrumentality of older workers. Of the three skill categories, craftsmen feature the highest proportion of older workers,[40] followed by support and assemblers. Thus, older workers appear less instrumental primarily due to the conditions of labour encountered.

EXTENDING THE INVESTIGATION

Table 15–5

Multiple Regression Model: Background Determinants to Instrumental Work Attachment

Variable Entered	Regression Coefficient		Simple R	F	S
	Unstandardized	Standardized			
1. Assemblers	.4931	.4697	.3729	43.06	p < .01
2. Support	.1877	.3562	.1260	27.55	p < .01
3. Size of community of birth	−.6486	−.1575	−.2513	6.45	p < .01
4. Type of dwelling	.2018	.1397	.2052	5.04	p < .01

Significance of complete regression equation. $F = 20.25$, $p < .01$

Already established is the powerful relationship between skill level and work instrumentalism, but not to be overlooked is the possibility that additional causes can be found. Other background sources revealed to exert significant zero-order effects include: (1) size of community of birth, (2) type of dwelling, (3) years worked in G.M., (4) downward occupational mobility, and (5) age. Along with the three skill categories, these variables are entered into a multiple regression equation[41] and the following manifest significant independent effects: (1) assemblers, (2) support, (3) size of community of birth and (4) apartment dwelling. The standardized regression coefficients in Table 15–5 indicate skill category to account for the greatest amount of explained variance, followed by size of community of birth and type of dwelling. These results attract interest because they can potentially broaden understanding if the meaning attached to these job-independent effects can be captured; Tables 15–6 and 15–7 represent attempts to do so.

Again, insight here is achieved by determining how a given variable relates to another. Locating the correlates of "small towners" and apartment dwellers should clarify the matter by creating opportunity to make intelligent guesses about it. A profile is constructed from each cluster of correlates, but it should be understood that they lack explanatory power in the strict sense of the term; rather, they provide a source from which a rough social image can be assembled — an image that will hopefully clarify the role played by these factors beyond the job setting.

The correlations in Table 15–6 reveal the social characteristics and attitudes of small towners. The powerful relationship between size of community of birth and geographic mobility indicates that mobile individuals originate primarily from smaller communities. However, these small towners

Table 15–6

Social Characteristics and Attitudes by Size of Community of Birth

Background Characteristics	Coefficient	Attitudes	Coefficient Uncorrected	Corrected
1. Geographic mobility	.58*	1. Work alienation	.17**	.20
2. Respondent's education	.26*	2. Strength workgroup affiliation	.23*	
3. Technological constraints	−.24*	3. Social isolation	.16**	
4. Social mobility	.15**			
5. Career mobility	.19*			
6. Adult relatives in Oshawa area	.17**			

All coefficients Pearson product-moment corrected for attenuation where applicable.
*S < .001
**S < .01

are relatively immobile socially and in terms of career; they have less education than those born and raised in larger communities, are more likely to be employed in G.M. as assemblers and least likely as craftsmen. As one might expect, they have fewer adult relatives living in the area. The attitudes of small towners reveal them to experience more work alienation and social isolation, while being more strongly affiliated with workmates on-the-job.

The impression created by this profile radically departs from Goldthorpe's view of the instrumental worker who is characterized as rationally assessing his current situation before reaching the decision to forego intrinsic job stimulation in favour of routinized labour paying higher wages. He then moves to areas experiencing new industrial growth and assumes a detached attitude toward job and workmates. By contrast, this study locates a group of geographically mobile workers with rural and semi-rural origins, relatively uneducated, immobile by generation and career: that is, they have maintained the class position conferred by family of origin. Work history is equally uneventful, featuring a succession of jobs ranked much the same by occupational prestige. The job-related malaise expressed by these workers probably derives from their rural origins, and from values which clash with the realities of an urban industrial environment. Once located in the industrial centre, they find themselves cut off from the extended network of kin and friends and a sense of social isolation ensues. The increased importance attributed to social contact at the workplace could represent an attempt to compensate for loneliness. Such findings underscore the trauma experienced by some rural men when exposed to the size, anonymity and impersonality of city life. It seems appropriate, therefore, to label this reaction a "traditional response."[42]

Table 15-7

Social Characteristics and Attitudes of Apartment Dwellers

Social Characteristics	Coefficient	Attitudes	Coefficient Uncorrected	Corrected
1. Age	−.20*	1. Ideological† coherence		
2. Years worked in G.M.	−.22*	2. Work alienation	.26*	.30
3. Father's education	.19*	3. Self-estrangement in work	.19*	
4. Years lived in Oshawa	−.20*	4. Contact frequency with workmates	.15**	
5. Terms of accommodation	.20*			
6. Respondent's education	.14**			
7. Marital status	.13**			
8. Technological constraints	−.22**			

All coefficients Pearson product-moment corrected for attenuation where applicable.
 *S < .001
**S < .01
†One-way ANOVA, F = 2.77, S < .06

The social characteristics and attitudes of apartment dwellers are shown in Table 15-7. They tend to be younger than house dwellers, have less seniority in G.M. and years residency in the Oshawa area. Apartment dwellers are more likely to be single, and significantly more likely to rent rather than own their place of residence; they are moderately more educated than other G.M. workers and significantly more educated than father; they are most likely to be assemblers and least likely craftsmen. Attitudinally, apartment dwellers are more likely to operate within an ideological framework radically inspired,[43] more likely to experience self-estrangement and alienation from work, and moderately more likely to fraternize with workmates during leisure time.

Significant among these results is a higher level of educational attainment than father. And yet despite this achievement, one generally rewarded with increased employment opportunity, apartment dwellers have not experienced upward career mobility. They tend to be employed as assemblers, a clear indication that educational success has gone unrewarded; they also tend to be young with lower seniority but higher education than other G.M. workers. These experiences suggest the existence of a group psychology dominated by unfulfilled expectations, frustration and resentment. Discontent finds further expression through adherence to radical ideology and readiness to define work as alienating, irrespective of working conditions. In other words, those individuals sharing the characteristics just mentioned, whether they are craftsmen, support or assemblers, still perceive work as unrewarding. Moreover, this perception is not produced by working conditions. The theoretical significance of this is that while the results of this study support technologism, and by extension Marxist tradition with its emphasis on work centrality, such support is qualified. Work centrality means that job exploitation can stimulate the latent radicalism of the working class, sensitizing it to the conditions of exploitation in society at large. In short, the material conditions of labour are held responsible for ideological formation. No support for this view is found here. Rather it appears that something like the reverse occurs, that political orientations are formed by conditions in society at large. When radical in nature, these beliefs act as perceptual filters through which the individual observes and interprets work experience. To avow a radical belief system is to simultaneously harbour a unified vision of existence. Proletarian workers are disenchanted and resentful of conditions found at work and in society at large. But the initial stimulus for this consolidated world view originates from a societal foundation. Marxist tradition, by contrast, places it squarely in the workplace.

In many respects, apartment dwellers resemble the proletarian variety of working class man. Those attached to proletarian images of society espouse left wing political sentiments, and tend to be well integrated within working class social networks revealed by council house living and maintenance of workmates for friends.[44] Although apartment dwellers lack some of these attributes, nevertheless they manifest proletarianization by renting rather than owning place of residence; they are more likely to fraternize with workmates and are ideologically radical. The characteristics used to identify the proletarian worker can now be supplemented by another — a tendency to view work as unpleasant, irrespective of actual work experience.

CONCLUSION

Current disagreement over the nature of the relationship existing between the manual worker and the job originates from two positions. On the one hand, the technological implications approach maintains job-oriented attitudes and behaviour to be most crucially shaped by the material conditions of labour. On the other hand, instrumental theory views job conditions as neutral because, in part, the worker is directed by a prior commitment. This instrumental commitment sees work as the means necessary to achieve economic ends, not as an activity which can provide intrinsic gratification. Due to the controversy surrounding instrumentalism, as well as the fact that it labours under tangible difficulty, the decision was taken to retest it. A supplementary feature of this strategy is also to contrive test conditions for technologism. This arrangement entails two outcomes: the acceptance of instrumentalism and rejection of technologism, or the rejection of instrumentalism and acceptance of technologism.

Unequivocally, the findings endorse acceptance of the second alternative. Instrumental values do not conform to Goldthorpe's explanation but are revealed to be an expression of alienated labour. As such, an instrumental job attachment is the product of job conditions rather than those located in society. But, while job orientations are mainly a function of work experience, two exceptions are noted. A traditional response to an urban industrial milieu is partially manifested by an aversion for factory labour, unrelated to the quality of working life (see Table 15–6). Similarly, a proletarian response to the industrial system arises remote from the task setting (see Table 15–7). In relative terms, these relationships are weakly expressed and the most powerful consequences are generated by the material conditions of labour.

NOTES

1. Although emphasis varies, those attributing primacy to technology as an intraorganizational variable include the following: J. Woodward, *Management and Technology*, London: Oxford University Press, 1965; R. Blauner, *Alienation and Freedom*, Chicago: University of Chicago Press, 1964; L.R. Sayles, "Managing Organizations: Old Textbooks Do Die," *Columbia J. World Business*, Vol. I, 1966, 81–6; C. Perrow, "A Framework for the Comparative Analysis of Organizations," *Amer. Sociol. Rev.*, Vol. 32, 1967, 194–208. E. Harvey, "Technology and the Structure of Organizations," *Amer. Sociol. Rev.*, Vol. 33, 1968, 247–59.

2. For a more complete discussion on the behavioural consequences of assembly-line labour see: C.R. Walker and R. Guest, *Man on the Assembly-Line*, Cambridge, Mass.: Harvard University Press, 1952; R. Blauner, op. cit., 1964, 89–123.

3. D. Lockwood, "Sources of Variation in Working-Class Images of Society," *Am. Sociol. Rev.*, Vol. 14, 1966, 249–67; J.H. Goldthorpe, "Attitudes and Behaviour of Car Assembly Workers: A Deviant Case and a Theoretical Critique," *Brit. J. Sociol.*, Vol. 17, 1966, 227–44; J.H. Goldthorpe et al., *The Affluent Worker: Industrial Attitudes and Behaviour*, Cambridge, Mass.; Harvard University Press, 1968a; J.H. Goldthorpe et al., *The Affluent Worker: Political Attitudes and Behaviour*, Cambridge, Mass.: Harvard University Press, 1968b; J.H. Goldthorpe et al., *The Affluent Worker in the Class Structure*, Cambridge, Mass.: Harvard University Press, 1969. J.H. Goldthorpe, "Class Status and Party in Modern Britain: Some Recent Interpretations, Marxist and Marxisant," *J. Europ. Sociol.*, Vol. 13, 1972, 342–72.

4. The following acknowledge varying degrees of recognition for the contribution made by instrumental theory: C. Pateman, *Participation and Democratic Theory*, Cambridge, Mass.: Harvard University Press, 1970, 54, 85; W.F. Form, "The Accommodation of Rural-Urban Workers to Industrial Discipline and Urban Living: A Four Nation Study," *Rural Sociol.*, Vol. 36, 1971, 488–508; W.F. Form, "The Internal Stratification of the Working Class: System Involvement of Auto Workers in Four Countries," *Amer. Sociol. Rev.*, Vol. 38, 1973, 697–711; W.F. Form, "Automobile Workers in Four Countries: The Relevance of System Participation," *Brit. J. Sociol.*, Vol. 23, 1972, 437–51; M. Harrington, "Old Working-Class, New Working-Class," in I. Howe (ed.), *The World of the Blue-Collar Worker*, New York: Quandrangle Books, 1972, 135–59; R. Scase, "Industrial Man: A Reassessment with English and Swedish Data," *Brit. J. Sociol.*, Vol. 23, 1972, 204–20; C. Chamberlain, "The Growth of Support for the Labour Party in Britain," *Brit. J. Sociol.*, Vol. 24, 1973, 474–89; J.W. Rinehart, *The Tyranny of Work*, Don Mills: Longman Canada Ltd., 1975, 66; M.L. Kohn, "Occupational Structure and Alienation," *Amer. J. Sociol.*, Vol. 82, 1976, 111–30.

   Like supporters, those opposed to instrumental theory state their views with varying degrees of intensity: R. Blackburn, *The Incompatibles: Trade Union Militancy and the Consensus*, Harmondsworth: Penguin Books Ltd., 1967, 15–55; W.W. Daniel, "Industrial Behaviour and Orientation to Work — A Critique," *J. Management Studies*, Vol. 6, 1969, 366–75; W.W. Daniel, "Productivity Bargaining and Orientation to Work — A Rejoinder to Goldthorpe," *J. Management Studies*, Vol. 8, 1971, 329–35; J. Platt, "Variations to Answers to Different Questions on

Perceptions of Class," *Sociol. Rev.*, Vol. 19, 1971, 409–19; M. Mann, *Consciousness and Action Among the Western Working Class*, London: The MacMillan Co., 1973, 27, 77; G. Strauss, "Workers: Attitudes and Adjustments," in J.M. Rosow (ed.), *The Worker and the Job: Coping with Change*, Englewood Cliffs, N.J.: Prentice-Hall, 1974, 73–98; J.M. Shepard, "Technology, Alienation and Job Satisfaction," *Annual Rev. Sociol.*, Vol. 3, 1977, 1–21; K. Roberts et al., *The Fragmentary Class Structure*, London: Heineman, 1977, 37–65.

5. That western man has abandoned ideological commitment was originally proposed by Bell. See D. Bell, *The End of Ideology*, New York: Collier Books, 1961. Goldthorpe agrees with this view but develops it further. Rather than deriving from ideology, the social imagery of the working class now arises from a pecuniary foundation — a concern for money and the commodities it can purchase. See Goldthorpe et al., op. cit., 1969, 146–7.

6. Mann, op. cit., 1973, 19–20.

7. Social Science Department, University of Liverpool, *The Dock Worker*, Liverpool, 1954.

8. G.D.H. Cole, *Labour in Coal Mining Industry*, 1914–21, Oxford: Clarendon Press, 1923. N. Dennis and F. Henriques, *Coal is Our Life*, London: Eyre and Spottiswoode, 1956.

9. G.W. Horobin, "Community and Occupation in the Hull Fishing Industry," *Brit. J. Sociol.*, Vol. 8, 1957, 55–72.

10. C. Kerr and A. Siegel, "The Inter-Industry Propensity to Strike: An International Comparison," in Dubin, Ross and Kornhauser (eds.), *Industrial Conflict*, Cambridge, Mass.: Harvard University Press, 1960, 49–68.

11. Lockwood, op. cit., 1966, 249–67.

12. M. Yonge and P. Wilmott, *Family and Kinship in East London*, London: Penguin Books, 1957, 121–69.

13. Goldthorpe et al., op. cit., 1968b, 76.

14. Downwardly mobiles are stated to experience "relative deprivation" and "status incongruency" resulting in the social devaluation of present position. This occurs because assessment derives from position held prior to slippage, a comparison downgrading present conditions of existence. A preoccupation with money and standard of living are extensions of this posture. Ibid., 158–9.

15. Ibid., 147.

16. Ibid., 38–9.

17. J.A.C. Brown, *The Social Psychology of Industry*, Harmondsworth: Penguin Books, 1954, 206; F.B. Herzberg et al., *The Motivation to Work*, John Wiley & Sons, 1959, 65–70. M. Patchen, "A Conceptual Framework and Some Empirical Data Regarding Comparisons of Social Rewards," *Sociometry*, 1961, Vol. 4, 136–56.

18. Goldthorpe et al., op. cit., 1968a, 114.

19. Ibid., 91.

20. Ibid., 162.

21. In this connection, the three background variables investigated are geographic, downward career and social mobility. The possibility of assessing the impact of age is precluded by limiting eligibility to the Luton sample to men aged between 21 and 46. The rationale underlying this strategy is twofold. First, it is hypothesized that younger men are more likely to be instrumental. Second, the decision taken is to design a study

maximizing the probability of locating instrumental workers in absolute terms, hence the exclusion of older men. It goes without saying that the original hypothesis can neither be confirmed nor denied by this strategy.

22. For a more complete discussion of Goldthorpe's investigation in this direction see: M. MacKinnon, "Work Instrumentalism Reconsidered: A Replication of Goldthorpe's Luton Project," *Brit. J. Sociol.*, Vol. 31, No. 1 (March 1980).

23. Goldthorpe et al., op. cit., 1968a, 162.

24. Ibid., 2–3.

25. Unlike Britain, government sponsored housing projects and council estates are not prevalent in Canada. The main alternative to home ownership is to rent either a house or apartment.

26. Goldthorpe et al., op. cit., 1968a, 3.

27. The city directory was used to locate G.M. workers and identify their occupational ranking in the plant. If an individual's name appeared non-British he was excluded. The advisability of this decision rests on the fact that the Luton sample is primarily comprised of those with British origins, a condition that should be matched by this study. In addition, a generalization firmly established in Canadian Studies is that ethnicity has a profound impact on attitudes and behaviour and the decision to omit those of apparently non-British origin serves to control this confounding effect. Effective implementation of this strategy is further guaranteed by having the respondent identify nationality of father. About one-fifth of the G.M. workers located have non-British ethnic origins and are thus ineligible for sample membership.

28. To some extent, selection procedures for occupational ranking lack precision; nevertheless, the process is governed by systematic criteria. An attempt is made to adhere to Blauner's framework of occupational powerlessness which exists when the worker is dominated by technological constraints like the following: (1) inability to control the pace of work; (2) inability to control the amount of work produced; (3) inability to control the quality of work; (4) inability to control job procedures and techniques; (5) inability to leave the immediate job station (Blauner, op. cit., 1964, 16–22). On occasion, an occupational label was discarded because knowledge of its task roles was lacking and ranking on the continuum of occupational powerlessness not possible. About one-fifth of all occupational titles located could not be ranked for this reason.

29. Another observation about the sample is required. An estimate given by a G.M. official claims that about one-third of hourly paid employees live beyond city limits. In consequence, this group is also excluded from the sampling frame.

30. Half the sample was contacted at place of residence, the project was explained, co-operation was requested, and a fixed-choice questionnaire was placed on approval. The remainder of the sample was simply reached through the mail.

31. Establishing the instrumentality of the sample in absolute as well as causal terms is also important because resolution of the causal question hinges on the sample characteristics of this study. Again, this requirement directs attention toward the independent and dependent variables comprising Goldthorpe's causal model. Of the former, do workers in Oshawa possess the social characteristics necessary to produce instrumental values? And latterly, do they subscribe to these values? The ideal situation is one in which proportional equivalence between the two studies

is found. If this similarity can be demonstrated, increased confidence is generated in the selection of Oshawa as a research site and in our claim that we are, in fact, examining instrumental workers as Goldthorpe defines them. Subsequent failure to establish a causal connection cannot then be attributed to the fact that we are not examining instrumental workers in the first place. Comparative results do reveal the proportions of both studies to be roughly similar but, unfortunately, space limitations prohibit a detailed presentation and review. Those interested in pursuing this matter should consult: MacKinnon, op. cit., 1980.

32. Unfortunately, worker attitudes toward company sponsored clubs and activities cannot be recorded because G.M. does not involve itself in this kind of social activity. Thus, we are reduced to using three variables to measure work instrumentalism, whereas Goldthorpe uses four.

33. Social mobility is computed by comparing respondent's socio-economic index for occupation with that of father. See B.R. Blishen and H.A. McRoberts, "A Revised Socio-Economic Index for Occupations in Canada," *Cdn. Rev. of Sociol. and Anthrop.*, Vol. 13, 1976, 71–9. The instrument used to assign scores being sensitive to gradations in prestige tends to blur the distinction between working and middle class jobs. In order to clearly establish this conceptual boundary lower middle class occupations are grouped with those of the working class, a technique matching the one used by Goldthorpe et al., op. cit., 1968a, 156.

34. The conventional explanation for this relationship, one widely reported in the literature, is that downwardly mobiles attempt to insulate themselves from the conditions of existence embedded in a working class lifestyle by continued subscription to middle class values. In this connection see: H.L. Wilensky, "The Skidder: Ideological Adjustment of Downwardly Mobile Workers," *Amer. Sociol. Rev.*, Vol. 24, 1959, 215–31; L. Lopreato and J.S. Chafetz, "The Political Orientation of Skidders: A Middle Range Theory," *Amer. Sociol. Rev.*, Vol. 35, 1970, 440–51. Additional research shows sliders to avoid working class social networks (participation in union affairs) by maintaining middle class social contacts; K. Roberts et al., op. cit., 1977, 56; S.M. Lipset and J. Gordon, "Mobility and Trade Union Membership," in Lipset and Bendix (eds.), *Class, Status and Power*, Glencoe, Ill.: Free Press of Glencoe, 1954, 491–500.

35. Scoring methods used for occupational mobility are identical to those for social mobility except that designation is now derived from comparing respondent's previous job index with present. Goldthorpe et al., op. cit., 1968a, 157.

36. The item used to measure work attachment is borrowed from a study by Seeman. See, "On the Personal Consequences of Alienation," *Amer. Sociol. Rev.*, Vol. 32, 1967, 273–85. Selection of response category one, four or seven indicates an intrinsic choice, the remainder an extrinsic affiliation. The item reads as follows:

From the following features about work, select the one from the list that you like the most as it applies to your job in G.M.

1. It's interesting work
2. It has high prestige
3. It has good working conditions
4. It's educational work
5. It's a secure job
6. It pays good wages
7. It uses my skills
8. It has good possibilities for promotion

37. In order to implement this test, implication variables measuring work alienation and estrangement are required. A work alienation scale comprised of six items is borrowed from Seeman's study (op. cit., 1967, 273–85). The scale reads as follows:

1. Is your job too simple to bring out the best of your abilities or not?
   1. Yes
   2. No

2. Can you do work on the job and keep your mind on other things or not?
   1. Yes
   2. No

3. Which one of the following statements comes closest to describing how you feel about your present job in G.M.?
   1. Interesting nearly all the time.
   2. Interesting some of the time.
   3. Hardly interesting at all.
   4. Completely dull and monotonous.

4. Does your job make you work too fast most of the time or not?
   1. Yes
   2. No

5. Does your job give you a chance to try out your own ideas or not?
   1. Yes
   2. No

6. On an ordinary working day, do you have the opportunity to make independent decisions when you are carrying out your tasks or is it rather routine work?
   1. Yes, I make independent decisions.
   2. No, it's rather routine work.

Self-estrangement from work is an item drawn from a social alienation scale devised by Middleton, "Alienation, Race and Education," *Amer. Sociol. Rev.,* Vol. 28, 1963, 973–77. Accompanied by Likert response categories, it reads: I really don't enjoy most of the work that I do but feel I must do it in order to have other things that I want and need.

38. Cronback's coefficient alpha (.78) is used to compute the internal consistency of the scale. Despite a good degree of consistency, some measurement error still occurs (the higher the coefficient of reliability the lower the error). An important feature of measurement error is that it attenuates the relationship between variables, a condition that can be corrected as shown in Table 15–4. For a more precise and extensive discussion of this issue, see: M. MacKinnon, op. cit., (March 1980).

39. The coefficient for Pearson product-moment recording the relationship between skill level and downward career mobility = .39, s < .001.

40. The same coefficient measuring the connection between age and technological constraints = .41, S < .001.

41. Skill level (response categories: (1) assemblers, (2) support, (3) craft), apartment dwelling (house, apartment), and the instrumental attachment (intrinsic, extrinsic) are entered into the regression equation as dummy variables.

42. C. Kerr et al., *Industrialism and Industrial Man*, Cambridge, Mass.:

Harvard University Press, 1960, 305–12, provides some supporting evidence for this finding when noting that rural-bred workers, because of traditional orientations, experience more industrial stress than urban workers. Another source reveals the factory system to produce deep feelings of insecurity widespread among industrial populations but especially severe among rural newcomers. See H.L. Wilensky & C.L. Lebeaux, *Industrial Society and Social Welfare*, New York: Free Press, 1958, 55. Although not directly applicable to the present case, additional evidence indicates traditional men to have universally resisted absorption by industrial forms of labour and coercive means often employed to achieve these ends. See J.H. Boeke, *The Structure of Netherlands Indian Economy*, New York: Institute of Pacific Relations, 1942 and W.E. Moore, *Industrialization and Labour: Social Aspects of Economic Development*, New York: Russell and Russell, 1965. Finally, in a compelling narrative, Rinehart (op. cit., 1975, 25–53) describes work and community in Canada before and after industrialization, and a particularly stark contrast is established. Summarized briefly, this evidence suggests the existence of a traditional response to an urban-industrial climate, one marked by a sense of isolation and despair.

43. Construction of the ideological coherence variable originates from a four-item scale of political conservatism (Cronbach's alpha = .69) and a five-item scale of radicalism (Cronbach's alpha = .66). This variable is represented by three nominal response categories reading as follows: (1) bourgeois imagery, (2) disorganized imagery, (3) proletarian imagery. Assignment to a given category is determined by computing an average score for each respondent on both scales, followed by a comparison of the two averages. Bourgeois designation results when average score on the conservatism scale (the lower the score, the more conservative) is lower than average score on the radicalism scale and the difference between the two exceeds a value of one. For instance, an average of two for conservatism and three for radicalism produces a bourgeois classification. A difference between the averages of less than one means assignment to the disorganized category. Proletarian imagery is decided when score on the radicalism scale is lower (the lower the score, the more radical) than the score on the conservatism scale and the difference between the scores exceeds a value of one.

    Underlying formulation of this variable is a conviction that ideological clarity represents a salient issue for sociological investigation. Adherence to a particular belief system is considered significant when it coincides with a "significant" measure of disavowal for a competing system. At the same time absence of coherence, to partake more or less equally of both, likewise has consequences of interest.

44. Roberts et al., op. cit., 1977, 50–2.

Chapter 16

Work Orientation and Mobility Ideology in the Working Class*

Graham Knight

INTRODUCTION

It is now generally recognized that the growth of white-collar labour which accompanied the shift from entrepreneurial to corporate capitalism has reshaped the structures of occupational mobility (cf. Thernstrom, 1973). What is less clear is the effect this change has had upon mobility ideologies. The marketplace of preindustrial capitalism, composed largely of farmers, peasants, a few professionals and artisans, merchant-entrepreneurs, and growing numbers of handicraft workers, gave rise to a mobility ideology of "entrepreneurial individualism" in which occupational success was seen to derive from striking out on one's own account as a small commodity or service producer. Success was seen to result largely from the possession of the requisite moral virtues of application, perseverance, and most importantly the willingness to take risks (together with a little fortuitous circumstance along the way). Sufficient will to succeed was seen to create its own means of realization; structural barriers and differential opportunity were overlooked as determining factors in the aetiology of success.

From the available evidence it appears that this ideology weathered the initial stage of industrialization relatively intact. Although the increasing proletarianization of labour restricted the opportunities for entrepreneurialism proper, the core theme of success through personal rectitude prevailed, albeit in more secularized form (cf. Thernstrom, 1964). This began to change chiefly with the second and particularly the third stage of industrialization as occupational mobility began to depend less upon morally informed striving in the labour market *per se*, as upon prior success in the school system. The growing dependency of occupational attainment upon educational success has formalized the occupational "career" within a work bureaucracy or a profession as the dominant mode of mobility, and has resulted in the generational differentiation and allocation of occupational aspirations and ambitions. Increasingly, students of mobility have found themselves devoting their analytic attentions to the school as a means of anticipatory socialization for the labour market, and to its role in mitigating the structure of unequal opportunity derived from family and class background.

This paper concerns the fate of the ideology of entrepreneurial mobility against this background of diminishing opportunities for successful self-employment and the emergence of "careerism" as the principal form of

---

*Reprinted with permission from *Canadian Journal of Sociology*, Vol. 4, No. 1 (1979).

occupational success. It is concerned particularly with the fate of entrepreneurialism among those for whom the pursuit of a career, in the sense of a projected occupational biography consisting of identifiable stages of promotion and advancement which can be preknown and prejudged, is largely inaccessible. In this sense, it concerns specifically the fate of entrepreneurialism, and the nature of mobility ideology generally, among the working-class, among those employed in industrial, manual, blue-collar work.

In order to accomplish this, we must initially situate the problem of mobility ideology within the general debate on the meanings of work among the working-class. On this score, there now exists a good deal of evidence that suggests that blue-collar work is now viewed primarily in "instrumental" terms by those who perform it. It is defined, in other words, as the means to ends of a largely financial nature rather than as an activity which is primarily rewarding in and of itself. Beginning in the mid 1950s with Robert Dubin's (1956) thesis that work was not a "central life interest" for most industrial workers, the general consensus to have emerged among professional researchers of the topic is that the workplace of modern capitalism does not enable many of its participants to find intrinsic meaning, fulfilment and creativity in their labour, and that the rewards of work are defined principally in terms of the enrichment of the individual as a consumer rather than as a producer (cf. Argyle, 1972; Blauner, 1964; Goldthorpe et al., 1968; Wedderburn and Crompton, 1972).

The relationship between mobility ideology and the general meaning attributed to work has, however, remained at issue. On the one hand are those who, following Marx's (1964) formulation of "estranged labour," interpret an instrumental attitude towards work as symptomatic of a broader sense of alienation (cf. Blauner, 1964). It is assumed that individuals seek intrinsic rewards from their work, and become alienated when these aspirations are subsequently frustrated. Alienation, then, consists in the contradiction between what is sought from work and what is actually gained. Implicit in this perspective is the proposition that an orientation to personal mobility will remain strong among the instrumentally oriented as one way to attenuate the underlying contradiction between aspirations and fulfilment, and that it will therefore be defined primarily as a means to enhance intrinsic rather than instrumental work rewards.

Some support for this proposition can be found in Chinoy's (1955) study of work and life aspirations among a sample of American auto workers. He found not only that ambitions for personal mobility remained strong among these workers, but also that they were framed more in terms of escape from the bureaucratic work world in the form of becoming self-employed entrepreneurs than in terms of successful mobility in that world as foremen, office workers, or even union officials. According to Chinoy, the main definition attached to these ambitions was political: self-employment offered the promise of escaping the domination of wage labour and enjoying autonomy over their work. For Chinoy's auto workers self-employment meant "becoming one's own boss." This, moreover, he attributed largely to the alienation these men typically suffered in their lives in the factory: "The alienation of [their] work does much to explain their widespread interest in a small business" (Chinoy, 1955: 86).

Additional support for the "political" or "autonomy" view of entrepreneur-ial ambitions among blue-collar workers can be found in Mackenzie's (1973) study of the work and home lives of a sample of American craftsmen. Although he did not find cause to tie the interest in self-employment to the alienation of wage labour, Mackenzie did find that it was associated chiefly with the promise of greater autonomy over all aspects of work. Similarly, although they attributed the reasons for entering self-employment by former blue-collar workers largely to a process of "drifting," the studies by Mayer and Goldstein (1964) and Berg and Rogers (1964) reaffirm the idea that "being-one's-own-boss" is an aspiration commonly associated with starting and running a small business.

The alternative view of work attitudes and mobility ideology among the working-class emerges chiefly from the "affluent worker" study undertaken by Goldthorpe et al. (1968; 1969) in the United Kingdom. They too found evidence of substantial instrumentalism toward work among a sample of blue-collar males, but they attributed this not to the frustrations of the work situation but to a prior orientation to work, established largely on the basis of experiences and considerations in the realm of family, home life, and consumption aspirations, and duly imported into the workplace where it was the major factor shaping the worker's attitudes to his job, his workmates, the firm and its management, the union, and his image of his own economic and occupational future. Work instrumentalism was associated with an orientation to affluence, with the experience of relatively frequent occupational and geographical mobility, with the worker's situation in the family life cycle (married with dependent family), and was seen to derive particularly from the experience of downward social mobility on the part of the worker with respect to either his parents or his siblings. In some cases, this had been "compounded" by downward intragenerational mobility on the part of some workers who had previously left their own less successful careers as white-collar workers in order to work in the factory. In this way, Goldthorpe et al. argued, these workers had reduced some of their sense of relative deprivation vis à vis their own successful kin by taking jobs that at least enabled them to consume at a comparable level to the latter.

The relationship between this instrumental orientation and mobility ideology is contained in the workers' attitudes toward their economic and occupational futures, in which, Goldthorpe et al. argued, a situation of "instrumental collectivism" prevailed. This meant that for the most part the workers in their sample saw their own futures in terms of a "logical" extension of the present — a continuing improvement in standard of living to be shared by all and acquired chiefly through the union and the collective bargaining system. To be sure, this did not preclude consideration of personal mobility through promotion or through self-employment as an option for the future (nearly half of the workers were attracted by the idea of becoming foremen; a quarter had "thought seriously" about starting their own business, another 12 per cent had actually tried to do so in the past). These ambitions, however, were framed in primarily economic terms — to "make more money," "to get ahead" — and were accorded little importance by Goldthorpe and his colleagues in the worker's realistic perceptions of his present and future situation: "... it is not typically part of their designs for the future that they should secure this rising consumer power through individual advancement in their occupational lives ... this lack of occupational ambition arose from the fact that, *given* the present economic situation of our affluent workers, neither promotion nor self-employment appeared as an objective which was now worth while for them to aim at." (Goldthorpe et al., 1968: 142–3, emphasis original). In other words, as long as wage labour continued to fulfill the primary orientation towards the enhancement of consumption standards, these workers were relatively content to remain put.

The purpose of the present research is to examine mobility attitudes and ideology among the working-class in light of these two views on the matter. Using a sample of Canadian male industrial workers the following discussion will address itself to these specific issues:

1. To what extent do industrial workers subscribe to an instrumental orientation to work, and what are the specific dimensions of this orientation?
2. To what extent is instrumentalism associated or not with a concern for personal mobility and how is that mobility conceived — promotion within the bureaucratic work order or advancement through self-employment?
3. What are the social correlates of mobility attitudes among the working-class, and how are the latter associated with the general meaning attached to work?

Table 16–1

Survey on Income, Education and Self-Rated Social Class

	Percentage		
	manager	skilled	semi-skilled
Earn more than $10,000 p.a. (1968)	72.8	8.1	0.4
Have finished at least high school	51.6*	24.5	17.8
Rate themselves upper/middle-class	92.5	54.9	39.9

*This figure is lower than might be expected, but the reason for this resides to a large extent with the fact that the managers are disproportionately older than the other two groups: 72% of them are over 40 as compared to 59% of the skilled and 53% of the semi-skilled. When we control for age we find that 74% of the younger managers have completed at least high school as compared to 46% of those over 40.

RESEARCH DESIGN

DATA BASE

To speak to the issues outlined above data were taken from a survey conducted in 1968 by J. Loubser and M. Fullan as part of the Parliamentary Task Force on Industrial Relations in Canada. The data are drawn from the responses to a face-sheet questionnaire by 2,827 male employees residing largely in Ontario, particularly in the Oshawa-Toronto-Hamilton area, and working in seventeen firms in six major industrial complexes: oil, chemicals, electricals, printing, autos, and steel. The sample was drawn from those engaged in either direct production, maintenance, or first level supervision, and is classified into four major occupational groupings: 147 managers; 274 foremen; 1,628 skilled workers; and 774 semi-skilled.

While the responses of the foremen and the handful of clerical and unskilled workers have been excluded from consideration below, those of the managers have been retained as a point of reference against which to compare the findings for the two blue-collar groups. The term "manager" is admittedly an ambiguous one; yet it is clear from the data provided in Table 16-1, the survey on income, education, and self-rated social class, that they can be legitimately situated in the lower middle-class.

DATA COLLECTION

The data were collected by means of a mailed questionnaire which was accompanied by the usual follow-up and reminder letters to the non-respondents. The final response rate reached 50.3 per cent of the target sample. This ranged from a low of 35.7 per cent for one of the electrical firms to a high of 78.2 per cent for one of those in printing. The proportion of the total possible labour force sampled in each firm varied according to the size of the enterprise and its occupational composition. This ranged from a high of 86.4 per cent of the workforce in the case of the smaller of the two electrical firms to a low of 9.2 per cent in the case of the steel firm (cf. Loubser and Fullan, 1970: 3–6).

DIMENSIONS OF WORK ORIENTATION

Goldthorpe et al. (1968) arrived at their conclusions about the incidence of work instrumentalism among their affluent workers on the basis of questions directed to the reasons these men had come to work in their present jobs and why they remained in them. Along similar lines Table 16–2 presents percentage cross-tabulations for occupation and the factor each respondent felt the most important in his relationship with his employer.

Table 16–2

The Factor Most Important to the Respondent in his Relationship with the Company

	Occupation		
Most important factor	manager	skilled	semi-skilled
Material benefits	35.9%	60.4%	69.3%
Social relationships	5.5	9.0	8.5
Sense of fulfilment and accomplishment	24.8	13.1	9.3
Feeling of belonging to a goal-oriented concern	33.8	17.6	12.8
Total	100.0	100.1	99.9
N	145	1606	763

Cramer's V = 0.178
$p \leq .05$

Editors' Note: Crammer's V *is a correlation coefficient which measures the degree of association among the variables in a table when the number of variables contained by the table is larger than 2 × 2. Thus Crammer's V is used in Table 16–2 because it assumes a 3 × 4 format; it seeks to measure the degree of association of the three job categories (managers, skilled and semi-skilled) with the four factors affecting the relationship between the employee and the company (material rewards, social relationships, sense of fulfillment and accomplishment and feeling of belonging to a goal oriented concern). The variables in Table 16–2 are called nominal variables because a name or a set of terms is used to define them. Crammer's V is thus a correlation coefficient used to measure the degree of association among nominal variables in a table larger than 2 × 2.*

But what is meant when we say that Crammer's V measures the degree of association among variables? Once again, Table 16–2 is used to illustrate the explanation. Respondents in the study (managers, skilled and semi-skilled) are given a question comprised of four alternatives and asked to select only ONE of these alternatives, the one that best explains their relationship with the company for whom they work. The results in Table 16–2 reveal that 35.9 per cent of the managers choose material rewards, 60.4 per cent of the skilled do so, followed by 69.3 per cent of the semi-skilled. This means that the relative importance assigned to material rewards varies with or is associated with occupation. The lower the level of skill, the greater the likelihood that material benefits will be selected. By contrast, the pattern of association is reversed when the distribution of percentages for "feeling of belonging to a goal-oriented concern" are examined. Nearly 34 per cent of the managers select this option, followed by 17.6 per cent of the skilled and 12.8 per cent of the semi-skilled. The lower the level of skill, the less likely people are to select this option.

Crammer's V therefore, is used to measure the degree of association for the table as a whole; it is up to the reader to determine the pattern or the direction of the relationships among the variables, a task that can be accomplished by examining the percentage distributions. The previously cited examples demonstrate how this can be done. In measuring the overall degree of association it should also be realized that Crammer's V can vary from 0 to 1.0. When Crammer's V = O, no relationship among the variables has been found. When Crammer's V = 1.0 a perfect degree of association exists but this type of relationship is never found in sociology. The magnitude of Crammer's V = .178 in Table 16–2 is a more likely possibility; it indicates a moderate degree of association among the variables contained by the table.

These data generally support the idea that work instrumentalism is the most prevalent orientation to work among the working-class. Sixty per cent of the skilled and 70 per cent of the semi-skilled identify wages and material benefits as the most important factor, as compared to about a third of the managers. For the latter, intrinsic factors like a sense of belonging and of accomplishment figure jointly as the most common factor. For all three groups, the social relations of the workplace are the least important.

The concept of work orientation, however, implies something more encompassing than the specific reasons for taking and keeping a specific job; it connotes a general meaning attached to work as well as specific, situational meanings. To measure this more general element of work orientation we can examine the responses of the three occupational groups to a question asking the respondents to identify which of seven factors they deemed the most important consideration when thinking of taking another job.

As we can see from the data in Table 16–3, measured in this manner we do not find any substantial change in the incidence of instrumentalism among the two blue-collar groups. We do, however, find a greater incidence of instrumentalism among the managers with the result that in terms of overall work orientation class differences all but disappear. At the same time, it is clear from both tables that although instrumentalism prevails as the modal orientation among the skilled and semi-skilled, a fairly substantial minority of both groups has retained some concern for work's intrinsic rewards. Instrumentalism may prevail, but it does not overwhelm.

MOBILITY INTEREST AND THE WORKING-CLASS

In contrast to the implications of the Goldthorpe study, however, the data do suggest that personal mobility is a concern of some salience among blue-collar workers. As we can see from Table 16–3, opportunity for advancement is the most, or second most, prominent component of work instrumentalism among all three groups. Indeed, it is the most, or second most, important of all seven job considerations, instrumental and intrinsic. This conclusion is further strengthened by responses to a question concerning satisfaction with advancement prospects. When asked to rate their satisfaction with the "chances for advancement" they considered their present employment offered, four-fifths of the managers reported they were satisfied as compared to barely two-fifths of the skilled workers and slightly more than a third of the semi-skilled. Combined, these two sets of data do not provide support for the implications of the thesis of "instrumental collectivism" as conceived by the Goldthorpe research. Rather, they indicate that far from being relatively accommodated to their present occupational lives, these Canadian workers are concerned with personal advancement and mobility.

Table 16–3

Most Important Consideration when Thinking of Taking Another Job

Most important consideration when thinking of taking another job	Occupation		
	managers	skilled	semi-skilled
Better pay and benefits	18.8%	23.5%	22.1%
More security	10.4	14.1	18.0
Better opportunities for advancement	28.5	24.0	18.9
Overall instrumental orientation	57.7	61.6	59.0
More interesting work	7.6%	9.8%	12.4%
More control over work pace and quality	0.7	2.0	5.9
Better chance to use abilities	16.7	16.3	14.0
Greater sense of accomplishment	17.4	10.3	8.7
Overall intrinsic orientation	42.3	38.4	41.0
Sample size	144	1523	715

Cramer's V = 0.110
$p \leq 0.05$

These data do not, however, tell us how these concerns are framed and defined. Do these workers see advancement in terms of promotion within the bureaucratic work world, or do they conceive of escape from that world and advancement through self-employment? Table 16–4 presents percentage cross-tabulations for occupation and future occupational expectations for those of the sample who do not expect to remain in their present job. Overall, we find that about a quarter of the sample expect to become mobile. This may appear low enough to validate the Goldthorpe conclusions, but it must be borne in mind that these data measure occupational *expectations* rather than simply aspirations or unqualified ambitions. Furthermore, it must also be noted that the majority (57 per cent) of the sample are over the age of forty, and, as Chinoy (1955) found, personal ambitions tend to level off, decline, and become displaced onto the next generation after this age.

Table 16–4

Future Job Expectations

Expected job	Occupation		
	manager	skilled	semi-skilled
White-collar	70.3%	21.2%	19.3%
Self-employed ("entrepreneur" or farmer)	8.1	25.2	36.5
Foreman	18.9	29.6	11.3
Skilled worker	2.7	20.0	21.5
Semi-skilled worker	—	4.0	11.3
Total	100.0	100.0	99.9
N	38	250	186

Cramer's V = 0.361
$p \leq 0.05$

For those managers who expect to become mobile the clear majority — over two-thirds — expect to remain in some form of salaried white-collar work. From their responses it is evident that "careerism" is the predominant ideology of occupational mobility in the salaried lower middle-class. Very few harbour expectations of striking out on their own account; indeed a larger proportion than this actually expect to "skid" down into foreman roles. Among the skilled and the semi-skilled, on the other hand, occupational expectations are more varied. For the former there is a fairly even division of expectations between foremanship, salaried white-collar work, self-employment, and some other form of skilled blue-collar work. Overall, nonetheless, the clear majority of those who expect to become occupationally mobile do expect to remain in some form of wage labour.

Among the semi-skilled, however, this conclusion, while still valid, is far less striking. For almost two-fifths the future is not envisioned in terms of continued wage labour but in terms of self-employment, either as "entrepreneurs" or as farmers. In their case, the ideology of "entrepreneurialism" has retained a certain poignancy that is less apparent among the skilled and almost totally absent among the managers. The conclusion these data point to is that the version of the "American Dream" found among his auto workers by Chinoy in the late 1940s is far from moribund among Canadian workers of the "affluent" late sixties, and particularly among those who, from the point of view of skill level, possess the least resources and opportunities to become successfully mobile from the pursuit of a bureaucratic or professional career.

THE ROOTS OF ENTREPRENEURIALISM

The origins of entrepreneurial ambitions and expectations among the working-class have been attributed to a number of factors. For Chinoy (1955) and to a lesser extent Mackenzie (1973) these were primarily factors that operated upon the worker in the work situation. Chinoy, as we have seen, attributed the desire for self-employment to the experience of work alienation under modern wage labour. For Mackenzie, the desire to become self-employed was seen largely to reflect the greater opportunity to do so on the part of the skilled for whom it was easier to do for themselves what they presently did for an employer. However, the present data do not support this proposition as the expectation of self-employment among the skilled is lower rather than higher than among the semi-skilled.

Table 16–5

Job Expectations[1] and Selected Social Background and Work Situation Characteristics (Cramer's V)

	Occupation	
Social background	skilled	semi-skilled
Age	.020	.179*
Marital status[2]	.111	.090
Education	.060	.253*
Community background[3]	.113	.246*
Extent of geographical mobility	0.94	.116
Father's occupation[4]	.089	.186*
Number of dependents	.040	.023
Work situation		
Income	.020	.020
Extent of job mobility	.057	.142
Job satisfaction	.157*	.070
Job interest	.126*	.047
Technology[5]	.020	.282*
Job history I[6]	.112	.210*
Job history II[7]	.110	.020

*p = .05
1. Those who expect self-employment vs. those with other expectations.
2. Married/Single.
3. Size of community in which respondent grew up.
4. White-collar, blue-collar, farmer.

5. Automation, skilled tool use, skill machine use, routine machine tending, assembly line, inspection.
6. Ever been self-employed.
7. Ever held a white-collar job.

An alternative view of the origins of mobility ambitions can be deduced from the Goldthorpe thesis. As we have seen, Goldthorpe et al. equated the widespread incidence of work instrumentalism on the part of the workers in their sample with an accommodation to their present employment, and by implication to a life of wage labour, at least to the extent that this fulfilled their consumer aspirations. This accommodationist posture was associated with continued affluence, relatively extensive geographical and occupational mobility, the existence of a dependent nuclear family, and the relative deprivation associated with downward intergenerational mobility. By implication, then, we should expect accommodationism to be weaker, and therewith an interest not only in personal mobility but also in self-employment to be stronger, among the less affluent, the less mobile, those without family dependents, and those whose class and status situations were relatively stable vis à vis the previous generation and their own work histories.[1]

Table 16–5 presents Cramer's V values for the association between future job expectations for those who expect to be mobile (dichotomised into those who expect some other form of wage labour and those who expect to become self-employed) and selected social background and work situation characteristics. The main support for the Chinoy thesis occurs among the skilled, for whom job satisfaction and job interest are the only factors to exert any statistically significant effect on job expectations. We find that expectations of self-employment, as opposed to continued wage labour, do indeed increase among those who are less satisfied with their jobs, and find them mostly dull and monotonous. Although we do not find that reported satisfaction and interest with work have any significant effect on job expectations among the semi-skilled, we do find some support for the Chinoy thesis with regard to technological work environment. Thus we find that those working in the more routinized work environments, particularly on the assembly-line, are more likely to expect self-employment in the future. The fact that technology has a significant effect upon the mobility attitudes of the semi-skilled, yet not upon those of the skilled, suggests greater structural, and therewith experiential, differentiation in the working environments of the former than of the latter, and offers some support for the thesis propounded by Mackenzie (1973) and Form (1976) of the increasing internal differentiation and stratification of the working-class in modern capitalism.

Support of a kind can also be found for the general implication of the Goldthorpe thesis that work attitudes generally are shaped principally by experiences and considerations in the nonwork realm. This support, however, is confined to the semi-skilled. Moreover we find that of the variables associated with mobility attitudes by the Goldthorpe research, only intergenerational mobility (as measured by father's main occupation) has any significant effect, and that this is not in the manner suggested. We do not find that the job expectations of those whose fathers were white-collar workers differ notably from those whose fathers were foremen, skilled, or semi-skilled workers; the former are neither more nor less accommodated to wage labour than the latter. About two-thirds of all those whose fathers were employees expect to remain employees themselves: about two-fifths as white-collar workers, a third as foremen or skilled workers, and the remaining tenth or so as semi-skilled workers.

The significant difference resides in the job expectations of the semi-skilled whose fathers were wage earners, regardless of type, as compared to those whose fathers were self-employed as farmers. Among the latter we find that a majority of almost three-fifths expect themselves to become self-employed at some future point in their lives; this compares to just under a third of those whose fathers were wage earners. This pattern is reinforced by the effect on job expectations of community background and the respondent's own occupational history; expectations for self-employment are greater among those who grew up in rural and small town areas and among those who have already been self-employed at some point. Although only six of the semi-skilled fall into the latter category, five of them express the expectation to do so again in the future. This tends to confirm the argument of Chinoy (1955) and Mayer and Goldstein (1964) that when blue-collarites-turned-entrepreneurs revert back to wage labour they do so more from lack of skills, capital, and general opportunity than from disenchantment with self-employment as a goal.

On the surface, these findings would suggest that self-employment expectations are greatest among those who have been most exposed to socializing influences conducive to the formation of such attitudes. This, however, is only part of the explanation. The transition from rural agrarian to urban industrial life, and particularly if this involves the shift from autonomous labour to wage labour, generally entails considerable problems of social readjustment. Not only have those from rural agrarian backgrounds been socialized into values and beliefs that are often inappropriate for urban life, they are also often less equipped in terms of occupational and general social skills to make the transition to industrial wage labour smoothly. In this respect, migrants also suffer from unequal opportunity, as well as inadequate socialization, to succeed on the terms that prevail in urban industrial society.

This is partly borne out when we examine the direction of the effect of the remaining variables whose impact upon the job expectations of the semi-skilled is statistically significant: age, education, and technology. We find that expectations for self-employment are greatest among the older workers, among those with the least education, and among those working on assembly lines, that is, among those with the least resources and opportunities to become successfully mobile by commencing and pursuing a bureaucratic or professional career. It appears, then, that rather than being the ideology of those who feel subjectively alienated in their work or of those whose home life commitments and aspirations do not foster an accommodationist work posture, entrepreneurialism is now the ideology of those effectively trapped in a socially and economically marginal class position. In this respect, an inversion may have taken place: if entrepreneurialism was once quintessentially bourgeois, it is now quintessentially an ideology of the working-class. However, it is, in its contemporary form, an ideology that connotes escape from the dominant institutions of the work world rather than a commitment to them.

THE MEANINGS OF ENTREPRENEURIALISM

The final aspect of the problem to be confronted is the social meaning of work associated with these expectations for self-employment on the part of the two blue-collar groups. Does self-employment mean, as it did for Goldthorpe's workers, a way to "get ahead," enjoy the full fruits of one's labour, and eliminate the alienation of the marketplace inherent in wage labour? Or does it mean, as it did for Chinoy's workers, the ability to become "one's own boss," enjoy the intrinsic rewards of one's labour, and eliminate the alienation of the workplace inherent in rationalized wage labour?

To assess the applicability of these two views we can examine the relationship between job expectations and the measure of work orientation and its dimensions employed in Table 16–3. The percentage cross-tabulations for this relationship are presented in Table 16–6. It is clear first of all that there is no relationship at all between overall orientation to work and job expectations among either the skilled or the semi-skilled. For the former about a quarter of both the instrumentally and the intrinsically oriented expect to become self-employed; for the semi-skilled the respective proportions are 36 per cent and 39 per cent. When we examine the relationship in greater detail, however, it becomes evident that important differences do exist.

Table 16–6

Work orientation and job expectations

Percent of instrumentally oriented who give priority to:	Skilled		Semi-skilled	
	expects self-employment	expects other job	expects self-employment	expects other job
Better pay and benefits	37.6%	24.4%	40.6%	35.7%
More job security	3.3	6.7	28.1	10.7
Better opportunities for advancement	60.0	68.9	31.3	53.6
Total	100.0	100.0	100.0	100.0
Subsample size	30.0	90	32	56
	Cramer's V = 0.126 p ≤ .05		Cramer's V = 0.261 p ≤ .05	
Percent of intrinsically oriented who give priority to:				
More interesting work	25.8%	25.5%	23.5%	23.1%
More control over work pace and quality	3.2	3.2	11.8	1.9
Better chance to use abilities	38.7	47.9	29.4	57.7
Greater sense of accomplishment	32.2	23.4	35.3	17.3
Total	100.0	100.0	100.0	100.0
Subsample size	31	94	34	52
	Cramer's V = 0.096 p ≤ .05		Cramer's V = 0.336 p ≤ .05	

Among the instrumentally oriented we find the conventional wisdom supported among the skilled for whom expectations of self-employment are clearly associated with advancement and income. In this respect, however, there is no significant difference between those who expect to become self-employed and those who expect some other form of wage labour than their present one. Among the semi-skilled, on the other hand, we find that although expectations of self-employment are still predominantly associated with an orientation to income and advancement, they are also more clearly associated with a concern for security, distinguishing them not only from the skilled but also from the semi-skilled who expect some other form of job in the future. This pattern corresponds to the fact that self-employment expectations generally increase among those for whom security also becomes a greater concern, namely the older, the less educated, and those from farm and small town backgrounds. This correlation, however, entails something of a contradiction between perception and prevailing reality. Self-employment is now a highly unstable form of occupational and economic status; the chances of striking out and succeeding on one's own account are particularly slim for those with little capital, few entrepreneurial skills, and a history of manual wage labour behind them (Cf. Mackenzie, 1973; Mayer and Goldstein, 1964). In Canada, for example, the proportion of the labour force composed of the individual self-employed (i.e., self-employed but not employing the labour of others) declined from 11.6 per cent in 1957 to 6.4 per cent in 1966 to 5.4 per cent in 1976 (Statistics Canada, 1976: 116). For relatively unskilled, older, uneducated workers to view self-employment as a means to countervail the vagaries of wage labour is to flirt with imminent failure for many, and with long hours, hard work, and some disillusionment for the few who succeed (cf. Berg and Rogers, 1964).

For the intrinsically oriented, both skilled and semi-skilled, we find that expectations for self-employment are associated more with feelings of accomplishment than is the case for those with other mobility expectations. Contrary to expectations, however, we find that even among those who expect to become self-employed, concern with more control over work pace and quality does not figure prominently. This is particularly true for the skilled, but also for the semi-skilled. This would tend to disconfirm the conventional wisdom that self-employment denotes the desire to become one's own boss; it seems, rather, to be associated with a search for greater enjoyment from the performance of one's labour.

Such a conclusion is, however, only partly warranted. It is clear when we examine other indicators that self-employment is more clearly related to the dimension of work control, especially so far as the semi-skilled are concerned. For example, we find that nearly 30 per cent of the semi-skilled as a whole express dissatisfaction with the amount of control they currently exercise over their work. This proportion doubles for those who expect to become self-employed, rendering the latter more dissatisfied than those with other occupational expectations. And when we control for overall job orientation we find that the proportion increases to over 70 per cent among those who endow work with an intrinsic meaning.

Nor should we conclude that the issue of control is confined to the level of the immediate work process as some writers such as Blauner (1964) have argued. As Marx pointed out, part of what has come to be called the ideological "hegemony" of capital resides in transforming socially determined relations grounded in the divisions of property and labour into "natural" and "necessary" features of the social order. Predominant in this respect are the rights accruing to private property. Thus we should not expect workers to articulate in a fully conscious manner the demand for control over property and the structures of political and economic decision-making which derive from it until greater control over the immediate work process has been accomplished. In a more empirical sense this means that sentiments which may evolve into more clearly expressed demands for control over property are likely initially to take the form of sentiments of a general critical nature towards abstractions like "management," the "corporation" and so on. For example, in the case of attitudes towards "big companies," among both the skilled and the semi-skilled those who think the latter are "bad" are significantly more likely to expect to become self-employed than to expect some other form of occupational future. Attitudes of this nature, while they may be manifested in a loose and unfocused manner, form an underlying "structure of sentiment" which may become articulated as demands for property control under more conducive conditions.

CONCLUSION

The data analysed confirm the view that instrumentalism is a widespread orientation to work among Canadian industrial workers. Moreover, if by work orientation we mean not only the meaning bestowed upon a specific, concrete job but also the general meaning associated with work, we find that it is common among the lower middle-class also. At the same time, it must be noted that the incidence of instrumentalism is not overwhelming, and that when we examine its more specific components the concern for advancement emerges as the most important consideration for the managers and the skilled, and the second most important for the semi-skilled. These facts, reinforced by data concerning satisfaction with current advancement opportunities, suggest that personal mobility is a strong interest for many of those in industrial manual jobs.

Although we found that a clear majority of all three occupational groups expect to remain occupationally immobile, significant differences do exist with respect to the patterning of expectations of those who do not. To be sure, the majority of managers, skilled, and semi-skilled expect to remain in wage labour of some form, a fact which reaffirms the view that careerism is the dominant mobility ideology of modern capitalism. Nonetheless, entre-preneurialism retains salience for a sizeable minority of the skilled and especially the semi-skilled. In the latter case this becomes an overall majority among those who have little schooling, who are older, who work in highly routinized jobs, and who are from farm backgrounds. These patterns suggest that mobility through self-employment is most important for those in the least advantageous position to succeed via a bureaucratic or professional career. The mobility ideology of early capitalism has today become an ideology of the marginal, the disadvantaged, the otherwise trapped.

Finally, the data suggest no relationship between job expectations and overall work orientation; the instrumentally oriented are neither more nor less likely to expect a future of self-employment than are those who endow work with an intrinsic meaning. However, significant differences are apparent in the case of the semi-skilled with respect to the relationship between job expectations and the specific components of work orientation. For the instrumentally oriented, self-employment expectations are associated with a greater, if somewhat contradictory, concern for security; for the intrinsically oriented, they are associated with a greater concern for feelings of accomplishment from and control over work.

In sum, the data offer limited support for the implications of Goldthorpe et al.'s notion of instrumentalism, and for Chinoy's view of entrepreneurialism as the quest for autonomy on the part of alienated wage labour. While entrepreneurialism remains a resilient concern in the working-class, it is evident that its incidence, roots, and meanings do vary, especially by skill level. This fact, in turn, does provide some support for the thesis of the internal differentiation of the working-class, and reminds us that the presence of similar attitudes among individuals does not mean that they are necessarily endowed with the same meanings and implications, or that they are derived from the same sources.

NOTES

1. Particularly, in so far as the attainment of relatively well-paying wage labour, especially in light of the financial "burdens" of a dependent family, can be said to represent an investment in one's social status quo, and in so far as embarking upon a course of self-employment entails risks even greater than those entailed in attempting advancement through promotion, we should expect those without such investments in their current work and life situations to be more likely to confront the risks of entrepreneurial mobility.

REFERENCES

Argyle, M.
1972   *The Social Psychology of Work*. Harmondsworth: Pelican Books.

Berg, I. and D. Rogers
1964   "Former Blue-Collarites in Small Business." In *Blue-Collar World*. A. Shostak and W. Gomberg (eds.) Englewood Cliffs, N.J.: Prentice-Hall.

Blauner, R.
1964   *Alienation and Freedom*. Chicago: University of Chicago Press.

Chinoy, E.
1955   *Automobile Workers and the American Dream*. New York: Random House.

Dubin, R.
1956   "Industrial Workers' Worlds." *Social Problems* 3.

Form, W.
1976   *Blue-Collar Stratification*. Princeton: Princeton University Press.

Goldthorpe, J. et al.

1968   *The Affluent Worker: Industrial Attitudes and Behaviour*. London: Cambridge University Press.

1969   *The Affluent Worker in the Class Structure*. London: Cambridge University Press.

Loubser, J., and M. Fullan

1970   *Industrial Conversion: Workers' Attitudes to Change in Different Industries*. Ottawa: Queen's Printer.

Marx, K.

1964   *Economic and Philosophical Manuscripts of 1844*. D. Struik (ed.). New York: International Publishers.

Mayer, K., and S. Goldstein

1964   "Manual Workers as Small Businessmen," in *Blue-Collar World*. A. Shostak and W. Gomberg (eds.). Englewood Cliffs, N.J.: Prentice-Hall.

Mackenzie, G.

1973   *The Aristocracy of Labour*. London: Cambridge University Press.

Statistics Canada

1977   *Perspectives Canada*. Ottawa: Information Canada.

Thermstrom, S.

1964   *Poverty and Progress*. Cambridge, Mass.: Harvard University Press.

1973   *The Other Bostonians*. Cambridge, Mass.: Harvard University Press.

Wedderburn, D., and R. Crompton

1972   *Workers' Attitudes and Technology*. London: Cambridge University Press.

Chapter 17

A Tragically Repeating Pattern: Issues of Industrial Safety

Lloyd Tataryn

Producers of murder mystery movies love fogs. There is nothing like a steamy fog to heighten suspense and hide the identity of the culprit until the climactic ending. But fogs have been useful in occupational health crises as well. They also have been used to hide the identity of the true culprits and fudge the unseemly plot.

Occupational health crises have consistently traced a tragically predictable pattern in this country — a pattern often hidden by a thick political fog of self-serving scientific and medical jargon. Government and industry have taken advantage of this murky scientific haze to obscure their role in the making of the tragedies.

Expressions of intense concern for human health and safety have tumbled out of the mouths of politicians and regulatory officials whenever an occupational problem has reached critical proportions. Industry spokesmen, in turn, have despairingly thrown up their hands and pointed to the millions spent on health studies and new technology that purportedly made the workplace safe. The plaintive cry from industry and government has always been: "we did our best." And if one accepts their approach to scientific research and risk assessment as valid and just, then it probably is correct to say "government and industry did their best."

But alligator tears and gnashing of teeth aside, the sad fact remains that in Canada we spend over 7,500 dollars a minute on workmen's compensation payments for job related deaths and disease. An average of three million more working days are lost in Canada each year through accident and illness than are lost through industrial disputes.[1]

In the fall of 1978, Labour Canada published a study on Canadian compliance with the International Labour Code developed by the International Labour Organization. Under the heading "Occupational Cancer" it observed that in Canada, "the present degree of compliance with the [International Labour Code] is minimal." The report noted that no Canadian jurisdiction ensures "that all exposed workers are provided with all available information of the dangers involved," and no jurisdiction has ever succeeded in "establishing appropriate medical examinations both during and after employment."[2]

When workers enter the workforce they are among the healthiest people in society. Companies simply refuse to hire people who fail their pre-employment medical examinations. And people in poor health usually choose to avoid physically taxing jobs and work where they must breathe dusts and fumes. Considering the state of their health upon entering employment, workers should ordinarily live well into their seventies and eighties, and even

293

nineties. Instead, a disproportionate number fall victim to occupational diseases such as cancer, and die by the thousands at much younger ages.[3]

Given these facts, it is hardly surprising that investigators have uncovered the same unhealthy thread of events weaving its way through almost all the carefully documented occupational and environmental health tragedies.[4] In almost every case, three key common features emerge: the victims have been drawn from the same social class; the victims have been lulled into accepting their lot in life and death by the presentation of tainted scientific and medical evidence purchased by industry; and the victims have had imposed on them someone else's definition of what constitutes an "acceptable" risk.

The observation on social class is almost a mundane point to make. One would have to be terribly obtuse not to notice that the principal victims of unsafe environments generally come from the ranks of the working class and the poorest segments of society.

The wealthy, like the tall, view the world from a different angle. Not only do the wealthy have more money than most people, they also possess the wherewithal to buy in and out of situations into which others are often locked for life. Their riches usually allow them to escape the unhealthy environments they or their colleagues have often been most responsible for creating. The health consequences are left to the less fortunate members of society to experience.

In 1943, Dr. Henry Sigerist of Johns Hopkins University observed:

> In any given society the incidence of illness is largely determined by economic factors. . . . A low living standard, lack of food, clothing and fuel, poor housing conditions and other symptoms of poverty, have always been major causes of disease.
>
> Health conditions have greatly improved, at least in the Western world, but this improvement has not equally benefited the various groups of the population. The process was in many cases as follows: a disease, such as tuberculosis or malaria, indiscriminately attacked all groups. With developing civilization the standard of living rose and medicine advanced. Groups in the higher income brackets were the first to profit from these gains, leaving the disease to continue its ravages among the people of low income.[5]

Preventable diseases continue to be unequally distributed. Those who reap the greatest benefits from our economic distribution of wealth seldom assume the environmental health risks experienced by people looking up at the world from society's under-class.[6]

Consider the evidence compiled by the U.S. National Cancer Institute and National Institute of Environmental Health Sciences on job-related cancers. The U.S. government agencies estimate that close to 40 per cent of cancers may be triggered by occupational factors.[7] The agencies reached this conclusion after tabulating the cancer risk ratios for exposure to a number of industrial substances: (A risk ratio of 2 means a doubling of the cancer risk.)[8]

(1) arsenic has a risk ratio of 2–8 for lung cancer.

(2) benzene has a risk ratio of 2–3 for leukemia.

(3) coal tar pitch volatiles and coke oven emissions have a risk ratio of 2–6 for cancer of the lung, larynx, skin and scrotum.

(4) vinyl chloride has risk ratios of 200, 4 and 1.9 respectively for hemangiosarcoma (a malignant tumour of cells lining the cavities of the heart), brain and lung cancer.

(5) chromium has risk ratios of 3–40 for lung and larynx cancers.

(6) nickel has risk ratios of 5–10 for lung cancer.

(7) petroleum distillates have risk ratios of 2–6 for lung and larynx cancers.

Industries take into consideration many costs when they launch an enterprise. They carefully estimate their construction, equipment, transportation, raw material and marketing costs. They tabulate wage rates, employee benefit plans and their probable return on the capital invested. They budget for management perks and public relations efforts. Nevertheless, as the disturbing statistics on production-related cancer indicate, industries have repeatedly failed to take into account the *full* costs of their operations. Industries have imposed additional costs on people who have never agreed to shoulder the expenses which are part and parcel of money-making endeavours. Social costs are seldom considered by entrepreneurs in their business planning, primarily because those most affected are from the economic groups least equipped to fight back.

Costs in environmental destruction, lost recreational opportunities, lifestyle changes and costs to future generations in the form of clean-up and rehabilitation expenses seldom appear in corporate ledger books. Neither do the costs in human health. And no one can realistically tabulate a going rate for the suffering experienced by a family who has lost its bread-winner to job-related cancer.

The pursuit of profits usually conflicts, at least in the short term, with occupational and environmental health demands. Health protection costs money — money which often only yields further expenses in equipment maintenance, rather than a profitable return on the capital invested. Professor Bruce Doern, Director of Carleton University's School of Public Administration, has examined the regulation of hazardous products in Canada. He observes that industries usually take exception to new standards. They claim that the technology to achieve the standard is unavailable, and that industry must be given more time to meet the new exposure goals. According to Doern:

> In some instances a time lag is clearly necessary. In others, time is merely another way of expressing the higher priority to be accorded to capital as opposed to labour. . . .[9]

Stated another way: when corporations protest against new exposure standards they are, in effect, arguing that money is a more important consideration than human lives.

And industries have been prone to finance the production of scientific and medical data suggesting that "unsafe" conditions are indeed "safe," in order to kill the introduction of strict exposure standards. According to the Science Council of Canada:

> The role of the medical profession in insisting on better protection for the
> workforce . . . has been less than distinguished in the recent past. Many
> people believe that the reason for this is that physicians are wholly
> employed by company management and that independent medical advice
> is therefore not available within the workplace. We have observed
> during the last few months an increasing tendency for workers in major
> industries involved with hazards to seek their own medical opinion from
> consultants outside the plant, and even from outside Canada. We regard
> this breakdown of confidence as particularly unfortunate, but easily
> understandable.[10]

Simply put: medical opinions and scientific data can be bought — a fact
most people do not seem to realize.

In most environmental health confrontations, the average citizen is forced
to place his trust in the hands of sophisticated specialists. Confused by
unfamiliar jargon and unable to follow the esoteric arguments employed by the
"experts," the citizen often shrugs and makes the assumption that eventually
scientific truth will win out and everything will be justly settled.

But this is not necessarily the case. The scientific truth must first run a
political gauntlet. For after the authorities give their advice, and all the
technical data are in, the decision arrived at is ultimately a political verdict. It
is merely masquerading as a purely scientific ruling.

Politicians, corporations, and unions are aware of this environmental fact
of life. And since in the long run they must rely upon the combined political
and scientific judgment of their technical advisors, they tend to choose as
advisors scientists whose biases are similar to their own — scientists who are
prone to ask the type of questions that produce answers which most often serve
the interests of their employers.

When confronted with conflicting scientific presentations on environmental health, the public is forced to decide whose argument is valid.
Unfortunately, the public is seldom informed of the political and economic as
well as scientific biases scientists in environmental health conflicts bring to
their investigations. Most of us have been led to believe that "science" and
"scientists" are above such considerations.[11]

But consider the history of the asbestos exposure standard as a case in
point. Asbestos has long been known to cause the lung scarring disease
asbestosis, as well as cancer.

The ways and means of eliminating asbestos dust have therefore long been
a subject of controversy. Doctors, health professionals and governments have
joined companies and unions in pitched battles over establishing asbestos dust
standards. The official "safe" exposure level has been lowered in fits and starts.
Since the early 1900s, asbestos workers have been repeatedly assured that
existing standards protect their health. Each time, diseased and dead bodies
suggested otherwise. After each tragedy was uncovered, another official "safe"
level of exposure was pronounced.

Great Britain made the earliest attempt to limit asbestos exposure. In
1906, Dr. H. Montague Murray optimistically informed a compensation
regulations hearing of vastly improved asbestos ventilation technology. "One
hears, generally speaking, that considerable trouble is now taken to prevent

the inhalation of dust," said Murray, "so the disease (asbestosis) is not likely to occur as heretofore."[12]

In spite of this assurance, asbestos workers continued to die at unconscionable rates — so much so, that in the late 1920s the British Factory Inspectorate required the asbestos industry to introduce more extensive environmental control technology. In 1930, another optimistic prediction was made: "The outlook . . . is good. . . . In the space of a decade, or thereabouts, the effect of energetic application of preventative measures should be apparent in a great reduction in the incidence of fibrosis."[13]

By 1938, it became clear that the much-touted improved ventilation technology remained inadequate. The United States Public Health Service then introduced an asbestos standard based on dust measurements. Asbestos exposure was limited to 5 million particles per cubic foot of air, which is roughly 30 fibers per cubic centimeter of air.[14]

When the standard was set, an announcement was issued by the United States Public Health Service: "It appears from these data that if asbestos dust concentrations in the air are kept below this limit, new cases of asbestosis would not appear."[15] Once again, the standard setters were wrong. Men continued to die because of dust conditions on the job.

In Canada these developments were ignored. Most of the asbestos mining and milling operations were located in the province of Quebec, and the Quebec asbestos industry steadfastly maintained that their work environments were as harmless as a baby's breath. After the famous 1949 asbestos strike where asbestos exposure was a strike issue,[16] the Quebec companies trotted out medical "experts" who loudly trumpeted the safety of asbestos.

At the 1949 Arbitration Tribunal, Dr. Arthur Vorwald testified on behalf of the companies that asbestos exposure was not related to the development of cancer:

> I do not think there is [an increase in cancer]. . . . I surveyed all the world's literature with respect to the incidence of cancer among individuals who are inhaling dust, and the literature included not only (X-ray) evidence collated from industries . . . but it also included autopsy statistics of the individuals who were examined.
>
> Also the study included an experimental approach wherein we tried to determine whether cancer in the lung was higher in our experimental animals exposed to asbestos fibers, than it was in normal animals. In both instances, I was unable to determine with accuracy that there was an increased incidence of pulmonary cancer in individuals exposed to asbestos fibers . . . the evidence certainly is not clear-cut.[17]

Dr. Vorwald also testified that workers should only worry about "long fibers" and those only at "high concentrations." According to Vorwald, his experiments showed that a "high concentration" was 183 million particles per cubic foot,[18] so the 5 million particle standard included a generous safety margin. Nevertheless, the standard was soon lowered to 12 fibers per cubic centimeter of air,[19] (the equivalent of 177 fibers per cubic foot) and then to 5 fibers per cubic centimeter of air when 12-fibers proved unsafe.

In 1968, however, the British Occupational Hygiene Society recommended the implementation of a 2-fiber standard. The 2-fiber recommendation was made after asbestos industry "experts" conducted an examination of X-ray abnormalities ravaging the lungs of 290 workers in a British asbestos factory at Rochdale. By comparing the X-ray abnormalities to the recorded dust concentrations, the company's industrial hygienists concluded that a worker had only a 1 per cent chance of contracting asbestosis at the 2-fiber level.[20]

In January 1977, Dr. Julian Peto of Oxford University's Cancer Epidemiology and Clinical Trials Unit made public his evaluation of the 2-fiber standard. Peto noted that fewer than one person in 100 supposedly ran the risk of disease at the 2-fiber standard. His calculations indicated, however, that at that standard, one asbestos worker in 14 would possibly die prematurely. Dr. Peto based his calculations on data provided to Oxford by the asbestos plant in Rochdale, England. Upon re-evaluating the Rochdale data, Peto also discovered that the lung cancer death rate in the plant was almost double the expected death rate.[21]

Since October 1975, the United States Department of Labor proposed an in-plant asbestos standard of one-half a fiber per cubic centimeter of air.[22] The United States proposed the one-half fiber standard because of evidence that the 2-fiber standard, *which was designed to prevent asbestosis, not cancer*, has proven inadequate for the prevention of asbestosis, let alone cancer. The United States Department of Labor does not attempt to suggest that the 2-fiber standard will prevent cancer. The National Institute for Occupational Safety and Health in the United States has since proposed that the asbestos exposure standard be reduced to .1 fibers per cubic centimeter of air.[23]

So we have seen the asbestos standard reduced from 5 million fibers per cubic foot of air to a recommended standard of .1 per cubic centimeter of air. And at every stage of the reduction process, scientists and doctors have confidently testified that this was finally a "safe" level of exposure. Unfortunately, workers have paid with their health and lives when the "experts' " calculated gamble did not pan out.

Scientists and doctors with a given set of biases examining a particular problem can ask a series of questions which produce certain answers. Scientists and doctors with another set of biases may examine the same problem and ask a different series of questions which produce very different answers. This is not to suggest that it is impossible to design a scientific or medical inquiry which will produce results acceptable to all parties. It merely suggests that many of the scientific inquiries posing as "pure" scientific and medical investigations have, in fact, been unduly influenced by political, social and economic factors generally considered outside the scientific realm.

Stephanie Shields of the University of California psychology department writes that scientific inquiry has always been influenced by the context from which it operates.

> As human beings engaged in science we bring to our work values and attitudes which, though [sometimes] unconscious, guide our selection of problems, methodology, and interpretation. Science fits comfortably with established social values and typically has been a champion of the *status quo*. As such, it is a highly adaptive social system. For the most part, this may be of little concern when the topic of investigation is far removed

from normal human social interaction. But the closer the topic to everyday life, the more problematic systems become.[24]

As the history of the asbestos exposure standard outlined has shown, one such problematic scientific topic complicating "normal human social interaction," has been the analysis of industrial contaminants.

Consider again the 1949 testimony of Dr. Arthur Vorwald. His testimony aptly illustrates the hard-nosed bias that medical and epidemiological professionals hired by industry have brought to their investigations. When Vorwald was questioned about workers' disabilities, particularly in relation to asbestos lung scarring, he replied:

> I would like to compare lungs with our two arms, two legs and our two eyes. When one goes bad we can use the other one, and we have two lungs in case of disease.[25]

The union lawyer grabbed the first opportunity to question Dr. Vorwald about his definition of disability.

Q: Nevertheless, when an eye is lost ... impairment is definitely detrimental to the man who has suffered this misfortune?

A: [Vorwald] Yes. So?

Q: So, possibly, it would be accurate to say that a man who lost an eye suffered from an impairment. Would not the condition of the worker who is suffering from a substantial degree of fibrosis in the lung be much the same?

A: No, I don't think so. He has an impairment of his lung tissue but he is not suffering from it.[26]

In a 1953 address to a medical symposium in Boston, Dr. Paul Cartier, the man who ran the asbestos companies' health clinic in Thetford Mines, outlined a personal philosophy of industrial medicine akin to Vorwald's. Cartier explained that asbestosis "remains a disease which can be tolerated for many years." He told the Boston assembly: "this disease may look more serious and cause important *medicolegal problems* if a too scientific medical concept or too liberal social interpretation is accepted by the medicolegal professions, labour and compensation bodies."[27]

When the Thetford asbestos issue flared again during a 1975 strike, Dr. Cartier openly stated that, on humanitarian grounds, he had not always informed workers suffering from asbestosis of the full extent of their illness: "I figured it was in their best interests to stay at their jobs. Besides, they didn't want to be reported ill and transferred to a lower-paying job where they might have earned as much as 50 dollars less a week." Cartier also noted that "even if they had left their work completely and gone on to drive cabs, for instance, it might not have arrested the progressive effects of asbestosis."

Paul Filteau, general manager and secretary of the Quebec Asbestos Mining Association, the organization which represents the Quebec asbestos industry, says the companies never encouraged Cartier to be wary of "medicolegal problems" when he examined Thetford workers and gave workers with impaired lungs "A" classifications. But Filteau admits that the companies' clinic had not always informed the workers about the state of their health: "Cartier told the workers they were all right, let them go back to their jobs, and, if he thought the case serious, recommended that they visit their family doctor. But the companies never told him to do this. It was his decision. We never interfered."

Neither did the Quebec government. The clinic's X-ray records were supposedly subject to government inspection. Until 1972, however, the government-appointed doctor responsible for monitoring the X-ray records of clinics in eastern Quebec was Dr. Paul Cartier. In the case of Thetford Mines, then, Cartier was in effect inspecting his own work.

The evidence continues to mount that asbestos companies hid from workers the diagnoses that they were suffering from asbestos-related diseases. They hid this until the men finally became physically disabled and the sickness could no longer be denied. In 1949, Dr. Kenneth Wallace Smith, then the medical officer for Johns-Manville Canada Inc. in Asbestos, Quebec, filed a health report with the asbestos company's head offices in the United States. The report indicates that Dr. Smith discussed the potential asbestos danger with Johns-Manville (JM) executives and records their reaction, which, according to Smith, was: "we know that we are producing disease in the employees who manufacture these products and there is no question in my (our) mind that disease is being produced in non-JM employees who may use certain of these products." Smith noted in his report that asbestosis was "irreversible and permanent" and added "but as long as a man is not disabled it is felt he should not be told of his condition so that he can live and work in peace and the company can benefit by his many years of experience."

Smith's report to Johns-Manville came to light through a series of recent lawsuits filed against U.S. asbestos companies by American asbestos-disease victims. The victims allege that asbestos companies deliberately withheld information on the deadly effects of asbestos exposure from them.[28]

Lawyers suing the asbestos firm on behalf of diseased workers filed another damaging sworn statement with a U.S. Congressional hearing on asbestos on May 2, 1979. Wilbur Ruff, the former Johns-Manville plant manager in Pittsburg, California swore that the company doctor was not allowed to refer workers to outside specialists, even if he found something in his physical examination "that he felt required evaluation by a chest specialist." Ruff stated it was company policy until the "early 1970s" not to warn workers if they had danger symptoms.[29]

The asbestos exposure fiasco ideally illustrates how blue-collar workers have been handicapped in occupational health battles. They have possessed neither the resources nor the sophisticated scientific and political tools that are essential in any campaign to alter their work environments. Consequently, blue-collar workers have generally had someone else's definition of an "acceptable" risk imposed upon them.

In the United States, all of the federal health agencies have adopted the approach that there is no threshold to carcinogenic exposures.[30] If a substance causes cancer, it is held that, ideally, the safest way to protect human health is to remove it from the environment. In Canada, occupational and environmental regulatory agencies have failed to develop any consistent policy on thresholds to carcinogens.

But, whether it be here or in the United States, industry now argues that exposure to cancer-causing agents is part of the price we pay for living in an industrial society. Since exposure to carcinogens involves some risk, it has been suggested that the concept of "safe" levels be replaced by that of a "socially acceptable level of risk."[31] Yet, once the concept of "acceptable" risk is raised, the question becomes "acceptable to whom?" From whose viewpoint is "acceptability" to be judged — from that of its creators, its victims, from experts or governments, or the community at large? Each viewpoint clearly defines its own, sometimes widely different, level of acceptability.[32]

Dr. Jerry Ravetz writes in the British publication, *New Scientist*, of a "risk triangle" which is present in standard-setting situations. He states "there are three sides involved in every hazard: those who create it; those who experience it; and those who regulate it. Sometimes all 'sides' (of the risk triangle) come together in the same person (say, a mountain climber). But for most technical risks the sides are largely separate." He notes that the values, expectations and goals of each side in the risk triangle are influenced by "wider social relations of power."

A hazardous environment (at work or at home) is a part of social powerlessness. Hence all debates on risks have an inevitable and inescapable element of politics in them.[33]

Science Council of Canada investigators have commented on a key political element associated with risk assessment in Canada:

A major difficulty with most risk-benefit analyses appears to be a lack of consideration of how risks and benefits are distributed among various social sectors. It seems that those at greatest health risk are often not those who derive major benefits. Since this is characteristic of our socio-economic system, it is often neglected [or merely assumed correct] by those engaged in risk-benefit analyses.[34]

Ideally, this need not be the case. The "risk triangle" should be contracted: those who create the risks could be required to suffer them, and those who make the regulatory decisions could be required to live with the consequences of their decisions.[35]

But Canadian wage earners have traditionally had little say in the creation of the environmental guidelines they work under, let alone a major say in the distribution of the wealth they produce. Above the 49th parallel "accountability" for regulatory decisions has been a problem as has "jurisdictional responsibility."[36] Workers have only been given a significant voice in occupational and environmental health matters when crises have erupted — then governments, eager to wriggle out of embarrassing political jams, have appointed royal commissions or task forces to assess the issues and give the decision-makers breathing space.

In the United States, workers are somewhat better off, at least in occupational health matters. There, the Occupational Safety and Health Administration (OSHA) holds extensive public hearings when occupational exposure standards are established. Although OSHA has been chastised by Americans for taking a leisurely approach to establishing certain occupational

302 Work in the Canadian Context

standards,[37] the agency has nevertheless accepted the view that it is impossible to detect threshold levels for carcinogens. OSHA's policy is that exposures must be controlled as tightly as possible, even at very high cost. Since OSHA is also required to consider the social and economic ramifications of its decisions, the agency has ruled that levels must be reduced to their lowest "feasible" level.[38] This approach, of course, means that policy makers must consider a morbid trade-off — the cost of controlling an economically valuable substance versus the threat to the lives of the people exposed to it. (This trade-off is made, of course, in Canada all the time. Canadians, however, do not have an OSHA to formalize the political and economic bartering process which is a very real part of occupational health exposure decisions.)

Industries now argue that if there is no "safe" exposure level to a carcinogen, there is no absolute "feasible" level either. Every time a standard is lowered 1 part per million, 1 fiber per cubic centimeter of air, it costs somebody a great deal of money. For example, chemical company representatives have disputed OSHA's proposal to lower occupational exposure to the cancer-causing polymer compound acrylonitrite to .2 parts per million on financial grounds. Industry spokesmen say the new standard will cost over 126 million dollars a year to save the life of one textile worker.[39]

As the debates over threshold levels indicate, the regulation of industrial health hazards remains essentially a social, economic and political question, rather than a scientific one. At issue is the price tag to be placed on a human life.[40]

The most humane and just solution to the risk–benefit dilemma is obvious: involve workers as the key element in health safety decisions. Only when the balance of industrial power is tilted toward those who toil to produce wealth and away from profit, will we begin to see major changes — changes which protect physical health and promote "well-being in a more comprehensive social sense."[41] Otherwise, the constant compromise between the money-making motive and health and safety will inevitably favour healthy profits as opposed to healthy workers.

As Sheldon Samuels, the director of Health, Safety and Environmental Affairs for the AFL–CIO's Industrial Union Department puts it:

> The economics of the situation are very simple. Nearly half of the male blue-collar work force is afflicted with chronic — and no doubt partly work-related — diseases that are largely paid for by the worker and the community as a whole. Even if all of the identifiable costs were placed on the employer, we cannot always be sure that it would not be cheaper for the employer to replace dead workers than to keep them alive. It may even be profitable, if only dollars and cents are counted. In the case of chronic occupational disease, it may be cheaper for any nation to sacrifice a life that has already achieved peak productivity.[42]

The accuracy of Samuels's disheartening description of the political economy of the work place is starkly apparent when one investigates any of the numerous occupational health crises Canada has experienced. The principal victims have been the "hewers of wood and drawers of water" who have built this nation's economy. As working-class people, they have generally not had the sophisticated scientific tools necessary to adequately analyse their work environments. When presented with scientific evidence designed to justify the existing work situation, the victims have not understood that the supposedly neutral evidence may have been designed to purposefully under-estimate the risks they faced. The victims have generally not realized that scientific evidence can be purchased. Working-class people have been trained to work with their hands, backs and brawn, and have been discouraged from using their critical faculties to question the assumptions and biases of degree-laden scientists. Consequently, the employers who have created the work place, purchased the labour, marshalled political support and bought the scientific justifications for the overall design, have been allowed to impose risks on their employees which have not been defined, explained or understood by the people who experience those risks.

The tragically repeating pattern of occupational illness is therefore once more set in motion — and will continue to be set in motion as long as the pattern remains unbroken.

NOTES

1. *Globe and Mail*. Feb. 16, 1977. *Globe and Mail*. Mar. 28, 1978. "Work-injury and cost in Canadian industry, 1967–1977," *The Labour Gazette*. Labour Canada, Ottawa, 1977.
2. *Canada and the International Labour Code*. Labour Canada, Ottawa, 1978, 55–56.
3. Agran, L., *The Cancer Connection*, Boston, Mass.: Houghton Mifflin Co., 1977, 25.
4. Tataryn, L., *Dying For A Living*, Ottawa: Deneau and Greenberg, 1979. This book cites scores of studies attesting to the above point.
5. Sigerist, H.E., *Civilization and Disease*, Ithaca, N.Y.: Cornell University Press, 1943, 55.
6. See Sterling, T.D., "Does Smoking Kill Workers or Working Kill Smokers," *International Journal of Health Services*, Vol. 8, 1978, 437–452 and *Policy and Poisons*, Science Council of Canada, Report No. 28, October 1977, 27.
7. "Estimates of the Fraction of Cancer Incidence in the United States Attributable to Occupational Factors," National Cancer Institute and National Institute of Environmental Health Sciences, Washington, C.B., Sept. 11, 1978, 4.
8. Ibid., 2–3.
9. Doern, G.B., "The Political Economy of Regulating Occupational Health: The Ham and Beaudry Reports," *Canadian Public Administration*, Vol. 20, 1977, 1–35.
10. *Policies and Poisons*, Science Council of Canada, Report No. 28, Oct. 1977, 47–48.
11. See Primack, J. and Von Hippel, F., *Advice and Dissent: Scientists in the Political Arena*, New York: Basic Books Inc., 1974.
12. Murray, H.M., *1907 Report of the Departmental Committee on Compensation for Industrial Disease*, 127, London, England: H.M. Stationery Office, 1907.
13. Merewether, E.R.A. and Price, C.V., *1930 Report on Effects of Asbestos Dust Suppression in the Asbestos Industry*, London, England: H.M. Stationery Office, 1930.

14. An absolutely accurate translation from the particles per cubic foot standard to the fibers per cubic centimetre standard is impossible. The particulate method of measurement included substances other than asbestos in its calculations. This means that a low particulate count could nevertheless include an extremely high amount of asbestos fibers, or that a high particulate count could include only a few asbestos fibers. Nevertheless, two million particles have been considered the equivalent of twelve asbestos fibers. See, Brodeur, P., *Expendable Americans*. 10–11, and 26.

15. Dreesson, W.C., Dallavalle, J.M., Edwards, T.I., Miller, J.W. and Sayers, R.R., *1938 U.S. Public Health Bulletin*. No. 241.

16. Isbister, F., "Asbestos 1949," in Abella, I. *On Strike*, Toronto: James Lewis and Samuel, 1974.

17. Tribunal D'Arbitrage institué pour régler le différend entre Asbestos Corporation Limited et Le Syndicat National Des Travailleurs De L'Asbestos Corporation Limited, Inc., Séance du 23 Septembre, 1949, *Volume 8*, 60–63.

18. Ibid., 52.

19. "Submission on behalf of Canadian Johns-Manville Co., Ltd. to the Comité d'étude de la salubrité dans l'industrie de l'amiante" Asbestos, Quebec, 1976, 14.

20. "British Occupational Hygiene Society — Subcommittee on Asbestosis Hygiene Standards for Chrysotile Asbestos Dust," *Annals of Occupational Hygiene*, Vol. 11, 1958, 47–49.

21. Gillie, O., Gillman, P. and May, D., "Official Safety Limit for Asbestos May Put One in Fourteen at Risk." *The Sunday Times*, (London) Jan. 30, 1977.

22. United States Department of Labor, Occupational Safety and Health Administration, "Occupational Exposure to Asbestos," *Federal Register*, Vol. 40, no. 197, Oct. 9, 1975.

23. United States Department of Health, Education and Welfare, National Institute for Occupational Safety and Health, "Revised Recommended Asbestos Standard," Publication no. 77–169, Dec. 1976.

24. Shields, S. "Sex and the Biased Scientist," *New Scientist*, December 7, 1978. See also Irvine, J., Miles, I. and Evans, J. *Demystifying Social Statistics*, London: Pluto Press Ltd., 1979.

25. Tribunal D'Arbitrage institué pour régler le différend entre Asbestos Corporation Limited et Le Syndicat National Des Travailleurs De L'Asbestos Corporation Limited, Inc. Séance du 23 Septembre 1949, *Volume 8*, 71.

26. Ibid., 83–84.

27. Cartier, P., "Some Clinical Observations of Asbestosis in Mine and Mill Workers," *Archives of Industrial Health*, Vol. 55, 1955, 204–207. (emphasis added).

28. Martin L., "Asbestos workers not told of hazards, papers indicate," *Globe and Mail*, November 23, 1978.

29. "Asbestos Firm Hid Workers' X-Rays," *Toronto Star*, May 3, 1979.

30. See "Identification, Classification and Regulation of Toxic Substances Posing a Potential Occupational Risk," Department of Labor, Occupational Safety and Health Administration. *Federal Register*, Vol. 42, no. 192, Oct. 4, 1977.

31. *Evaluation of Environmental Carcinogens*, Report to the Surgeon General, Ad Hoc Committee on the Evaluation of Low Levels of Environmental

Chemical Carcinogens, U.S. Department of Health, Education and Welfare, April 22, 1970, 7.

32. McGinty, L. and Atherley, G., "Acceptability versus Democracy," *New Scientist*, Sept. 8, 1977.
33. Ravetz, J., "The Political Economy of Risk," *New Scientist*, Sept. 8, 1977.
34. *Policies and Poisons*, Science Council of Canada, Report no. 28, Oct. 1977, 27.
35. Remarks taken from an address made to a conference on Science and Politics of the Environment at York University, Nov. 10, 1977, by Ursula Franklin, Chairperson of the Science Council of Canada's investigation into a "Conserver Society." (Report no. 27, Sept. 1977.)
36. *Policies and Poisons*, Science Council of Canada, Report no. 28, Oct. 1977, 44.
37. While Richard Nixon was President of the United States, OSHA was used as part of the Nixon re-election strategy. A 1972 memo from the chief administrator of OSHA to Nixon's staff recommended that the promulgation of "highly controversial standards" be avoided, and that "four more years of properly managed OSHA" should be used "as a sales point for fund raising and general support by employers." See Berman, D. *Death on the Job*, New York, N.Y.: Monthly Review Press, 1979, 33–34.
38. See "Occupational Exposure to Inorganic Arsenic — Final Standard," Department of Labor, Occupational Safety and Health Administration, *Federal Register*, Vol. 43, no. 88, May 5, 1978, 19600.
39. Behr, P., "Controlling Chemical Hazards," *Environment*, July/August 1978 and Lang, R.A., "Keep an Eye on OSHA," *Enterprise*, Journal of the National Association of Manufacturers, June 1978. See also Kletz, T., "What Risks Should We Run," *New Scientist*, May 12, 1977 and Gehring, P., "The Threshold Controversy," *New Scientist*, Aug. 18, 1977.
40. Hapgood, F., "Risk-Benefit Analysis," *The Atlantic*, Jan. 1979.
41. Kronlund, J., "Organizing for Safety," *New Scientist*, June 14, 1979. In Sweden experiments have shown that health and safety in the workplace is dramatically improved when workers made the decisions on "acceptable" risk.
42. Brodeur, P., *Expendable Americans*, New York: Viking Press, 1973, 207.

REFERENCES

Agran, L.
1977   *The Cancer Connection*. Boston, Mass.: Houghton Mifflin, 25.

Toronto Star
1979   "Asbestos Firm Hid Workers' X-Rays." (May 3).

Behr, P.
1978   "Controlling Chemical Hazards," in *Environment* (July–August) and R.A. Lang "Keep an Eye on OSHA," in *Enterprise* (June) the Journal of the National Association of Manufacturers.

Berman, D.
1979   *Death on the Job*. New York, N.Y.: Monthly Review Press, 33–34.

British Occupational Hygiene Society
       Subcommittee on Asbestosis Hygiene Standards for Chrysotile Asbestos Dust. *Annals of Occupational Hygiene* 11: 47–49.

Brodeur, P.
1973   *Expendable Americans*. New York, N.Y.: Viking Press, 207.

Canada and the International Labour Code
1978   Ottawa: Labour Canada, 55–56.

Cartier, P.
1955   "Some Clinical Observations of Asbestosis in Mine and Mill Workers," in *Archives of Industrial Health* 55: 204–207 (emphasis added).

Doern, G.B.
1977   "The Political Economy of Regulating Occupational Health: The Ham and Beaudry Reports," in *Canadian Public Administration* 20: 1–35.

Dreeson, W.C. et al.
1938   *1938 U.S. Public Health Bulletin*. No. 241.

Gehring, P.
1977   "The Threshold Controversy," in *New Scientist* (Aug. 18).

Gillie, O., P. Gillman and D. May
1977   "Official Safety Limit for Asbestos May Put One in Fourteen at Risk," in the *Sunday Times*. London (Jan. 30).

Globe and Mail
1977   February 16.

Globe and Mail
1978   March 28.

Hapgood, F.
1979   "Risk-Benefit Analysis," in *The Atlantic* (Jan.)

Isbister, F.
1974   "Asbestos 1949," in I. Abella (ed.) *On Strike*. Toronto: James Lewis and Samuel.

Kletz, T.
1977   "What Risks Should We Run," in *New Scientist* (May 12).

Kronlund, J.
1979   "Organizing for Safety," in *New Scientist* (June 14).

Labour Canada
1977   "Identification, Classification and Regulation of Toxic Substances Posing a Potential Occupational Risk," in *Federal Register* Vol. 42, No. 192 (Oct. 4).

1977   "Work-Injury and Cost in Canadian Industry, 1967–1977," in *The Labour Gazette*.

1978   "Occupational Exposure to Inorganic Arsenic — Final Standard," in Federal Register Vol. 43, No. 88 (May 5): 19600.

McGinty, L. and G. Atherley
1977   "Acceptability versus Democracy," in *New Scientist* (Sept. 8).

Martin, L.
1978   "Asbestos Workers Not Told of Hazards, Papers Indicate," in the *Globe and Mail* (Nov. 23).

Merewether, E.R.A. and C.V. Price
1930   *1930 Report on Effects of Asbestos Dust Suppression in the Asbestos Industry*. London: H.M.S.O.

Murray, H.M.
1907   *1907 Report of the Departmental Committee on Compensation for Industrial Disease*. No. 127. London: H.M.S.O.

National Cancer Institute and National Institute of Environmental Health
Sciences
1978   "Estimates of the Fraction of Cancer Incidence in the United States
Attributable to Occupational Factors." Washington, C.B. (Sept. 11): 4.

Primack, J. and Von Hippel, F.
1974   *Advice and Dissent: Scientists in the Political Arena.* New York, N.Y.:
Basic Books.

Ravetz, J.
1977   "The Political Economy of Risk," in *New Scientist* (Sept. 8).

Science Council of Canada
1977   *Policies and Poisons.* Report No. 28. (October): 47–48.

Shields, S.
1978   "Sex and the Biased Scientist," in *New Scientist* (Dec. 7). See also J.
Irvine, I. Miles and J. Evans (1979) *Demystifying Social Statistics.*
London: Pluto Press.

Sigerist, H.E.
1943   *Civilization and Disease.* Ithaca, N.Y.: Cornell University Press, 55.

Sterling, T.D.
1978   "Does Smoking Kill Workers or Working Kill Smokers?" in *International Journal of Health Services* 8: 437–452.

1976   "Submission on Behalf of Canadian Johns-Manville Co. Ltd. to the
Comité d'étude de la salubrité dans l'industrie de l'amiante." Asbestos,
Québec, 14.

Tataryn, L.
1979   *Dying for a Living.* Ottawa: Deneau and Greenberg.

1949   Tribunal D'Arbitrage institué pour régler la différend entre Asbestos
Corporation Limited et Le Syndicat National Des Travailleurs De
L'Asbestos Corporation Inc. Séance du 23 Sept., Vol. 8, 60–63.

United States
1970   *Evaluation of Environmental Carcinogens.* Report to the Surgeon
General, Ad Hoc Committee on the Evaluation of Low Levels of
Environmental Chemical Carcinogens prepared by Department of
Health, Education and Welfare. (April 22): 7.

1976   "Revised Recommended Asbestos Standards." Department of Health,
Education and Welfare; National Institute for Occupational Safety and
Health. Publication No. 77–169 (Dec.)

Chapter 18

Discrimination Against Indians: Issues and Policies*

Harish C. Jain

Minority employment is perhaps the most significant and complex human resource problem faced by policymakers, at least since the early 1960s. Today, it is public policy in all jurisdictions in Canada to eliminate discrimination in the workplace on the basis of race, colour, sex and numerous other grounds. Employment barriers based on homosexuality are increasingly being called into question; at least one province has already outlawed such discrimination. Affirmative-action programs are coming into vogue to increase the employment, training and promotion opportunities of minorities and women.

Discrimination is not confined to any one group, but native people are clearly the most disadvantaged group in our society. In order to gain an appreciation of the labour market problems (e.g., unemployment, low earnings) faced by Native People, it is important to examine their economic and social conditions.

INTRODUCTION

In this paper, we will analyse demographic, cultural, economic, institutional and legal factors that affect the labour market activities of Indians in Canada.

THE POPULATION

Status Indians accounted for approximately 287,000 or 1.2 per cent of Canada's population in 1976;[1] in 1979, there were 300,000 Indians in 573 bands, (*Indian Conditions*, 1980). Ontario has the greatest number of status Indians relative to any other jurisdiction in Canada; the total population of Ontario registered Indians in 1976 was 61,621 or approximately 1 per cent of Ontario's population.[2] Indians represent a higher proportion of the provincial population in western provinces. For example, in Saskatchewan, the proportion of Indians in the provincial population was 5.0 per cent in 1976; in Manitoba it was 4.3 per cent in the same year (*Indian Conditions*, 1980).

At present, both the Ontario and the Canadian Indian population is young and growing[3] rapidly (Ontario Statistics, 1976). For instance, 54 per cent of the registered Indian population in 1976 was under 20 years of age, compared with only 36 per cent for the rest of Canada (*Perspectives Canada*, 1980).

It is these young people who will swell the ranks of young adults in the 1980s, and put great pressure on the employment and housing capacity of many Indian communities. It may result in more Indians being forced to leave

---

*Editors' Note: In this article, the terms "Indians" and "Native Peoples" are used interchangeably, unless it is essential to differentiate between them.

reserves and Native communities in search of opportunities in non-Native communities. The Census data and the data provided by the Department of Indian and Northern Affairs indicate that a growing number of Indians are moving from reserves to urban areas; between 1966 and 1976, for example, the number of registered Indians living off reserves increased by 81 per cent while the on-reserve population grew by only 15 per cent (*Perspectives Canada,* 1980). Some 30 per cent of Indians were living outside reserves in 1979 (*Indian Conditions,* 1980).

EDUCATION

The educational attainment of Canadian Indians is far below that of other Canadians. However, some improvements have taken place. In recent years, both the percentage of all registered Indian students going to school who are enrolled in high school, and the number of these attending university have increased markedly[4] (*Perspectives Canada,* 1980). Despite the rise in enrolment, the retention rates (the number enrolled in grade two that completed grade 12) of Indians compared to non-Indians are low. The Indian retention rate is less than one-quarter of the national rate (*Indian Conditions,* 1980: 49). This suggests that the needs of many Native students are not being met. A report by the OECD suggests that until recently, the majority of Indians on reserves were educated with books and other material that seldom related to their own culture, but rather reflected that of middle class Canadian society. There was lack of appropriate curricula, and inadequate participation by Native People; there are still far too few (about 15 per cent) Native teachers, and schools that are Native controlled. It is only recently (1973) that an increasing number of bands are being allowed by the federal government to assume control of their schools and their educational programs. There are now over one hundred band schools, largely in western provinces (*Indian Conditions,* 1980). Many Indian children seem to have been alienated from their own ways of life, without having been prepared in any significant fashion for a different society; they lack motivation, have poor self images, and a low level of aspiration (Hawthorne, 1967; *Northern Frontier,* 1977; *Perspectives Canada,* 1980).

Similarly, higher education has a short history among Indians. Their proportion in professional and vocational courses and on-the-job training programs is negligible (Jain, December 1977; *Indian Conditions,* 1980).

LABOUR FORCE

The working-age population of status Indians will increase faster in the decade 1975–85 than during any previous decade. The 5 to 14 year olds who will come of working age in 1975–85 will number 83,506, or almost 30 per cent of the status Indian population. In 1975, 150,720, or 53.3 per cent, of the status Indians were of working age. Of the 150,720 in 1975, 107,311 were on reserves including Crown land and the remaining 43,409 off reserve. The labour force participation rate (persons of working age, either working or actively seeking work) of Indians is approximately two-thirds of the national rate, viz. 40 per cent for Indians as opposed to 60 per cent for the national population in 1976 (*Indian Conditions,* 1980: 58).

EMPLOYMENT AND EARNINGS[5]

According to the Canada Employment and Immigration Commission (CE&IC) study referred to earlier (The Development of an Employment Policy. . .), the employment rate of the Indian population and its per worker income vary greatly from community to community, from year to year, and from season to season. In every province and territory, there exists a substantial gap between the place of the Native People in the labour market and that of other ethnic groups. A 1973 survey undertaken by the Department of Indian Affairs and Northern Development (DIAND) established the general unemployment rate of reserves at 48 per cent[6] (The Development of an Employment Policy. . .). Other surveys suggest that Indian labour force participation is about 40 per cent and employment rates about 32 per cent of the working age population, compared to about 60 per cent and 56 per cent for the national population. Based on this information, Indian unemployment would be over 18 per cent compared to 8 per cent of the national labour force (*Indian Conditions,* 1980: 59).

A part of the reason for the abnormally high unemployment rates of Indians may be that an average Indian is employed only part of the year; both in Ontario and Canada, the average duration of employment for the native worker is less than six months (First session, Thirtieth Parliament, 1974–75: issue no. 21). Two explanatory factors are involved:

(a) The work accessible to Indians by dint of education, geographic location and cultural tradition may be seasonal in nature, for example logging and construction.

(b) They may engage in sporadic work patterns in order to be free to participate in their traditional activities, such as fishing and trapping, which are seasonal in nature.

Moreover, it is estimated that 10 to 15 per cent of the Indian working-age population is involved in nonwage "traditional" pursuits (*Indian Conditions,* 1980).

Even for those who do work, the rate of remuneration received is very low.[7] A 1971 DREE survey of the on-reserve work force in Manitoba established that only 4 per cent of the on-reserve work force earned $4,000 or more, compared to almost 50 per cent for the workers of that province as a whole (*The Development of an Employment Policy. . .*). Similarly, information from the 1971 and 1976 Census suggests that average wages and incomes for Indians, even when employed, are still well below national levels (*Indian Conditions,* 1980).

The extensive unemployment among Indians results from a variety of factors which include inadequate technology, isolation from markets, lack of capital and credit, and limited business-related training and experience (*Perspectives Canada,* 1980).

INDUSTRIAL AND OCCUPATIONAL DISTRIBUTION[8]

The majority of Indians in Ontario and Canada are employed in primary economic activity, such as agriculture, fishing, forestry, arts and crafts, and wildlife, and therefore they are over-represented in primary and unskilled occupational categories (compared to non-Indians) and under-represented in skilled, managerial and professional categories (*Perspectives Canada,* 1974; 1971 Census of Canada). They are, however, becoming more involved in white-collar work in the commercial and social service sectors; this work is unsuited to that part of the Indian population located on reserves (*Indian Conditions,* 1980: 61).

SOURCES OF DISCRIMINATION AGAINST OFF-RESERVE INDIANS

As stated earlier, a growing number of Native People are moving off-reserves to urban areas. Studies of migration from reserves indicate that the predominant reason for the movement to urban areas is employment (Nagler, 1970; Stanbury, 1975).

Some of the job barriers that the Indians face include inflated or artificial educational requirements, arbitrary test scores, occupational licensing and other restrictive entry requirements. For instance, employers demand educational requirements, even for entry-level jobs, which are high and often unrelated to actual job performance. Moreover, occupational licensing and other restrictive entry requirements, such as courses in the skilled trades which can only be taken upon completion of grades 11 or 12, depending on the jurisdiction, have an adverse impact on Indians. Thus, a majority receive no training in the trades, such as carpentry and plumbing, since their educational level attained, in most cases, is too low. In these circumstances, if the employer establishes educational and other standards as conditions for employment, he will necessarily exclude from consideration proportionately more minority group members than general population. This exclusion becomes even more pronounced in the face of research evidence that little direct connection exists between education as presently practised and the objective requirements of most jobs, especially entry level jobs (Berg, 1970).

In a recent study for the Department of Manpower and Immigration, Michel Alain (1976) interviewed both counsellors and Native People to evaluate the perceptions of cultural biases found in the testing and counselling services offered to Native People in a number of Canada Employment Centres. The researcher found that, despite the fact that both counsellors and Native People agreed that the tests were inadequate and unreliable, the counsellors continued to use them.

Another example of perhaps unintentionally biased selection procedures is the recent publicity surrounding selection of police officers in Ontario. Police departments require certain height and weight standards of their candidates. A case cited in April 1980, in the *Canadian Human Rights Reporter*, indicates that the Ottawa Police department has required 5' 10'' and 160 lbs., while the Toronto police force has required 5' 8'' and 160 lbs. Numerous reports, including this writer's testimony before the Solicitor General's Task Force on Police Recruitment, Training and Promotion (1980), have indicated that height and weight requirements unduly discourage some Native People, among other minorities, from applying for these jobs, even though they may be qualified to do the job. An "obvious" but unmeasured relationship between selection standards and qualities thought necessary for job performance is not enough to justify the imposition of restrictive standards, such as those pertaining to height and/or weight.

In a pilot study conducted by this author, consisting of interviews with personnel managers of pulp and paper, woodland operations, and mining in Brantford, Thunder Bay and several other rural areas (such as Red Rock, and Nipigon) in Northern Ontario, it is remarkable to note that, without exception, employers were satisfied with the performance (as measured by criteria such as rate of production, absenteeism and alcohol consumption) of the Indians they had hired, but still held on to the stereotypes of Indians as "irresponsible," "unreliable," "lacking in drive," and so on. They were reluctant to hire them for any supervisory or white-collar jobs. In addition, they characterized the Native workers they had hired as lacking in ambition, and did not anticipate promoting them. In our interviews with Indians, we gained the distinct impression that the image of them as hewers of wood and drawers of water is distorted. While the opportunity to work outdoors is important to some, it does not take precedence over employment and income. In fact, in a recent study, it was discovered that the opportunity to work outdoors ranks behind income, proximity to home and job regularity (Jain, 1979).

It is important to determine, first, what "important elements of work behaviour are," by doing a careful job analysis; and second, to demonstrate that selection devices are "predictive or significantly correlated" with the elements of work behaviour that have been identified as important.

RECRUITMENT

Apart from arbitrary selection standards, another problem of entry discrimination relates to recruitment procedures. Certain employers tend to rely on a narrow set of recruitment channels. Some of these are incumbent employees who refer friends and relatives to the firm. Stymeist's (1975) study found that informal exclusion processes prevent Indians from working in northern towns. As he points out, ". . .one hears about jobs and apartments not through the newspapers or notices on bulletin boards, but through friends and acquaintances" (Stymeist, 1975).

Similarly, a 1977 investigation by the Saskatchewan Human Rights Commission revealed that the recruiting methods of the Department of Northern Saskatchewan (DNS) were structured so that "the result produces the same effect as if there were a deliberate and conscious effort to discriminate on racial grounds" (Powers, 1977). The report criticized such DNS employment practices as the method of advertising job openings, absence of on-the-job training, and lack of opportunities for promotion (Jackson, 1979).

POST-EMPLOYMENT DISCRIMINATION

At the post-employment level, that is, after the individual has been hired, discrimination can take several forms. For example, it can occur at (a) the level and wage/salary rate at which an individual is hired, (b) the rate of wage/salary increase once hired, and (c) the pace at which an individual moves up through the organizational hierarchy. The Canadian Civil Liberties Education Trust (1974) reported, for example, that Native People in Northern Ontario tourist camps were found to be receiving about one-quarter of the wage rates of non-Natives for fire fighting (Jackson, 1979). In another instance, Montagnais Indians at the Iron Ore Company of Canada near Sept

314 Work in the Canadian Context

Isles, Quebec, walked out protesting discriminatory promotion policies, and won their case (Jackson, 1979).

A 1977 study on Native People and employment in the public service of Canada found that Native People felt that the public service offers them few job or career opportunities (Impact Research, 1977). The major goal of the newly created Office of Native Employment (ONE) is to increase the number of responsible positions held by Native People in the public service. The major problems facing the ONE have been identified as: (1) the discriminatory attitudes of personnel managers, (2) the need for cabinet support; (3) complex and jargon-dominated job descriptions; and the unchanging nature of public service work (Jackson, 1979).

In order to overcome some of the employment barriers outlined above, all Canadian jurisdictions have human rights/EEO legislation designed to eliminate discrimination in access to employment and careers. The aim is to remove both unintentional and intentional discrimination in the recruitment and staffing policies and practices of employers which have adverse or disproportionate effects on the utilization of certain groups. Such employer policies are typically based on characteristics such as colour, age and sex, which may not be correlated with actual or potential job performance. Presumably, the objective of the anti-discrimination legislation is to promote a more equitable distribution of employment and career opportunities for minority groups who are discriminated against for nonfunctional reasons.[9]

One might ask why positive laws need to be enacted and why all this cannot be done through voluntary efforts. A recent example will help to provide an answer to this question. In this case, Marlene Bloedel complained against the University of Calgary for reverse discrimination. The Board of Governors of the University had a program for nonmatriculated mature students which was directed in large part at people of Indian ancestry. There was a separate admissions process for these people; they received a special support service program, funded federally, by the Department of Indian Affairs and Northern Development (DIAND). Thus, any Indian person admitted to this program received financial support and tutoring support. Marlene Bloedel was not a person of Indian ancestry. She attempted and failed to get into this program and hence lodged her complaint. The Board of Inquiry upheld her complaint on the ground that Alberta's Individual Rights Protection Act, unlike that in some other provinces, contained no provision which allowed special programs, however meritorious they might be and however great the need (Norman, 1980). As Professor Norman points out, "that a perfectly defensible program, where there is an enormous need among Native People based on reserves in that province, is brought to its knees by an adjudication on the footing that the law does not specifically give its blessing to it, is surely a sorry state of affairs" (Norman 1980).

HUMAN RIGHTS LEGISLATION

In the light of this case and numerous others like it, it might be instructive to examine the existing human rights legislation in Canada. As we pointed out earlier, all Canadian jurisdictions have human rights legislation.[10]

The Canadian Human Rights Act, which became effective in March 1978, has borrowed several features from United States legislation and case law and British anti-discrimination legislation (Jain and Sloane, 1978). Two of these are the concepts of indirect discrimination and affirmative-action programs. The third feature pertaining to class-action suits and strategic systemic investigation of industries, firms or institutions, is likely to be incorporated in the not too distant future. Each of these is outlined briefly below:

(1) *The concept of indirect discrimination*: This concept is borrowed from U.S. case law and British anti-discrimination legislation (Sex Discrimination Act and Race Relations Law). In the United States, the concept was articulated by the Supreme Court in the *Griggs v. Duke Power Co.* case in 1971. The Court unanimously endorsed a results-oriented definition of what constitutes employment discrimination. The Court indicated that intent to discriminate does not matter; it is the consequences of an employer's actions that determine whether it may have discriminated under Title VII of the Civil Rights Act. In this case, the Court struck down educational requirements and employment tests on two grounds.

(a) These requirements could not be justified on the grounds of business necessity, since they were not valid or related to job performance.

(b) They had an adverse impact since they screened out a greater proportion of blacks than whites. However, if business necessity could be proved, that is, if the educational and testing requirements that had disproportionate or adverse impact on minorities were in fact related to job performance, then the practice was not prohibited. Thus, disproportionate or adverse impact is not sufficient to outlaw credentialism, tests and other hiring standards. Business necessity is the prime criterion in hiring and promotion decisions.

The U.S. case law has already had some impact in Canada. In 1978, in Ontario, a Board of Inquiry hearing the complaint of *Mr. Ishar Singh v. Security Investigation Services Ltd.* ruled in favour of Mr. Singh. He was refused a job as a security guard because he wore the turban and beard required by his Sikh faith. The Board of Inquiry found that the "employer bore no ill will towards Sikh people . . . had no intention to insult or act with malice . . . and did not have the intention or motive of discrimination." The Board, however, found that the effect of the employer's policy which required that their security guards be clean shaven and wear caps, was to deny employment to Sikhs. It ruled that intention was not necessary to establish a contravention of human rights legislation.

(2) *Class-Action Suits and strategic investigation of industries, firms or institutions*: In the United States, class-action suits can be filed on behalf of a large number of persons, in addition to the individual actually filing the charge. This ability to file a class-action suit has enlarged the scope of both investigation and remedies to cover all persons "similarly situated" who have suffered as a result of the same discriminatory practices. One notable example was the class-action suit filed on behalf of discriminatees by an employee of the Bowman Transportation Co. In this case, the company had discriminated against black workers in hiring, transfer, and discharge. The United States Supreme Court declared that the remedy for in-hire discrimination is the employment of the discriminatees with full seniority, back to the date of their

application for work. This is but one example of a number of cases brought by an individual employee, and decided in favour of the affected class of employees in a particular company or industry.

The concept of strategic investigation in Britain is similar to the "practice or pattern" suits in the U.S. Such suits under Title VII of the U.S. Civil Rights Act can be brought only by the government; this form of action is not available to private parties. The AT&T and the Steel industry cases based on several years of massive investigation by federal agencies in the United States are typical of such suits.

(3) *Affirmative-Action Programs*: One of the important features of the Canadian Human Rights Act is its provision of affirmative-action programs borrowed directly from the pertinent U.S. legislation. Affirmative action is a deliberate, structured approach to improving work opportunities for minority groups and women. This approach involves a series of positive steps undertaken by employers to remove barriers to employment and achieve measurable improvement in recruiting, hiring, training, and promoting qualified workers who have in the past been denied access to certain jobs.

Several provincial laws also allow for special or affirmative-action programs, which promote the interests of minorities and provide training for women, Native People and others, in order to increase the supply of qualified Native People and other minorities. The Canadian Human Rights Commission (CHRC) is authorized to encourage affirmative-action programs, to give out information about them, to promote their use and to "make clear legal rulings as to their legality and determine that they are not discriminatory programs in themselves," according to Ron Basford, formerly Minister of Justice and Attorney General of Canada. In addition, Basford stated, the Commission could give approval to an affirmative-action program in advance and approval would be binding.

Federal and provincial human rights legislation stresses the voluntary aspects of affirmative-action programs. In other words, employers in the public and private sectors are encouraged to set up goals voluntarily in order to recruit, train and promote women and minorities. The federal Act makes a provision for a mandatory affirmative-action program to be ordered by a tribunal only if there is actual proof of discrimination. The Charter of the French Language (Bill 101) enacted in Quebec is the only legislation in Canada that comes close to requiring mandatory affirmative action on the part of employers, via its requirements of francization certificates.

In the provinces, the mandatory affirmative-action programs have been used rarely and only in cases where the employer's discriminatory actions have been blatant. In such cases, affirmative-action programs have been used as only one of the several remedies. This is because the Human Rights Commissions in Canada have concentrated on conciliation and on effecting a satisfactory settlement.

There is some evidence that the voluntary approach to affirmative-action programs is encouraging at least some employers to establish special programs to provide and accelerate training and promotional opportunities for women. These employers include the federal and Ontario governments, and several large business organizations, such as the Royal Bank of Canada, Canadian

National and Bell Canada. The Women's Bureau in Ontario has been providing consultative services to employers.

Despite these voluntary programs, some critics have charged that the majority of Canadian organizations have taken little or no affirmative action for women. In an article entitled, "Affirmative Action: a Sadly Passive Event," for instance, Joy Moore and Frank Laverty have criticized the human rights legislation in Canada for its insufficient clout in stimulating affirmative-action programs. They go on to comment that unless corporations take positive action, "we expect more explicit legislation which will lead to increased sex bias complaints, legal suits, fines, compensatory settlements and forced rather than suggested affirmative-action programs" (*Business Quarterly*, Autumn 1976).

In our opinion, legal remedies are only a partial answer to eliminating institutional discrimination in employment; legislation is necessary but not sufficient. For instance, empirical studies suggest that the employment effects of affirmative-action programs in the United States were positive but quantitatively small, and that the effect in terms of relative occupational position was negligible (Jain and Sloane, 1978). Legal approaches are limited because they operate only on the demand side of the problem (i.e., institutional or employer side) and do little to change supply (namely, the education and training of minorities).

DISCUSSION

Education and training of minorities and women for professional and managerial jobs require lead time. Thus, the lowering of racial and sexual barriers does not in itself ensure a supply of qualified people to take advantage of new opportunities. While employers, unions and other institutions can be compelled to stop discrimination against minorities and women, they cannot be compelled to recruit them actively, or to train them. This is true despite the monumental legal efforts in the United States. The evolution of law and legal principles is a slow process; the case-by-case approach adopted thus far in Canada and the United States (in seniority cases, for example), illustrates this point.

In the case of Indians on reserves, a move such as dismantling the reserve system, which the federal government proposed in 1969, would possibly only transfer the dependency of reserves to urban welfare living. Canadian Natives constitute a distinct social group whose values and patterns of social organization are quite different from those of the rest of Canada. Such solutions as improving education and facilitating occupational and career mobility are based solely on an economic development model, and are clearly inadequate. Both cultural survival and socio-economic development need to be taken into account.

What policy options are, then, available to preserve the Indian way of life and promote socio-economic development, especially on reserves?

(1) Indians on the reserves could be encouraged to gain economic independence by financial assistance in the form of loans and incentives, such as under the Economic Development Fund referred to earlier, to develop reserve-based industries which utilize their traditional skills and resources in

and around the reserves. This could be done by maintaining opportunities for traditional pursuits (hunting, fishing, trapping) and encouraging a shift to analogous activities (campsite supervisors, tourist guides, game and fire wardens) for Native Peoples.[11]

(2) Commuter operations from reserves are feasible. For geographically isolated reserves, landing strips for twin otter aircraft could be constructed to fly the natives to the place of work and back.

Commuting, with rotation schedules, needs to be explored with Northern reserve Indians, in order to provide employment in wood-lands operations (which require living in camps for long periods of time without any family contact), pulp and paper and mining industries. Such a project by Gulf Oil Canada in Coppermine, N.W.T., did not seem to create adverse effects on the family and communal life of the Inuits. What needs to be examined is whether a successful transference of such a project is possible for Northern reserve residents in Ontario and elsewhere in Canada.

POLICY OPTIONS — NATIVES OFF-RESERVE

As pointed out earlier, it seems likely that an increasing proportion of Native People will be coming to our urban centers in search of job opportunities. The single most important reason for the growing movement of Natives to urban areas is to obtain employment. Some of the policy options for their gainful employment are listed below.

It is necessary to have anti-discrimination clauses in all contracts with the various levels of government. In addition, programs of compensatory employment or "positive discrimination," allowing employers in the public and private sectors to provide special training facilities to Native workers and to encourage them to take advantage of opportunities for doing particular work as well as anti-discrimination legislation, are necessary in order to overcome past discrimination and barriers to employment, such as credentialism.

(2) Another approach which complements programs of compensatory employment is the "new careers" approach. This is a manpower development approach which is particularly suitable to Native People. It offers unemployed or underemployed persons of a disadvantaged background an opportunity, through alternative systems of education and on-the-job training as well as work experience, to gain meaningful employment in both public and private sectors. The private sector could be encouraged to undertake programs such as "new careers" for Native People if wage subsidies or tax incentives were made available. In the public sector, job descriptions which emphasize knowledge of Native languages, the need for understanding Native concepts, culture, goals and lifestyles can help create jobs for those departments and operations of the government that serve Native populations.

(3) Training is a major vehicle for upgrading the productivity of disadvantaged workers. Experience with training programs in North America suggests that many minority workers are isolated and alienated from existing social and labour market institutions. They lack motivation to seek employment. This is because the job satisfaction and performance of these workers is influenced by a number of factors in the social system, including the organization providing training or job, community organizations, peer groups

and family circumstances. In order for such a worker to be productive, he must internalize a wide range of middle-class values. His performance is a function of three major types of skills — adaptive, functional and specific. Most Native workers probably lack the adaptive skills which enable an individual to meet demands for conformity (such as punctuality and dress requirements) and the demands for change due to the physical, interpersonal and organizational arrangements and conditions of a job.

(4) Recurrent education and training are capable of providing continuing opportunity for those who are most disadvantaged in the labour market, to have a second and even a third chance to improve their relative position in the occupational and income hierarchy, rather than being dependent on early (youth) education alone.

CONCLUSION

In this paper we have sought to convey that any effective policy-making process must be grounded in an understanding of how social, cultural and economic factors may interact to create a vicious circle. This vicious circle may serve to entrap Native People in the most menial jobs, thereby validating their own and society's perception of them as failures.

NOTES

1. When nonstatus Indians are included, Native People could well represent almost 5 per cent of Canada's population, according to Frideres (1974). A recent study, *The Development of an Employment Policy for Indian, Inuit and Métis People* (undated) by the Canada Employment and Immigration Commission (CE&IC) puts the Native population at 600,000; it includes 300,000 Métis and nonstatus Indians, 282,000 status Indians and 18,000 Inuit (see Page 1 and Table 1 of this study). The figures on Métis and nonstatus Indians were compiled by regional manpower directorates of the Canada Employment and Immigration Commission in consultation with Métis and nonstatus Indian Associations.

2. 51.5 per cent of Ontario Indians lived in Northern Ontario and the remaining 48.5 per cent in Southern Ontario in 1971. Ontario had 50,000 Métis and nonstatus Indians and 800 Inuit people. In terms of the population of status Indians, B.C. was next to Ontario (52,724), followed by Saskatchewan (42,420) and Manitoba (41,187). North West Territories had 11,400 Inuits of a total of 17,877 in Canada, followed by Quebec (4,037) and Newfoundland (1,100).

   Of the 300,000 Métis and nonstatus Indians, Saskatchewan had 64,400, followed by 62,000 in Manitoba, 50,000 in Ontario, 45,000 in Alberta and 40,000 in B.C. (see Table 1, *The Development of an Employment Policy for Indian, Inuit and Métis People*).

3. This trend is expected to continue in the future. The Canadian Indian population is expected to increase by 43 per cent from 1973 to 1985 (*Economic Circumstances of Indians 1974*, December 1975). New entrants into the labour force, the age group 15–29, will be approximately 34 per cent of the Indian population by the mid 1980s, compared to 25 per cent of the national population (*Indian Conditions*, 1980: 10).

4. In the 25 years between 1949–50 and 1974–75, Indian school enrolment

jumped from 330 (in 1949–50) to 3,118 (in 1974–75) in grade 9 and above in Ontario and from 739 to 11,247 for the same years in Canada. In grade XII–XIII, the figures were 28 in 1949–50 and 365 in 1974–75 in Ontario, and 50 and 922 respectively for Canada (Jain, 1979). A recent report indicates that elementary participation by Indians is now virtually the same as national levels, and secondary participation is about 12 per cent below. While university enrolment of Indians has risen from 57 in 1963 to 2,700 in 1979, their participation is less than one-half the national levels (*Indian Conditions,* 1980).

5. In these two areas of employment and earnings, the problem of limited data is acute. There are two reasons for this. One is that most Native communities are isolated and widely dispersed; for instance, 4 out of 10 reserves in Ontario in 1970 were accessible by water only, another 3 by road and rail and the remaining 3 by road (*Economic Circumstances of Indians 1974,* December 1975). Therefore, comprehensive surveys are extremely expensive and time-consuming to conduct. Second, the concept and definition of many indicators which are relevant to the analysis of urban industrial life — such as labour force participation, unemployment rates and family income — are not totally appropriate measures of the lifestyles experienced by a significant part of the native community (*Perspectives Canada,* 1980).

6. The same survey showed the following unemployment rates of Indians on reserves by region: Atlantic 49 per cent, Ontario 39 per cent, Manitoba 44 per cent, Saskatchewan 44 per cent, Alberta 68 per cent and British Columbia 45 per cent (*The Development of an Employment Policy. . .*). A rapid increase in the size of the Indian working-age population is projected over the next ten years; therefore, in the absence of expanded job creation, there will be between 30,000 and 40,000 unemployed Indian workers (*Indian Conditions,* 1980).

7. The average weekly earned income for employed Natives (Métis and nonstatus Indians) was 84 per cent of the mean income of all Canadian industrial wage earners, (*Perspectives Canada,* 1980). Similarly, Stanbury found that 63 per cent of Indian families living off reserves in B.C. in 1970 had incomes below the 1969 Senate poverty line; this was two and a half times the national average (Stanbury, 1975).

8. A survey of Métis and nonstatus Indians conducted jointly in 1976 by the Native Council of Canada and the CE&IC found that the largest occupational categories of Métis and nonstatus Indians were: service occupations, 16 per cent; construction 13 per cent; clerical 10 per cent; forestry and logging 6 per cent; product fabricating 6 per cent and transportation and transport mechanics 5 per cent. These occupations are characterized by declining labour demand and are at the lower end of the pay and prestige scales (*Perspectives Canada,* 1980).

9. Canada has both legal and moral commitments to take special measures to overcome the disadvantages suffered by minority groups and women. Canada is a party signatory to *The International Convention to Eliminate All Forms of Racial Discrimination, 1966.* In addition, in December 1979, the General Assembly of the United Nations in its 34th Session approved, with Canada's vote in support, the *Convention On The Elimination of Discrimination Against Women.* In April 1980, The Throne Speech to the Canadian Parliament talked about affirmative action for disadvantaged groups. One excerpt from that speech stated "Expanding Native opportunities and training women for new occupations will receive strong emphasis. . .".

10. In Canada, employment and industrial relations legislation falls primarily under provincial jurisdiction. Federal legislation covers only 10 per cent of the labour force, while the remaining 90 per cent is covered by the provincial statutes. However, we will discuss the Canadian Human Rights Act for two reasons. First, the provisions of this Act reflect some of the best features of the relevant U.S. and British legislation. Second, federal legislation tends to be emulated by the Provinces. This has already taken place in Saskatchewan. The 1979 Spring session of the Saskatchewan legislature passed a new Human Rights code which was proclaimed in August 1979. The Code has incorporated some of the features of the federal Act and has broken new ground.

11. Another factor which could assist at least some reserves is the recent phenomenon of land claims. The federal government is assisting Native bands in the form of grants, contributions and loans to enable them to research, develop and negotiate land claims. Land claims alone, for instance, involve nearly one-third of Canada's land mass and federal money estimated at more than 3 billion dollars from the mid 1980s to the year 2000. According to a report in the *Canadian Business Magazine* (April 1980), land claims and royalties are creating a new social force: red capitalism. Native People now own everything from airlines to shopping plazas. Those Indians that have valuable oil and mineral resources are becoming Bay-Street wise and putting together the experts (at chartered banks, financial institutions and management consulting firms) resources, leadership, land and dollars, (*Canadian Business Magazine*, April 1980). This experience would assist these Indians and others to gain self confidence, independence, initiative and esteem which are so necessary to break away from dependence on social welfare. It will also provide role models for other Indian communities and aspiring Native businessmen.

REFERENCES

Alain, Michel
1976   *A Study of the Testing and Counselling Services Offered to the Canadian Native Population by Canada Manpower Centres*, Ottawa: Dept. of Manpower and Immigration, February.

Berg, Ivar
1970   *Education and Jobs: The Great Training Robbery*. New York: Praeger.

Canada
1975   *Economic Circumstances of Indians* 1974. Ottawa: Department of Indian Affairs and Northern Development, December.

1975   *First Session (Proceedings) Thirtieth Parliament* 1974–75, Issue No. 21, Ottawa, March 25.

1980   *Indian Conditions: A Survey*. Ottawa: Indian Affairs and Northern Development.

Frideres, J.S.
1974   *Canada's Indians: Contemporary Conflicts*. Scarborough, Ontario: Prentice-Hall.

Hawthorne, H.B. et al.
1966   *A Survey of the Contemporary Indians of Canada*. Ottawa: Indian Affairs Branch, Vol. 1, October.

Indian Life and Canadian Law.
1974   Toronto: Canadian Civil Liberties Education Trust.

Jackson, Ted
1979 "Institutional Discrimination in Employment." A background paper, Atlantic Regional Conference of the Canadian Human Rights Commission, June 22–24.

Jain, H.C.
1977 *Labour Market Problems of Native People in Ontario.* Research and Working Paper No. 139, McMaster University, December.

Jain, H.C. and P.J. Sloane
1978 "Race, Sex and Minority Group Discrimination Legislation in North America and Britain," in *Industrial Relations Journal* Vol. 9 (Summer).

Jain, H.C.
1979 "Employment Problems of the Native People in Ontario," *Relations Industrielles* Vol. 34, No. 2.

Moore, Joy and Frank Laverty
1976 "Affirmative Action: a sadly passive event," in *Business Quarterly* (Autumn).

Nagler, Mark
1970 *Indians in the City.* Ottawa: St. Paul Press.

Native People and Employment in the Public Service of Canada.
1977 Ottawa: Impact Research.

Norman, Ken
1980 An Address to the conference on "Human Rights and the Corporation." Organized by the Public Affairs International, Toronto, April 23.

Northern Frontier, Northern Homeland
1977 The Report of the MacKenzie Valley Pipeline Inquiry, Vol. 1, Ottawa.

O'Malley, Martin
1980 "Red Capitalism: Self Sufficiency for Native Peoples," in *Canadian Business Magazine* (April).

Ontario Statistics
1976 Vol. 1, Toronto, Ontario.

Perspectives Canada II
1974 Ottawa, Information Canada, July.

Perspectives Canada III
1980 "Indians and Métis of Canada," by Colin Lindsay, Ottawa, Statistics Canada.

Powers N.
1977 "Amid Signs of Western Bigotry," in the *Globe and Mail* (September 24).

Reviews of National Policies for Education, Canada
1976 Paris, OECD.

Stanbury, W.T.
1975 *Success and Failure: Indians in Urban Society.* Vancouver: University of British Columbia Press.

Stymeist, D.
1975 *Ethnics and Indians.* Toronto: Peter Martin Associates.

The Development of an Employment Policy for Indian, Inuit and Métis People, Ottawa, Employment and Immigration Canada (Undated).

Chapter 19

Networks, Education and Occupational Success

Grace M. Anderson

The popular press has frequently emphasized the importance of "having an education" in order to obtain and to hold a remunerative occupational position. More recently, now that relatively large numbers of well-educated persons are without employment, the question is being asked, "Just how important is education in the job market today?"[1]

The viewpoint that education is of overriding significance in the world of work ignores the favourable influence which is exerted through contacting others with network connections who may know of job opportunities, or who may "put in a favourable word" to the boss. Networks have been popularly described by Boissevain (1974) as consisting of "friends of friends." Obviously, persons with a large circle of friends and relatives, who also have ever-widening circles of contacts, are in a very favoured position in certain sectors of the job market. Messages may pass through many links in these chains of connections in order to reach target persons (Milgram, 1967; Killworth and Bernard, 1979). This puts certain ethnic groups with many kin connections, who have probably immigrated through sponsorships, at an advantage over other groups who tend to immigrate independently (Hawkins, 1972).

At certain job levels, networks may be the dominant mode of obtaining a position in the work force. Graves (1970) has indicated that these are not a factor where there is the potential for serious and costly errors, as occurs with specific jobs in pipeline laying, since the pipe segments must accurately join. Covey has indicated that in other circumstances, where safety is a factor, for example, in a salvage diving team, it is advantageous to have close friends and relatives working together.[2]

In the unskilled labour market, since "what you know" is not a factor, "who you know" assumes paramount importance in the job search. In many unskilled positions, strength and stamina are necessary prerequisites. Compatibility with workmates assures a smooth-running operation. This may be assured through recommendations (often verbal) by friends and relatives of present employees. In the case of poor job performance, peer group pressure can be applied and this is a powerful incentive to perform well, for friendship may hinge upon not "letting down" the work group.

Turrittin (1979) in a study of West Indian women from Montserrat, who are employed as domestics in Canada, has demonstrated how these coloured women are able to use their network contacts to secure white patrons. They put a high priority on education and, as soon as they are able in Canada, they "upgrade their educational credentials considerably." While these immigrants use the enhanced educational route to success, other immigrants manage to get ahead financially without educational upgrading. The Macedonians in Toronto advance through learning on-the-job skills in the restaurant industry and then opening their own businesses (Herman, 1978). Still others, such as Portuguese immigrants, enter trades in the construction industry, which can be learned on the job. One example of this is the job of cement finisher in subway or sewer tunnel construction. So there are many routes to either upward job mobility or enhanced occupational earnings.

The data in this study have been gathered by the author in a series of studies dating from the late sixties until the present time in the early eighties. In the first study (Anderson, 1974), a random sample of 250 Portuguese male manual workers was selected from both unionized and nonunionized subsamples in Toronto. The unionized workers were chosen from trade union membership lists of one construction union and one building services union. The nonunion sample was obtained through selection of Portuguese surnames from tax assessment lists of census tract 59, the Kensington Market area. The selected respondents were asked whether they belonged to a trade union. Only nonunionized workers were interviewed further in this portion of the sample. Of the original sample, 201 (80.4 per cent) were successfully interviewed. A total of 182 respondents, that is 90.5 per cent, have four years of formal education or less. One-hour interviews were carried out in the homes of the respondents.

Table 19–1

Income and Years of Formal Education*

		1–4 years	5 years and over
Low Income	n	85	7
	%	52.8%	50.0%
High Income	n	76	7
	%	47.2%	50.0%
Total	N	(161)	(14)
	%	100.0%	100.0%
Rate Per	Mean	$2.84	$2.80
Hour	S.D.	1.34	1.29

*x^2 = 0. (1 d.f.), with Yates correction and continuity corrected, not significant.
Source: Anderson, 1971: 14.

Income, as an indicator of economic integration, was measured in terms of rate per hour. Since there is a bimodal distribution of income in the sample, it is logical to use only two income categories: (1) "low income" for the purposes of this study was defined as occupational income of less than $3.00 per hour in 1969; (2) "high income," $3.00 per hour and over. (There was no statistically significant difference between the groups in the amount of unemployment experienced in the preceding 12 months.)

In an analysis of these data, it was found that there is no significant difference in income attainment between those respondents who have had five years or more of formal education and those who have received from one to four years of formal schooling. It should be emphasized that numbers of respondents are small in categories of "other than 1–4 years" of education. Therefore, interpretation of the table should be considered with caution.

Research by Briones and Waisanen (1969: 256, 263) indicates it is possible that an educational level of grade 8 or 10 may be necessary before "economic take-off" can take place.

> The relationship between parental educational achievement and educational aspirations for children could be expressed as an "s" curve, with a significant point of aspirational "take-off" occurring somewhere between the fifth year of elementary and the second year of secondary school. At this point, a kind of rupture with traditional belief systems may occur and a more "modern" or urban outlook, committed to processes of ascent and accompanied by perception of opportunities, may start to take form.
> . . .
> The data in this Santiago case suggest, although by no means conclusively, that this point of attitudinal "take-off" may occur between the fifth year of elementary and the first year of secondary school.

Jencks et al. (1979), in a substantial analysis of five American national surveys of 25- to 64-year-old men, found that

> The best readily observable predictor of a young man's eventual status or earnings is the amount of schooling he has had. This could be an arbitrary rationing device for allocating scarce jobs; or because schooling imparts skills, knowledge or attitudes that employers value; or because schooling alters men's aspirations. Our data do not allow us to choose between these alternate explanations. We did find, however, that the first and last years of high school and college are usually worth more than intervening years. (230)

The one hint of the part which networks play in the process of job allocation was contained in the summary sentence, "In the absence of 'meritocratic' criteria, managers usually give such jobs to their friends" (Jencks, 1979: 309). But this avenue was not explored further.

Jencks' study demonstrates that "the highest grade of school or college he [the interviewee] has completed is the best single predictor of his eventual occupational status" (223), and "the first and last years of both high school and college raise earnings twice as much as the intervening years" (227), and "nonetheless, our data do not suggest that the economic benefits of education depend *primarily* on certification effects. Any year of schooling raises earnings to some extent" (227–28).

These various studies can be viewed as complementary rather than contradictory. They can be taken to apply to different segments of the labour market, each competing from separate or overlapping labour pools. A generalization based on an intuitive knowledge of the job market might include the following labour pools:

(1) The unskilled labour market, educational level up to grade 8 or 9.

(2) The semi-skilled and skilled labour market, grade 8, 9 or 10 up to and including community college and 1 year of university.
(3) White-collar market, junior levels, grade 10 to 4 years of university.
(4) Senior white-collar job market, managerial level, grade 10 to 6 years of university.
(5) Professional job market, 1 to 10 years of university.

The above scheme is speculative in nature and would need to be examined in further research studies.

Anderson (1971, 1974) demonstrates that for unskilled immigrant workers in Canada there may be no advantage in increased years of education, unless the workers have sufficient education (grades 8 to 10) to make the leap into semi-skilled or skilled occupations. This study limited its sample to workers in minimal skill occupations, whereas Briones and Waisanen (1969), and Jencks (1979), had more diverse occupational samples. Their averages could be skewed by the relatively few lower education persons who became entrepreneurs. Anderson and Higgs (1976) document many Portuguese immigrant cases, without quantifying their data. However, looking at the ethnic communities as a whole, the entrepreneurs are usually the exceptional cases, rather than being indicative of a general trend.

Education has traditionally been used to explain the major portion of variance in occupationally-attained economic success (Meyer, 1966: 34–38). However, it is possible that the generalizations about the relationship of education and income may not be equally applicable to the native born and to immigrants from the less industrialized countries. Those immigrants who originate from rural regions with a low level of industrialization, may have encountered severe difficulties in obtaining anything past a rudimentary level of formal education. Frequently, it is only the highly urbanized segment of the population or the relatively "well-to-do" who can keep their children in school beyond the primary school level. In highly industrialized countries, where secondary school education is readily available, the lack of high school training is frequently indicative of lack of motivation or ability on the part of the individual concerned; by contrast, it is probable that many immigrants with little or no formal education from overseas may be more highly motivated than many native-born Canadians and, in general, may form a more intellectually-able category than their native-born North American educational counterparts.

If, on the other hand, the differences between having no formal education and having some is examined, it can be seen that having at least a little education appears to be important to economic success. Literacy should be distinguished, therefore, as a factor contributing to occupational success, even though years of schooling are few. Although the numbers in the "no formal education" are small, the results are in the anticipated direction. The mean income for no formal education is $2.01 (S.D. = 0.75), which is much below the income of the remainder of the sample.

In an analysis of the individual cases, there are several major reasons why persons with more education than the 1–4 years of the majority of the respondents would accept jobs which have a low pay scale: (1) they regard their time spent in this country as temporary and therefore are not "career" oriented, although they may eventually remain here for a lifetime; (2) they are unwilling or unable to accept jobs with strenuous physical requirements; (3) they commenced work in this country in a "stagnant" occupational channel; (4) they wish to work in an occupation in which the spouse can also be employed. It is possible that, for a small minority, the prestige attached to certain institutions is a factor to be taken into consideration, although the data collected in this study do not give any indication one way or the other whether this is actually a significant factor to these immigrants. Further research would be needed in this regard.

Table 19–2

Income and Number of Years of Formal Education

		None	1–4 years	5–7 years	8 years and over
Low Income	n	10	85	5	2
	%	90.9%	52.8%	41.7%	100.0%
High Income	n	1	76	7	0
	%	9.1%	47.2%	58.3%	0.0%
Total	N	(11)	(161)	(12)	(2)
	%	100.0%	100.0%	100.0%	100.0%

*x^2 = 8.538 (3 d.f.), significant at the .05 level.
Source: Anderson, 1971: 17.

Networks may be activated by the job-seeker through asking relatives and friends to be on the lookout for a job vacancy. The initiative need not always come from the job-seeker. In discussing the higher echelons of the occupational hierarchy, Granovetter (1974) has indicated that sometimes business acquaintances approach a potential executive recruit and ask whether he would be interested in moving. On other occasions, the white-collar worker may drop a hint that he would like to move if the right opportunity occurs. The "strength of weak ties," to quote Granovetter, or knowing a large number of acquaintances, is a potent factor in the male white-collar job market.

It has been suggested that women have fewer opportunities for upward mobility because they lack ready access to male-dominated occupational networks (Clement, 1975). However, this may be changing, although at a very gradual pace. The influential role of secretaries in casually passing along information to their bosses has been largely ignored, in spite of much research into other aspects of elite networks (Mills, 1959; Porter, 1965; Clement, 1975; Kelner, 1971).

At the other end of the scale, among Portuguese immigrants with minimal formal education, the role of women in the occupational mobility of their menfolk is another facet of this subject. Studies have shown that young male immigrants frequently write home to female kin, and especially mothers, asking if they know of anyone in the home village who has a son in Vancouver or Toronto and whether they would obtain an address for contacting in regard to lodging or employment (Anderson and Higgs, 1976). Smith (1976) has explored the many roles of immigrant Portuguese women.

Table 19–3

Income and Sources of Assistance in Finding First Job in Canada[a]

Finding First Job		Through Relatives	Friends	Relatives & Friends	Wide Ranging Tactics	Immigration Department	Trade Union	Job Already Promised	Other
Low Income	%	50.0	65.8	72.7	66.7	51.4		47.5	75.0
	N	(50)	(38)	(11)	(9)	(35)	(1)	(40)	(4)
Rate Per Hour	Mean	$2.85	2.52	2.55	2.62	2.97	3.70	2.88	2.35
	S.D.	1.29	1.17	1.24	1.30	1.49	0.	1.41	0.96

[a] $x^2 = 7.144$ (7 d.f.), not significant at 0.1 level.
Source: Anderson, 1974: 102

However, a network may lead to a dead-end or trap job, rather than to a remunerative career. In Anderson (1974), it was demonstrated that initial jobs for immigrants in Canada, on a farm or as part of a railway section-hand gang, could lead to either a progressive channel or a stagnant channel. But if the immigrants first entered janitorial or cleaning jobs or were employed in a kitchen or bakery, they were seldom able to advance significantly in terms of income. This is unlike the Macedonian case in the restaurant industry, where Macedonian immigrants entered an established ethnic network in situations leading to eventual entrepreneurship. But the latter have the advantage of many Macedonian restaurant owners and hence employers who are willing and able to teach them, and also kin who would pool resources to finance them in their own businesses.

To return to the Portuguese case, the major influence exerted by the first job in Canada has a long-term bearing on career development and ultimate achievement. A parallel case is observed among white-collar native-born workers where paramount importance is noted of the first job for subsequent career development in the case of academics (Caplow and McGee, 1961) and among medical students (Hall, 1948). Networks established during training in prestige institutions are also a feature of successful career development in these studies.

Another route to occupational success consists in deliberately entering a highly-remunerative but frequently-uncongenial job in order to accumulate the necessary capital to go into business for oneself. Anderson and Higgs (1976, 1979) have documented the way in which Portuguese immigrants of little formal education entered the construction industry in Kitimat, British Columbia, through ethnic networks. After construction in the area was largely completed, they remained to work in the local smelter until sufficient capital

Table 19-4

Income and Type of Initial Job, Controlled by Means of Finding First Job in Canada

Means of Finding First Job		Through Friends and Relatives[a]		
Type of Initial Job		Trap	Interim	Step
Low	%	91.7	58.3	13.3
Income	N	(24)	(12)	(30)
Rate	Mean	$2.19	$2.77	$3.35
per				
Hour	S.D.	0.65	1.21	0.91
			Through Other Means[b]	
Low	%	0.0	54.3	30.0
Income	N	(1)	(46)	(10)
Rate	Mean	$3.10	$2.87	$3.16
per				
Hour	S.D.	0.	1.31	1.29

[a] $x^2 = 33.133$ (2 d.f.), significant at the 0.000 level.
[b] $x^2 = 2.931$ (2 d.f.), not significant at the 0.10 level.
Source: Anderson, 1974: 98

had been accumulated, then they purchased fruit or vegetable farms in the Okanagan valley and settled there with their families.

Ethnic occupational networks function to establish enclaves in particular regions, towns or cities. Anderson and Higgs (1976: 56-59 and 1979: 70-73) have documented the establishment of these settlements. Influences upon the occupational and residential networks include:
—Initial direction by government or private enterprise
—Streaming by crucial gatekeepers
—Economic pull to new regions or urban areas
—Economic pull to the proximate city from rural areas
—Chance meetings and the establishment of new networks
—Socially-organized pressure to move (e.g., through the church)
—Congruence of employment with former occupation
—Congruence of climatic conditions
—Eastward trend across country for European immigrants [and Westward trend for Asian immigrants]—nearer to the homeland.
Once a nucleus from the ethnic group is established in a new location, the networks usually operate to attract other immigrants from the same ethnic group, often in similar occupational settings and sometimes from the same small town or village. Pineo's study (1964) discovered the settlement of Italians from the village of Racamulto in the North End of Hamilton, and is a case in point.

The importance of the initial settler who "anchors down" a new network by attracting other like ethnic members should not be ignored. This theme of

Figure 19-1

Ethnic Networks as Assets

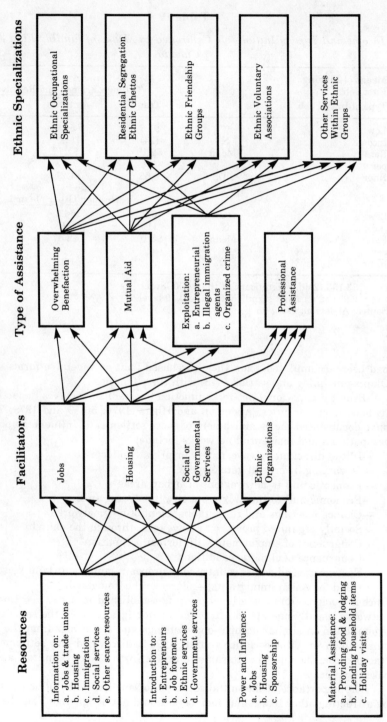

| Resources | Facilitators | Type of Assistance | Ethnic Specializations |

Ethnic Occupational Specializations

Residential Segregation Ethnic Ghettos

Ethnic Friendship Groups

Ethnic Voluntary Associations

Other Services Within Ethnic Groups

Overwhelming Benefaction

Mutual Aid

Exploitation:
a. Entrepreneurial
b. Illegal immigration agents
c. Organized crime

Professional Assistance

Jobs

Housing

Social or Governmental Services

Ethnic Organizations

Information on:
a. Jobs & trade unions
b. Housing
c. Immigration
d. Social services
e. Other scarce resources

Introduction to:
a. Entrepreneurs
b. Job foremen
c. Ethnic services
d. Government services

Power and Influence:
a. Jobs
b. Housing
c. Sponsorship

Material Assistance:
a. Providing food & lodging
b. Lending household items
c. Holiday visits

Source: Anderson and Christie, 1978: 26

spearhead anchorages and the initiation of networks has been further developed by Anderson (in Kovacs, 1978).

Networks function to allow the possibility of job mobility for persons in our society who might not otherwise risk career or geographical changes. They enable the persons to "try out" for different jobs, in situations where they are assured assistance in learning new skills and role requirements in a congenial and supportive atmosphere. The employer can locate new employees rapidly and with minimal expense and trouble, by merely asking his present employees if they know of suitable workers. He is thus assured of a reasonably congenial work group who will exert peer group pressure for adequate job performance. New immigrants experience a cushioning effect by working among kin and friends, so that the adverse effects of culture shock are minimized.

On the other hand, the gaining of employment through networks is not universally beneficial to employees or to their bosses. Integration with members of the host society is usually reduced, and opportunities to learn the host language on the job may be minimal, or the new immigrants may acquire only a highly job-specific vocabulary. There are cases of Spanish-speaking workers in Kitchener who learned German on the job, but still know little English after a period of several years (Anderson and Clarke, 1973).

Several further dysfunctions of occupational networks are apparent. For the employers, when one person moves to another company, several other employees in the same personal network may also move to the new firm (Anderson, 1978: 385).

Networks of communication frequently present a problem to industry, for when one person moves, often a large proportion of the work force also moves. At times they leave suddenly to go to a better paying job in the same industry, and often without waiting for wages due, departing at a moment's notice.

From the viewpoint of the employees, the immigrants may be inadvertently assisted into a trap job by the ethnic network (Anderson, 1974: 71 ff.). Or the immigrants may be exploited, by working for a sweatshop. Certain segments of the garment industry are notorious in this regard. The worst kind of exploitation occurs among illegal immigrants and this has been amply documented elsewhere (Anderson, 1974; Anderson *et al.,* forthcoming; Montero, 1977). The forms of entrapment vary from forcing the illegal immigrants to work for less than the minimum wage during prolonged working hours in unsafe conditions, to violence or demands for sexual favours, threats, or even systematic rape of women by their employers. These immigrants are a captive workforce who feel that they have no recourse to justice because of their illegal status in the country.

As Herman (1978) has suggested, ethnic networks may be either assets or liabilities in the work world. Anderson and Christie (1978) have summarized the various outcomes of utilizing ethnic networks in Figures 19–1 to 19–3.

Figure 19-2

Truncated Ethnic Networks as Liabilities

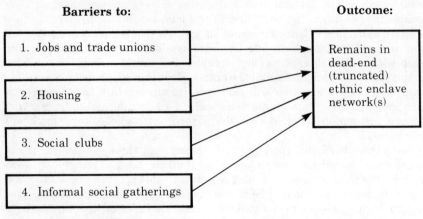

Barriers to: **Outcome:**

1. Jobs and trade unions   Remains in
                                             dead-end
                                             (truncated)
2. Housing   ethnic enclave
                                             network(s)

3. Social clubs

4. Informal social gatherings

Source: Anderson & Christie, 1978: 27

In conclusion, the research studies to date indicate that there is a relationship between education and income from occupational sources, although it is not a straight linear one. This relationship is sometimes depicted as having a "take-off" point, which is variously pegged at initial literacy (although only grade 2 might be attained), and a further take-off at grades 8 to 10 (Anderson, 1971, 1974; Anderson and Higgs, 1976, 1979); at grades 5 to 9, that is, second year of secondary school (Briones and Waisanen, 1969); or a relationship between each year's education and income at all levels, with the first and last years of high school and college being worth nearly twice as much as the intervening years (Jencks et al., 1979). The difference in these results may be derived from differences in the composition of the samples, in terms of other skill levels and of predominantly native-born versus immigrant populations.

Personal networks, or the lack thereof, of the various ethnic and racial groups may provide further explanations of occupational success of one category in comparison to another. Moreover, there are many dysfunctions of occupational networks, and ethnic members may be inadvertently "assisted" into "trap" jobs (Anderson, 1974), or may be aided to occupational mobility (Turritin, 1979; Herman, 1978). In Canada the elitist groups are usually white, Anglo-Saxon Protestant (Porter, 1965; Clement, 1975; Kelner, 1971). Social class and religious backgrounds are thus added to ethnic–racial categories, and all these usually precede education. "Years of schooling" becomes the intervening variable, although it is frequently used as an explanation of higher income attainment and occupational success.

Figure 19–3

Establishing Extra-Ethnic Network Connections

Forming new network ties:

Outcome: Assimilation

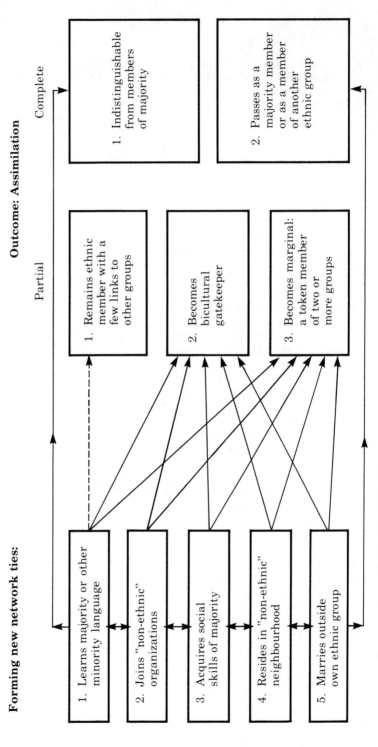

Source: Anderson & Christie, 1978: 27

NOTES

1. An earlier version of the introductory section of this paper was first published in the *Journal of the American Portuguese Cultural Society,* Summer–Fall, 1971.
2. Art Covey, Department of Manpower and Immigration, Windsor, personal communication.

REFERENCES

Books

Anderson, Grace M.
1974 *Networks of Contact: The Portuguese in Toronto.* Waterloo: Wilfrid Laurier University Press.

Anderson, Grace M. and David Higgs
1976 *A Future to Inherit: The Portuguese Communities of Canada.* Toronto: McClelland and Stewart and Ottawa, Multiculturalism Program, Secretary of State, and Supply and Services, Canada.

1979 *L'Heritage du Futur:* Les Communautés Portugaises au Canada, Montréal, Le Circle du Livre de France for Ottawa, Multiculturalism Program, Secretary of State, and Supply and Services, Canada.

Anderson, Grace M. with Juanne Clarke, Sara Keith and Joyce Lorimer
forthcoming *A Fragile Unity: Spanish-speaking Immigrants in Anglophone Canada.* Waterloo: Wilfrid Laurier University Press.

Caplow, Theodore and Reece J. McGee
1961 *The Academic Market Place.* New York: Science Editions.

Clement, Wallace
1975 *The Canadian Corporate Elite: An Analysis of Economic Power.* Toronto: McClelland and Stewart. Carleton Library No. 89.

Hawkins, Freda
1972 *Canada and Immigration: Public Policy and Public Concerns.* Montreal and Kingston: McGill-Queen's University Press.

Herman, Harry Vjekoslav
1978 *Men in White Aprons: A Study of Ethnicity and Occupation.* Toronto: Peter Martin.

Jencks, Christopher et al.
1979 *Who Gets Ahead? The Determinants of Economic Success in America.* New York: Basic Books.

Granovetter, Mark S.
1974 *Getting a Job: A Study of Contacts and Careers.* Cambridge, Mass.: Harvard University Press.

Mills, C. Wright
1959 *The Power Elite.* New York, Oxford University Press. (1967 edition, New York: Galaxy).

Montero, Gloria
1977 *The Immigrants.* Toronto: James Lorimer.

Porter, John
1965   *The Vertical Mosaic: An Analysis of Social Class and Power in Canada.*
Toronto: University of Toronto Press.

Periodicals

Anderson, Grace M.
1971   "The Educational Ladder and Success," in *American Portuguese
Cultural Society Journal* (Fall): 13–18 and 50.

Anderson, Grace M. and T. Laird Christie
1978   "Ethnic Networks: North American Perspectives," in *Connections:
Bulletin of the International Network for Social Network Analysis* Vol.,
II No. 1: 25–34.

Graves, Bennie
1970   "Particularism, Exchange and Organizational Efficiency: A Case Study
of a Construction Industry," *Social Forces* Vol. 49 No. 1: 72–81.

Hall, Oswald
1948   "The Stages of a Medical Career," in *American Journal of Sociology* Vol.
53 No. 5: 327–36.

Killworth, Peter D. and H. Russell Bernard
1979   "A Pseudomodel of the Small World Problem," in *Social Forces* Vol. 58
No. 2: 477–505.

Milgram, S.
1967   "The Small World Problem," in *Psychology Today* Vol. 1: 61–7.

Smith, M. Estelle
1976   "Networks and Migration Resettlement: Cherchez la Femme," in
Anthropological Quarterly Vol. 48 No. 1: 20–27.

Collections

Anderson, Grace M.
1978   "Spearhead Anchorages and Initiation of Networks, with Special
Reference to the Portuguese Case" in Martin L. Kovacs (ed.) *Ethnic
Canadians: Culture and Education.* Regina: Canadian Plains Studies, 8:
381–87.

Briones, Guillermo and F.B. Waisanen
1969   "Educational Aspirations, Modernization and Urban Integration," in
Paul Meadows and Ephraim H. Miztuchi (eds.) *Urbanism, Urbanization
and Change: Comparative Perspectives.* Reading, Mass.: Addison-
Wesley, 252 –64.

Kelner, Merrijoy
1971   "Ethnic Penetration into Toronto's Elite Structure," in Craig L.
Boydell, Carl F. Gridstaff, Paul C. Whitehead (eds.) *Critical Issues in
Canadian Society.* Toronto and Montreal: Holt, Rinehart and Winston,
329–37.

Meyer, Kurt
1966   "Class and Education" in *Class and Society.* Revised edition. New York:
Random House, 34–38.

Pineo, Peter C.
1964   "The Extended Family in a Working-Class Area of Hamilton," in
Bernard R. Blishen et al. (eds) *Canadian Society: Sociological Perspectives.* Revised edition Toronto: MacMillan, 135–45.

Turrittin, Jane Sayer
1979 "'We Don't Look for Prejudice': Migrant Mobility Culture among Lower Status West Indian Women from Montserrat," in Jean Elliott Leonard (ed.) *Two Nations, Many Cultures: Ethnic Groups in Canada.* Scarborough, Ont.: Prentice-Hall, 311–24.

Unpublished

Anderson, Grace M. and Juanne Clarke
1973 "Double-hyphenated Canadians: Spanish-speaking Immigrants of German Background in Kitchener. Waterloo Urban Area of Ontario." Waterloo: Waterloo Lutheran University (now Wilfrid Laurier University) paper presented to Canadian Sociology and Anthropology Association, Kingston. (Partially incorporated in Anderson et al. forthcoming book).

Chapter 20

Her View from the Executive Suite: Canadian Women in Management*

G.L. Symons

INTRODUCTION

It is a well-documented fact that the Canadian labour force is segregated by sex, with men predominating in the occupations carrying authority, high wages, job security, opportunities for career advancement and prestige. Women cluster in low-prestige, low-paying, dead-end jobs, which tend to be repetitious and routine (Armstrong and Armstrong, 1978). In this study, women have been chosen who have managed to avoid occupational segregation, and to develop a career line in essentially masculine occupations.

The purpose of this paper is to examine how occupational segregation was avoided, to analyse the ways in which women cope with operating in an essentially masculine environment, and to study the implications for equality of opportunity of the presence of women in managerial positions.

Three models which have been used to explain the position of women in the work world will be drawn upon. Issues raised by these models include early socialization experiences, the effects of marital and parental statuses on women in the work force, and social structural variables peculiar to the organizational environment which affect the position of women.

THREE EXPLANATORY MODELS

Kanter (1976) outlines three models which have been used to explain the position of women in the occupational world. They are based on different assumptions, and focus the research perspective in different directions. She calls these models the "temperamental," the "role related," and the "social structural." The temperamental model focuses on the individual's character and personality traits, and makes generalizations about sex differences. Kanter (1976: 283) overstates the assumptions of this model as follows:

Women differ from men in their character, temperament, attitudes,

*A paper presented at the Canadian Sociology and Anthropology Association Meetings, Saskatoon, June, 1979.

My sincere appreciation is extended to the women who participated in this study. I would like to thank Dr. L. Riznek who contributed to the conceptualization of the study, and conducted the interviews with the Toronto sample. The work of G. Hall, J. Hillmo, L. Meadows, B. Pengelly, and J. Tregaskis is also gratefully acknowledged.

This research was funded by an operating grant from the University of Calgary.

self-esteem, language, gestures, and interpersonal orientations, whether by nature, early socialization or accumulated learning as a result of coping with an inferior position.

This model lends itself to the danger of sex stereotyping, whether positive or negative, with respect to women and men. Consider, for example, the stereotype of women as expressive, nurturing and supportive. One could argue, given the essentially "masculine" nature of the business world, with its values of instrumentality, rationality and application of universalistic criteria in the bureaucratic setting, that women are therefore unsuited to work and succeed in this environment. (Here, of course, the argument is limited to the management sector, since women have been extensively employed in clerical and service roles in business.) One could then turn this argument around and suggest that it is precisely these characteristics of women that are important for business. It is time we countered the bureaucratic features of the work world and created a more "humane" and "sane" environment. Enter women. Their nurturing and expressive qualities will be a positive factor in management. Both these lines of reasoning make assumptions about women's characteristics which can lead to stereotyping.

The second model is "role related" and focuses on the sexual division of labour in both the family and the work world. Studies of this nature analyse cases of role strain and conflict for women (Mackie, 1976), and explain occupational segregation in terms of difficulties for women in coping with the dual roles of wife/mother and worker. As Kanter notes, the problem with this model is that more attention is given to the family, and less to the workplace, than is warranted.

The third model, which Kanter feels is the most fruitful for analysis of the position of women at work is "social structural." This model examines the structural nature of the work setting, considering variables such as opportunity structures, internal labour markets, dominance structures, and sex ratios. Kanter (1976: 287) explains:

> These [variables] determine or highly influence the likelihood that women on the job will have high motivation, will be able to demonstrate competence and confidence, will be seen as promotable, will be productive, and will be effective in leadership roles.

Kanter notes the relationship between the three models, in that social structural variables also impact on individual attitudes and family roles. In this analysis, questions raised by these three models will be examined with respect to the position of women in management in Canadian business.

METHODOLOGY

Subjects were located through snowball sampling, contacted by letter or telephone during the months of August 1978 until February 1979, and asked to participate in the study. Interviews lasting from one to three hours were conducted with the respondents. All but one (at the request of the respondent) of the interviews were taped, and then transcribed. These interviews provide the data base for the present analysis.

THE SAMPLE

The sample consists of 20 women (5 in Toronto and 15 in Calgary); six senior managers, six entrepreneurs (women who own and manage their own companies), five supervisors and three professionals. The industries in which these women are employed are the following: advertising, consulting, finance, manufacturing, oil and gas, real estate, retail and ranching.

The subjects range in age from 26 to 62, with a mean age of 38 years. Four have high school education or less, one has some university training, ten have bachelor's degrees, three have master's degrees, and two have technical diplomas.

Table 20-1 presents some background characteristics of the sample, and compares them with those of a larger sample of women managers in Canada (van der Merwe, 1978). The first column presents data from van der Merwe's study. She chose a sample of 100 women managers (above supervisory level) across Canada. The second column presents data from the total sample of this study. The third column presents data on women managers and entrepreneurs only, to more closely approximate van der Merwe's sample. The ages of the women in the total sample are similar to those of van der Merwe's study, with most women falling into the 30–40 year old age group. Marital and parental statuses of the women in the samples are also similar, with less than half of the women being married, and the majority (64 per cent and 65 per cent respectively) being without children. The women in this sample are more highly educated than van der Merwe's group, with 75 per cent of the former group and 50 per cent of the latter group having university degrees or technical diplomas. When one excludes the supervisors and professionals from the sample, the educational levels more closely approximate those of van der Merwe's sample.

The mean number of years of work experience is 14, and the respondents have been at their present jobs for an average of four years. Thirty-five per cent of the women have been at their present jobs for five years or more. Half of the sample has been at their present jobs for one to four years, and the remaining 15 per cent have worked in their present positions for less than one year. This distribution differs from van der Merwe's study, where only 8 per cent of her sample had been in their present positions for five years or more, 49 per cent for one to four years, and 43 per cent for less than one year. When one separates out the managers and entrepreneurs from the present sample, the differences become more pronounced between the two samples. One-half of the sample of managers and entrepreneurs have been at their present jobs for five years or more, one-third from one to four years, and 17 per cent have been in their present jobs for less than one year.

CAREER HISTORIES

The career histories of the women in the sample are both interesting and informative. Four of the women who now hold senior managerial positions began their careers in traditional female occupations—as secretaries or support staff. They worked their way up through the company, or its subsidiaries, and only recently (in the last 6 years or less) have reached the

Table 20–1

Some Demographic Characteristics of Women in Management in Two Canadian Samples

Demographic Characteristics	van der Merwe's Sample (%)	(%) Total	Symons's Sample (%) Managers/ Entrepreneurs
	N=100	N=20	N=12
Age			
Under 30	18	15	8
30–40	38	50	33
41–50	22	30	50
Over 50	22	5	8
Marital Status			
Married	38	40	50
Single	34	40	33
Divorced	20	20	16
Widowed	8	0	0
Parental Status			
Have children	36	35	42
No children	64	65	58
Education			
Degree or diploma	50	75	58
Some university	13	5	8
High school or less	37	20	33

managerial level. These women developed a commitment to the organization in which they worked, knew the business and the employees well and developed systems of trust within the organization. They also had the sponsorship of senior members of the firm who recognized their talents after their many years in the company, and promoted them to senior positions. They attribute their success to their willingness to take on all types of jobs within the organization, to work hard and long hours, and to accept new demands as a challenge. One woman explains,

> I've always counselled people who have worked for me never to be reluctant to do anything in any office, no matter how menial it seemed at the time. Because, I said, the more you know the more it will help you as you move along. Never be reluctant to learn anything, anything at all. If they want to train you in another job, grab it, even if it's on a part-time basis. Don't ever think that you don't want to do it, because somewhere along the line it will help. You never know when it might be important to know, and don't ever turn down an opportunity to learn.

Another woman notes her experience, and the advice given her by a sponsor. When she first joined the company, she inquired into the opportunities for advancement for women. The man who became her mentor responded,

There isn't any, but, I'll tell you what, there will be, I'm sure. So, if you want to assist me in every possible way—it will mean working late, it may mean coming in early, it will mean extra duties. I will give you as much training as I possibly can.

Taking his advice, and following his direction, she learned all the routines of the business. She had no title, and "hopped from desk to desk for a period of about 2 and ½ years." Two managers attained their present positions by virtue of their educational and professional expertise, as well as by sponsorship in the company. One woman, who appears to be an exceptional case, being very young to have such a senior position, has outstanding credentials, and strong sponsorship.

Four of the entrepreneurs started their own companies with the moral and financial support of their husbands, and set themselves up as presidents, thus managing to avoid occupational segregation. One of the women entrepreneurs is independently wealthy, and used her capital to start her business. One of the entrepreneurs began her career in a traditionally female occupation of teaching, switched into personnel work, and has just recently rechannelled her skills to develop her own counselling firm.

Of the five supervisors and three professionals, all are professionally trained. These skills, as well as assertive job searches, assisted them in obtaining their present positions. Two women note that when they applied for the job, typing skills were required. One accepted the position, and managed to avoid taking the typing course. Six months later when asked about the typing, she noted that she had a degree, that it was unfair of them to request that she take a typing course, and that she would have to leave. The typing issue was dropped. Another woman was told that no work was available, but she requested an interview nonetheless. Within a few weeks the company had hired her. Another woman, after taking tests required for a certain position, was turned down. Not satisfied with the response, she went in to see the manager and requested an explanation, asking if the fact that she was a woman had anything to do with it. The manager was impressed with her determination and gave her the job. In about three months she was leading the country in terms of production. There is no doubt that individual qualities of assertiveness can play an important role in career development.

All of these women have a strong career orientation, and see their work as an integral part of their self-concept. One woman, who had recently been off work due to an operation states,

> Work is an important part of my life. I probably didn't realize how important, until I was away for 3 weeks. It was very difficult—I got so frustrated; I felt inadequate; I couldn't do anything. Then I realized, I never could quit work. I realized why I work—I need people. I need people around me, and work is important to me for my own personal self. The end result is that I'm content and I'm hopefully going to make other people content and happy.

Another woman notes the importance of a challenge in her work, and describes her career in the following fashion:

Work is very important to my self-definition. I don't see my career basically as being separated from me as a human being. They are pretty intertwined. If I can do a good job and present myself professionally in a good, healthy way, then that means a lot to my self-esteem—a tremendous amount. I recognized that as soon as I changed jobs. My self-esteem went up about 75% the minute I left the old job I was in. I left a place that was cushy, comfortable and conforming, and went into a gamble, into an industry that I know nothing about, into a subject area I have never even looked at, but taking a tool with me to achieve an end, and finding out that I could do it. I took a gamble and I think I am winning.

SOCIALIZATION EXPERIENCES

The temperamental model focuses, among other things, on socialization experiences, and explains differences between men and women in terms of gender role socialization. Women are brought up to be person-oriented, to lack career orientation, and to be channelled into traditionally feminine areas of study, if they receive higher education. Feminine qualities of submissiveness and nurturance are taught. Boys, on the other hand, are taught mastery of their environment from an early age, emotional expression is curtailed, and they develop a career orientation, with which to fulfill their traditional adult role of provider for wife and children. If women manage to succeed in non-traditional occupations, proponents of the temperamental theory will examine, among other things, socialization patterns among this group, to see if aspects of their development affected their present work orientation.

Only three women state that their childhood socialization experiences did not have any influence on their career orientation. All of the others suggest aspects of this training period which may have been influential. Four of the women come from wealthy families, where their fathers owned their own companies. These women note the effect of living in a home where business was a main topic of conversation. They learned business values and were made aware of at least some aspects of the business world. As one woman recalls,

I came from a family that took for granted that women could assume the responsibility that gave them equality with men.

Three of the five entrepreneurs who reside in Calgary came from pioneer backgrounds, and suggest that the pioneer spirit might have influenced them in starting their own businesses. One woman, whose family came to Western Canada in a cart in 1905, says,

As pioneers of this area, there were things that had to be done, and my parents went out and did them. This sort of gave me the idea of being master of my own destiny. If it's cold you go out and get something to keep you warm; you build a shelter. Nobody was there to supply it.

Three women came from poor families, where "there were no handouts." These women note that they learned early to fend for themselves, and were imbued with the Protestant work ethic early in life. Most women spoke of specific parental influence, either from fathers, mothers, or both parents, who encouraged them to continue with their education, and to develop a career orientation. One woman describes the female influence in the following manner. Her mother, grandmother and great aunt were university-educated, and her mother had her own business for some 20 years.

> I guess all the roles that women have played in my close immediate family have been very liberated ones, and very ahead of their time. . . . I think that in some ways my mother created a very unrealistic world for me, but one that has made me quite capable of coping at the place that I want to be, because I don't ever remember her saying it was wrong for women to work, and that it was something that shouldn't be done, or that it was wrong to get divorced, and something that shouldn't be done, or anything like that. And she pretty much protected me from anyone who said otherwise.

Others note the influence of being brought up with brothers, playing sports, and escaping some of the traditional aspects of female socialization. One woman, the eldest of six children, notes:

> My mother was a hard-working, ambitious woman. There wasn't the man–woman thing in the house. Women could always take care of themselves.

Hence, using the temperamental model, the nontraditional socialization experiences of these women managers can be seen to contribute to at least part of the explanation for the development of a career orientation.

MARITAL AND PARENTAL STATUSES

The role related model of women's participation in the labour force addresses the question of women's dual roles of wife/mother and worker. In spite of the principles laid out in the Royal Commission on the Status of Women (1970), women in Canada still take the major responsibility for home and child care. If the married woman decides to pursue a career outside the home, she in fact takes on two jobs. Meissner et al. (1975), for example, found that women still do the majority of the household labour, and this does not change when they go out to work.

Eleven of the women do not face this problem of dual role commitments, since they are single, separated, or divorced. As noted earlier, Canadian women managers tend to be more often single than not. However, one should not be quick to conclude that because role conflict is alleviated, the single life is without drawbacks. One single woman notes,

> Being single gives great leisure. I never had to consider what somebody else might like to do. I could be directed in one area in terms of the time it took, or the mental concentration, or the energy. On the other hand, I am also the first to maintain that it's exceedingly lonely, because you have to stand by all your own decisions, and you have to stand by the fact that there is nobody really concerned whether you succeed, or whether you don't. You do it entirely for yourself. There's no back-up.

Eight of the remaining nine women are married, and one is co-habiting. Five have children, and one was pregnant at the time of the interview. Of the women with children, one has a pre-schooler. The mothers coped (or are presently coping) with child rearing by not working outside the home, or by working part-time when the children were (or are) young, and combining this with some form of baby-sitting. This technique for managing the dual role is not easy. One woman notes the difficulty of this arrangement, and the problems she had staying at home when her child was young.

> The emotional factor was difficult. There I was in suburbia, and I was the one that went out to work. And not only did I go to work but I couldn't get my sheets straight on the line. . . . The lady next door was a fabulous cook and she always had cookies and squares, and cakes. I remember one night when we had company, I ran in and borrowed a dish of cookies, and shamed myself.
> I had this kid who had the colic and every other thing, and he was almost a year old before I did anything. . . . Sometime during this time I felt I had lost all my skills, I couldn't do anything anymore. I said, "I can't cope with this house, I can't hang the sheets straight, I can't make the cookies," so I went out and applied for a job.

The woman with the pre-schooler notes that the main disadvantage for women in the work force is that they do not have wives. She has many time constraints, and even though her husband helps out at home, she has only about one hour leisure time a day. However, other women note, reflecting back on the early years of child-rearing, that they feel their outside employment had a positive effect on the children, in terms of giving the children time and space to develop, without being overly supervised. One woman recalls those years:

> When he went to kindergarten, the school bus dropped him off at the office. When he went to school I worked full-time and came home at noon hours. We both [husband and respondent] came home many times and all had lunch together. He was a latch key kid from 4:00 to 6:00. When we got home he would say, "You know, it was a lovely time." He would come in and unlock the door, turn on the TV and lie on the floor. The cat would get up on his chest and they would just have a lovely time watching TV. And he said, in later years, how glad he is that we had it that way, and what a nice life it was.

Another woman notes the positive effects of her employment on child-rearing.

> I think that the fact that I have gone to work, and I have done these things, has been particularly good for my boys, because there is no way that you can come home and wait for someone to cook dinner. In this house you darn well cook it or you don't eat, and it is quite acceptable. They keep their rooms tidy and it makes it much easier.

In coping with her teenage children, this woman notes:

> Now it is much simpler because as the children become teenagers, they resent you asking them a lot of questions. So, you sort of give up and don't do it, because you can learn to say, "I'm going out too."

All of the married women state that their spouses help with the labour in the home. They do not appear to have a strict division of labour, but chores are shared equally, and some of the husbands help with the child-rearing. These women appear to be able to compartmentalize their dual role. One respondent summed it up as follows, "The first thing to do that is a paramount rule for any woman going to work is to forget about the ironing."

THE WORK SETTING

The social structural model focuses on the organizational environment, and attempts to understand the position of women in the labour force in terms of structural variables. This paper will examine three structural variables which affect women in management positions, namely the sponsorship system, sex ratios, and the effect of the presence of women in management positions for greater equality.

SPONSORSHIP

The opportunity structure in the work world is very much influenced by the operation of the sponsorship system. The importance of this system has been noted in the literature (Hennig and Jardim, 1977; Thompson, 1978; Williams, 1977). The sponsorship system acts in such a way that a powerful person in the organization supports and encourages a protégé, gives him/her career advice, and demonstrates the operation of office politics. Kanter (1975: 63) notes the importance of sponsorship for women.

> A high-status man bringing the woman up behind him may provide the visible sign that the woman does have influence upward. While sponsors serve multiple functions (e.g., coaching and socialization in the informal routines) and are found in the careers of men, the "reflected power" they provide may be even more pivotal for women.

For the most part, the respondents were well aware of this system, and noted its importance for career advancement. One woman defines a sponsor as someone who "has some investment in seeing that you do well." A reciprocal relationship is developed between sponsor and protégé. Another respondent noted the significance of sponsorship in large corporations.

> Sponsorship is vital, absolutely vital. In a large corporation, if you're not sponsored, you're not going to make it.

Only three of the respondents claimed that they were without sponsorship, and two of these were at the professional level. The large majority received encouragement and support from present superiors, whether senior partners, vice-presidents or presidents of the company. Others report sponsorship from former superiors. Two of the entrepreneurs note the help and support, as well as the business advice they received from their husbands. One woman explains the relationship she had with a former superior who acted as her sponsor. She relates a comment he made to her:

> I will interview 300 people probably to fill jobs—I will interview 300 in a year. Maybe 50 of them I will hire, or want to hire, or will feel that they

are competent to hire. Five of those will be put in management. I would get perhaps one I would consider an executive of these guys—and you are the one.

The importance the sponsorship system can have for developing self-confidence is evident from this comment.

SEX RATIOS

As Kanter (1977) points out, sex ratios in the organization may have important implications for those who find themselves in a statistical minority. Being the lone (or token) woman in a group can affect how the female manager operates. In this case there is more opportunity for sex to become salient in interpersonal interaction for the woman than for the man. By "salient status" is meant that status which

> is focused upon—made salient—in the interaction under analysis. The salient status may be the one that is most germane to the interaction but it may be one that is inappropriate to the situation (Epstein, 1971: 68).

A status may become salient in interaction if it is culturally defined as inappropriate when held in conjunction with certain other statuses, for example, an occupational status. As Epstein (1971: 53) notes,

> those persons whose status-sets do not conform to the expected and preferred configuration cause discordant impressions on members of the occupational network and the society at large.

Hence, women in masculine occupations may find that their sex status becomes salient in interaction when it is inappropriate to consider in a particular situation. Hughes (1971) refers to this phenomenon as "status contradictions," which arise when the master-status trait is present (i.e., professional certification, or managerial status), but the auxiliary-status traits (i.e., male sex) are not. For example, many women tell of experiences of being mistaken for a secretary. One woman entrepreneur, the president of her company, reports an experience she had with a client, during a telephone conversation. She was speaking with the general manager and began to explain the problem. His response was something to the effect of "Listen dearie, you just have somebody call me about that."

Coping mechanisms must be developed to deal with status contradictions. Some of the women have dealt with this issue with subordinates by addressing the question directly at the time of hiring. One woman entrepreneur explains:

> One thing you always have to ask your men is whether it was going to worry them that they were taking a woman's paycheck. It was always a thing you settled right at the time you hired them. If it was going to worry them let's get it out and know it right then and there. I never had any of them say that it was a problem because I bet that very, very carefully. But by the same token I sign all cheques with my initials, because a woman is not supposed to be in this business.

Another technique used by the women in the sample is to work harder to get ahead. While recognizing that both men and women must demonstrate competence, the women agree (with two exceptions), that women must work harder to prove their worth. It is never taken for granted. Similar results were found by van der Merwe (1978: 50) in her profile of Canadian women managers. One woman, in finance, recalls being specifically told that she was expected to perform in a fashion superior to her male peers. She notes:

> I don't know about other industries, but in this industry, I'll tell you, you have to do better than the men. I don't care what they do, if you're not better than them, it's not good enough. I know because I was told, "Well, I'll rely on you, but you had better prove yourself, and you have to show that you can do better than the guys. You can be good, but good is not good enough for you, you have to do better." So, I have to always over-quota the men, you know, to do more than they do.

Another woman notes the importance of this coping strategy for women who are in the minority. She says:

> I firmly and honestly believe that I am better than a lot of people here. I believe still that women have to be exceptional to get ahead, which is unfortunate. I don't think the chances for the average woman are as good as they are for the average man. . . . I look at the women around here, they're all just exceptional women, exceptional! I think you could take any one of the women in this firm, pit them against a guy at an equal level and more likely than not the woman would do the better job. The women are exceptional and some of the men here are average. There are no average women here.

The impact of the skewed sex ratio means that women may be treated differently than their male colleagues, and they therefore work harder. As one woman colourfully put it:

> It has taken me seven years to get to the point where I'm not treated differently. I had to work harder, I had to dig in more—everything I did had to be better. There's just no question about it, it did. However, this doesn't still apply, because I think that I have proven that I will do a good job in spite of this terrible pox that I have on my head or between my legs.

Another significant impact of being a lone woman is visibility. Many women in the sample note both the positive and negative effects of this phenomenon, as does Kanter (1977). Because there are so few women, they tend to stand out, and their progress is more visible. This means that they have the opportunity of greater recognition than men might have. On the other hand, visibility can work against them, since their mistakes also get wide publication.

One way of coping with this issue is to avoid any association with other women or with women's groups, which may tend to increase visibility. This tactic has the latent function of isolating women even further, and restricting access to possible support groups. Three women expressed the view that an association with women's groups may not be politically wise for them in terms of their careers. As one woman explains:

The game is not for women to get together to promote themselves. The game is to be part of your little clique wherever you work.

Another woman did not want to be affiliated with the women's movement and declined to participate in an association of women professionals. Some of the respondents' attitudes towards the women's movement are highly critical. While some 40 per cent of the group feel that the movement is a positive influence for women in business, helping to clarify women's issues, and redefining some of the negative stereotypes, others were less positive. These women support equal opportunities and equal pay for women, but prefaced their remarks with the phrase "I'm not a women's libber." They feel that the women's movement is too radical, and that it does more harm than good. The feeling is that women should stop bitching, and focusing on the issues, and get on with their jobs. One woman is particularly adamant about this. She states:

I'm ashamed when I read literature written by the movement. If they spent their energies and time doing their job well so they would be recognized for it they would receive more recognition and more promotions than they ever will by campaigning. And I don't believe in liberation, I believe in equality.

Expressing the views of many of the respondents, this woman feels that militancy and defensive attitudes are inappropriate.

Other women, two in particular, while recognizing the dangers of association with women's groups, continue to openly express their views. One woman is vocal and active in the movement. She will post notices of women's events, although she believes it is seen as inappropriate. She states:

They call me a women's libber as though they were calling me a leper. You know, it's the same connotation to them—and to a lot of women here too.

One of the managers notes that a possible problem for her career advancement would be her feminist views. She says:

Men are very leary of women who are very strongly advocating women's rights, and I do. If there is any detriment I would have in my advancement it would probably be that it's humorously said that I carry a flag for women. And so that remains to be seen. I see that as the one possible detriment, but it certainly is not enough to stop me.

All of the women realize that in a conservative environment like the business world, militant tactics are usually counterproductive, and can act to isolate women even more. They note it is necessary to present rational arguments, and be capable of seeing the other's point of view. Some women expressed the opinion that there is no use in raising women's issues, or defining problems in terms of sex. They feel that this is received as self-serving—crying in one's milk—and is used only as an excuse. One manager states:

There is no sense in making any point of one's being the only female. They [male managers] don't see discrimination, they won't recognize discrimination, and they regard it as seeking special favours, I suspect.

However, the respondents are in agreement that women should not try to hide their femininity or attempt to become masculine. They feel that their femininity is a positive thing, and can be used in a constructive fashion. Says one woman supervisor:

> We were born women and we should bloody well not be putting ourselves down for it. And we shouldn't be trying to change it. We shouldn't be trying to become like men, although we can learn from them. I think that we can use our femininity in a very practical sense.

The women do not feel it is necessary to somehow suppress their femininity in order to succeed, but recognize that traditional tactics attributed to women such as manipulation and feigned helplessness are counterproductive.

EFFECTS OF THE PRESENCE OF WOMEN—GREATER EQUALITY?

In her paper entitled "Sex Equality and Public Participation of Women in Canada. Some Survey Results," Eichler (1978) raises the issue of the "double edged nature" of the participation of women in decision-making positions. That is, women power holders may be seen both as a result of equalization of opportunity, as well as a precondition for greater equality. Eichler questioned 150 female and 150 male decision-makers in top positions in Canada in political, economic, trade union, cultural, educational and religious institutions, and 150 feminist activists. Among the issues raised were awareness of sex inequalities, and commitment to the notion of sex equality. As she notes, Eichler is tapping only attitudes, and respondents need not manifest any behavioural correlates of either a commitment to, or lack of concern for, sex equality. The results of her study show that feminist activists are most aware of sex inequality, and most committed to the notion of sex equality. Moreover, female decision-makers score higher on these issues than do their male counterparts. Eichler concludes that increased participation of women in decision-making positions is a necessary prerequisite to sex equality. She states:

> Since male decision-makers are less aware and care less than do female decision-makers, we cannot expect as much progress as we could if we had more women in decision-making positions (Eichler, 1978: 30, 31).

This study attempts to address these issues, not only in attitudinal terms, but also by examining actual behaviour of female decision-makers.

Most of the women in the sample (18 out of 20) are aware of sex inequality in the business world, whether in their present company or in others where they have worked. They state that they themselves have experienced it in terms of pay differentials, blocked mobility, or attitudes towards women on the job. One woman recalls her experience in over 20 years in the business world. Speaking of a particular job change she made due to blocked mobility, she notes:

> I decided that all things being equal it was time to make a move, because

there was no room for women in a promotional capacity. I had gone as far as I was going to go, unless I wanted to go back to straight secretarial work, and sort of move up the chain, which I did not want to do. But there was no way they would have ever promoted me, because in that company they just wouldn't put a woman in that job. . . . I just accepted it, it was no big deal. I didn't like what was happening to me there, mind you. I was a little resentful, I must admit, I didn't like it. But I knew there was nothing I could do about it. . . . Had I been a man, I probably would have been the manager.

Speaking of salary inequities, she notes:

I would support the theory of equal pay for equal work. I have come the hard way, because I know I've been shorted. I've been burned so badly over the years with money that it's unreal, simply because I'm a girl in the job. I have always believed, long before women's lib ever came into existence, that you should get equal pay for equal work. You should get equal recognition for equal work. It doesn't work, unfortunately, but you should get it. They pay lip service to it now, but it still isn't there. I know what the salaries are in this entire organization and I know that it still isn't there.

With respect to attitudes towards women on the job, one entrepreneur notes:

You find that you run into discrimination when you least expect it. People assume that a woman does not have administrative responsibility, or that it's a fluke, or that she inherited it, because it was a family business, which is not my case.

Two of the women interviewed do not feel that women are unfairly treated, and one suggests that if they do in fact receive unequal treatment, it is their own fault. It was noted that women tend to want promotions immediately, and do not realize that one has to be patient, work hard, and demonstrate competence, rather than complain and campaign.

Commitment to the notion of sex equality is measured in both attitudinal and behavioural terms. Most of the women feel that women should support other women in the business world. They note that men support each other, and women should do the same. Moreover, they feel that, because of the disadvantages of being a woman in a masculine world of work ("they are unprepared for what they encounter"), women need support from one another. They have to build up networks, support systems, and information systems. One woman suggests that every woman she supports will in turn support other women. Women have to be prepared to give recognition, and avoid the Queen Bee Syndrome. One woman commented on this:

It is my observation that older women are still in the so called Queen Bee Syndrome, that women cannot expect help from them, that they are so busy conforming to the rules laid out by the organization that they have no time to think about changing them, and they certainly don't intend to be compromised by being associated with people who are somehow different from the organization.

Five women comment that women should not necessarily support other women in the business world, but that competent people, both men and women, should get sponsorship.

It is a well-known fact that expressed attitudes and behaviour may not coincide (Deutscher, 1973). One may express egalitarian notions without acting on them. If the presence of women in decision-making positions is to have an impact, women must act on their beliefs and actually support one another in the business world.

Seven of the women in the sample gave explicit examples of assisting other women, in terms of grooming them for jobs, hiring them and supporting them, counselling them, and fighting for equal pay and opportunities for advancement within the company. One woman notes that women need sponsors just as men do:

> It's a combination of being in the right place at the right time with the right people. Generally, women do not get that kind of sponsorship.

She spoke of cases where the management was going to hire a man for a certain position, but she recommended a woman for the job. She describes one such situation:

> They were going to hire a male and bring him in from the outside, and I said "no." We had quite a sitdown discussion and I said she deserves a shot at it, she's doing well and you just can't walk by her. She deserves the opportunity and if she finds she can't do it, fine, but first of all, she deserves a shot. I really stuck up for her and she sure hasn't let me down.

These data support the conclusion of Eichler (1978), in both attitudinal and behaviour terms, that the presence of women in management positions will increase the degree of equality for women in business.

IMPLICATIONS

This study of women in managerial positions has attempted to address the question of how they managed to avoid occupational segregation and succeed in a masculine work environment. Aspects of the three models articulated above have been addressed to answer this question. It appears that socialization experiences that are not sex-typed help in developing a career orientation. The dual roles of wife/mother and worker are managed by either remaining single, (thus, in effect, eliminating one role) or by having the support of husband and/or remaining at home, or working part-time when the children are young.

In the work world, strong, positive self-concepts are important, as are assertive job searches, and sponsorship. All these features combine to make for a promising career. However, sex ratios affect members of a minority, and coping strategies must be developed. Women experience status contradictions, which they manage by working harder than men, and excelling.

Finally, the issue of the implications for sex equality of the presence of women in managerial positions is raised. Eichler's (1978) attitudinal data suggest that such a presence is important for greater equality of opportunity for women. The data presented here, both attitudinal and behavioural, corroborate her findings. Women will support and sponsor other women (competence, of course, being a given), and will assist them in their career advancement. One woman manager sums up this sentiment succinctly:

I feel I should use this opportunity for all women because I want to see the day not when exceptional women get opportunity for advancement, but the day when the average woman has the right to advance as quickly as the average man.

REFERENCES

Armstrong, P. and H. Armstrong
1978   *The Double Ghetto: Canadian Women and Their Segregated Work.* Toronto: McClelland and Stewart.

Deutscher, I.
1973   *What We Say/What We Do.* Glenview, Illinois: Scott, Foresman and Company.

Eichler, M.
1978   "Sex Equality and Public Participation of Women in Canada. Some Survey Results." Paper given at the Conference on Women in Eastern Europe and the USSR, University of Alberta, Edmonton, Alberta (October).

Epstein, C.F.
1971   "Encountering the Male Establishment: Sex-Status Limits on Women's Careers in the Professions," in A. Theodore (ed.) *The Professional Woman.* Cambridge, Mass.: Schenkman, 52–73.

Hennig, M. and A. Jardim
1977   *The Managerial Woman.* New York: Anchor.

Hughes, E.C.
1971   *The Sociological Eye.* Chicago: Aldine.

Kanter, Rosabeth Moss
1975   "Woman and the Structure of Organizations: Explorations in Theory and Behavior," in M. Millman and R. M. Kanter (eds.) *Another Voice.* Garden City, N.J.: Anchor, 34–74.

1976   "Presentation VI," in *Signs* 1(3) Part 2 (Spring): 282–291.

1977   *Men and Women of the Corporation.* New York: Basic Books.

Mackie, M.
1976   "The Role Constraints of Working Wives." Unpublished paper. Revised version of a paper presented at the Symposium on "The Working Sexes," University of British Columbia (October).

Meissner, M., E. W. Humphreys, S. C. Meis and W. J. Scheu
1975   "No Exit for Wives: Sexual Division of Labour and the Accumulation of Household Demands, in *The Canadian Review of Sociology and Anthropology* 12(4) Part 1 (November): 424–439.

Report of the Royal Commission on the Status of Women in Canada
1970   Ottawa: Information Canada.

Thompson, J.
1978   "Patrons, Rabbis, Mentors—Whatever You Call Them, Women Need Them Too," in B.A. Stead (ed.) *Women in Management.* Englewood Cliffs, New Jersey: Prentice-Hall, 66–74.

van der Merwe, Sandra
1978   "A Portrait of the Canadian Woman Manager," in *The Business Quarterly* 43(3) (Autumn): 45–52.

Williams, M. G.
1977   *The New Executive Woman. A Guide to Business Success.* Randor, Pennsylvania: Chilton.

Chapter 21

The Transformation of Labour Relations in Quebec: An Analysis*

Michael R. Smith

Quebec's trade union movement has changed markedly over the postwar period. In the 1950s, it appears to have been more conservative than the labour movement of the rest of Canada. By the 1970s, Quebec's union centrals had become distinctively radical. In 1971, those centrals issued a series of manifestoes which presented a diagnosis of the ills of Quebec workers, the cures of which ills would require a radical transformation of the Quebec economy and society.[1] In 1972, the "Common Front" strike of public sector unions generated a crisis in the relations between the government and organized labour, which in turn led to strikes and disorders involving both public and private sector workers. Quebec labour also became more prone to strike than labour in the rest of Canada during the 1970s. What I want to stress here as my starting point is that the Quebec labour movement is, without question, different; it displays traits which demarcate it from the labour movements in the rest of Canada and of North America as a whole. In this it is interesting in precisely the same way that the rise to power of the CCF in Saskatchewan in 1944 was and remains interesting (cf. Lipset, 1955). The electoral success of the CCF was achieved in a sub-continent where equivalent socialist successes have been few and far between; Quebec labour centrals have adopted a more or less explicitly Marxist rhetoric against the background of a resolutely pragmatic North American labour movement, whose ideological inspiration varies between the vaguely social democratic sympathies of the CLC and the apolitical business unionism that predominates in the United States.

Consequently, recent Quebec labour history both invites and has received close attention. In this essay, I examine the explanations that have been given for the distinctive evolution of Quebec labour during the latter postwar period. I will argue that there are two kinds of serious problem with the interpretations most often given (although they are partly adequate); first, there are some serious ambiguities in their formulations and, second, they are not entirely consistent with the available facts. Having reviewed the difficulties with the explanations most often given, I will try to construct a more adequate and complete explanation. But before getting to the problem of explanation, it is worth reviewing the facts for which the explanations are designed to account.

*Research support for this paper came from the Canada Department of Labour to whom I am indebted.

IDEOLOGICAL SHIFTS WITHIN THE UNION MOVEMENT

Alone in North America, in Quebec, confessional trade unionism played an important part in the early development of the labour movement.[2] The Confédération des Travailleurs Catholiques du Canada (CTCC) was led by people trained in Catholic lay organizations, and its self-defined mission in its early years was to protect Catholic workers against the corrupting effects of industrialization in general and of American-based international unions in particular. Over the postwar period, these "social" concerns of the CTCC tended to progressively decline in favour of the more orthodox economic concerns of the international unions. But still, in the 1950s, the CTCC continued to officially express ambivalence about the need for strikes as a routine part of labour relations. There was, into the 1950s, a residuum of the old corporatist ideology upon which the union was founded, an ideology which stressed the shared rather than the conflicting interests of workers and employers (Tremblay, 1972: 115–16; Saint Pierre, 1975; Monière, 1977: 258–61). This is not to say that there were no CTCC strikes in this period. There were a number, including the bitter one at Asbestos (Trudeau, 1974). But still, into the 1950s, the CTCC remained a rather conservative union confederation.

About two-thirds of the unionized population belonged to unions outside of the CTCC. Many craft workers were affiliated with the Fédération Provinciale du Travail du Québec (FPTQ). The unions affiliated to the FPTQ fitted the more general business union model as, one would assume, did some of the other affiliates of the international unions who were not also affiliated to the FPTQ. That business union model involves pragmatic economic and political conduct which concerns itself above all with securing the establishment of favourable bargaining conditions (through legislation guaranteeing union security), and then aggressively advancing the wages and fringe benefits of its members in the collective bargaining process. But, even there, the result was a rather tepid version of business unionism. For it can be argued that Quebec workers, or at least the francophone ones, were not well served by trade unions whose leaders did not understand the language of the workers from whom they collected dues (Bernard, 1969: 54). Certainly, the leaders of the FPTQ managed to maintain cozy relations with the markedly anti-labour administration of Maurice Duplessis (Tremblay, 1972: 130).

By the late 1950s, things had already started to change. The Fédération des Unions Industrielles du Québec (FUIQ) was founded in 1952 and its leadership had a conception of government as a more active intervenor in the economic process. That is, the role of the Quebec government should not be to simply guarantee union security and then allow the collective bargaining process to establish wage levels; it should actively intervene in the economy to remove the gap between Quebec's wage level and that of Ontario.

These larger aspirations had become general throughout the leadership of the Quebec labour movement by the time the Quiet Revolution started. By 1960, the leadership of the CTCC decided that it had to substantially detach the union federation from its Catholic roots and turn it into a more orthodox labour organization, concerned above all with the economic interests of its members. In this, it was no doubt encouraged by the relative decline in the

CTCC's membership during the late 1950s, as compared to the Fédération des Travailleurs du Québec (FTQ), newly created from a merger between the FUIQ and the FPTQ. So the CTCC deconfessionalized and became the CSN. Meanwhile, the constituent unions of the FTQ were endowing themselves with a stronger Quebec presence at the same time that the FTQ itself had been strengthening its capacity to assist its affiliates (Bernard, 1969; Dofny and Bernard, 1968: 63–64; Hamelin and Harvey, 1976: 377).

In the early years of the Quiet Revolution, then, tendencies that had been revealing themselves for some years were consolidated. Both the FTQ and the CSN unions became aggressive in pursuit of their members' economic interests and, especially in the case of the CSN, endowed themselves with the staff and organization which would support that aggressiveness.[3] They also adopted the old FUIQ's preference for active government involvement in the economy to raise average living standards in Quebec to those of Ontario. But the evolution of Quebec labour did not come to an end with the Quiet Revolution. From the rather conservative unionism of the CTCC and the FPTQ, the Quebec labour movement became economically aggressive and better organized in the early years of the Quiet Revolution. Subsequently, it has become increasingly radical. This is true not only of the CSN and the FTQ but also of the Centrale de l'Enseignement du Québec (CEQ). At the beginning of the 1970s, each of these union centrals issued a manifesto and each of the manifestoes was couched in terms of class conflict.[4] The CSN manifesto, in fact, had an unambiguously Marxist flavour; it stressed contradictory class interests and treated the problems of working people in Quebec as irremediable within a capitalist economic system. In 1975, the CEQ published its "Manuel du 1er Mai," a teaching aid which was designed to assist teachers in explaining to their pupils how the schools were part of the total system of bourgeois oppression in Quebec. By 1970, in other words, Quebec union centrals were issuing documents whose radicalness clearly demarcated them from the approved sentiments throughout most of the rest of the North American labour movement. Quebec's labour centrals in the early 1970s endorsed views which one would have difficulty in imagining being expressed by either Dennis McDermott of the CLC or the late George Meany of the AFL–CIO.

STRIKES IN QUEBEC

A number of writers have emphasized the increase in the amount of industrial conflict in Quebec since the mid-1960s (e.g., Milner and Milner, 1973: 188; Willox, 1979: 269).[5] In Table 21–1, I have assembled five-year averages (arithmetical means) describing trends in the extent of industrial conflict in Quebec, Ontario and in Canada as a whole. The comparison between Quebec and Ontario is particularly interesting, since those two provinces remain the industrial centre of Canada. Since one would expect the amount of industrial conflict to increase with the numbers of workers available to go on strike, the measures of industrial conflict are deflated by labour force. What Table 21–1 makes clear is that the propensities for industrial conflict have indeed increased in Quebec relative to Ontario, and relative to Canada as a whole. The average strike rate in Quebec was about half that in Ontario in the three five-year periods from 1951 to 1965. The differential diminished from 1966 to

1970. In the 1970s, the strike rate in Quebec exceeded that of Ontario, by increasing amounts. By the end of the 1970s, Quebec's strike propensity was almost twice that of Ontario's. The man days lost rate follows a similar pattern. The trend in overall strike propensity clearly demarcates Quebec from Canada as a whole, and from Ontario in particular. The trend in the strike propensity of Quebec relative to that in Ontario is made still clearer in Figure 21–1 which plots the ratio of strike propensity in Quebec to that in Ontario. It shows that the propensity to strike in Quebec started to increase relative to that in Ontario from the very beginning of the Quiet Revolution.

Table 21–1

Industrial Conflict in Quebec, Ontario and Canada

	Strikes per 100,000 workers[1]			Man days lost per 1000 workers[1]		
	Quebec	Ontario	Cànada	Quebec	Ontario	Canada
1946–50	4.4	5.2	4.7	368.1	410.1	530.4
1951–55	3.1	5.9	4.4	372.6	449.4	364.6
1956–60	3.0	6.0	4.6	266.7	359.3	318.2
1961–65	4.4	8.3	5.7	320.2	300.3	245.4
1966–70	7.2	9.1	7.8	790.6	966.6	769.5
1971–75	11.2	7.5	9.6	1002.4	634.5	817.6
1976–78[2]	12.1	6.9	9.6	1200.4	490.8	745.6

[1] To be specific, this refers to the nonagricultural labour force. Data from *Historical Labour Force Statistics* (71-201); *The Labour Force*: Supplement to September 1960 issue (71-001); *Labour Force Reference Paper #58* (71-502). Data on industrial conflict from Strikes and Lockouts (Department of Labour).

[2] Note: this is for three years only.

We can examine a little more closely what has gone on with the help of Figure 21–2 which is derived from the date presented in Table 21–2. We know from Table 21–1 that the propensity to strike in Quebec has increased relative to Ontario. It is in the 1970 to 1978 period that Quebec overtook Ontario, and so Figure 21–2 focuses on this period. It shows where the relative growth in industrial conflict in Quebec was located by plotting the differences in the number of strikes between Quebec and Ontario by industrial sector. You should remember two things in examining this graph; the first is that it describes differences in numbers of strikes, not propensities. In fact, the labour force in Ontario is larger than that in Quebec in each industrial category. Secondly, the graph is inverted; that is, the negative numbers that result when the number of strikes in an industrial sector in Quebec exceeds that in Ontario are in the upper half of the graph.

Figure 21–2 shows that, while the totals oscillate from year to year, in all industries except two, the difference shifts in Quebec's favour (so to speak) from the first few years of the period to the last. The two exceptions are mining and construction. In neither of these cases is there any trend. But while the number of strikes from 1970 to 1973 was markedly lower in manufacturing in Quebec than in Ontario, from 1974 to 1978 the difference is much smaller. In

Figure 21-1

The Ratio of Strikes Per Thousand Workers in Quebec to Strikes Per Thousand Workers in Ontario

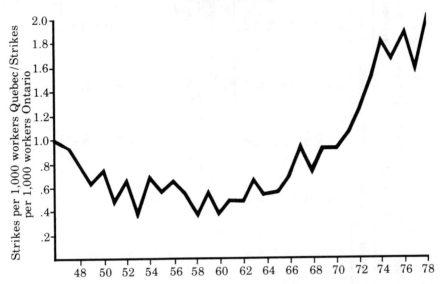

the other five industries, trade, services, transport, finance, and public administration, Quebec starts in 1970 with about as many strikes as Ontario (despite a smaller labour force), but accumulates a larger balance in its favour over the latter five years. What Figure 21-2 tells us, then, is that the increase in the number of strikes in Quebec relative to Ontario over the 1970s was widely spread throughout industrial sectors; only construction and mining display no trend.

THE COMMON FRONT STRIKE OF 1972

We have seen that the rate of industrial conflict in Quebec started to increase in about 1960, both absolutely and in relation to Ontario and the rest of Canada. We have also seen that the programmatic statements that Quebec's unions made started out being relatively conservative, became more or less social democratic and then, more recently, Marxist. The increase in the rate of industrial conflict and the ideological shift of Quebec union centrals are eloquent testimony to the fact that something interesting has been going on in the Quebec Labour movement over the postwar period. The events that have most caught the imagination of observers, however, are those related to the Common Front Strike of 1972.[6]

In 1964 and 1965, Quebec labour law was changed to legalize strikes in the public and para-public sectors. By the end of 1965, only policemen and firemen were prohibited from striking; public servants, teachers, and hospital and welfare workers henceforth had the legal right to use work stoppages to add

Table 21-2

Number of Strikes in Quebec, Ontario and Canada as a Whole, by Industrial Sector[1]

	Mines			Manufacturing			Construction			Transport		
	Quebec	Ontario	Canada	Quebec	Ontario	Canada	Quebec	Ontario	Canada	Quebec	Ontario	Canada
1970	4	1	15	72	127	263	6	42	109	14	12	48
1971	6	0	19	73	137	278	8	20	72	9	11	55
1972	12	0	32	70	127	290	5	21	81	11	8	59
1973	6	2	33	130	138	384	7	20	62	8	8	74
1974	7	5	60	243	249	687	7	18	70	38	11	126
1975	13	13	46	174	208	523	11	58	122	30	17	114
1976	7	8	49	180	172	457	7	21	76	39	10	142
1977	3	5	28	134	148	342	3	29	84	17	13	98
1978	11	5	39	172	179	459	4	30	108	29	10	126

	Trade			Finance			Services			Public Administration		
	Quebec	Ontario	Canada	Quebec	Ontario	Canada	Quebec	Ontario	Canada	Quebec	Ontario	Canada
1970	10	14	42	0	0	0	15	17	47	5	2	13
1971	12	16	46	1	0	1	15	9	43	9	8	27
1972	20	14	47	2	0	2	12	11	37	14	5	37
1973	29	18	71	2	2	2	10	12	49	5	5	23
1974	36	14	82	4	2	6	23	34	105	26	4	59
1975	40	17	89	8	1	10	43	38	164	36	7	87
1976	44	17	93	6	2	8	54	40	147	17	9	59
1977	27	18	70	3	2	7	45	18	96	28	10	56
1978	47	14	91	15	1	16	53	25	143	18	8	55

[1] Data from Strikes and Lockouts (Department of Labour).

Figure 21–2

Number of Strikes in Ontario Minus Number of Strikes in Quebec, by Industrial Sector, 1970–1978

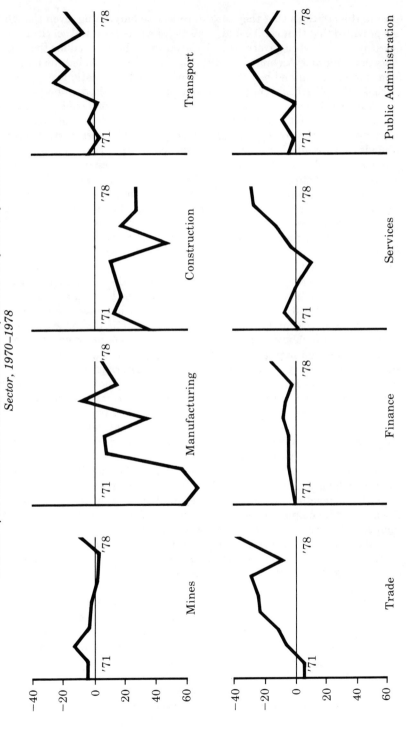

force to the positions that they took in collective bargaining, even though the law provided that that right could be abridged where essential services were in jeopardy. The Quebec government, however, was ill-prepared for the negotiations that followed. Among other difficulties, while it provided the bulk of the funds for education and health institutions, actual negotiations remained the responsibility of school commissions and boards of directors of hospitals.

From 1965 onwards, there were three broad sets of developments. First, the government felt obliged to resort on a number of occasions to court injunctions to prevent or end public or para-public sector strikes on the grounds that essential services were being jeopardized. Second, the direct role of the provincial government in the negotiations was progressively increased. It was not willing to confine its role to the provision of revenues to cover labour costs incurred in local negotiations.[7] It moved, in other words, to unite the responsibilities for spending and taxing. Third, the relations between the government and the unions became increasingly strained.

For the government, public and para-public sector salaries were one among a number of budgetary items. Larger salary costs in the public sector meant less available for equipment improvements in hospitals and schools, and for other government expenditures such as the construction of roads, incentives for industrial relocations and welfare payments, among other things. The implication of this is that the critical issue for the trade unions with which the government negotiated was the *salary mass* made available for public and para-public services. Unless the unions were to increase the salaries of some public and para-public sector workers[8] at the expense of other public and para-public sector workers, they had no alternative but to press the government on its overall budgetary decisions. The logic of the situation made union collective bargaining, accompanied with the right to strike, a struggle over state priorities.

Quebec's union leaders were fully aware of this (Ethier et al., 1975: 43). At the initiative of the CSN, and after some negotiating difficulties, the principal union centrals incorporating public and para-public service workers formed a common front, in order to facilitate the direct negotiation of government salary policy and, by implication, to negotiate the government's budgetary priorities.[9] In 1972, the negotiations between the government and the common front broke down and the unions called a legal strike. The government obtained an injunction that required the hospital workers to return to work, on the grounds that they provided an essential service. But the leaders of the three union centrals involved, Marcel Pépin, Louis Laberge, and Yvon Charbonneau, counselled defiance of the law and were sent to prison. These jailings generated a week of wildcat strikes which involved private as well as public sector workers. They also generated a quite substantial amount of public disorder, including the occupation of some radio stations.[10] The common front negotiations in 1970, in other words, ended in a serious crisis. It was a crisis, moreover, whose distinctive character was that labour relations had become intensely politicized. The *raison d'être* of the common front was that it was a vehicle through which organized labour could attempt to directly negotiate the bulk of the provincial budget. Furthermore, it is clear that the imprisonment of the union leaders engendered a quite passionate response on the part of a significant number of unionized workers—a response which had an overtly political character, since it was directed against an assertion on the part of the government of its own authority. I will return to the more general meaning of all this later in this essay.

WHERE IS THE DIFFERENCE LOCATED?

Manifestly, there is something special about the Quebec labour movement. It has produced ideological writings which have no counterpart in the ideological products of the major unions within English Canada. Furthermore, it generates a lot of strikes. In 1972, it participated in a major confrontation with the provincial government. The ideological pronouncements, at least, suggest a very real radical *élan* as compared to the labour movement of English Canada. Now, the increasing propensity to strike and the events of 1972 are sometimes interpreted as somehow linked to the ideological convictions of Quebec trade unionists. But those ideological convictions have been located in different places by different writers. There are descriptions of the importance of rank and file pressure in the radicalization of the Quebec labour movement (e.g., Isbester, 1971: 262; Brunelle, 1978: 196, Willox, 1979: 269). But there are other descriptions which stress a substantial gulf between a radical union leadership and a more pragmatic rank and file (Dupont and Tremblay, 1976: 19; Milner, 1977: 110). In short, while everybody agrees that the Quebec labour movement has displayed a remarkable radicalism over the last decade or so, there is no clear agreement on the distribution of that radicalism within the movement. Yet, if we are to understand adequately the mechanisms that lie behind the distinctiveness of recent Quebec labour history, we need to know where, within the labour movement, "advanced" sentiments are located.

What I wish to stress here is that the three critical features of recent Quebec labour history that I identified at the beginning of this paper do not tell us whether it is a union membership or a union leadership distinctive from that found in English Canada in general and Ontario in particular, that accounts for the ideological shift in Quebec's unions, the increasing relative propensity to strike, and the events of 1972.[11] It should be immediately clear that the much cited manifestoes do not necessarily indicate a radical rank and file. The recruitment of "intellectuals" into Quebec labour centrals (especially the CSN and the CEQ) has been noted in a number of places (e.g., Milner and Milner, 1973: 186; Smucker, 1980: 235). The CSN manifesto has all the hallmarks of the work of somebody trained within one of the more dogmatic branches of the social science disciplines. It is quite likely that it has been more avidly consumed by university professors than by the CSN's rank and file. The rank and file could be largely indifferent to the publication of documents of this sort, except insofar as the larger political preoccupations of the union leadership expressed in these documents led to a neglect, or inadequate treatment, of bread and butter issues. There is, as a matter of fact, some evidence that this is precisely what happened. The aftermath of the CSN's manifesto, *Ne Comptons Que Sur Nos Propres Moyens,* and all that it seems to suggest about the sentiments of the CSN's leadership, was a very real haemorrhage of members from the CSN, starting with the breakaway of the Confédération des Syndicats Démocratiques (CSD)[12] after the common front strike (cf. Dupont and Tremblay, 1976: 17–39). In the CEQ, Yvon Charbonneau and a good part of the union executive that shared his ideological dispositions were voted out of office in favour of more pragmatic candidates.[13] The manifestoes simply do not tell us very much about the state of mind of the rank and file.

The increasing relative propensity to strike in Quebec is similarly ambiguous. It is true that the decision to strike requires some sort of majority among the members of a bargaining unit. But the decision to vote in favour of a strike is also likely to be affected both by the recommendations of a union executive, and the degree of access to strike funds. This remains generally true even though, on occasion, workers vote to go on strike against the recommendations of their executive. In practice, union leaders act to regulate the incidence of strike decisions for one of two reasons. First, they may deter workers from striking because to do so is not tactically prudent; for example, markets for the product they produce may be soft and their firm may have large enough stocks on hand that it would not in the least be dismayed by a strike (cf. Ulman, 1955: 426–28). Second, union leaders may deter workers from striking because those leaders have become conservative. Michels (1962), of course, presented a set of reasons why one might expect union leaders routinely to become conservative.[14] The point of all this is that one could have a relatively higher strike propensity among one group of workers as compared to another, not because the attitudes of the workers themselves were much different, but either because their union leaders did not exercise as much tactical control over the members, or because the union leaders had not become conservative. A higher strike propensity does not necessarily betray difference in rank and file sentiments.

Only the events of 1972 are inconsistent with the notion that radical initiatives within the Quebec labour movement are based in the doctrinal commitments and decisions of the leadership, rather than the rank and file. For all that the data on these events are not hugely reliable, the fact remains that many Quebec workers struck spontaneously, or with only a little prompting, and a number participated in disorderly events. Yet even here, the comparison with English Canada is not clear. We simply do not know what would happen if Dennis McDermott and assorted English Canadian union leaders were to be imprisoned. Moreover, the arrest and imprisonment of the leader of the Canadian Union of Postal Workers (Jean-Claude Parrot) does not appear to have generated any more aggressive response in Quebec than in English Canada.[15] It has not generated much of a response at all. What happened in 1972 after the union leaders were imprisoned may indicate a distinctively radical rank and file. But without a comparable incident in English Canada, it is hard to be sure.

SURVEY EVIDENCE

If the distinctiveness of recent Quebec labour history (as compared to that of English Canada) has its origins in the sentiments of the rank and file, there should be evidence of that in the responses of Quebec trade unionists to survey questions. As a matter of fact, that is the only kind of evidence that can settle the issue. Some use has been made of survey data to depict the rank and file

Table 21-3

The Attitudes of Union Members by Region

		Atlantic	Quebec	Ontario	Prairies	B.C.	English Canada
(1) There is too much differ- ence between rich and poor.	Agree	70.7	78.1	62.5	62.9	67.8	64.4
	Neither	11.8	13.1	21.3	20.2	7.3	17.6
	Disagree	17.5	8.7	16.2	16.9	24.9	18.0
		(N=44)	(N=219)	(N=230)	(N=77)	(N=78)	(N=429)
(2) High income people should pay more taxes.	Agree	57.2	71.3	62.4	52.5	65.2	60.6
	Neither	7.5	12.6	11.0	13.7	9.3	10.8
	Disagree	35.3	16.1	26.6	33.8	25.5	28.6
		(N=44)	(N=215)	(N=232)	(N=79)	(N=73)	(N=428)
(3) Teachers should not have the right to strike.	Agree	44.3	79.1	52.7	48.4	32.9	47.4
	Neither	14.9	15.8	11.0	11.0	18.0	12.7
	Disagree	40.8	5.1	36.3	40.5	49.1	39.9
		(N=44)	(N=214)	(N=231)	(N=78)	(N=79)	(N=432)
(4) During a strike managers should be prohibited by law from hiring workers to take the place of strikers.	Agree	68.9	75.9	79.4	70.4	64.9	74.1
	Neither	14.5	9.4	8.4	9.7	3.4	8.4
	Disagree	16.6	14.7	12.2	19.8	31.7	17.5
		(N=43)	(N=213)	(N=230)	(N=80)	(N=77)	(N=430)
(5) Workers should have positions on the board of directors of the organization for which they work.	Agree	80.5	77.9	67.6	73.1	84.3	72.9
	Neither	13.8	10.9	18.2	7.4	11.8	14.6
	Disagree	5.8	11.2	14.3	19.5	3.8	12.5

Table 21-3 — Continued

The Attitudes of Union Members by Region

		Atlantic	Quebec	Ontario	Prairies	B.C.	English Canada
		(N=44)	(N=210)	(N=227)	(N=76)	(N=74)	(N=421)
(6) Do you think labour unions have too much or too little power for the good of the country?	Too Much	64.9	65.6	49.0	69.9	58.4	56.0
	About Right	23.2	27.3	39.4	22.4	35.8	34.1
	Too Little	11.8	7.1	11.6	7.6	5.8	9.9
		(N=43)	(N=217)	(N=230)	(N=76)	(N=77)	(N=426)
(7) Do you think corporations have too much or too little power for the good of the country?	Too Much	72.7	76.2	76.0	91.6	83.3	79.7
	About Right	26.7	18.9	23.0	8.4	15.8	19.6
	Too Little	0.6	4.9	1.1	0	0.9	0.9
		(N=43)	(N=205)	(N=226)	(N=72)	(N=75)	(N=416)
(8) Can strikes be justified as a form of protest to change government policies?	Often	17.4	24.2	12.8	7.7	12.0	12.2
	Sometimes	66.5	62.6	61.0	70.9	73.3	65.6
	Never	16.1	13.2	26.2	21.4	14.7	22.2

Table 21-3 — Continued

The Attitudes of Union Members by Region

	Atlantic	Quebec	Ontario	Prairies	B.C.	English Canada
	(N=44)	(N=219)	(N=234)	(N=80)	(N=80)	(N=438)
(9) Can legal and peaceful demonstrations like marches, rallies, and picketing be justified as a form of protest to change government policies?						
Often	19.7	32.0	17.9	24.4	27.5	21.0
Sometimes	61.6	45.8	62.6	57.2	48.1	58.9
Never	18.7	22.2	19.5	18.4	24.4	20.1
	(N=43)	(N=216)	(N=229)	(N=80)	(N=78)	(N=430)
(10) Can illegal but peaceful demonstrations like sit-ins be justified as a form of protest to change government policies?						
Often	8.9	7.6	5.6	11.3	14.5	8.6
Sometimes	47.9	38.1	35.2	49.4	47.2	41.2
Never	43.2	54.4	59.2	39.3	38.3	50.2
	(N=40)	(N=208)	(N=229)	(N=79)	(N=76)	(N=424)
(11) Can violent protests be justified as a way to change government policy?						
Often	0.0	5.8	0.2	8.0	1.7	1.9
Sometimes	15.9	14.1	9.3	7.1	7.2	9.2
Never	84.1	80.1	90.5	84.9	91.1	88.9
	(N=44)	(N=216)	(N=230)	(N=80)	(N=80)	(N=434)

Quebec union member as distinctively radical (e.g., Bennett, 1974), but the data heretofore used have been rather unconvincing.[16] We can, however, get a good picture of the attitudinal differences between the union members of Quebec and other Canadian provinces using data from the 1977 Quality of Life Survey.[17] These data are presented in Table 21-3. There are three different kinds of attitude represented in Table 21-3. Questions 1 and 2 deal with the attitudes of Canadian union members towards the general question of inequality. Questions 4 to 7 deal with their attitude towards the actors and institutions of the industrial relations system. Questions 8 to 11 deal with their attitude towards what constitute justifiable methods of protest.

The picture presented in this table is rather mixed. Questions 1 and 2 suggest that Quebec union members are substantially more likely to be resentful toward income inequality than union members in Ontario, or English Canada as a whole.[18] They also appear from Questions 7 to 11 to be more likely to favour more aggressive forms of protest. These seven questions together tend to suggest that there is indeed a more radical trade union rank and file in Quebec. On Questions 3 to 6, on the other hand, the distribution of attitudes of Quebec labour union members appears rather similar to that in the rest of Canada, or somewhat more conservative. Bitter experience (presumably) has made Quebec unionists more hostile than unionists in other provinces to the right of teachers to strike. Their distribution of views on the need to prohibit the use of scabs in labour disputes is similar to that in Ontario and British Columbia, and not markedly different from that of English Canada as a whole. They are slightly more likely to favour workers on boards of directors, and slightly less likely to think that corporations have too much power. On the question of trade union power, on the other hand, the distribution of attitudes among Quebec trade unionists is markedly more conservative than that of English Canadian unionists.[19]

ACCOUNTING FOR THE FACTS: A FIRST ATTEMPT

We have seen that the propensity to strike in Quebec has increased relative to that in Ontario; that it started to do so during the Quiet Revolution; that it overtook Ontario in 1970; that the difference between its propensity and that of Ontario widened at a very fast rate thereafter; and that this increase in strike propensity relative to Ontario was widely dispersed throughout most, although not all, industrial sectors. We have also seen that the ideological statements emanating from Quebec trade unions tended to become increasingly radical, with a climax in the early 1970s. Furthermore, in the Common Front Strike, the Quebec labour movement was embroiled in a direct confrontation with political authority which resulted in fairly widespread disorders. These are the irreducible facts with which an interpretation of the Quebec labour movement in the postwar period must come to terms. It should be clear that accounting for these facts would require an explanation or set of explanations based, first, upon factors which demarcate Quebec from Ontario and the rest of Canada and, second, which designate changes that came into play during the early 1960s, for it was during the Quiet Revolution that the relative strike propensity of Quebec began to shift, and it was after the Quiet Revolution that the Quebec union centrals started to adopt publicly radical postures.

One explanation that has wide currency, and does clearly demarcate Quebec from Ontario and the rest of Canada, stresses the coincidence of class and language.[20] In Quebec, large private employers have been disproportionately anglophone and workers disproportionately francophone. This means that the normal class cleavage in industrial societies is overlaid by a linguistic cleavage. As a result, according to this view, the working class is unambiguously demarcated, and its members have a sense of their distinctive identity. There is here a stronger basis for "class consciousness" than one would find in a linguistically homogeneous society. This argument would suggest that the distinctive features of Quebec labour relations reflect the greater class consciousness rooted in the experiences provided by the coincidence of class and language in Quebec.[21]

It should be clear that, on its own, this explanation will not do. The linguistic cleavage between management and labour in important sectors of Quebec industry is of long standing, while the Quebec labour movement has only relatively recently become radicalized. But it is conceivable that the coincidence of class and language *in conjunction with* some other factor that came into play at about the time of the Quiet Revolution accounts for what has subsequently happened. One fairly widely cited such factor is the "failure" of the Quiet Revolution. At the beginning of the Quiet Revolution, average earnings in Quebec were below those in Ontario, and rates of unemployment were higher. The aggressive state intervention in the economy, and the expanded social and educational facilities of the Quiet Revolution were advertised, in part, as attempts to eliminate this disparity. But by the end of the Quiet Revolution, Quebec was still economically weaker than Ontario, and there was an accumulating government debt to boot. From the point of view of workers, the real legacy of the Quiet Revolution was higher taxes. The lesson for them to draw, or for intellectuals to draw for them, was that it was the impersonal workings of international capitalism which dictated economic conditions, and that a government which took the private enterprise structure of the economy for granted, like the Liberal government of the Quiet Revolution, was incapable of significantly improving the conditions of workers.[22]

Our next question is, to what extent do the "coincidence of class and language" and the "failure of the Quiet Revolution" provide an adequate explanation for the distinctive features of recent Quebec labour history? It is fairly clear that the union manifestoes can be accounted for in this way. The manifestoes of the CSN and the FTQ put considerable stress on the weaknesses of the government economic interventions of the 1960s, and the CSN manifesto directly interprets the Quiet Revolution as an instructive lesson in the limits of capitalist reformism. One also finds within the manifestoes some discussion of the "imperialism" of both American and Anglo-Canadian capital, which tends to suggest a sensitivity to the coincidence of class and language. Furthermore, the fact that the union leadership approved the publication of these manifestoes would presumably indicate that they reflected, to some extent, either their own sentiments or those of many of the union militants (or both). We do, in fact, know that a substantial proportion of trade union militants in Quebec combine their left-wing sentiments with a strong nationalism. Thus, at a time when support for the Parti Québécois was low, a large proportion of the delegates to an FTQ conference were Parti Québécois supporters (Milner, 1978: 166). Moreover, the leaders of each of the three big union centrals in the mid-1970s all expressed themselves in favour of some form of political independence for Quebec (Dupont and Tremblay, 1976).

But if we can account for the content of the manifestoes in terms of the "failure of the Quiet Revolution" and the "coincidence of class and language," this is less easily done for the other two distinguishing features of recent Quebec labour history, upon which commentaries on Quebec labour relations have focused. The survey data in Table 21-3 suggested that, in Quebec, there is somewhat more widespread resentment at inequality. It is reasonable to assume, I think, that resentment is more widespread because "the rich" are identified with a particular linguistic group.

One might be tempted to conclude, therefore, that this resentment at inequality, fuelled by the linguistic gap between workers and their employers, and by disillusionment with the "failure" of the Quiet Revolution, has been translated into a greater willingness to vote to go on strike. There may be something to this, but there are some difficulties. First, as we saw in Table 21-3 (Questions 3 to 7), when it comes to specific questions on the institutions and actors of the labour relations system, Quebec workers appear no more radical than their English-Canadian counterparts. It is hard to tell how this would work itself out in the strike vote decision. Which would be more important in an individual strike vote decision—a generalized resentment at inequality or the view that, for instance, trade unions are too powerful?[23] Perhaps more importantly, the fact that Quebec workers are no more likely to be antagonistic towards corporations (Question 7) does suggest a hiatus between generalized resentment at inequality and the specific antagonism towards capital which one might expect to influence their strike vote decision.

Furthermore, in the strikes and disorders that have occurred over the last decade or so, including the common front strike, public and para-public sector workers have been full participants, and in some respects the vanguard. But workers in those sectors generally confront francophone employers. Teachers, hospital workers and provincial civil servants are least likely to have any practical experience of linguistic inequality. Mining, on the other hand, is an industry where, very generally, Anglo-Canadian or American companies deal with a francophone labour force.[24] But as we saw in Figure 21-2, that is one industry in which the propensity to strike in Quebec relative to that in Ontario has not been increasing over the last decade. This is the opposite of what one would expect if linguistic inequality had been a critical factor in determining Quebec's relative strike propensity. Another consideration is that, as Figure 21-1 shows, the upward tendency in relative strike propensity started *with* the Quiet Revolution.[25] It can be seen that, while the ratio of Quebec to Ontario strike propensities shifts about from year to year, *each subsequent low point is higher than the preceding low point.* Notwithstanding year to year fluctuations, then, the increasing propensity to strike seems to have been underway before the Quiet Revolution can be deemed to have "failed."

Overall, it is difficult to have any confidence in an explanation of the relatively high strike propensity in Quebec of recent years which is based on the effect of the "coincidence of class and language" or the "failure of the Quiet Revolution," particularly if that effect is supposed to have operated through the pressure of rank and file union sentiments on the union leadership. What of the events of 1972? There were two aspects to those events: the immense scale of the conflict between the government and the unions and the disorders that followed. With respect to the second of these aspects, I have already pointed out earlier that one cannot be sure that they demarcate Quebec's union members from those of English Canada in recent years. The closest event to such a comparable conflict was the imprisonment of Jean-Claude Parrot, and that does not seem to have generated any more aggressive response in Quebec than in the rest of Canada. With respect to the immense scale, it should be clear that it was based on initiatives on the part of the provincial government to centralize labour negotiations. The decision to form a common front on the part of the unions was a tactical reaction to that centralization. The *scale* of the dispute, then, was generated by some specific industrial relations institutions developed in Quebec. I will expand on this in the next section.

ACCOUNTING FOR THE FACTS: ANOTHER TRY

If the contents of the manifestoes of the early 1970s reflect, albeit crudely and distantly, real sentiments held by some Quebec union leaders and militants (and I am willing to assume that they do), it is reasonable to conclude that the coincidence of class and language, and the limited accomplishments of the Quiet Revolution substantially account for the content of those manifestoes. But the previous section showed that those factors are not sufficient to account for the changing strike propensity in Quebec and for the events of 1972. Once again, however, we must seek an explanation which demarcates Quebec from the other provinces, and the timing of which "fits." We need explanations that account for the fact that the increasing relative strike propensity in Quebec started *with* the Quiet Revolution. We need another explanation that accounts for the fact that it was at the end of the 1960s that tension in public sector labour negotiations built up.

One factor which distinguishes Quebec from other provinces, and which came into effect at about the time of the Quiet Revolution, is the existence of two vigorous, approximately equal-sized labour centrals, actively competing for membership within most industries. The CTCC, as we noted earlier, started out as a rival to the unions that later came together to form the FTQ. But by the 1950s, its antiquated ideological baggage made it a somewhat anaemic rival to the FTQ, as its dwindling relative share of union membership in Quebec during the 1950s shows. At the end of the 1950s, however, an attempt to merge the two centrals broke down and generated a period of intense intercentral competition, but a competition in which the CSN, the newly secularized reincarnation of the CTCC, was a vigorous participant, unencumbered with the restraining ideology of its Catholic heritage. This is important, since one would assume that, other things being equal, competing unions are unions that are more likely to strike. Striking gives a union a high profile; it can be seen as a form of advertising.[26] And, in addition, competing unions are also likely to be particularly attentive to the economic discontents of their members, and enthusiastic to see those discontents expressed forcibly to employers.[27] In short, I am arguing that the increasing relative propensity to strike in Quebec since 1960 can best be interpreted as an outcome of the existence of two union federations, aspiring to increase their memberships among the same groups of workers and, consequently, aggressively competing for attention. That the upward tendency in strikes started in 1960, shortly after the breakdown of merger attempts between the CTCC and the FTQ, gives additional credence to this interpretation.

What of the events of 1972? This was a public sector dispute. In what way have public sector negotiations become different in Quebec as compared to the rest of Canada? They became different because, in Quebec, the government went farther than most other provinces (and certainly than Ontario) in extending the right to strike to public and para-public sector workers.[28] At the same time, the movement to the centralization of public sector bargaining that I described earlier in this paper has raised the stakes in any dispute. In public sector negotiations, the authority to determine budgetary priorities of the government in Quebec is at issue. And the right to strike that was granted to public and para-public sector workers in the context of services that can often be described as "essential," makes public sector collective bargaining in Quebec a very delicate process indeed, a process which really can "blow up." In 1972, it did so.

I am suggesting that what happened in 1972 can be substantially explained in terms of the distinctive public sector industrial relations institutions with which Quebec endowed itself.[29] The state confronted a very real crisis because of the tensions inherent in public sector negotiations *in conjunction with* the particular public sector industrial relations institutions with which it had endowed itself. Because it confronted a crisis,[30] it took a hard line with Laberge, Pépin, and Charbonneau, and sent them to prison. Sending the leaders of all three Quebec centrals to prison precipitated the disorders that followed. A more complete explanation of the events of 1972, however, does seem to me to require a consideration of the political positions of Quebec's labour leaders, which political positions may well have been affected by the "coincidence of class and language" and the "failure of the Quiet Revolution." After all, Pépin, Laberge and Charbonneau did not need to counsel defiance of the law; that they did so, one suspects, was partially rooted in their rather distinctive (for union leaders in North America) doctrinal commitments. It is also possible that the "spontaneous" walkouts[31] after the imprisonments were facilitated by the existence of a core of militants with an "advanced" ideology, which core either does not exist or is less substantial in the rest of Canada. Questions 8 to 11 of Table 21–3, which showed that larger percentages of Quebec trade unionists favoured more extreme forms of protest, would tend to be consistent with this notion.

CONCLUSION

In this essay, I have been concerned with why recent Quebec labour history has been so different from that in the rest of Canada. I have suggested that it is reasonable to interpret the ideological pronouncements that have come out of Quebec's labour centrals as linked to the effects of the coincidence of class and language, and disappointment at the modest accomplishments of the Quiet

Revolution, on some union leaders and militants. But I have also argued that, if one is concerned with the attributes of recent Quebec labour history that have more practical relevance, the increasing relative strike propensity, and the events of 1972, one can best seek an explanation within the distinctive industrial relations institutions found in Quebec, within the acute interunion rivalry in the case of the increasing relative strike propensity, and within the right to strike *in conjunction with* a highly centralized negotiating process in the case of the events of 1972. In making this argument, I have suggested that Quebec union members do not seem to be consistently more likely to hold radical views than union members in the rest of Canada, so that an explanation of recent Quebec labour history's distinctiveness that is couched *principally* in terms of the special structural location of Quebec's working class is inevitably dubious, except insofar as it shows that those industrial relations institutions have their origins in that special structural location. That has yet to be done. An adequate analysis of industrial conflict, in other words, cannot ignore the fact that strikes are framed by the industrial relations institutions[32] in which they are set, as well as by the class structure.

NOTES

1. For general analyses of the politicization of the Quebec labour movement, see the essays in Dion (1973).
2. What follows is largely based on the analysis by Tremblay (1972) of ideological shifts within the Quebec labour movement.
3. The difference between the size of the staff of the CSN and that of the FTQ has always been, and remains, enormous (cf. Dupont and Tremblay, 1976).
4. The early manifestoes are collected in Drache (1972).
5. The treatments of the increasing propensity to strike have been rather unsatisfactory. Milner and Milner, for instance, present data on the very short period from 1964 to 1966. Willox presents data covering the only slightly longer period from 1966 to 1970. It should be recognized, however, that there are always substantial year-to-year fluctuations in the extent of industrial conflict, and it is hazardous to make assertions about trends on the basis of data from a short time period. Furthermore, from the mid-1960s, the extent of industrial conflict increased throughout Canada. In short, if one is trying to make assertions about the distinctiveness of the pattern of industrial conflict in Quebec, the data presented by Milner and Milner and by Willox are wholly inadequate.
6. The account that follows is based principally on Ethier et al. (1975) and Goldenberg (1975a).
7. The reaction on the part of the union federations to this centralization of the negotiating process was divided. The CEQ thought a decentralized structure was in its interests; the CSN, on the other hand, was in favour of centralization (Ethier et al., 1975: 34–35).
8. In fact the CEQ, despite its progressive ideology, was at first reticent to join the Common Front, precisely because the CSN was in favour of a settlement in which the lower-paid workers would receive the largest pay increases (Ethier et al., 1975: 55–63).
9. Goldenberg (1975a: 16) estimates that "nearly half the gross provincial budget was involved."

10. The most detailed narrative can be found in *Radical America* (1972). How reliable the figures quoted on pages 102-105 of that publication are is not clear. Certainly, given the ideological presuppositions of the authors, it is unlikely that they have underestimated the participation. Another useful account can be found in Chodos and Auf der Maur (1972: 109–142).

11. Willox (1979: 269) has written that "a significant and growing minority of Quebec workers came to explicitly identify themselves as an exploited class whose interests are separate from and opposed to the interests of industrial owners and their governmental supporters," and uses the amount of industrial conflict as one piece of evidence in support of this. I am arguing here that this is, quite simply, an illegitimate inference.

12. Smucker (1980: 235) makes the interesting point that "the leaders of the CSD came up through the ranks of labour, while Pépin and his predecessor in the CSN were university graduates."

13. Charbonneau's electoral defeat and the campaign leading up to it are described in a series of reports by Francoy Roberge in *Le Devoir*. These are listed in the reference section at the end of this essay.

14. In brief, Michels argued that union leaders have both a strong motivation to stay in office (their next most likely job is considerably less attractive), and the resources to make it very difficult for opponents to dislodge them (for example, control of union funds and of the union organization). Given their strong motivation to stay in office, they are unlikely, according to Michels, to take politically dangerous—that is radical — courses of action. For a general analysis of this issue see Hyman (1971).

15. The weakness of the response to the imprisonment of Jean-Claude Parrot is bemoaned in "The State of the Unions" in *Canadian Dimension,* Vol. 14, No. 7 (June 1980): 3–12.

16. The data cited by Bennett show that, in 1973, Quebecers, unlike other Canadians, were substantially more likely to hold management rather than unions responsible for strikes. The problem with these data is that they do not deal directly with the attitudes of workers, or more particularly, trade unionists. If one wishes to infer a link between the conduct of unions in Quebec as compared to the rest of Canada, and the attitudes of the members of those unions, one needs data specifically comparing the attitudes of union members.

17. These data were generated by the Social Change in Canada Project directed by Tom Atkinson, Bernard Blishen, Michael Ornstein and H. Michael Stevenson of York University. This project was supported by the Social Sciences and Humanities Research Council of Canada (Grant #S75-0332). The data files were made available by the Institute for Behavioural Research of York University. Any errors of interpretation, however, are my own.

18. Although, even here, the fact that the Quebec pattern is similar to that in the Atlantic provinces does rather suggest that this pattern of responses may substantially reflect a resentment at regional rather than class inequality.

19. For a detailed analysis of regional differences in attitudes, using the same data set as used here, see Ornstein et al. (1980).

20. Roback (1973: 19–20) has suggested one structural condition which demarcates Quebec from Ontario (and other provinces) and provides an impulse towards the politicization of the union movement; in Quebec there has been no socialist party to express working-class political concerns. The NDP has never succeeded in taking root in Quebec, and the more normal

condition in provincial politics has been the alternation of two parties of the right. Hence, on the left, there has been a political vacuum in Quebec and it is understandable that the union movement, or at least its leaders, would feel obliged to fill that vacuum by providing or sponsoring their own explicitly political analyses of unfolding events in Quebec. That, however, still leaves open the question of the specific content of the programmatic statements issued by the unions in the early 1970s. Why so radical?

21. This argument is developed at great length in Milner and Milner (1973). It can also be found in Willox (1979: 277). There is a general analysis of left-wing nationalism in Quebec in Denis (1979).

22. This argument can be found in Hamelin and Harvey (1976: 376), Willox (1979: 268–69); and Milner and Milner (1973: 224–25). There is a general discussion of the limitedness of the accomplishments of the Quiet Revolution in Brunelle (1978). I would note in passing that I regard the historical judgment that the Quiet Revolution somehow "failed" as not well established.

23. It would not, of course, be surprising if people made a radical distinction between their own trade union and that of other people. I have argued that workers tend to dissociate their own position from that of other workers, in significant ways (Smith, 1978).

24. The table on page 56 of Book 3 of the *Report of the Royal Commission on Bilingualism and Biculturalism* is suggestive in this respect.

25. For a more sophisticated analysis of temporal shifts in industrial conflict in Quebec, see Smith (1979).

26. The importance of inter-federation competition is stressed in Tremblay (1974). Willox (1979: 277) also stresses this, and I use inter-federation competition as part of my interpretation of the results reported in Smith (1979). Dumas (1968) stresses the benefits of union competition for union members.

27. I am arguing, in other words, that inter-federation competition tends to provide a counterbalance to any Michelsian tendencies towards increased conservatism on the part of union leaders.

28. As of 1975, only Saskatchewan, New Brunswick and Quebec had granted public employees the right to strike. Quebec, moreover, was distinguished by the absence of an arbitration provision (Goldenberg, 1975b). Additional relevant information can be found in Crispo (1978: 56–57) and Woods (1972: 294–335).

29. The question of what structural conditions *generated* the particular industrial relations institutions found in Quebec remains, of course. Certainly, the special national status of francophone trade unionists in Quebec accounts for the formation of the CTCC, which in turn provided the basis for the intense inter-federation rivalry that developed at the beginning of the 1960s. But I have yet to see an adequate sociological analysis of the development of the particular legal framework for collective bargaining in the public sector that is found in Quebec.

30. The Quebec government in 1972 may also have been forced to be rigid by a precarious financial situation. But none of the standard sources (Lemoine, 1973; Milner, 1977) establish that Quebec's government in 1972 was in a shakier financial state than any other provincial government. Indeed, considering the importance of a "fiscal crisis of the state" in recent Marxist political interpretations, the superficiality of the analysis of public accounts, upon which many of those interpretations are based, is quite staggering.

31. The word "spontaneity" is frequently used to describe the events of 1972. But that term should be used with some caution. Strikes in France in 1968 were similarly described as "spontaneous." Yet, as Erbès-Seguin's (1970) research makes clear, local militants played an important role in prompting walk-outs. In the words of Shorter and Tilly (1974: 141), "it would be inexact to call the May–June Days 'spontaneous'; they were perhaps without overall direction from a central place, and they were certainly not planned in advance; yet they were guided by local structures rather than unfolding in some kind of 'Hey-boys-lets-go-on-strike' pattern." We lack detailed descriptions of the walk-outs of 1972, but it seems likely that they would be similar in important ways to those of France in 1968.

32. For a general analysis of industrial relations systems, see Dunlop (1958).

REFERENCES

Bennett, Arnold
1974   "Labour and the Québec elections/1973," in Dimitrios I. Roussopoulos (ed.) *Québec and Radical Social Change*. Montreal: Black Rose Books, 119–27.

Bernard, P.
1969   *Structures et Pouvoirs de la Fédération des Travailleurs du Québec*. Task Force on Labour Relations, Study No. 13. Ottawa: Queen's Printer.

Brunelle, Dorval
1978   *La Désillusion Tranquille*. Montreal: Hurtubise HMH.

Chodos, Robert and Nick Auf der Maur
1972   *Quebec: A Chronicle 1968–1972*. Toronto: James Lewis and Samuel.

Crispo, John
1978   *The Canadian Industrial Relations System*. Toronto: McGraw-Hill Ryerson.

Denis, Roch
1979   *Luttes de Classes et Question Nationale au Québec 1948–1968*. Montreal: Presses Socialistes Internationales.

Dion, Gérard (ed.)
1973   *La Politisation des Relations du Travail*. Québec: Les Presses de l'Université Laval.

Dofny, J. and P. Bernard
1968   *Le Syndicalisme au Québec: Structure et Mouvement*. Task Force on Labour Relations, Study No. 9. Ottawa: Queen's Printer.

Drache, D. (ed.)
1972   *Quebec—Only the Beginning*. Toronto: New Press.

Dumas, Evelyn
1968   "Les Rivalités Syndicales: Force ou Faiblesse," in Gérard Dion (ed.) *Le Syndicalisme Canadien: Une Réévaluation*. Québec: Les Presses de l'Université Laval, 99–118.

Dunlop, John T.
1958   *Industrial Relations Systems*. New York: Holt.

Dupont, Pierre and Gisèle Tremblay
1976   *Les Syndicats en Crise*. Montreal: Editions Quinze.

Erbès-Seguin, Sabine
1970 "Le Déclenchement des Grèves de Mai: Spontanéité des Masses et Rôle des Syndicats," in *Sociologie du Travail* 12: 177–89.

Ethier, Diane, Jean-Marc Piotte and Jean Reynolds
1975 *Les Travailleurs Contre L'Etat Bourgeois, Avril et Mai 1972*. Montréal: Les Editions de l'Aurore.

Goldenberg, Shirley B.
1975a *Industrial Relations in Quebec: Past and Present*. Kingston: Industrial Relations Centre, Queen's University.
1975b "Dispute Settlement Legislation in the Public Sector: An Interprovincial Comparison," in H. C. Jain (ed.) *Canadian Labour and Industrial Relations: Public and Private Sectors*. Toronto: McGraw-Hill Ryerson, 291–300.

Hamelin, Jean and Fernand Harvey
1976 *Les Travailleurs Québécois, 1941–1971: Dossier*. Quebec: Institut Supérieur des Sciences Humaines, Université Laval.

Hyman, Richard
1971 *Marxism and the Sociology of Trade Unionism*. London: Pluto Press.

Isbester, Fraser
1971 "Quebec Labour in Perspective: 1949–1969," in Richard Ulric Miller and Fraser Isbester (eds.) *Canadian Labour in Transition*. Scarborough, Ontario: Prentice-Hall of Canada, 240–66.

Lemoine, B. Roy
1973 "The Growth of the State in Québec," in Dimitrios I. Roussopoulos (ed.) *The Political Economy of the State*. Montreal: Black Rose Books, 59–87.

Lipset, Seymour Martin
1950 *Agrarian Socialism: The Cooperative Commonwealth Federation in Saskatchewan*. Berkeley and Los Angeles: University of California Press.

Michels, Robert
1962 *Political Parties: A Sociological Study of the Oligarchical Tendencies of Modern Democracy*. New York: Crowell-Collier.

Milner, Henry
1977 "The Decline and Fall of the Quebec Liberal Regime: Contradictions in the Modern Quebec State," in Leo Panitch (ed.) *The Canadian State: Political Economy and Political Power*. Toronto: University of Toronto Press, 101–132.
1978 *Politics in the New Quebec*. Toronto: McClelland and Stewart.

Milner, Henry and Sheilagh Hodgins Milner
1973 *The Decolonization of Quebec: An Analysis of Left-Wing Nationalism*. Toronto: McClelland and Stewart.

Monière, Denis
1977 *Le Développement des Idéologies au Québec des Origines à Nos Jours*. Montréal: Editions Québec/Amérique.

Ornstein, Michael D., H. Michael Stevenson and A. Paul Williams
1980 "Region, Class and Political Culture in Canada," in *Canadian Journal of Political Science* 13: 227–72.

Radical America
1972 "Special Issue: Quebec." Radical America 6.

Roback, Léo
1973 "Les Formes Historiques de Politisation du Syndicalisme au Québec,"
in Gérard Dion (ed.) *La Politisation des Relations du Travail.* Québec:
Les Presses de l'Université Laval, 15–44.

Roberge, Francoy
1978a "Non au Dogmatisme de la CEO," in *Le Devoir* (June 15): 9.
1978b "La Rivalité Charbonneau-Gaulin Polarisera la Discussion à la CEQ,"
in *Le Devoir* (June 26): 3.
1978c "La Politisation Charbonneau-Gaulin s'Accentue à la CEQ," in *Le
Devoir* (June 28): 2.
1978d "Le Congrès de la CEQ Marqué par la Prudence," in *Le Devoir* (July 3):
2.

Saint-Pierre, Céline
1975 "Idéologies et Pratiques Syndicales au Québec dans les Années '30: La
Loi de l'Extension Juridique de la Convention Collective de Travail," in
Sociologie et Sociétés 7: 5–32.

Shorter, Edward and Charles Tilly
1974 *Strikes in France 1830–1968.* Cambridge: Cambridge University Press.

Smith, Michael R.
1978 "The Effects of Strikes on Workers: A Critical Analysis," in *Canadian
Journal of Sociology* 3: 457–72.
1979 "Institutional Setting and Industrial Conflict in Quebec," in *American
Journal of Sociology* 80: 109–134.

Smucker, Joseph
1980 *Industrialization in Canada.* Scarborough, Ontario: Prentice-Hall.

Tremblay, Louis-Marie
1972 *Le Syndicalisme Québécois: Idéologies de la C.S.N. et de la F.T.Q.
1940–1970.* Montréal: Les Presses de l'Université de Montréal.
1974 "Panorama du syndicalisme Québécois," in *Annuaire du Québec.*
Québec: Editeur Officiel du Québec, 578–585.

Trudeau, Pierre Elliot (ed.)
1974 *The Asbestos Strike.* Translated by James Boake. Toronto: Butterworths.

Ulman, Lloyd
1955 *The Rise of the National Trade Union: The Development and
Significance of Its Structure, Governing Institutions and Economic
Policies.* Cambridge, Mass.: Harvard University Press.

Woods, H.D.
1972 *Labour Policy in Canada* (2nd ed.). Toronto: Macmillan of Canada.

Chapter 22

Trade Union Reactions to Women Workers and Their Concerns*

Maureen Baker
Mary-Anne Robeson

The literature on women and trade unions is permeated with comments concerning the negative reactions or apathy of unions to working women. Studies from Australia, Canada, Great Britain, and the United States reveal the same trend: at the beginning of the trade union movement during the last century, many unions were openly hostile to the influx of women workers into the labour force and trade unions. After the Second World War, unions became more tolerant of female workers, but still seemed reluctant to assist them or give priority to "women's issues," such as equal pay, equal work, child care, and maternity leave. Despite the differences in the collective bargaining systems of these countries and their different rates of unionization, many authors have come to the same conclusion: that the union movement has shown little interest in working women and their concerns (O'Neill, 1969; Auchmuty, 1975; Ryan and Rowse, 1975; Marchak, 1973; McFarland, 1979).

The main purpose of this paper is to analyse the reasons behind the historical and contemporary reaction of trade unions to women workers. Although we are presenting no new empirical data, we are searching for a synthesis from the complexity of factors mentioned in the literature which influenced the treatment of women by the labour movement. Four potential explanations will be analysed, weighing the available evidence and assessing the argument. These four explanations include: viewing unions as vehicles of sexism; unions as threatened by cheap labour; the difficulty of organizing women who are mainly white-collar workers; and the nature of the collective bargaining system which benefits the majority of members.

UNIONS AS VEHICLES OF SEXISM

Sexism can be defined as conclusions about the nature or potential of men and women drawn from inadequate and stereotypic sources, such as biology or traditional roles. With respect to the role of women, unions have not shaped societal attitudes and mores, but mirrored traditional standards. Like other organizations, unions have operated within the prevailing ideology emphasizing women's primary role within the family (White, 1980). Moreover, the membership of unions has been dominated by blue-collar men, who are alleged to be more traditional than white-collar men in their attitudes towards women (Rainwater, 1960; Komarovsky, 1964).

Several Australian writers have articulated the "sexism position" by

---

*Reprinted with permission from *Canadian Journal of Sociology*, Vol. 6, No. 1.

providing historical evidence of men's view that women should not work outside the home for money (Summers, 1975; Dixson, 1976). This resistance to women entering the labour force in Australia was particularly evident prior to the Second World War.

The belief among male workers that women's place is in the home is prevalent in the Canadian writing as well. In 1907, an article in the "Toronto Labour Day Souvenir Book" appeals to women as consumers, wives, and mothers. The stress is placed on females "carrying on the educational work beyond the union and into the home," because it is the *women* and not the men who spend their sons', fathers', and husbands' money. As Klein and Roberts (1974: 220) assert, women's primary role was not as legitimate workers, but rather as consumers and homemakers.

More recently, the Geoffroy and Saint-Marie study (1971) of the attitudes of union men in Quebec clearly illustrates that male perceptions in some regions have changed little in sixty years. Using both questionnaires and interviews, they documented union men's traditional attitudes towards women. For example, 85 per cent were not in favour of married women with children working outside the home, and 68 per cent felt that most men would dislike having a woman boss. The authors concluded that "when unionists discuss women at work, it is never quite the same way they discuss men at work. There always seem to be implications that . . . women's role is elsewhere." And while these workers acknowledge that women may have to work out of economic necessity, they view it as a "deplorable circumstance" that they would not wish on *their wives.*

To compound this domestic stereotyping, male workers also thought that women who were in the labour force had different abilities and rights than themselves. As a result, they sought to segregate the sexes into different kinds of jobs, with varying pay scales. Ryan and Rowse (1975), reported that prior to 1940, Australian men retained the skilled, higher-paid jobs which covered all shifts. Women's work was unskilled, routine, lower-paid, and excluded the more lucrative night shift. Separate wages were endorsed by unions for each sex, with the "female wage" at about one half the "male wage." Ryan and Rowse (1975) argued that men's opposition to women's entrance into the labour force and union membership during the inter-war period in Australia was motivated by a desire to protect the male bread-winner. In those times of high unemployment, the job security of men was maintained at the expense of women workers, who were considered more transitory and in less need. Although some Australian unions fought for equal pay (Clothing Trades Union, 1926 and Clerks Union, 1937), the Australian Labor Movement did not contest women's secondary right to work. The Amalgamated Wireless of Australia and the Sheet Metal Trades Union stated in 1944 that after the war, men and boys would be given job preference over women (Ryan & Rowse, 1975). Spearitt (1975) also documents the marked lack of co-operation by these trade unions and the Labour Party, during the first half of this century. He specifically refers to the Sydney textile workers' strike of 1941 in which mainly women workers struck for better wages in defiance of the male union officials. And he comments that even today in Australia, women workers are faced with economic cutbacks which affect them more than male workers because of less assistance from the Labor Party and the union movement. A Canadian parallel to this specific strike is the 1972 Dare Food Factories strike in Kitchener–Waterloo (Bourne, 1978: 104).

Townson (1975) cites examples of Canadian collective agreements which have recently been negotiated with separate pay scales for men and women, such as Local 630 of the United Rubber, Cork, Linoleum and Plastic Workers of America (1974), the Service Employees International Union (1975), and the Tobacco Workers International Union (1974). These separate pay scales included lower wages for female workers.

McFarland (1979) studied 59 agreements in New Brunswick to examine their orientation to women's issues such as equal pay, maternity leave, non-sexist language in contracts, a no-discrimination clause, and support for part-time work. She found that five contracts explicitly discriminated against women; many discriminated against part-time workers (who are mainly women); and most collective agreements in the province showed no awareness of women's issues. Female majority unions were slightly more favourable to women but female minority unions had better fringe benefits for all workers. She concludes that most trade unions have not helped female workers to gain employment equality, although female-dominated professional unions appear to be most attuned to women's concerns.

In their early efforts to organize, women in America and Britain at the turn of the century were granted little money or encouragement from the union movement and were sometimes barred from membership (O'Neill, 1969). This situation is explained by O'Neill as being due to women's lower commitment to work, the transitory nature of their jobs, their low pay and subsequent lower union dues, the unskilled nature of their jobs (which created problems for union organizers), and men's traditional attitudes about "women's place."

Auchmuty (1975) discussed the limited success of attempts by middle class feminist "spinsters" to organize working women in Victorian Britain. There were financial difficulties as well as narrow attitudes. For example, British women attended every Trade Union Congress after 1876, even though they were not allowed to participate on the rationale that "under the influence of emotion they might vote for things which they would regret in cooler moments (Auchmuty, 1975: 117)."

This bias and lack of support is further documented by the fact that female trade unionists were forced to form separate organizations to organize women and fight opposition to female union membership. In 1874, the Women's Protective and Provident League was established to assist working women. It later became the Women's Trade Union League, which organized women, fought for equal pay and lobbied for equal membership in the trade movement. A similar group was founded in 1903 in the United States, but lack of money and support from organized labour meant that it had to depend upon private donors and align with the feminists to survive (O'Neill, 1969: 66).

The female workers' perception of lack of support from male-dominated unions persists today, as trade union women (aligned with the feminists) continue to organize their own groups to provide women workers with political socialization and aid. Organized Working Women in Ontario perceives that the union movement has done little for women workers, and has resolved to "confront our oppression as women and to convince the organized labour movement to take up the cause of working women (Organized Working Women, 1976)." An American group, the Coalition of Labour Union Women, formed in 1974, "is committed to encourage unions to be more aggressive in their efforts to organize women who are still not union members; to strengthen women's participation in unions, especially at the policy-making level; and to encourage unions to take positive action against sex discrimination in pay, hiring, job classification and promotion" (Townson, 1975: 352). In summary, the very existence of these organizations is an indication that women believe that they cannot further their cause within the established union movement.

Earlier protective legislation for women, promoted by both the unionists and the evangelicals in various countries, was designed to ameliorate working conditions, shorten long hours, and reduce both heavy and night work (Cook, 1968; Klein and Roberts, 1974; Lansbury, 1972). It is questionable, though, whether the motives and the results were in the best interests of the female workers. As Klein and Roberts stress, "the trade unionists' definition of the problems of women workers was dominated by their acceptance of the traditional moralistic definition of woman's place (Klein and Roberts, 1974: 219). The rationale was that the female workers' constitutions were weaker and their morals in danger; the result was that women were successfully excluded from the most lucrative forms of employment. Lansbury (1972: 290) believes Australian women in the early 1900s were seduced into acceptance of protective legislation by aspirations to respectability and gentility, despite the early feminist attempts to gain employment equality for women. And Cook states that, despite the continued opposition by feminists, most American unions still advocate protective legislation today (Cook, 1968).

Many male unionists, as other men, have questioned women's right to work. Clearly, numerous unions have not sought equal pay and opportunity but rather have advanced exclusion, segregation, and "protection." However, we are suggesting that it is not primarily "sexism" that prompted unionists to support protective legislation and other discriminatory behaviour. A more cogent and fundamental reason for their behaviour is fear of economic competition in the labour market. Women were and are often discriminated against because they constitute a source of cheap labour. It will be shown that unions react negatively to all workers who pose economic threats, and in this regard unions' treatment of women is not unique. We argue in the next section that sex *per se* is not the major variable influencing poor treatment, but rather, fear of economic competition in the labour market.

THREAT OF CHEAP LABOUR

Lansbury (1972) argued in her discussion of the early suffrage movement in Australia that unions supported protective legislation for women workers in order to retain the higher-paying positions for men. The fact that employers used women as a source of cheap labour led to retaliation by union men in creating ways to keep women away from the more lucrative jobs. Consequently, unions supported women's exclusion from the higher-paying night shift. But Lansbury hastened to argue that unions reacted in a similar way to other threats of cheap labour, such as the Chinese working in the Australian goldfields.

In Canada in the early twentieth century, craft union consciousness merged with traditional perspectives of the female role, resulting in blocked female entrance to craft unions. It was stated emphatically by one union that "women should not be allowed to lower the wages of men and to keep a number of young men out of work" (Klein and Roberts, 1974: 220). In other words, the ideology of a woman's place being in the home and of her need for protection in the workplace, ensured her exclusion from skilled jobs and higher wages.

There is ample evidence from the historical literature that women were used as cheap labour and that male workers reacted against this trend by attempting to exclude women from unions and the labour force (O'Neill, 1969; Roberts, 1976; White, 1980). MacLeod (1974: 316) discusses how employers in the garment industry in Toronto fired men during the Depression in order to hire women at one-half the wage. However, racial minorities and recent immigrants have also been used as cheap labour and have been the object of exclusion and discrimination by unions.

Evidence from the literature on American blacks and the labour movement verifies that discriminatory practices were experienced by blacks (Karson and Radosh, 1968; Rosen, 1968). In 1861, the American Federation of Labour began with a policy of nondiscrimination against black workers, but modified it within a few years because so many of their members were opposed to admitting blacks to their unions. Black workers were either excluded explicitly by constitutional provision or by high initiation fees, examinations designed to fail black applicants, or exclusion from apprenticeship programs. Black workers were further exploited because employers knew that they were not backed by international unions, as were whites (Karson and Radosh, 1968).

According to Rosen (1968), the CIO literature attacked the craft unions for their racial practices, but it was mainly a rhetorical commitment rather than a part of the CIO's active policy. By the time of the AFL-CIO merger, the CIO had given up its commitment to improve the position of American blacks through collective bargaining or internal reform, and did not try to implant CIO standards of union conduct in the newly merged organization.

Krauter and Davis (1968) provide similar information concerning unions and the Chinese on the west coast of Canada at the turn of the century. They claim that organized labour supported job discrimination against both the Japanese and the Chinese out of economic self-interest. Instead of using their collective power to improve the wages of the Orientals, the unions sought to exclude them, and allied with such racist organizations as the White Canadian Association and the Asiatic Exclusion League. Until World War II, craft union membership was closed to people of Chinese and Japanese descent (Krauter and Davis, 1968: 76).

It seems that trade unions have reflected the prevailing ideologies concerning women and minorities, and as general attitudes changed, so did the policies of trade unions. World War II seems to be a "watershed," in that after the war, views concerning minority groups and women gradually became more liberal. The interesting question is why men did not quickly include women in their unions and insist that women be paid the same wages as men, thus eliminating the threat. Part of the answer to this question goes back to the discussion of sexist attitudes and stereotyped views of woman's role. Two further aspects to be considered are the difficulty union men experienced in organizing women, and the nature of the collective bargaining process itself.

DIFFICULTIES IN ORGANIZING WOMEN WORKERS

O'Neill (1969) attributed part of the historical problem of organizing working women to the temporary and unskilled nature of women's jobs and to their low job commitment. Wertheimer and Nelson (1975) argued that American union leaders as well as female members feel that women lack the assertiveness necessary for union office. They claimed that organizing problems are related to socialization differences in the sexes. Cook (1968) spoke of competing domestic duties, intermittent work lives, and the unskilled nature of women's jobs which relates to lower commitment to work, as contributing factors to women's lower rates of unionization. In order to assess these arguments, one has to look more closely at the nature of women's jobs and where they are located in the labour force.

Prior to widespread use of contraception, women's worklives were interrupted by frequent and unexpected pregnancies. In addition to this, marriage and paid employment were considered to be incompatible, so that many women were expected to quit work after their weddings, even before they had children. Prior to World War I, gainful employment was largely restricted to single women, poorer wives, or sole-support mothers. Middle-class women did not "have to" work but were used as a reserve labour force (Connelly, 1978). Therefore, women's worklives were sporadic, and varied with their life-cycles or economic situation. Consequently, they were less interested than permanent workers in long-term employment benefits accrued from unionization. But in the last two decades, as more married women have entered the labour force, women are less likely to see their jobs as temporary and more likely to support unionization. Yet women are still segregated into lower-paid, dead-end jobs (Armstrong and Armstrong, 1978).

Although 37 per cent of the Canadian labour force was composed of women workers in 1977, not all were working full-time. About 22 per cent of female workers, compared to 5 per cent of male workers, are employed on a part-time basis (Labour Canada, 1977: 62, 29). Working part-time sometimes means less personal involvement with the job and less permanence, but also lower rates of unionization regardless of sex (Dewey, 1971). Women's greater tendency to work part-time contributes to their lesser involvement in unions, which they often see as working towards long-term goals (Howe, 1977). Although almost a quarter of women workers have been involved with part-time work, many unions have neither encouraged the creation of part-time jobs, nor have they supported people in these kinds of positions (Geoffroy and Sainte-Marie, 1971; McFarland, 1979). Industries with the highest proportion of female workers are services, finance, insurance, and real estate (Labour Canada, 1977: 62). Women in these occupations are clustered in clerical positions, with low mobility and job control. Table 22–1 relates the degree of female participation in these industries with the degree of union membership. Industries with a high percentage of white-collar female workers generally have the *lowest* rates of unionization among women employees.

Table 22–1

Female Participation and Union Membership By Industrial Distribution,
Canada 1976

Industry	Females as % of all workers	Females as % of all female workers	% of females unionized
Community, Business, Personal Service	59.0	43.4	30.1[b]
Finance, Insurance, Real Estate	57.5	8.1	2.2
Trade	39.9	18.7	7.4
Public Administration	32.0	6.2	63.3
Manufacturing	25.6	14.1	36.2
Transportation, Communication and Other Utilities	19.3	4.6	45.6
Agriculture[a]	24.3	3.3	1.1

[a]The figures here vary from the pattern; of 24,000 women only 270 are unionized, representing 1.1 per cent; similarly, the men, too, are poorly organized as of 82,000 male employees 2,734 are organized, representing only 3.3 per cent of all male employees. This suggests that other reasons exist to explain not only a very low degree of female unionization but also a low degree in the entire industry.

[b]This statistic, on the surface, may appear high; however, of all unionized women, 42.6 per cent form a majority in their union. These unions include the Quebec Teachers Corporation, Service Amalgamated Clothing and Textile Workers, Hospital Employees Union, Service Employees International Union, Alberta Assoc. of Registered Nurses, Ontario Public Service Employees, Registered Nurses Association of British Columbia, etc. These unions, predominantly female, are all service-oriented and generally white-collar. It is these unions that account for the comparatively high figure of 30 per cent. Thus the writers feel that the argument holds true, that where there is a large percentage of female workers, unionization, *particularly in male-dominated organizations*, is low. (Corporations and Labour Unions Returns Act, Part II, 1976, p. 49.)

Source: Derived from *Women in the Labour Force; Facts and Figures*. Women's Bureau, Labour Canada, Ottawa, Canada. 1977 edition, page 62 and 1976 edition pages 7–8.

Conversely, those industries with a high degree of unionization are those with low numbers of women workers. For example, Public Administration, with the lowest proportion of women (6 per cent), has the highest rate of female unionization. It is apparent that unions have not been successful in organizing the white-collar sector of the labour force (Labour Canada, 1976: 7, 8; 1977: 62). Yet 62 per cent of women occupy these white-collar positions (Marchak, 1973a).

White-collar workers have been notoriously difficult to unionize, and consequently both sexes have lower rates of unionization than other workers. Clerical workers are easily replaceable, and therefore have a weak bargaining position (Marchak, 1973). They work closely with management and sometimes see their interests as similar to those of their bosses. Low upward mobility, low control over work processes, and low incomes mark this sector of the workforce (Marchak, 1973). In spite of varying approaches and organizing drives, efforts of blue-collar industrial and craft unions to organize white-collar workers have not succeeded. Even though white-collar work has been increasingly routinized and downgraded, with relatively low wages and opportunities for promotion, white-collar workers still view themselves as "better off" than manual workers. White-collar workers often reject unionism because of its association with manual labour, uniformity, destruction of the merit system, and alienation from their bosses (Mills, 1951; Strauss, 1954). Traditionally, white-collar workers have maintained both higher status and higher incomes than blue-collar workers. But the entry of women into white-collar work coincided with the decline in both status and income. In recent years, blue-collar wages have risen relative to white-collar wages. Marchak (1973a) argued that blue-collar workers are reluctant to lose their new-found equality by actively attempting to unionize white-collar workers.

In summary, because women are largely clustered in white-collar clerical positions with weak bargaining power, unions have experienced difficulty in organizing them. There may also have been reluctance on the part of unions themselves to organize white-collar workers, for fear of reinstating the advantages they had historically enjoyed vis-a-vis blue-collar workers. This discussion, however, has addressed recruiting problems and the lower rates of unionization among women. But how do unions treat their members, once organized? The next section analyses the nature of the collective bargaining process and majority rule, which allows lower priority to women's issues.

THE COLLECTIVE BARGAINING PROCESS: MAJORITY RULES

To explain why trade unions have not responded enthusiastically to women workers demands a firm understanding of the collective bargaining process. The main purpose of a union is to bargain for those issues which the majority supports. Successful collective bargaining involves trade-offs and concessions, and negotiators will stress only those items which are lobbied for and demanded by the majority of employees in the bargaining unit. That means the process of "inter-organizational" bargaining must reconcile competing and conflicting factions and achieve consensus within the union. In the final analysis, a negotiator cannot fight for any item unless he/she has the strong support of a majority of members who are willing to enhance their demands with unified economic action. Otherwise, he/she risks his/her credibility at the bargaining table. In other words, union members will only get what they are willing to strike for. Also, some items are more attainable than others. Costly day-care centres and equal pay for work of equal value are much more difficult to achieve from a cost-conscious employer than maternity leave without pay or equal fringe benefits. Even at their most successful, union negotiators cannot achieve many costly items within the same contract. Bargaining is a continuing process with advances made slowly.

Geoffroy and Sainte-Marie (1971) found that 65.5 per cent of male workers felt a pregnant employee had a right to paid maternity leave; 85 per cent supported her regaining her position; and 85.4 per cent felt she should maintain seniority. However, only 32.1 per cent were prepared to go on strike in order to secure for female workers maternity leave with pay (Geoffroy, 1971: 68, 29). In such a system, collective bargaining is an inappropriate mechanism for responding to minority issues or interests. To explain why this system is disadvantageous for women is simply to state that women, as workers and as unionists, are a comparatively small, powerless group.

In 1977, 26.8 per cent of Canadian women workers were union members. These unionized women constituted 27.6 per cent of all union members. This means that women, already a minority in the general workforce, form an even smaller minority within the trade unions. Although only 42.9 per cent of male workers are organized, the fact still remains that three-quarters of the unionized population in Canada is male (Labour Canada, 1977: 6).

Union leadership in Canada is also predominantly male. Women are most likely to be represented on the executives of national unions (7.5 per cent) and least likely to be in international unions (4.2 per cent) (C.A.L.U.R.A., 1976: 54). A similar proportion of women are in leadership positions in American unions (Safilios-Rothschild, 1974) and an even lower proportion in Australia (Ryan, 1976). These figures emphasize that although women are under-represented as union members, their involvement in decision-making positions is even less representative.

In 1976, Canadian women union members were in the minority in 80 per cent of labour organizations (C.A.L.U.R.A., 1976: 54). Those unions which are dominated in numbers by women, contain 42.6 per cent of women union members. This reflects the segregated nature of the labour force. The fact that most unions have a majority of male members has led to the comment that the collective bargaining process "is not an ideal instrument through which to redress the wrongs suffered by women" (Finn, 1976: 47).

Nor can we assume that all women workers possess the same needs, demands, or outlooks, and that "women's issues" are of equal interest and import to all working women. Class differences, differences in marital status, and child-bearing create barriers to homogeneity and collective action. The conflict of interest groups within a union does not preclude women. But the fact that women's bargaining power is already low because of the nature of their jobs and their minority membership means that any division among women affects them to a greater extent than it would affect men. Marchak (1973) concluded that trade unions are of greatest benefit to those whose bargaining power is already the strongest, and of least benefit to those who are easily replaceable.

Many women writing about trade unions have emphasized the male "world view" that predominates in the union movement's policies and priorities (Safilios-Rothschild, 1974: 154; Hartman, 1976; Howe, 1977). Women's apparent lack of interest in unions may be largely related to their competing family responsibilities, but could also be a way of expressing their dissatisfaction with the priorities of union men. Unions tend to bargain for those issues considered important by the majority of members, and the majority is largely blue-collar men.

CONCLUSION

Of the four explanations analysing the negative reactions of trade unions to women workers, we feel that the nature of the collective bargaining process, with its reliance on majority rule, explains much of the reaction. Women are under-represented in the labour force compared to men, less likely to be unionized when gainfully employed, and far less likely to occupy decision-making positions within the union organization. Consequently, women as a group have low bargaining power. Moreover, those in the majority (blue-collar men) have lobbied for other issues. To understand why blue-collar men have not been concerned about child care or equality for women workers, we must return to the sexism argument. Blue-collar men have tended to accept the traditional ideology that women with children should not be in the labour force. Although middle class men have supported women's rights with greater enthusiasm than working class men (Tolson, 1977), the impetus for change has come from women themselves. Historically, women have been more likely than men to push for equal pay, equal work, child care, and maternity leave (Auchmuty, 1975; O'Neill, 1969). Considering that unions are dominated in membership by blue-collar men, we cannot expect them to be leaders in women's rights.

In fact, women as well as men have generally accepted the idea that women's place is in the home. Women's double burden — working for pay during the day and doing housework for no pay at home — has discouraged many women from spending more time than necessary on the job. Union participation requires extra time at work rather than at home. Canadian studies by Meissner et al. (1975) and Clark and Harvey (1976) indicate that working wives retain most of their housewife tasks. In addition to the home responsibilities that many women carry, women's socialization has not encouraged them to see themselves as assertive, politically efficacious, confronting, or even career-oriented. The more nurturant characteristics socialized into many girls do not naturally direct them into leadership positions, and lack of encouragement from husbands and fellow workers reinforces their socialization. Thus, women are unlikely to aggressively voice their concerns within unions.

However, traditional attitudes about women's roles explain only a part of their lesser tendency to unionize. The nature of women's work is such that the labour movement has been both less interested and less successful in organizing them. Women are clustered in low-status white-collar jobs, are more likely than men to be part-time workers, and are in positions with low job control. A search for reasons for these job characteristics of women workers highlights the idea that women are more "exploitable" through their "feminine" socialization, their family responsibilities, and discrimination against them.

Finally, women have historically been used as a source of cheap labour, and the union movement has not been successful in assisting women out of this position. In fact, in the early years of unionization, union men fought the threat of cheap labour by trying to exclude women from the labour movement, using arguments of women's secondary right to work. There seems to be the double-edged threat to men: that women workers are difficult to organize *and* have less right to be in the labour force than men. Discriminatory attitudes towards women and racial minorities kept these workers in weak bargaining positions. The fact that union members often harboured the same prejudices as employers meant that the labour movement preferred to eliminate the threat rather than to assist these workers, until after the Second World War when societal attitudes became more liberal toward minority groups in general. However, the early union movement was not powerful enough to resist the practices of employers with respect to women workers. With high rates of immigration and a surplus of labour, unions found it easier to exclude women than to force employers to pay all workers a fair wage (White, 1980: 19).

Although women's minority position within the union movement seems to be a crucial factor, all four explanations are interdependent and interconnected. As more married women enter full-time employment, there will be a greater demand for both maternity leave clauses and some form of employer-funded child care. And if middle-class women continue their trend toward "careers" rather than "jobs," "equal work" may become more of an issue. If women can increase their union membership throughout these trends, and increase their participation in decision-making, "women's issues" will rise in priority in collective bargaining.

Separate women's departments within unions may segregate "women's issues," but they also serve to unite women. Similarly, organizations of women unionists can provide each other with assurance that their concerns are valid and provide political socialization for female union members. But perhaps more important, these bodies are attempting to convince union men that women have been used as a source of cheap labour and as a reserve labour force, and only with the union's support can they improve their status as workers.

This comparative analysis of the historical and contemporary treatment of women workers by trade unions shows that there are many similarities in unions' reactions to women workers and their concerns in Canada, Australia, Britain, and the United States. But most of the literature does not delve deeply enough into the reasons behind this treatment. Viewing unions as "sexist" is not an adequate explanation of unions' negative reaction to women workers, nor is the argument that women were a threat of cheap labour. The fact that unions chose to exclude women rather than actively unionize them and fight for better wages for all workers was related to the lack of power of the union movement at the time. But unions have also historically been dominated in numbers by blue-collar men, and *their* interests rather than women's have been the focus of negotiations.

A question that the literature on trade unions and women does not adequately answer is: how different are unions which are dominated by women members and leaders? McFarland suggests that they have been more concerned with women's issues, but have not provided fringe benefits comparable to those of male-dominated unions. Secondly, what are the specific problems of organizing predominantly white-collar women workers? Marchak (1973) implies that the "union potential" among white-collar women is high, and that unions have not made great efforts to attract them. And, finally, we need more careful documentation of which unions are most likely to be sympathetic to women workers and their concerns. Historically, the craft unions were most exclusive. Until further research is completed, the research on women and trade unions remains sketchy and rather journalistic.

REFERENCES

Armstrong, Pat and Hugh Armstrong
1978 *The Double Ghetto: Canadian Women and Their Segregated Work*. Toronto: McClelland and Stewart.

Auchmuty, Rosemary
1975 "Spinsters and Trade Unions in Victorian Britain," in Curthoys et al.: 109–122.

Bourne, Paula
1979 *Women in Canadian Society*. Toronto: Ontario Institute for Studies in Education.

C.A.L.U.R.A. (See Statistics Canada).

Clark, Susan and Harvey Andrew
1976 "The Sexual Division of Labour: The Use of Time," in *Atlantis* 2 (1) (Fall).

Connelly, Patricia
1978 *Last Hired First Fired. Women and the Canadian Labour Force*. Toronto: The Women's Press.

Cook, Alice
1968 "Women and American Trade Unions," in *Annals of the American Academy of Political and Social Science* 375: 124–132.

Curthoys, Ann, Susan Eade and Peter Spearritt
1975 *Women at Work*. Canberra, Australia: Australian Society for the Study of Labour History.

Dewey, Lucretia M.
1971 "Women in Labor Unions," in *Monthly Labor Review* 94 (Feb.): 42–48.

Dixson, Miriam
1976 *The Real Matilda*. Melbourne, Australia: Penguin.

Finn, Ed
1978 "Equal Rights: Fact or Fantasy?" in *The Labour Gazette* (May).

Geoffroy, Renee and Paula Sainte-Marie
1971 *Attitudes of Union Workers to Women in Industry*. Study 9 of Studies of the Royal Commission on the Status of Women in Canada. Ottawa: Information Canada.

Hartman, Grace
1976 "Women and the Unions," in Gwen Matheson (ed.) *Women in the Canadian Mosaic*. Toronto: Peter Martin.

Howe, Louise Kapp
1977 *Pink Collar Workers*. New York: Avon Books.

Jacobson, Julius (ed.)
1968 *The Negro and the Labor Movement*. New York: Anchor Books.

Karson, Marc and Ronald Radosh
1968 "The American Federation of Labor and the Negro Worker, 1894–1949," in Jacobson: 155–187.

Klein, Alice and Wayne Roberts
1974 "Besieged Innocence: The "Problem" and Problems of Working Women — Toronto, 1896–1914," in *Women at Work, Ontario 1850–1930* by Acton et al., Toronto: Canadian Women's Educational Press.

Komarovsky, Mirra
1964   *Blue Collar Marriage*. New York: Random House.

Krauter, Joseph and Morris Davis
1978   *Minority Canadians: Ethnic Groups*, Toronto: Methuen.

Labour Canada
1976–77   *Women in the Labour Force, Facts and Figures*. Ottawa: Supply and Services.

Lansbury, Coral
1972   "The Feminine Frontier: Women's Suffrage and Economic Reality," — *Meanjin Quarterly* 3.

Macleod, Catherine
1974   "Women in Production: The Toronto Dressmakers' Strike of 1931," in *Women at Work, Ontario 1850–1930*. Edited by Janice Acton, Penny Goldsmith, and Bonnie Shepard. Toronto: Women's Press.

Marchak, M. Patricia
1973   "Women Workers and White Collar Unions," in *Canadian Review of Sociology and Anthropology* Vol. 10, No. 2 (May): 134–147.

1973a   "The Canadian Labour Force: Jobs for Women," in *Women in Canada*. Edited by Marylee Stephenson. Toronto: New Press.

McFarland, Joan
1979   "Women and Unions: Help or Hindrance?" in *Atlantis* Vol. 4, No. 2 (Spring).

Meissner, Martin et al.
1975   "No Exit for Wives: Sexual Division of Labour and the Cumulation of Household Demands," in *Canadian Review of Sociology and Anthropology* Vol. 12, No. 4 (Part I).

Mills, C. Wright
1951   *White Collar*. New York: Oxford University Press.

O'Neill, William (ed.)
1969   *The Woman Movement, Feminism in the United States and England*. Chicago: Quadrangle Books.

Organized Working Women
1976–79   *Reports, Pamphlets and Papers*. Don Mills, Ontario.

Rainwater, Lee
1960   *And the Poor Get Children*. Chicago: Quadrangle.

Robeson, Mary-Anne
1979   "Are Women Workers and Their Issues Represented in the Trade Unions: A Practical Study of the Canadian Airline Employees Association." Unpublished paper, Department of Sociology, University of Toronto.

Rosen, Sumner
1968   "The C.I.O. Era 1935–1955," in Jacobson: 183–208.

Ryan, Penny and Tim Rowse
1975   "Women, Arbitration and the Family," in Curthoys et al.: 15–30.

Safilios-Rothschild, Constantina
1974   *Women and Social Policy*. New Jersey: Prentice-Hall.

Statistics Canada
1979   *Corporations and Labour Unions Returns Act*. Report for 1976, Parts 1 and 2.

392 *Work in the Canadian Context*

Spearritt, Peter
1975 "Women in Sydney Factories 1920–1950" in Curthoys et al.: 31–46.
Strauss, George
1954 "White Collar Unions are Different," in *Harvard Business Review* 32 (Sept.): 73–82.
Summers, Anne
1975 *Damned Whores and God's Police: The Colonization of Women in Australia*. Melbourne: Penguin.
Tolson, Andrew
1977 *The Limits of Masculinity*. London: Tavistock.
Townson, Monica
1975 "Organizing Working Women," in *The Labour Gazette* (June): 349–ʳ 53.
Wertheimer, Barbara and Anne H. Nelson
1975 *Trade Union Women, A Study of their Participation in New Yor' Locals*. New York: Praeger.
White, Julie
1980 *Women and Unions*. Ottawa: Canadian Advisory Council on the Status of Women.